North American Borders in Comparative Perspective

NORTH AMERICAN BORDERS

IN COMPARATIVE PERSPECTIVE

Edited by
GUADALUPE CORREA-CABRERA AND VICTOR KONRAD

THE UNIVERSITY OF
ARIZONA PRESS
TUCSON

The University of Arizona Press
www.uapress.arizona.edu

ISBN-13: 978-0-8165-4104-1 (hardcover)
ISBN-13: 978-0-8165-3952-9 (paper)

Cover design by Derek Thornton, Notch Design
Interior design and typesetting by Sara Thaxton
Typeset in 10/14 Adobe Caslon Pro, Mongoose, Alternate Gothic, and ITC American Typewritter

Library of Congress Cataloging-in-Publication Data
Names: Correa-Cabrera, Guadalupe, editor. | Konrad, Victor A., editor.
Title: North American borders in comparative perspective / edited by Guadalupe Correa-Cabrera and
    Victor Konrad.
Description: Tucson : University of Arizona Press, 2020. | Includes bibliographical references and index.
Identifiers: LCCN 2019036799 | ISBN 9780816539529 (paperback) | ISBN 9780816541041 (hardcover)
Subjects: LCSH: United States—Boundaries—Canada. | Canada—Boundaries—United States. |
    United States—Boundaries—Mexico. | Mexico—Boundaries—United States. | United States—
    Foreign relations—Canada. | Canada—Foreign relations—United States. | United States—
    Foreign relations—Mexico. | Mexico—Foreign relations—United States.
Classification: LCC E179.5 .N66 2020 | DDC 327.73071—dc23
LC record available at https://lccn.loc.gov/2019036799

Printed in the United States of America
♾ This paper meets the requirements of ANSI/NISO Z39.48-1992 (Permanence of Paper).

This book is dedicated to Professor Alan F. J. Artibise

Alan F. J. Artibise is provost emeritus at the University of Texas Rio Grande Valley. His career accomplishments in higher education are immense and exemplary. In addition to scholarship and academic leadership in history, political science, and multidisciplinary fields, Professor Artibise has inspired and supported extensive research about borders and borderlands throughout North America. Artibise was among the leaders of the Borderlands Project established in the 1980s and a researcher and commentator about Cascadia, arguably the vanguard borderland initiative between Canada and the United States. Although Professor Artibise dedicated the last several decades of his career to universities along the southern boundary of the United States—from Louisiana to Arizona—his formative experience in research, teaching, and administration was in Canada, where he worked in institutions in British Columbia, Manitoba, and Ontario. Professor Artibise epitomizes the North American scholarly curiosity, experience, and accomplishment that extends across borders throughout the continent. In this era of barriers and walls, we need to acknowledge those who work to understand borders and take us beyond them. Thank you, Alan.

Contents

Foreword

This is a timely and insightful volume on an increasingly important topic for North American residents. There are several aspects of the volume that deserve to be highlighted.

The first is the makeup of the participants. Geographically, they come from many borderland regions, including the state of Washington, the province of British Columbia, the capitals of Canada and the United States, the state of New Mexico, the state of Texas, the state of Arizona, and several from Mexico Studies centers in both the United States and Mexico. The participants represent a wide variety of expertise and experience ranging from political science, planning, border studies, Canadian Studies, and Mexican Studies, and they include not only academics but border policy experts, former government officials, and active members of the Association for Borderland Studies. It is difficult to envision a more impressive group to discuss borders and borderlands in North America.

Also notable is the location of the conference. Few places in North America are as conscious—on a daily basis—of the border as Brownsville, Texas. Indeed, during the conference, participants could literally see Mexico and the partially completed border wall that was by then causing distress and concern among many in the region.

In May 2015, I had just retired after serving five years as provost of the University of Texas, Brownsville (UTB, soon to be joined with the University of Texas Pan American to become a new institution, the University of Texas Rio Grande Valley). In that relatively short period of time, living so close to the border with Mexico, change was everywhere evident. Many of my colleagues at UTB used to cross the border daily or weekly to visit family and relatives in Matamoros, Mexico, the sister city of Brownsville, or to have lunch or dinner in "real" Mexican restaurants. By 2015, these habits had changed, largely because of growing violence as a result of the drug cartels and because of increasing difficulties in crossing the border.

Notably at UTB (a borderlands institution of the first order), the students were over 90 percent Hispanic, and several hundred crossed the border daily to attend classes. This pattern has by now been severely disrupted, and more difficulties in crossing the border can be expected.

So what have the last two decades of border relations taught us? It is, of course, hard to say with complete confidence, but what this collection of essays does reveal is a massive shift in border relations on both the northern and southern borders of the United States. As a dual American and Canadian citizen, someone who has lived in four U.S.-Mexico border states (Texas, Arizona, Louisiana, and Florida), and as a Canadian, I had always lived close to the border in British Columbia, Ontario, and Manitoba. My deep involvement in the Cascadia region exposed me to the complexities of borderlands and to the inadequacies of border policy. In all North American countries, border policies are made in national capitals with little sensibility of the hopes and desires of any region's residents. As Bruce Agnew notes in his contribution to this volume, a cross-border governance policy formulated with regional concerns in mind could bring about many of the national goals. It remains to be seen, however, in an era of American xenophobic rhetoric espoused almost daily by the American president, whether this goal is possible. But stranger things have happened, and as the last few years have taught us, change can occur rapidly and dramatically.

In short, the essays in this volume provide scholars, policy makers, communities, institutions, and corporations with ample fodder to contemplate the next decade or two of borderlands and border development. Optimists will look to examples of successful borderland cooperation and integration in the past and hope for continued progress. Pessimists will note how much of the work of the past several decades has been dismantled in a few short years since the U.S. election of 2016. In my view, I believe the current "noise" about the border will fade as more thoughtful heads prevail. If this hope is realized, we must be ready with a deep understanding of borderlands and borders. This volume is a major step in that direction.

Alan F. J. Artibise
Provost Emeritus
University of Texas Rio Grande Valley

Preface

T he contributions to this book place border research and practice on North America in comparative perspective to further an advanced, comprehensive, and current understanding of this continent's borders and borderlands. In order to complement previous efforts and add to the regional analysis of North American borders and borderlands, this book cuts across disciplinary and topical areas. Overall, this edited volume provides a balanced and comparative view of borders in the dynamic and diverse region formed by Canada, the United States, and Mexico. The book conveys a unique perspective on current research and understanding of the U.S. borders with its immediate neighbors by offering insights from scholars, policy makers, and practitioners. The chapters included in this volume engage and develop current border studies thinking and theory. Also, these chapters combined address border issues that are timely, practical, and significant to our understanding and management of North American borders and borderlands.

A substantial comparative overview and assessment of North America's borders and borderlands requires the contributions of experts in many fields across the continent. We have been fortunate to draw on the expertise and insights of a formidable team of internationally acclaimed scholars and practitioners in border research and policy. To each and every contributor to this book, we say thank you for your commitment to this project. All of your chapters convey significant and engaging studies in their own right, and, when assembled in this book, the chapters combine to form a fresh and timely look at North America's borders.

A special thanks to Dr. Laurie Trautman and Roxanne Medina at the Border Policy Research Institute, Western Washington University, for the research and production of the maps accompanying this book. We also acknowledge and thank Dr. Alan Artibise, provost emeritus at the University of the Rio Grande Valley, for his initial interest in this project and for his support of the conference that spawned this book.

When we sent the manuscript to publishers, the University of Arizona Press was quick to respond and to recognize the potential of this project. The encouragement of the University of Arizona Press convinced us that we had a special book in the making, and the anonymous reviewers of the manuscript agreed. The entire University of Arizona Press team then expedited the project. Kristen Buckles, editor-in-chief at UAP, has worked closely with us on every phase of the project. Our project coordinator, Stacey A. Wujcik, has been in contact with us constantly to ensure a smooth and effective publication process. Thanks to the production team—Amanda Krause (editorial, design, and production manager), Leigh McDonald (art director), Sara Thaxton (book production coordinator), and Abby Mogollon (marketing manager)—the book moved very quickly through the production process. A special thanks to Steve LaRue for his attention to detail in the copyediting process. It has been our privilege and joy to work with everyone at the University of Arizona Press to publish *North American Borders in Comparative Perspective*.

Victor Konrad, Ottawa, Canada
Guadalupe Correa-Cabrera, Washington, D.C.
September 2019

North American Borders in Comparative Perspective

The International Boundary Perimeter of the United States of America

Two Borders and Many Borderlands

GUADALUPE CORREA-CABRERA AND VICTOR KONRAD

For a brief time after the terrorist events of September 11, 2001, and the subsequent creation of the U.S. Department of Homeland Security (DHS), the United States experimented with the notion that the nation-state was contained within one territorial boundary and that Americans maintained a consistent border around the country. It became apparent to the G. W. Bush and Obama administrations that one border policy did not suffice and that borders with Canada and Mexico required policies of border control and management tailored to the nature of the two bilateral relationships. Moreover, it was apparent as well that adjacent to both the southern and northern boundaries and across them, regional borderlands of interaction that emerged over centuries remained viable and vital even in the face of enhanced security and its effects on cross-border mobility.

The northern and southern borders and borderlands had become the hinges of the North American relationship because they allowed independent yet coordinated articulation of two of America's most important relationships. The centuries-long regional borderlands facilitated the immense volume of north-south trade, allowed energy sharing, and filtered flows of information and people. Concerns over illicit drugs, terrorism, and irregular migration had incentivized the borderlands in the American psyche, and the resulting security emphasis required efforts to enhance borderlands mobility but also brought about greater constrictions. With the inauguration of the Trump administration in 2017, the U.S. border policy showed signs of more and even greater change. The 2018 presidential election in Mexico added some uncertainty to the future of Mexico-U.S. border relations. The deteriorating relationship between President Donald Trump and Prime Minister Justin Trudeau marked a straining of relations between the United States and Canada with a potential for further tightening of border procedures. Nevertheless, the borders and borderlands continue to do their work and may become even more central to the articulation of relationships and engagements in North America.

Our comparative perspective on North American borders begins with selected stories to reveal the distinctive nature of first the overportrayed Mexico-U.S. border and then the largely overlooked Canada-U.S. border. The unbalanced and slanted view of the two borders in the American imagination has been explored somewhat in the media and by scholars of border studies. Yet the perspectives on either border are rarely compared. Essentially, the view gaining momentum is that the Mexico-U.S. border is too porous and that that is not good, and so a wall is necessary to keep out people and influences alien to America. Canada is not scrutinized as intensively mainly because "Canadians are like us," but recently, as Canada has become more evidently multicultural, the United States has viewed the Canada-U.S. border with greater suspicion and concern. This study aims not to extend stereotypes, assumptions, and misconceptions inherent in these portrayals but rather to seek commonalities, parallels, alignments, and shared characteristics to enable a North American perspective on how borders serve the United States, Mexico, and Canada at various scales extending from the local to the global.

Mexico-U.S. Border Stories

President Donald Trump signed an executive order during his first week as president authorizing the construction of a 1,900-mile-long border wall to replace the fence that now runs along a fraction of the Mexico-U.S. border. President Trump also signed executive orders increasing the number of Border Patrol agents by five thousand, tripling immigration officers, targeting so-called sanctuary cities for immigrants, and other related ones. His administration has also implemented the Migration Protection Protocols—the so-called Stay in Mexico Program—through which asylum seekers are returned to Mexico and have to wait outside the United States for the duration of their immigration proceedings. These measures are allegedly designed to stop "illegal immigration" and the possible accompanying drugs and gang violence coming from the south. The actual implementation of such policies has increased deportations of undocumented immigrants, raised human rights violations, and heightened tensions within the United States and between the United States and Mexico.

Aside from the economic and political effects of the deterioration in relations between the United States and Mexico, geography dictates that Mexico, which is caught between the massive migration force from the global south and the enhanced antimigration force in the United States, will be most affected by a continuing immigration crisis. But the United States will suffer too.

The United States has invested heavily in a plan to halt the irregular flow of immigrants. In the past decade and a half, the U.S. Border Patrol has doubled its agent force. Congress has authorized massive spending on fencing, infrastructure, and technology to secure the Mexico-U.S. border. Mexico recently supported the extensive U.S. deportation efforts with its own Southern Border Plan (*Plan Frontera Sur*), which was backed by the United States. The situation changed after the 2018 Mexican presidential election, but Mexico and the United States continue to cooperate to some extent. Nevertheless, transnational networks of migrant smugglers and drug traffickers seem to operate jointly and with impunity in these allegedly "more secure" and militarized border zones. The current U.S. and Mexican administrations do not offer a different plan but rather an expansion of continuing policies and a reinforcement of current trends, and all of these directions promise to lead to deficient results.

In 2018, Mexico held historic elections that gave a landslide victory to the country's political left. In the same year, Mexico faced tough trade negotiations with the United States. In this context, many influential Mexican citizens, political analysts, entrepreneurs, and politicians urged the Mexican government to take a hard line with the Trump administration on different bilateral issues. Among other things, they advised Mexico to suspend cooperation with the United States on immigration. This has not happened, but the recent "caravanization" of Central American migration gives the impression of a crisis at the border and puts further pressure on Mexico. The "wall," adorned with all the administration's rhetoric and imaginary construction in an era of looming migrant caravans, has become pivotal in long-term political and trade negotiations.

The reality is that there is no crisis at the border and no national emergency as Trump alleges. And even if there were one, it does not seem that a border wall could fix it. "The wall is not the answer," insists Texas sheriff Joe Frank

Martínez. Martínez is president of the Southwest Border Sheriffs' Coalition, whose members oppose the wall because the Trump administration has failed to reconcile the complex environmental and cultural conditions inherent to the border that make such a massive undertaking impractical (Johnson 2017). His colleague Sheriff Estrada of Santa Cruz County, Arizona, goes even further and calls Trump's "great, great wall," an "insult" to the people who live on each side of the border. John Doyle, the mayor of Nogales, Arizona, says, "A wall would represent a slap to the face of our Mexican neighbors," and "it sends the wrong signal to the rest of the world." "People don't want more walls, they want more exchange," explains Graco Ramírez, former governor of the Mexican state of Morelos and ex-president of the Mexican Governors' Conference. Mexico is the top trading partner of Arizona, New Mexico, and Texas and ranks as the United States' third largest trading partner after Canada and China.

The underlying problem, according to the sheriffs and many other borderland officials, is the "D.C. 'disconnect' at the border" (Johnson 2017). Washington develops border policy in Washington, not at the border. Alternatively, local authorities living and operating close to the border understand that citizens, not politicians, cannot see through a wall. They emphasize that "at least you can see your neighbor through a fence" and that there is something "unhealthy" about not seeing across the border. Inevitably, a wall is just another obstacle, a hurdle to cross, and according to Sheriff Estrada, it might be the easiest one to overcome for the millions of migrants—men, women, and children—who arrive at the U.S. border after long journeys with much greater challenges along the way.

Canada-U.S. Border Stories

Canada-U.S. border stories are also about endemic and growing problems with heightened border security and the specter of a less visible and tangible but still insidious wall construction. A recent online search for border-crossing stories concerning the Canada-U.S. border produced an astounding 1,550,000 hits in a few seconds. Examination of the first several hundred postings showed a pattern of personal and group vignettes about border-crossing mishaps, delays, encounters with authorities, and "horror" stories about the now formidable border. It seems that almost anyone who crosses the border encounters at some time a problem to be recounted on social media. Although most of the stories examined did not tell of arrest or deportation, the majority complained of ill treatment by officials and affronts to "civil" rights. In essence, the border was deemed more intimidating and unpredictable than it should be, and both Americans and Canadians, when crossing the border, expected less of a barrier and more of an expedited formality. The idea of the "longest undefended border in the world," once the image that guided our sense of the Canada-U.S. border, no longer prevails, and Canadians in particular do not like this change. Accordingly, the stories continue to accumulate.

One story was sparked by comments from Wisconsin governor Scott Walker, who insisted in 2016 that it was "legitimate" to discuss building a wall separating the United States from Canada as well as constructing the wall along the Mexican border advocated by then presidential candidate Donald Trump. Published by the *Huffington Post*'s David Martin, who was inspired by Walker's comments to write a fictional news account of a Canada-U.S. wall, the story is an anticipatory look to 2020, when a wall is completed between the United States and Canada. Martin writes of possible positive political and economic consequences for Canada of a Canada-U.S. border wall. In January 2020, after three years of "feverish" construction, the United States completes the wall unilaterally built by Americans because Canadians, having experienced decades of peaceful cooperation, saw no sense in spending billions of dollars on a border wall. "At a dedication ceremony held at the heavily fortified Detroit-Windsor border crossing, President Donald Trump and the Canadian Prime Minister jointly conducted a ribbon cutting. Due to security concerns, however, the ribbon cutting was carried out via simultaneous video transmissions."

In March 2020, evidence shows that the new wall structure benefits Canada because it stems the tide of illegal firearms that once easily crossed the border into Canada, and as a result gun crime and deaths in Canada declined. In May 2020, the wall halts so-called U.S. medical tourists who take advantage of Canada's universal health care coverage, and Canada's taxpayers save millions of dollars. Although the wall cuts the southern flow of oil and natural gas from Canada's wells to American markets, Canadian producers shift flows to China. Canada's sports and tourism, once dependent on the U.S. market, wean themselves of this dependence and move toward internal consolidation and international partnerships so that by the end of 2020, "the law of unintended consequences has come into play and it looks like the United States is no longer as keen on keeping the new border structure."

Although this story may have seemed far-fetched in 2016 when Donald Trump was still viewed as a long-shot contender for the White House, the story now appears plausible amid the uncertainties swirling after two years of the Trump administration. However, the issue is not whether a wall will be constructed or not. Today, the United States and Canada share a technologically sophisticated boundary-zone monitoring system. The question is, how far will the United States go to utilize this system and enhancements to the system in order to restrict trade and travel between the two countries? Canada's citizens depend on the United States to buy 70 percent of their exports, and they became, at some point, clearly anxious about the future of the U.S. trade relationship. Furthermore, Canadians were concerned about the effects of new travel restrictions imposed by the United States on foreigners.

One of President Trump's initial executive orders banned any travel to the United States by citizens of six Muslim nations. This affects citizens of these countries currently visiting or living in Canada. Suddenly, Canadians are witnessing and experiencing the new "wall" taking shape as the United States embarks on a strident, singular, isolationist travel and trade path. This virtual wall has several characteristics. The new wall along the Canada-U.S. border is a construct of the rapidly evolving U.S. imagination built on fear of anything non-American and the exclusion of everything non-American. This imaginary has long been nurtured by elements of far-right politics, xenophobia, hate groups, and neonationalism in the United States. Now, this imaginary is invested with immense power to construct both virtual and real walls. Although the real walls may be reserved for the southern boundary of the United States, the virtual wall with Canada may prove to be substantial in its own right by restricting Canada's goods and services from flowing into the United States, excluding Canadians who are connected if only by lineage to countries and cultures deemed enemies of the United States, and assuring that Canadian values, institutions, practices, and ideas are not allowed into the United States. In effect, the Canada-U.S. border imagined and promoted by the Trump administration may well configure the virtual wall emerging between the United States and Canada.

North American Borders: From Divergence to Alignment and Back

The year 2017 ended with divergent Canada-U.S. border policies and promises. At the beginning of his administration, President Donald Trump vowed to build a wall on the Mexico-U.S. border and end, or reshape substantially, the North American Free Trade Agreement (then NAFTA, now the United States–Mexico–Canada Agreement, or USMCA). At the same time, the U.S. Congress passed legislation to expedite Canada-U.S. border crossing, and the Trump administration gave the Keystone XL pipeline its key federal permit, which makes significant progress toward North American energy integration. Canada, the United States, and Mexico may share the North American continent with long established boundaries, yet the borders constructed and reconstructed among the three countries change constantly in their roles, effects, and significance to life and mobility on the continent. In 2019, North American borders are both diverging and realigning.

For more than three decades, North American borders have experienced extensive rethinking as the United States, Mexico, and Canada have grappled to manage the increasing flow of goods, people, information, and power in one of the most fluid continental exchange systems on the planet. The international boundaries have been the continent's steadfast control lines and the floodgates, yet the international boundaries work in very different ways. The northern boundary is distinguished by cooperation and connection whereas the southern boundary is defined by its fortified barrier. Moreover, both of these borders are differentiated more than at any time in the past three decades as political differences between the countries are accentuated.

Why are these borders so different in an ostensibly fluid continent in the vanguard of globalization? This question leads us to explore some fundamental premises in the thinking about what North America is and where it is headed. First, we must examine more closely and critically the state of continental integration in North America. What is actually integrating in North America? We need to dissect flows and differentiate movements from the actual transfer of ideas, culture, and norms. The process of globalization in North America needs to be better understood and differentiated from what is generally regarded as a worldwide process engaging all parts of the world, albeit in varying degrees.

There is an enticement to view a global process as perhaps more pervasive and encompassing than it really is. Scholars have done this with industrialization and metropolitanization only to acknowledge that the processes are much more variable than envisioned, with residuals that abound to challenge the generalizations and offer substantive insight. Is there a unique form of globalization in North America? How does it work? What part do borders play in the articulation of the process? These questions lead to the interrogation of the very idea of North America. How durable is this idea? Is the idea of North America adequate and appropriate to conceptualize an incisively bordered continent? All of these questions are fundamental to understanding North America. Furthermore, the questions are all linked to the role of borders in both dividing and linking North American components into a system and network that both works and yet grates constantly with seismic force and unpredictability.

This book aims to affirm that North America is not a level playing field for trade, migration, and other forms of exchange. North America is not integrated. Now, more than ever, borders articulate a divided and differentiated North America. These borders are both the traditional national and regional boundaries and the sustained yet metamorphosed lines between people in North America and some national markers that are increasingly based on wealth, race, education, and politics. It appears that the movement toward North American integration has been shattered. Yet the book also sustains the notion that the idea of a more integrated and aligned North America remains as a leitmotif to a more viable interaction on the continent, to a linkage that extends beyond connections for profit to cooperation for a common good.

Perhaps the greatest legacy of the "free-trade" initiatives of the FTA and NAFTA (now USMCA) is the comprehension, if not explicit acknowledgment among people in North America, that there is a common standard possible and desirable for environmental sustainability, technology sharing, health, social welfare, and security. In a sense, people in North America—Mexicans, Americans, and Canadians—realize yet negate their commonalities and use symbolic boundaries to reinforce distinctions. This growing dialectic is most disturbing, invasive, and disruptive in the enlarged borderlands of interaction where people experience the border constantly. These borderlands, although significant in the United States, are even more important to the economy, prosperity, and well-being of Canada and Mexico. Understanding North American borderlands, then, leads to a more effective understanding of the coincident differentiation and integration through bordering in North America.

North American Borderlands

North America works because North American borderlands work. Yet the idea of borderlands remains largely an intellectual construct regardless of the fact that it is used extensively in both academic and popular media accounts of North American border regions, particularly along the southern border.

Acknowledgment and acceptance of a concept that implies both division and integration is academically challenging and complex, and it is a difficult step indeed for policy makers. Nevertheless, there are indications that policy makers in the highest level of government in Canada recognize the emergence of cross-border regions between Canada and the United States (Government of Canada 2006). Along the Mexico-U.S. border, "borderlands" is a time-honored concept with roots in the Bolton School of historical scholarship and significant explication in recent years by scholars and cultural activists (Martínez 1994; Anzaldua [1987] 2012). Policy makers, particularly those engaged in transborder environment planning and management, have developed the concept in an ecological framework (López-Hoffman et al. 2010).

The concept of borderlands, however, remains beyond the public policy discourse because it implies a blurring of state territorial boundaries, the very boundaries that contain the mandates and regulatory frameworks of policy making. Whereas the public policy community may acknowledge the concept of borderlands intuitively, this same community will not accept the transnational overlay and fusion of constituencies divided by the boundary. The fundamental acknowledgment of "third space" (Dear 2013) is lacking, and without this recognition, policies to secure, expedite, and manage borderlands will never achieve the efficacy of policy measures aimed at territory contained entirely and exclusively within the nation-state.

In the 1990s after NAFTA was crafted, proclaimed, endorsed, and finally implemented, it appeared that the third space identified by theorists, observers, and researchers could actually be characterized and articulated in the border regions of North America. Environmental policies for management of water, clean air, and wildlife, already based on cross-border ecological models, subsequently invoked broader borderland frameworks. Great Lakes environmental management, Rio Grande Valley water management, and Yukon-Alaska caribou herd management regimes engaged not only collaborative mechanisms for policy integration but also defined borderland contexts for these engagements.

Furthermore, borderlands were described as cross-border culture regions of both Indigenous and non-Indigenous populations; they were integrated economic zones; some were developing as transportation corridors; others were urban cross-border complexes; and still others were isolated and interdependent communities. Even the enhancement of border security in the era subsequent to 9/11 could not erase the growing significance and recognition that third space or borderlands gained within the thinking and writing and policy implementation surrounding borders in North America. In fact, the implementation of enhanced security actually defined one-hundred-mile security zones adjacent to the U.S. international boundary to extend border policing and thus formalized the security borderlands.

The challenge now is to sustain the momentum toward recognition that North America works not only as a strong, central, and hegemonic power flanked by two lesser states secured from it by impenetrable borders but also through the enlightened and sensitive engagement among the three states at the borderlands. Borderlands work at all times. They operate as effective conduits in situations of enhanced trade and migration. In addition, they sustain communication, linkage, and all forms of engagement even under conditions of substantive bordering and rebordering. Understanding borderlands is the key to understanding the role of North American borders.

North America's Borders: A Comparative Perspective

The chapters in this book offer a comprehensive look at border research on this continent. The essays represent a comparative perspective and give a greater understanding of North American borders and borderlands. North American borders and borderlands have been analyzed extensively, but usually separately. The Mexico-U.S. border has received considerable attention by scholars throughout the twentieth century, but this work became more extensive and significant in the decade of the 1980s when North American ideas about border studies emerged in this southern border region. The work of Oscar Martínez and other scholars in Mexico and the United States paved the way to expanded research throughout the social sciences and the humanities, and the institutionalization of border studies in the United States. In recent years, the literature has become extensive, with hundreds of scholars contributing to journals in the field and publishing numerous volumes devoted to the southern border focusing on either the Mexican or the U.S. side or a specific cross-border region (Elizondo Griest 2017; Córdova 2010; Valenzuela Arce 2013; Anderson and Gerber 2008; Ganster and Lorey 2007). Some academics and policy analysts have focused on specific aspects of the broader region (Payan 2016; Andreas 2009; Staudt and Payan 2009; Staudt and Coronado 2002; Staudt 1998). Particular attention has been directed to matters of trade, security, and immigration.

Culture, trade, migration, and the environment have become the primary emphasis in more recent scholarship about the Canada-U.S. border and borderlands. Characteristically, the work is led by scholars and policy analysts who live and do their research along the extensive border regions shared between the United States and Canada (Nicol 2015; Bryce and Freund 2015; King, Mosher, and Lynch 2014; Moore 2014; Norman, Cohen, and Bakker 2013; Chang 2012; Konrad and Nicol 2008; Widdis 1999). Border studies emerged in this region as trade between Canada and the United States became more formalized in the 1980s, and as scholars in Canada looked beyond "Canada First" approaches nurtured in the shadow of U.S. hegemony, to recognize the immense significance of cross-border interaction rather than just repudiate the vision of integration with the United States. These particular scholars realized the parallels, parallaxes, dialectics, and liminalities inherent in borderland life because Canada, with approximately 90 percent of its population living within one hundred kilometers of the U.S. border, is a borderland.

Only a few volumes of North American continental history (Hämäläinen and Johnson 2011), the continent in general (Chávez 2012), and particular issues or policy areas (Andreas and Biersteker 2003; UNEP 2002) focus on borders. Even fewer studies compare the two borders or assess main issues or policy areas in comparative perspective (Nischik 2016; Johnson and Graybill 2010; Brunet-Jailly 2007). These approaches to broader North American analyses received greater attention in the 1990s, particularly when NAFTA was under discussion and initially implemented. Further studies focused on the effects of economic integration in the North American region (Bersin 2012; Brunet-Jailly 2007). At that time, immense optimism prevailed regarding the benefits of trade and greater integration among Mexico, the United States and Canada. This sentiment changed dramatically after the events of 9/11. Further changes have taken place in recent years to incise the boundaries and draw distinctions between the North American neighbors.

Books analyzing or comparing North American borders focus mainly on the topics of energy, the environment, trade, transportation, migration, security, and politics. All have a particular focus, and all speak to a specialist audience in those fields. In summary, studies of North American borders have been conducted largely along thematic lines, and this leaves a vacuum to fill in the comprehensive analysis and comparison of North American borders in all of its dimensions and key border policy areas.

In order to complement previous efforts and add to the regional analysis of North American borders and borderlands, this book aims to cut across disciplinary and topical areas. *North American Borders in Comparative Perspective* provides a balanced and comparative view of borders in the region formed by

Canada, the United States, and Mexico. The book conveys information on current research and understanding of the U.S. borders with Canada and Mexico. The chapters engage or develop current border studies thinking and theory and address timely border issues significant to our understanding of North American borders and borderlands.

"Rebordering" Canada, the United States, and Mexico in the Twenty-First Century

The material included in this book is based on the presentations at a conference organized with the aim of advancing our understanding of borders in a variety of theoretical and empirical contexts as they pertain to the North American region. The conference took place at the University of Texas at Brownsville on May 7–8, 2015, and involved the participation of a group of nine contributors consisting of border scholars and policy makers and analysts specializing in diverse border issues and focusing on different North American regions. Familiar with the work of their colleagues, the participants contributed to an intense exchange of knowledge, ideas, and perspectives concerning North American borders that is revealed in the chapters of this book.

The May 2015 conference and this book constitute an opportunity to affect public policy related to the two North American borders at a time when borders are being constantly evaluated and contested, represented in government policies, and addressed by the media at all scales across the North American continent. The articles offered herein assess the connections between theoretical approaches and public policy applications. Utilizing a comparative approach is one of the book's key elements. To create a better understanding of North American borders and borderlands, the contributions place border research into a comparative perspective. This comparative approach is expanded visually with a set of graphic representations of North American borders and crossings, infrastructures that are essentially continental in their extent, environments that are shared, and the flows (including human migration, information, goods and services) that cross North America in all directions.

Since the May 2015 conference, many circumstances have changed in North America. The 2016 U.S. presidential election represents a major shift in the way North American borders are defined and conceived. The 2018 presidential election in Mexico might add to the current border dilemmas. Up to and including NAFTA, which was inaugurated January, 1, 1994 (and was recently renamed USMCA), the economic integration of the three countries that signed the agreement and the gradual elimination of the barriers that divided the countries were the dominant trends. However, during this period of linkage building, a host of problems related to cohesiveness and comprehensive integration in North America were evident. More specifically, the North American continent was in transition between "isolation" and "integration," which is a phenomenon now understood as a move toward globalization and transnationalism. Simultaneously, we observe a resilience and even a reimposition of borders today. David Newman has stated, "Lines continue to separate us" (Newman 2006, 143), and while this seems to be a contradiction, North American citizens have found themselves caught between a more globalized world order and the complicated expansion of borders for more than a decade.

Drawing on an idea of "transition" and based on the broader contradiction between globalization and borders, the purpose of the May 2015 conference was to explore and question this idea as it relates to borders and borderlands. The participants concluded that to build an effective and viable North America, both political will and a certain amount of hope were needed. The scholars and policy analysts who participated in the effort proposed new insights and ideas related to borders with the aim of advancing a more integrated and developed region. The goal was to bring theory and policy together. The interaction between academic and nonacademic sectors has been proven important to solve very complex problems in border studies projects in Europe (border regions, borderscapes) and North America (borders in globalization). Generally, the participants advocated for integration of innovative approaches. Many advocated specific policies and directions that still resonate despite the shift in 2016.

In 2016, the election of Donald J. Trump as the forty-fifth president of the United States of America changed, perhaps fundamentally, the trends and the analysis applied to North American borders. The election may affect the future of the region as a whole and the relationship between the three countries astride North America. The relationship between the United States and Mexico could suffer the greatest change and ultimately alter the perception of the role and validity of Mexico in a so-called region of North America. Integration appears to have given way dramatically to separation. The border dynamic between Canada and the United States appears less volatile. Yet as stated already, borders and borderlands will remain in place as they have always been since they were established as North American divisions and connections. If anything, the task of border specialists has become more fascinating and important as they explore the workings of North American borders and borderlands. The changes in leadership, direction, and politics in North America, which only make the study of borders more timely and significant, is the primary focus of this book.

A Book on North American Borders in Comparative Perspective

This book is divided into four sections that analyze and compare the two North American borders, their people (sometimes referred to as *borderlanders* in the United States and Canada and *fronterizos* in Mexico), main issues, policies, current trends, and perspectives on policy directions and cooperation. Such an analysis covers the two sides of each border and concludes by posing two plausible and also uncertain and diverging scenarios: (1) one that proposes further North American integration and greater collaboration in the future notwithstanding the most recent changes in U.S. politics and proposed policies, and (2) a less positive one that redirects the current trends toward isolation and disintegration of the existing bilateral and trilateral agreements and cooperation.

Part 1 includes three chapters that describe the two North American borders and place them in the present era and within the current debates within borderlands studies. The first chapter was written by Tony Payan, director of the Mexico Center at the Baker Institute of Rice University. By using the so-called theory of action fields, Payan examines the character and nature of governance at the Mexico-U.S. border primarily through an in-depth analysis of the actors who populate and interact on the border. Subsequently, Victor Konrad, a geography professor at Carleton University and former director of the Canada--U.S. Fulbright Commission, offers a conceptual framework for reimagining the border between the United States and Canada. The third chapter, by Rick Van Schoik, portfolio director of the North American Research Partnership (NARP), describes twenty-first-century North American borders and draws lessons from around the world. Advocating for the reduction of transactional costs of and at borders, Van Schoik argues that "borders are shaped and rebordered by modern forces leading to necessary sovereignty shifts and sharing."

Part 2 of this book analyzes spaces, divisions, and interrelations among the different actors in the two North American borderlands. Chapter 4, by Francisco Lara-Valencia, associate professor of the School of Transborder Studies at

Arizona State University and executive secretary and treasurer of the Association for Borderlands Studies (ABS), explores transborder space formation in the Canada-U.S. and Mexico-U.S. borders from a comparative perspective. Considering postpositivist paradigms of region building, his analysis aims to understand "the construction of transborder spaces for development planning and cooperation in North America." In chapter 5, Donald K. Alper, professor emeritus of political science and founding director of the Border Policy Research Institute, Western Washington University, analyzes the shifting meanings of borders in North America. By acknowledging border thickening and the significant differences between the two North American borders, he suggests that these two spaces "are marked by two kinds of bordering: territorial divisive bordering and connective spatial bordering." In chapter 6, Alan Bersin, former assistant secretary for international affairs and chief diplomatic officer for the U.S. Department of Homeland Security (DHS) Office of Policy (and former "Border Czar"), explains how the nature of borders in today's global context has changed radically. According to his perspective, borders must be viewed as global "flows" of goods and people as much as "lines" on a map marking the transition from one sovereignty to another. This perspective fundamentally alters the understanding of the relationship between security and economic competitiveness.

Part 3 analyzes border governance in North America. Chapter 7 examines border governance in the context of twenty-first-century globalization. Here Emmanuel Brunet-Jailly, professor and Jean Monnet Chair at the University of Victoria and current president of ABS, reflects on China's current "Road and Belt Initiative" to illustrate his central argument: "In the 21st century borders are either territorial or they are functional." His analysis is then applied to an understanding of the complexity of North American borders. In order to analyze the positive side of border governance, the subsequent two chapters capture the reality of one segment of each North American border. In chapter 8, Kathleen Staudt, professor emerita at the University of Texas, El Paso, examines the central Mexico-U.S. borderlands and proposes short- and long-term actions to promote democratic cross-border governance with the aim of reducing economic inequalities and boosting wage prosperity for more people on both sides of the border. In chapter 9, Bruce Agnew, director of the Discovery Institute's Cascadia Center for Regional Development, looks to the Cascadia borderland and the Pacific Northwest Economic Region (PNWER) for a comprehensive example of successful binational governance with a history of environmental action and a talent for innovation.

Part 4, on integration and border policy directions in North America, includes four chapters that highlight issues of border cooperation and existing inequalities. Chapter 10, by Guadalupe Correa-Cabrera and Michelle Keck, associate professors at George Mason University and University of Texas Rio Grande Valley, respectively, is a comparative analysis of energy developments on both the Canada-U.S. and Mexico-U.S. borderlands regarding economic integration for the purpose of energy production. Their essay examines advances toward energy integration in both border regions, highlighting the differences and limitations of these processes as well as regional inequalities. Also stressing economic inequalities, chapter 11 examines cross-border cooperation for economic development. In this chapter, Christopher Wilson, deputy director of the Mexico Institute at the Woodrow Wilson International Center for Scholars, complements prior research on this subject by documenting the qualitative experiences of various actors that have been on the forefront of the process of cross-border cooperation for economic development in the U.S.-Mexico borderlands in the recent past. Chapter 12, by Christopher Brown, associate professor at New Mexico State University and president of the Western Social Science Association, is a comparative examination of watershed management efforts that have been advanced on "the arid region of the southwestern U.S.-Mexico borderlands and the humid region of the Canada-U.S. borderlands." The final essay of the edited collection, by Irasema Coronado, professor and director of the School of Transborder Studies, Arizona State University, and former executive director of the North American Commission for Environmental Cooperation, is not a comparative analysis of the two North American borders but an examination of the key aspects of trilateral collaboration. In her piece, Coronado recognizes that the commission "had a modicum of success in achieving its goals" and believes that it "is an excellent model for future environmental cooperation internationally."

The Role of North American Borders

Current thought about borders and their role in globalization is evolving rapidly as more social scientists and humanists direct their attention to what borders are, how they have evolved, and, particularly how they work. In this book we explore not only how borders work in theory in North America but also how these borders work in practice. First, borders are historically and culturally contingent. They are lines with temporal as well as spatial location, and history is very important in understanding where and how borders have been placed. It is also important to understand how the line divides different or the same peoples in the border space. These are border essentials in North America where Indigenous peoples still prevail in areas rebordered over centuries of colonial and state-building processes by newcomers to the continent and where successive waves of immigration have reconfigured borderlands' history and culture. These processes have shaped as well the imaginaries of the border in the borderlands and in the national territory at large.

Characteristically, in North America, the visions of the border are different in the borderlands and in the "heartland," thus contributing to everything from differences of opinion to outright conflict between those who inhabit the borderlands and those who control the border as a territorial boundary. One very practical consideration is to understand that borderlands have spatial extent (even though these areas are rarely designated or defined by the state) and that distinctive activities and actors operate within these zones. In North America, these border regions or borderlands have now been defined as cross-border regions.

These regions facilitate and articulate balanced and graduated interaction and to a degree integration. Also designated are the many corridors and conduits that operate as the arterials of the continent. True, these are often formed in and are vital to the infrastructure of the three countries, but their connection and extension create a truly North American ligature that is now firmly in place. Within this framework, the operation of the border and the borderlands is affected by the vagaries of agency, political will and clout, economic cycles, and other forces both inside the borderlands and outside. The resulting patterns of border operation and management and borderlands efficacy and viability are mainly defined regionally and locally. Borders and borderlands, then, are best understood and operationalized through a coordination of scale, because borders and borderlands are increasingly evocative of scalar pluralism and mobility.

When the scalar recognition and articulation is not evident, there is something missing or out of balance in the borderlands. The borderlands recede, and the border takes precedence in statist, territorial definition, most certainly, but also in the holding of the line to constrain, stratify, and prohibit crossing and integration. Borders that do not work are costly and require substantial securitization, eventually with walls. Yet when walls are constructed, it is a definitive sign of a border that has failed. In an era of globalization, such failure is even more devastating because it is exhaustive of state resources that are required to sort, select, and protect flows, resources that could be utilized elsewhere to provide more effective well-being and prosperity.

Borders have now become critical to understanding North American relations. Borders have been institutionalized in the federal government structures and operations of all three countries. Massive sums have been allocated to fund expanding cohorts of personnel to manage borders, infrastructure, technology, and security apparatus. Most of this enhancement is in the name of heightening security and control of the southern and northern land borders of the United States as well as the ports and airports that are increasingly international entry and exit spaces in a global network. All of the apertures are "ports" in a continental as well as a global exchange system. These apertures and the edges that they penetrate—on land, sea, or in the air—are vital connections in these systems at the same time that they are potential boundaries that may be breached by flows of undesirable goods and people. North American relations must encompass the understanding of how borders work in order to convey how North America now works. Border studies, then, have a tremendous potential to contribute to our understanding of continental dynamics and of how to implement this knowledge in facilitating effective border operation.

The Future of North American Borders

Where are North American borders headed? Clearly, the trend toward securitization, initiated substantially after the events of 9/11, has not yet run its course. Indeed, the construction of fences and barriers appears to be inclined toward new heights as President Trump begins to fulfill his campaign promise to build a great wall, sends over 5,200 troops to the border with Mexico, and declares a national emergency with the aim of achieving his goal. As the barriers accumulate, the material and virtual walls will affect the economies and well-being of all three countries in ways we can only now imagine. What is certain is that "new" borders will play a major role in changing North America.

In order to understand this emerging North America, it is incumbent on us to understand as much as we can about borders and how they work in continental as well as global contexts. We need to understand the confrontation between neonationalism and the cross-border structures, institutions, and cultures that have evolved during the past three decades. This knowledge of borders, borderlands, and the way in which these concepts have both galvanized opposition to integration and transition and support for North American and global ideals is quite necessary. In the process of rethinking North American borders in comparative perspective, we may move closer to understanding not only how North America works but how it may work better.

REFERENCES

Anderson, Joan B., and James Gerber. 2008. *Fifty Years of Change on the US-Mexico Border: Growth, Development, and Quality of Life.* Austin: University of Texas Press.

Andreas, Peter. 2009. *Border Games: Policing the US-Mexico Divide.* 2nd ed. Ithaca, NY: Cornell University Press.

Andreas, Peter, and Thomas J. Biersteker, eds. 2003. *The Rebordering of North America: Integration and Exclusion in a New Security Context.* New York: Routledge.

Anzaldua, Gloria E. (1987) 2012. *Borderlands/La Frontera: The New Mestiza.* 4th ed. San Francisco: Aunt Lute Books.

Bersin, Alan. 2012. "Lines and Flows: The Beginning and End of Borders." *Brooklyn Journal of International Law* 37 (2): 389–406.

Brunet-Jailly, Emmanuel, ed. 2007. *Borderlands: Comparing Border Security in North America and Europe.* Ottawa: Ottawa University Press.

Bryce, Benjamin, and Alexander Freund, eds. 2015. *Entangling Migration History: Borderlands and Transnationalism in the United States and Canada.* Gainesville: University Press of Florida.

Chang, Kornel. 2012. *Pacific Connections: The Making of the US-Canadian Borderlands.* Berkeley: University of California Press.

Chávez, Manuel. 2012. "Border Theories and the Realities of Daily Public Exchanges in North America." *Eurasia Border Review* 3 (1): 101–14.

Córdova, Ana. 2010. *Muro fronterizo entre México y Estados Unidos.* Tijuana: Colegio de la Frontera Norte.

Dear, Michael. 2013. *Why Walls Won't Work: Repairing the US-Mexico Divide.* New York: Oxford University Press.

Elizondo Griest, Stephanie. 2017. *All the Agents and Saints: Dispatches from the US Borderlands.* Chapel Hill: University of North Carolina Press.

Ganster, Paul, and David Lorey, eds. 2007. *The US-Mexican Border into the Twenty-First Century.* 2nd ed. Lanham, Md.: Rowman and Littlefield.

Government of Canada. 2006. "The Emergence of Cross-Border Regions Between Canada and the US: Roundtable Synthesis Report." Ottawa: Policy Research Initiative (PRI). Accessed August 8, 2008 (no longer posted). http://www.policyresearch.gc.ca /doclib/SR_NAL_CrossBorder_200605_e.pdf.

Hämäläinen, Pekka, and Benjamin Johnson, eds. 2011. *Major Problems in the History of North American Borderlands.* Belmont, Calif.: Wadsworth.

Johnson, Benjamin, and Andrew R. Graybill, eds. 2010. *Bridging National Borders in North America: Transnational and Comparative Histories.* Durham, N.C.: Duke University Press.

Johnson, Kevin. 2017. "The Lawman Challenging Trump's Border Wall." *USA Today*, March 5. https://www.usatoday.com/story/news/2017/03/05/arizona-lawman -challenging-president-trumps-border-wall/98492128/.

King, Thomas, Howard F. Mosher, and Jim Lynch. 2014. *Narrating North American Borderlands*. Frankfurt: Peter Lang.

Konrad, Victor, and Heather N. Nicol. 2008. *Beyond Walls: Re-Inventing the Canada–United States Borderlands*. Burlington, Vt.: Ashgate.

Lopez-Hoffman, Laura, Robert G. Varaday, Karl W. Flessa, and Patricia Balvanera. 2010. "Ecosystem Services Across Borders: A Framework for Transboundary Conservation Policy." *Frontiers in Ecology and Environment* 8 (2): 84–91.

Martínez, Oscar J. 1994. *Border People: Life and Society in the US-Mexico Borderlands*. Tucson: University of Arizona Press.

Moore, Stephen T. 2014. *Bootleggers and Borders: The Paradox of Prohibition on a Canada-US Borderland*. Lincoln: University of Nebraska Press.

Newman, David. 2006. The Lines That Continue to Separate Us: Borders in our Borderless World. *Progress in Human Geography* 30 (2): 143–61.

Nicol, Heather N. 2015. *The Fence and the Bridge: Geopolitics and Identity Along the Canada-US Border*. Waterloo, ON: Wilfrid Laurier University Press.

Nischik, Reingard M. 2016. *Comparative North American Studies: Transnational Approaches to American and Canadian Literature and Culture*. New York: Palgrave Macmillan.

Norman, Emma S., Alice Cohen, and Karen Bakker, eds. 2013. *Water Without Borders? Canada, the United States, and Shared Waters*. Toronto: University of Toronto Press.

Payan, Tony. 2016. *The Three US-Mexico Border Wars: Drugs, Immigration, and Homeland Security*. 2nd ed. Santa Barbara, Calif.: Praeger Security International.

Staudt, Kathleen. 1998. *Free Trade? Informal Economies at the US-Mexico Border*. Philadelphia: Temple University Press.

Staudt, Kathleen, and Irasema Coronado. 2002. *Fronteras no más: Toward Social Justice at the US-Mexico Border*. New York: Palgrave Macmillan.

Staudt, Kathleen, and Tony Payan. 2009. *Human Rights Along the US-Mexico Border: Gendered Violence and Insecurity*. Tucson: University of Arizona Press.

United Nations Environment Programme (UNEP). 2002. *North America's Environment: A Thirty-Year State of the Environment*. Washington, D.C.: UNEP.

Valenzuela Arce, José Manuel. 2013. *Nosotros: Arte, cultura e identidad en la frontera México–Estados Unidos*. Mexico City: Educal.

Widdis, Randy William. 1999. *With Scarcely a Ripple: Anglo-Canadian Migration into the United States and Western Canada, 1880–1920*. Kingston: McGill-Queen's University Press.

North American Borders in Maps

MAPS BY LAURIE TRAUTMAN AND ROXANNE MEDINA, BORDER POLICY
RESEARCH INSTITUTE, WESTERN WASHINGTON UNIVERSITY

Port of Entry

These maps display all of the ports of entry between the United States and
Canada (127) and between the United States and Mexico (44), including commercial and passenger crossings. As the maps highlight, there are regions of
both borders that consist of a dense network of multiple crossings as well as
areas where crossings are sparse. The maps include the Canadian, Mexican, and
U.S. crossing names and annual truck- and train-crossing volumes. The data
are based on annual transportation information from 2017 provided by the U.S.
Bureau of Transportation Statistics, part of the U.S. Department of Transportation. Roads and railroad data are from the Commission for Environmental
Cooperation (CEC) *North American Environmental Atlas* and are for reference
purposes only. Cities and provincial and state capital data are provided by Natural Earth Data, which utilizes up-to-date LANSCAN population data sets
maintained and distributed by the Oak Ridge National Laboratory. Country,
state, and provincial borders as well as international borders data used for the
base maps are also from Natural Earth Data. All main maps are presented in
the North American Datum 1983 Contiguous USA Albers projection, while
all locator maps are present in a modified North Pole Lambert Azimuth Equal
Area projection to maintain a North American focus.

Supporting Online Links/References: https://hifld-geoplatform.opendata
.arcgis.com/datasets/canada-and-mexico-border-crossings (for Shapefile for
points); https://www.naturalearthdata.com/downloads/10m-cultural-vectors/
(for roads, railroads, states, provinces, countries, populated places).

USA – Canada: Ports of Entry – Northwest

Annual Truck Crossings (U.S. entry only)

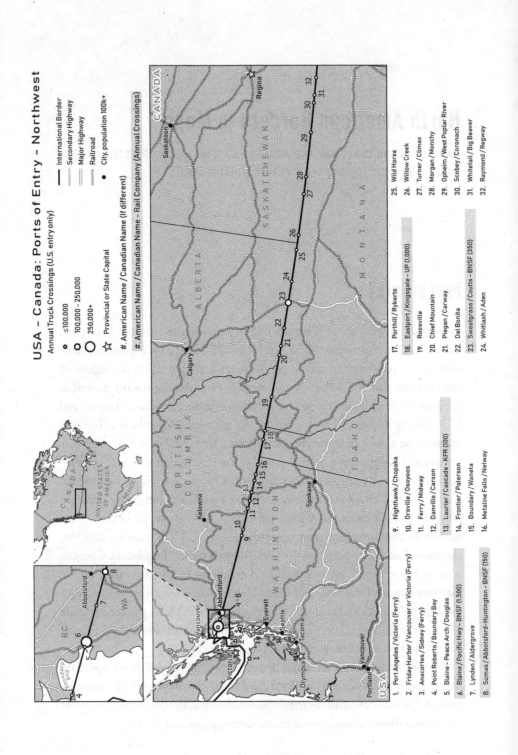

Legend:
- ——— International Border
- ——— Secondary Highway
- ——— Major Highway
- ········· Railroad
- ● City, population 100k+

○ ≤100,000
◎ 100,000 – 250,000
◯ 250,000+
☆ Provincial or State Capital

\# American Name / Canadian Name (If different)

\# American Name / Canadian Name – Rail Company (Annual Crossings)

1. Port Angeles / Victoria (Ferry)
2. Friday Harbor / Vancouver or Victoria (Ferry)
3. Anacortes / Sidney (Ferry)
4. Point Roberts / Boundary Bay
5. Blaine – Peace Arch / Douglas
6. Blaine / Pacific Hwy – BNSF (1,500)
7. Lynden / Aldergrove
8. Sumas / Abbotsford-Huntington – BNSF (150)
9. Nighthawk / Chopaka
10. Oroville / Osoyoos
11. Ferry / Midway
12. Danville / Carson
13. Laurier / Cascade – KFR (100)
14. Frontier / Paterson
15. Boundary / Waneta
16. Metaline Falls / Nelway
17. Porthill / Rykerts
18. Eastport / Kingsgate – UP (1,000)
19. Roosville
20. Chief Mountain
21. Piegan / Carway
22. Del Bonita
23. Sweetgrass / Coutts – BNSF (350)
24. Whitlash / Aden
25. Wild Horse
26. Willow Creek
27. Turner / Climax
28. Morgan / Monchy
29. Opheim / West Poplar River
30. Scobey / Coronach
31. Whitetail / Big Beaver
32. Raymond / Regway

USA – Canada: Ports of Entry – Midwest

Annual Truck Crossings (U.S. entry only)

- ○ ≤100,000
- ○ 100,000 - 250,000
- ○ 250,000+
- ☆ Provincial or State Capital

— International Border
— Secondary Highway
═ Major Highway
····· Railroad
● City, population 100k+

#. American Name / Canadian Name (If different)

#. American Name / Canadian Name – Rail Company (Annual Crossings)

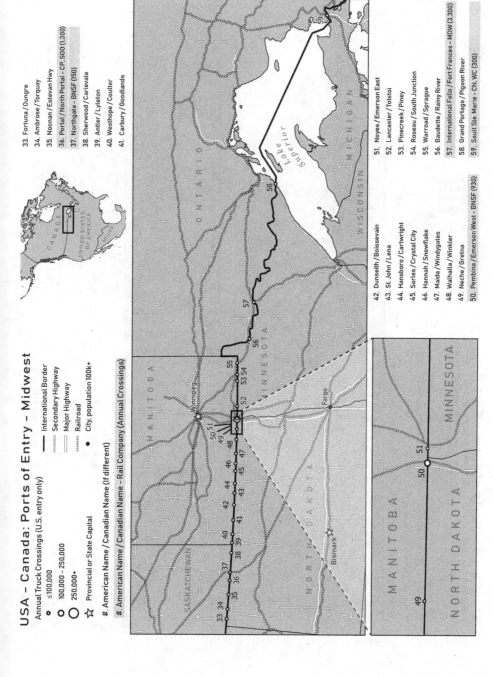

33. Fortuna / Oungre
34. Ambrose / Torquay
35. Noonan / Estevan Hwy
36. Portal / North Portal - CP. SOO (1,300)
37. Northgate - BNSF (150)
38. Sherwood / Carievale
39. Antler / Lyleton
40. Westhope / Coulter
41. Carbury / Goodlands

42. Dunseith / Boissevain
43. St. John / Lena
44. Hansboro / Cartwright
45. Sarles / Crystal City
46. Hannah / Snowflake
47. Maida / Windygates
48. Walhalla / Winkler
49. Neche / Gretna
50. Pembina / Emerson West - BNSF (930)

51. Noyes / Emerson East
52. Lancaster / Tolstoi
53. Pinecreek / Piney
54. Roseau / South Junction
55. Warroad / Sprague
56. Baudette / Rainy River
57. International Falls / Fort Frances - MDW (3,300)
58. Grand Portage / Pigeon River
59. Sault Ste Marie - CN. WC (300)

USA – Canada: Ports of Entry – East

Annual Truck Crossings

- ○ ≤100,000
- ○ 100,000 – 250,000
- ○ 250,000+
- ☆ Provincial or State Capital
- ★ National Capital

— International Border
‖ Secondary Highway
═ Major Highway
┄ Railroad
• City, population 100k+
★ National Capital

#. American Name / Canadian Name (if different)

#. American Name / Canadian Name – Rail Company (Annual Crossings)

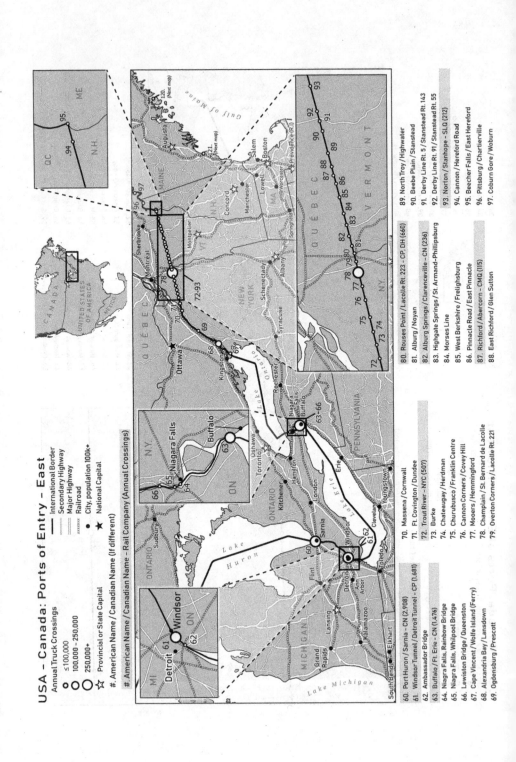

60. Port Huron / Sarnia – CN (2,908)
61. Windsor Tunnel / Detroit Tunnel – CP (1,681)
62. Ambassador Bridge
63. Buffalo / Ft. Erie – CN (1,476)
64. Niagara Falls, Rainbow Bridge
65. Niagara Falls, Whirlpool Bridge
66. Lewiston Bridge / Queenston
67. Cape Vincent / Wolfe Island (Ferry)
68. Alexandria Bay / Lansdown
69. Ogdensburg / Prescott

70. Massena / Cornwall
71. Ft. Covington / Dundee
72. Trout River – NYC (507)
73. Burke
74. Chateaugay / Herdman
75. Churubusco / Franklin Centre
76. Cannon Corners / Covey Hill
77. Mooers / Hemmingford
78. Champlain / St. Bernard de Lacolle
79. Overton Corners / Lacolle Rt. 221

80. Rouses Point / Lacolle Rt. 223 – CP, DH (660)
81. Alburg / Noyan
82. Alburg Springs / Clarenceville – CN (236)
83. Highgate Springs / St. Armand–Phillipsburg
84. Morses Line
85. West Berkshire / Frelighsburg
86. Pinnacle Road / East Pinnacle
87. Richford / Abercorn – CMQ (115)
88. East Richford / Glen Sutton

89. North Troy / Highwater
90. Beebe Plain / Stanstead
91. Derby Line Rt. 5 / Stanstead Rt. 143
92. Derby Line Rt. 91 / Stanstead Rt. 55
93. Norton / Stanhope – SLQ (212)
94. Cannon / Hereford Road
95. Beecher Falls / East Hereford
96. Pittsburg / Chartierville
97. Coburn Gore / Woburn

USA – Canada: Ports of Entry – East/Alaska/Yukon

Annual Truck Crossings (U.S. entry only) ——— International Border

○ ≤100,000   ⋯⋯⋯ Secondary Highway
○ 100,000–250,000   ⋯⋯⋯ Major Highway
○ 250,000+ (None this map)   ⋯⋯⋯ Railroad
☆ Provincial or State Capital – – – Ferry Route
                                ● City, population 100k+

American Name / Canadian Name (if different)

American Name / Canadian Name – Rail Company (Annual Crossings)

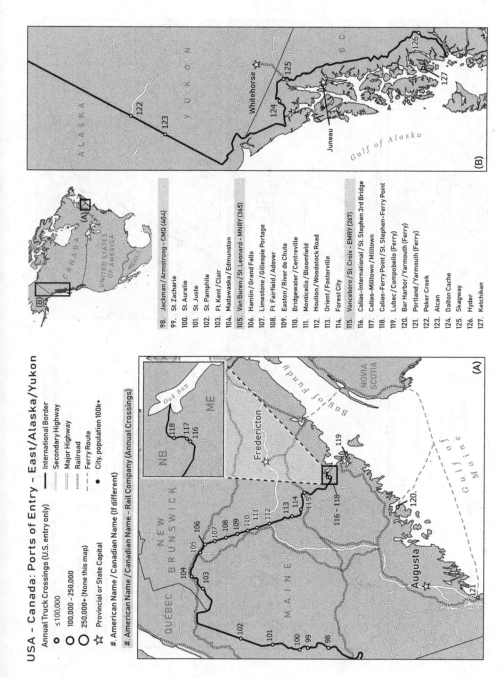

98. Jackman / Armstrong – CMQ (404)
99. St. Zacharie
100. St. Aurelie
101. St. Juste
102. St. Pamphile
103. Ft. Kent / Clair
104. Madawaska / Edmunston
105. Van Buren / St. Leonard – MNRY (365)
106. Hamlin / Grand Falls
107. Limestone / Gillespie Portage
108. Ft. Fairfield / Adover
109. Easton / River de Chute
110. Bridgewater / Centreville
111. Monticello / Bloomfield
112. Houlton / Woodstock Road
113. Orient / Fosterville
114. Forest City
115. Vanceboro / St. Croix – EMRY (267)
116. Calias–International / St. Stephen 3rd Bridge
117. Calias–Milltown / Milltown
118. Calias–Ferry Point / St. Stephen–Ferry Point
119. Lubec / Campobello (Ferry)
120. Bar Harbor / Yarmouth (Ferry)
121. Portland / Yarmouth (Ferry)
122. Poker Creek
123. Alcan
124. Dalton Cache
125. Skagway
126. Hyder
127. Ketchikan

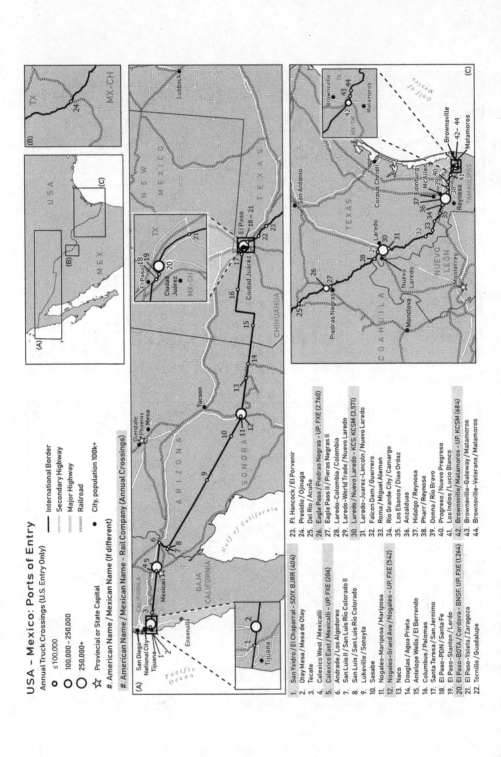

USA – Mexico: Ports of Entry

Annual Truck Crossings (U.S. Entry Only)

○ ≤100,000
○ 100,000 – 250,000
◯ 250,000+

☆ Provincial or State Capital
● City, population 100k+

— International Border
⫶⫶⫶ Secondary Highway
⫶⫶⫶ Major Highway
xxxxxxx Railroad

#. American Name / Mexican Name (if different)

#. American Name / Mexican Name – Rail Company (Annual Crossings)

1. San Ysidro / El Chaparral – SDIY, BJRR (404)
2. Otay Mesa / Mesa de Otay
3. Tecate
4. Calexico West / Mexicalli
5. Calexico East / Mexicalli – UP, FXE (206)
6. Andrade / Los Algodores
7. San Luis II / San Luis Río Colorado II
8. San Luis / San Luis Río Colorado
9. Sasabe
10. Lukeville / Sonoyta
11. Nogales–Mariposa / Mariposa
12. Nogales–Grand Ave / Nogales – UP, FXE (542)
13. Naco
14. Douglas / Agua Prieta
15. Antelope Wells / El Berrendo
16. Columbus / Palomas
17. Santa Teresa / San Jernimo
18. El Paso–PDN / Santa Fe
19. El Paso–Stanton / Lerdo
20. El Paso–BOTA / Cordova – BNSF, UP, FXE (1,264)
21. El Paso–Ysleta / Zaragoza
22. Tornillo / Guadalupe
23. Ft. Hancock / El Porvenir
24. Presidio / Ojinaga
25. Del Río / Acuña
26. Eagle Pass / Piedras Negras – UP, FXE (2,760)
27. Eagle Pass II / Pieras Negras II
28. Laredo–Colombia / Colombia
29. Laredo–World Trade / Nuevo Laredo
30. Laredo / Nuevo Laredo – KCS, KCSM (3,571)
31. Laredo–Juarez–Lincoln / Nuevo Laredo
32. Falcon Dam / Guerrero
33. Roma / Miguel Aleman
34. Rio Grande City / Camargo
35. Los Ebanos / Dias Ordaz
36. Anzalduas
37. Hidalgo / Reynosa
38. Pharr / Reynosa
39. Donna / Río Bravo
40. Progreso / Nuevo Pregreso
41. Los Indios / Lucio Blanco
42. Brownsville / Matamoros – UP, KCSM (684)
43. Brownsville–Gateway / Matamoros
44. Brownsville–Veterans / Matamoros

North American Drainage Basins and Subwatersheds

There are sixty-three unique drainage basins and subwatersheds that overlap borders in North America. As the map displays, many of these areas are large in size and are thus critical to natural resource management in a binational context. Published in 2010, the data are from Natural Resources Canada, Mapping Information Branch, *The Atlas of Canada*; Instituto Nacional de Estadística y Geografía (National Institute of Statistics and Geography of Mexico); and the United States Department of the Interior, U.S. Geological Survey, and are provided by the CEC's *North American Environmental Atlas*. Country, state, and provincial borders as well as international borders data used for the base map are from Natural Earth Data. This map and all its corresponding locator and inset maps are presented in the same modified North Pole Lambert Azimuth Equal Area projection used in other maps.

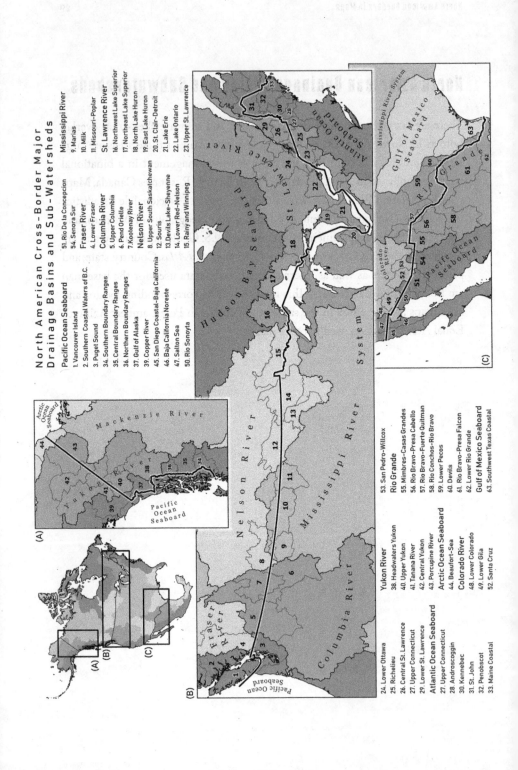

North American Cross-Border Major Drainage Basins and Sub-Watersheds

Pacific Ocean Seaboard
1. Vancouver Island
2. Southern Coastal Waters of B.C.
3. Puget Sound
Southern Boundary Ranges
34. Southern Boundary Ranges
35. Central Boundary Ranges
36. Northern Boundary Ranges
37. Gulf of Alaska
39. Copper River
45. San Diego Coastal–Baja California
46. Baja California Noreste
47. Salton Sea
50. Rio Sonoyta
51. Rio De la Concepcion
54. Senora Sur

Fraser River
4. Lower Fraser

Columbia River
5. Upper Columbia
6. Pend Orielle
7. Kootenay River

Nelson River
8. Upper South Saskatchewan
12. Souris
13. Devils Lake–Sheyenne
14. Lower Red–Nelson
15. Rainy and Winnipeg

Mississippi River
9. Marias
10. Milk
11. Missouri–Poplar

St. Lawrence River
16. Northwest Lake Superior
17. Northeast Lake Superior
18. North Lake Huron
19. East Lake Huron
20. St. Clair–Detroit
21. Lake Erie
22. Lake Ontario
23. Upper St. Lawrence
24. Lower Ottawa
25. Richelieu
26. Central St. Lawrence
29. Upper Connecticut
29. Lower St. Lawrence

Atlantic Ocean Seaboard
27. Upper Connecticut
28. Androscoggin
30. Kennebec
31. St. John
32. Penobscot
33. Maine Coastal

Yukon River
38. Headwaters Yukon
40. Upper Yukon
41. Tanana River
42. Central Yukon
43. Porcupine River

Arctic Ocean Seaboard
44. Beaufort–Sea

Colorado River
48. Lower Colorado
49. Lower Gila
52. Santa Cruz
53. San Pedro–Willcox

Rio Grande
55. Mimbres–Casas Grandes
56. Rio Bravo–Presa Cabello
57. Rio Bravo–Fuerte Quitman
58. Rio Conchos–Rio Bravo
59. Lower Pecos
60. Devils
61. Rio Bravo–Presa Falcon
62. Lower Rio Grande

Gulf of Mexico Seaboard
63. Southwest Texas Coastal

Energy Infrastructure

There is a dense and vast network of energy infrastructure throughout North America. This map displays electric transmission ties, natural gas pipelines, and liquids pipelines that cross the Canada-U.S. border and the Mexico-U.S. border. Liquids pipelines include the movement of crude oil, hydrocarbons, and petroleum products. Points of border crossing for all three of these energy resources are from information made available by the U.S. Energy Information Administration (EIA) based on 2017 data. This map also displays major pipelines that span all three countries. All pipelines were hand digitized by georeferencing static images of pipeline maps found online from various sources including the Canadian Association of Petroleum Producers, the U.S. Energy Information Administration, and Canadian Energy. Images were downloaded and brought into GIS software, georeferenced to a prepared states and provinces line layer, and then hand traced to create a custom North America pipelines layer. The pipelines presented in this map are thus not spatially accurate and are meant only to represent the network of interconnected pipelines that span North America through a visualization of their general geographic locations. This map and all its inset maps are presented in the same modified North Pole Lambert Azimuth Equal Area projection used in other maps.

Supporting Online Links/References: https://www.eia.gov/maps/layer_info -m.php (for points); https://pgjonline.com/old_assets/wp-content/uploads /sites/2/2015/07/Canada_figure1.png (for pipelines).

North American Cross-Border Energy Infrastructure and Major Pipelines

✛ Electric Transmission: USA/Canada

1. Belden Power / Stewart Hyder
2. Blaine / Ingledow
3. Netway
4. Netway 2
5. Montana Alberta Tie
6. Basin Electric / Boundary Dam–Tioga
7. Northern States / Manitoba Hydro–Electric
8. Northern States Power / Letellier–Prairie
9. Roseau County 508 / Dorsey–Chisago County
10. Roseau County 230 / Richer–Shannon
11. Minnesota Power / Ft. Frances
12. Int'l Transmission Co / Keith–Waterman
13. Int'l Transmission Co / Lambton–St. Clair L4D
14. Int'l Transmission Co / Bunce Creek–St. Clair LSID
15. Int'l Transmission Co / Sarnia Scott–Bunce Creek
16. Niagara Mohawk / Rainbow Bridge
17. Sir Adam Beck / New York Power
18. Niagara Mohawk / Peace Bridge
19. New York Power / Cornwall–Massena
20. New York Power / Chateauguay–Massena
21. Joint Owners of Highgate / Bedford–Vermont
22. Vermont Electric Power Co / Derby Line
23. Vermont Electric / Des Cantons
24. Maine Public Service / Edmunston–Madawaska
25. Maine Public Service / Beachwood Flo's Inn
26. Maine Electric / Keswick–Orrington
27. Maine Public Service / Circuit 6901 Tinker Plant
28. Maine Public Service / Circuit 6914 Tinker Plant
29. Bangor Hydro–Electric / New Brunswick Power
30. Maine Electric Power Co / Milltown Calais

✛ Electric Transmission: USA/Mexico

1. San Diego Gas and Electric / Tijuana I
2. Baja California Power / La Rosita I
3. Termoeléctrica US
4. San Diego Gas and Electric / La Rosita II
5. El Paso Electric Co / Anapra
6. El Paso Electric Co / Rivereña
7. AEP Texas Central / Piedras Negras–Eagle Pass
8. AEP Texas Central / Cd. Industrial–Laredo
9. Frontera Generation / Cumbres Frontera
10. Sharyland Utilities / Cumbres Frontera–Rail Road
11. AEP Texas Central / Matamoros–Military Highway
12. Brownsville Public Utilities Board

▲ Natural Gas Pipeline: USA/Canada

1. Northwest Pipeline / Hipco Import–Export Line
2. Puget Sound Energy / Hipco Import–Export Line
3. Cascade Natural Gas / Hipco Import–Export Line
4. Gas Transmission NW / ANG Mainline
5. Northwestern Energy / Carway Line
6. Northwestern Energy / Aden Pipeline
7. Havre Pipeline / Loomis–Herbert
8. Northern Border Pipeline / Line 1 – Zone 9
9. Williston Basin / Elmore–Portal / Steelman–North Portal
10. Alliance Pipeline / Mainline
11. Alliance / Mainline
12. Great Lakes Transmission
13. Viking Gas Transmission
14. Central Pipeline Minnesota / Sprague Pipeline
15. Central Pipeline Minnesota / Rainy River–Ft. Frances
16. Central Pipeline Minnesota / Ft. Frances
17. Panhandle Eastern / Detroit River–Windsor
18. Vector Pipeline / Vector
19. Michigan Consolidated Gas / St. Clair River Crossing
20. Great Lakes Transmission / Line 500-1 and 2
21. ANR Pipeline / The Link Pipeline
22. Bluewater Pipeline / Bluewater River Crossing
23. Tennessee Gas Pipeline / Line 200-1 and 2
24. Empire Pipeline / Line 400-1
25. Iroquois Pipeline / Line 1400-1
26. St. Lawrence Gas / Cornwall Pipe
27. North County Pipeline / Line 1600-1
28. Vermont Gas System / Line 800-1
29. Portland Gas Transmission / PNGTS
30. Maritimes & Northeast Pipeline / Mainline

▲ Natural Gas Pipeline: USA/Mexico

1. San Diego Gas and Electric / Baja California
2. Southern California Gas / Ecogas México
3. North Baja Pipeline / Gasoducto Rosarito
4. Sierrita Gas Pipeline / Gasoducto de Aguaprieta
5. Western States Power / Autoabastecedores de Gas Natural de Nogales
6. El Paso Natural Gas Pipeline / Naco
7. El Paso Natural Gas Pipeline / Gasoducto de Aguaprieta
8. Norteno Pipeline / Gas Natural de Juárez
9. El Paso Natural Gas Pipeline / Tarahumara Pipeline
10. Gasoductos de Chihuahua / Tarahumara Pipeline
11. Compañía de Autoabastecedores de Gas Natural de Acuña
12. West Texas Gas / Compañía Nacional de Gas (Río Bravo)
13. Kinder Morgan Texas / Kinder Morgan Gas Natural de Mexico
14. NET Mexico Pipeline / Gasoducto Noreste
15. Houston Pipeline / Argüelles Pipeline
16. Tennessee Gas Pipeline / Reynosa–Tennessee
17. Texas Eastern Pipeline / Reynosa–TETCO
18. Tennessee Gas Pipeline / Gasoducto del Río

☐ Liquids Pipeline: USA/Canada

1. Trans Mountain Pipeline
2. Phillips 66 / Carway
3. Front Range Pipeline / Milk River
4. Express Pipeline
5. Manline / Wascana
6. Vantage Pipeline
7. North Dakota / Line Ex-02
8. Cochin / Canadian Western Section
9. Keystone Pipeline / Keystone
10. Line 1, 2, 3, 4, 5, 67 Alberta Clipper
11. Southern Lights / Line 13
12. LSr Line 65
13. Dearoll Pipeline / Eastern Delivery System
14. Salmon A
15. Mariner West / Sun-Canadian
16. Genesis Pipeline / St. Clair River
17. Line 5
18. Line 6
19. Line 10
20. Portland Pipeline / Highwater

☐ Liquids Pipeline: USA/Mexico

1. Magellan Pipeline, Rio Grande Pipeline / Ciudad Juárez
2. Dos Laredos Pipeline / Nuevo Laredo
3. Burgos Pipeline / Burgos–Peñitas
4. Diamond Pipeline / Matamoros–Brownsville

Indigenous Lands and Protected Areas

These two maps illustrate the patchwork of Indigenous lands and protected areas that exist in the borderlands of North America. There are seventeen officially recognized lands and areas in the Canada-U.S. borderlands, the largest of which are located in the Alaska-Yukon wilderness. In the Mexico-U.S. borderlands, there are eighteen similar designations.

There are important differences in both terminology and recognition that Indigenous populations have in each country. In the United States, tribes have dedicated reservations, while in Canada, First Nations have reserves. In Mexico, however, Indigenous populations do not have designated and protected lands and thus are not presented in this map. It is important to note that both the Canada-U.S. and Mexico-U.S. borderlands are inhabited by Indigenous populations that are bifurcated by the border and face unique challenges to mobility and cohesion.

In Mexico, the Comisión Nacional de Áreas Naturales Protegidas (CONANP), or National Commission of Protected Natural Areas, is the federal agency that administers Mexico's 182 protected natural areas. These areas are categorized as national parks, biosphere reserves, protected flora and fauna areas, natural sanctuaries, protected natural resources areas, and natural monuments. Data for these maps are provided by the CEC's *North American Environmental Atlas* using data from the USGS Protected Areas Database of the United States. Additional Indigenous lands data sets for the U.S. and Canada are from the U.S. Census Bureau and Natural Resources Canada, provided by DataBasin.org. This map and all its inset maps are presented in the same modified North Pole Lambert Azimuth Equal Area projection used in other maps.

Supporting Online Links/References: http://www.cec.org/tools-and-resources/map-files/north-american-protected-areas-2017 (for Shapefile for all categories); https://commons.wikimedia.org/wiki/File:Mapa_de_lenguas_de_M%C3%A9xico_%2B_100_000.png (for Mexico, for reference).

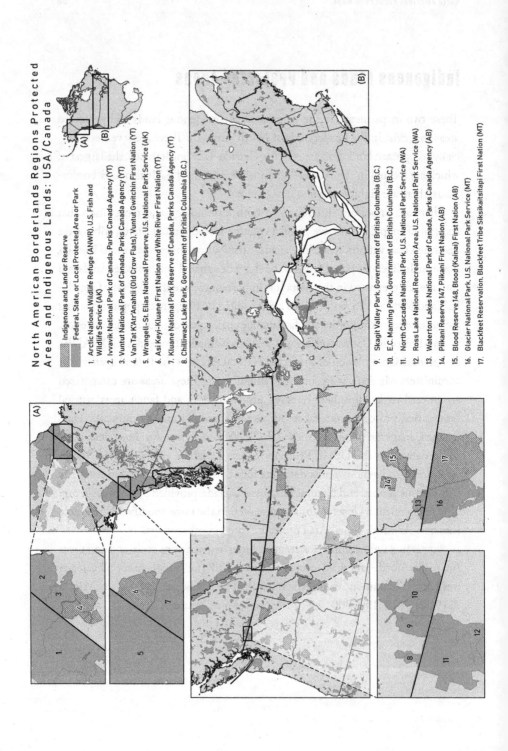

North American Borderlands Regions Protected Areas and Indigenous Lands: USA/Canada

Indigenous and Land or Reserve

Federal, State, or Local Protected Area or Park

1. Arctic National Wildlife Refuge (ANWR), U.S. Fish and Wildlife Service (AK)
2. Ivvavik National Park of Canada, Parks Canada Agency (YT)
3. Vuntut National Park of Canada, Parks Canada Agency (YT)
4. Van Tat K'Atr'Anahii (Old Crow Flats), Vuntut Gwitchin First Nation (YT)
5. Wrangell–St. Elias National Preserve, U.S. National Park Service (AK)
6. Asi Keyi–Kluane First Nation and White River First Nation (YT)
7. Kluane National Park Reserve of Canada, Parks Canada Agency (YT)
8. Chilliwack Lake Park, Government of British Columbia (B.C.)

9. Skagit Valley Park, Government of British Columbia (B.C.)
10. E.C. Manning Park, Government of British Columbia (B.C.)
11. North Cascades National Park, U.S. National Park Service (WA)
12. Ross Lake National Recreation Area, U.S. National Park Service (WA)
13. Waterton Lakes National Park of Canada, Parks Canada Agency (AB)
14. Piikani Reserve 147, Piikani First Nation (AB)
15. Blood Reserve 148, Blood (Kainai) First Nation (AB)
16. Glacier National Park, U.S. National Park Service (MT)
17. Blackfeet Reservation, Blackfeet Tribe Siksikaitsitapi First Nation (MT)

North American Borderlands Regions Protected Areas and Indigenous Lands: USA/Mexico

Indigenous Land or Reserve

Federal, State, or Local Protected Area or Park

1. Navajo Nation Reservation, Navajo Nation (AZ)
2. San Carlos Reservation, San Carlos Apache Nation (AZ)
3. Kofa National Wildlife Refuge, U.S. Fish and Wildlife Service (AZ)
4. Organ Pipe Cactus National Monument, U.S. National Park Service (AZ)
5. Gila River Reservation, Pima and Maricopa Tribes (AZ)
6. Tohono O'odham Nation Reservation, Tohono O'odham Nation (AZ)
7. El Pinacate y Gran Desierto de Altar Core Zone, National Commission of Natural Protected Areas (SO)
8. Janos Biosphere Preserve, Natural Commission of Natural Protected Areas (CH)
9. Cañón de Santa Elena, National Commission of Natural Protected Areas (CH)
10. Big Bend National Park, U.S. National Park Service (TX)
11. Ocampo, National Commission of Natural Protected Areas (CO)
12. Maderas del Carmen, National Commission of Natural Protected Areas (CO)
13. C.A.D.N.R. 004 Don Martín, National Commission of Natural Protected Areas (CO)
14. Cheyenne–Arapaho Reservation, Cheyenne and Arapaho Nations (OK)
15. Kiowa–Comanche–Apache Fort Sill Apache, Apache Nation (OK)
16. Chickasaw Reservation, Chickasaw Nation (OK)
17. Creek Reservation, Muscogee Nation (OK)
18. Cherokee Reservation, Cherokee Nation (OK)
19. Choctaw Reservation, Choctaw Nation (OK)

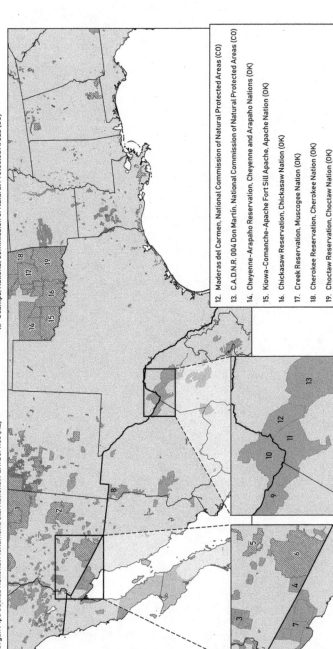

PART I

Replacing Borders Between Mexico, the United States, and Canada

CHAPTER 1

Actors, Strategic Fields, and Game Rules

Examining Governance at the U.S.-Mexico Border in the Twenty-First Century

TONY PAYAN

T he end of the Cold War profoundly affected the nature of governance at the U.S.-Mexico border. By 1990, as the iron curtain was falling in Europe and the Soviet Union was collapsing, Mexico and the United States moved to deepen their strategic relationship through one of the most avant-garde trade agreements of its time, the North American Free Trade Agreement (NAFTA). The two countries then sought to achieve unprecedented cooperation on public safety and security issues. Simultaneously, and unilaterally, however, the United States moved to vastly expand its surveillance and control of all border flows, legal and illegal, by deploying a security apparatus that would turn the borderlands into a region under the dominance of an increasingly well-articulated security and law enforcement apparatus. These contradictory actions, the economic and commercial opening of the border and the security-motivated closing of the border, reconfigured the border's governance system in a way that prevails to this day. Although the Trump administration has brought NAFTA under scrutiny and has called for a border wall—moves that challenge the idea of a binational strategic partnership—the treaty is likely to survive and border security, with or without a wall, is likely to harden further. Using concepts from *A Theory of Fields* by Fligstein and McAdam (2015), this essay examines the character and nature of governance at the border primarily through an in-depth examination of the actors who populate and interact on the border.

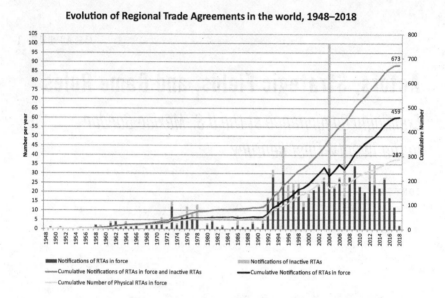

FIGURE 1.1 Number of free trade agreements in the world (Source: World Trade Organization, https://www.wto.org/english/tratop_e/region_e/regfac_e.htm)

Introduction

The last decade of the twentieth century was a decade of great optimism. Globally, the end of the Cold War in 1990 brought about a renewed push for international liberalism, including unprecedented economic openness, measured by a flurry of regional cross-border commercial activity (fig. 1.1) and a wave of democratic transitions (Huntington 1991). The apparent triumph of commercial and political liberalism made some proclaim that we had reached "the end of history" (Fukuyama 1992). In North America, the 1994 NAFTA—negotiated by Canada, the United States, and Mexico—was in fact one of the greatest symbols of the newfound faith in commercial regional integration and debordering. Mexico also began a push for democratic openness, seeking to join the club of industrialized democracies—a club to which the United States and Canada already belonged.

Not all was well at the U.S.-Mexico border, however. Even as NAFTA was providing new cross-border business opportunities, Mexico was engaged in a democratic transition, and optimism about regional integration was growing, the United States moved aggressively to reinforce its border with Mexico. Washington began putting in place a set of policies and building infrastructure to control tightly all border flows. As these measures paradoxically advanced through the 1990s and accelerated after the terrorist attacks of September 11, 2001, they would have a profound influence in transforming the U.S.-Mexico border— how it is governed and who governs it. In this new hardened border landscape, different actors would seek to position themselves to push for their own vision of the border. Some were favored by this trend; others would simply be left to react.

Who are these actors vying for influence at the U.S.-Mexico border? What are their interests? What are their strategies? Four collective actors are identified as the central players in the border strategic field. First, as NAFTA accelerated trade and business opportunities across the border, economic actors reaffirmed their view of the border as a strategic resource (Sohn 2014). Transnational corporations and investors, many of whom had already dotted the border through the maquiladora industry, moved to take advantage of the new commercial rules. Their vision was one of an open, flexible, and maybe even seamless border to take advantage of labor cost differentials and reduce transaction costs.

Second, border civil society—borderlanders in general—was another important collective actor. They, too, advocated for a more open order, pushing for worker rights, reduction of violence, an increase in the borderlands' quality of life, and bureaucratic accountability of government agencies operating along the border. They saw the reconfiguration of the border as affecting borderlanders and civil society organizations the most. Their lives and opportunities for cross-border activity were in effect reshaped dramatically by the new rigid conditions of the borderlands and the increase in border law enforcement discretionary power and lack of accountability.

Third, criminal organizations—from drug trafficking organizations to human smuggling groups—asserted themselves as strategic actors in the field. They proved themselves to be capable of learning and adapting to a changed border and to be very effective in dealing with the new environment in order to continue to conduct their black-market business.

Finally, anticipating strategic behavior by less desirable actors—for example, human smugglers, undocumented migrants, drug trafficking organizations, and others—U.S. government principals (politicians) and agents (bureaucracies) deployed unprecedented resources to control border flows, erected new barriers and fencing, introduced novel technologies to stem illegal flows, and added thousands of border patrol and customs agents (Maril 2004; Payan 2006; Chomsky 2009; Dunn 2010; Andreas 2012; Payan 2016). In this atmosphere of increased cross-border flows and unprecedented efforts to control them, law enforcement agencies became the central players, well above the rest of the other collective actors populating the border strategic field. Their vision of the border was one where they controlled all flows across the borderline with little or no liability (table 1.1).

The reshuffling of actors and interests at the border constituted the most important factor restructuring the border space (Flynn 2000) and provided the impetus for the cross-border governance system that prevails to this day. The cross-border governance system of the last quarter century has also experienced three key moments that have served to consolidate its composition: the mid-1990s military-style law enforcement operations, the terrorist attacks of September 11, and the 2016 election of Donald Trump to the presidency of the United States. Faced with these external shocks, each actor was forced to reassess its position in the border action field and to act strategically to preserve (defensive) or expand (offensive) its vision and its prerogatives and privileges in the borderlands. Because all players—economic actors, cross-border civil society, criminal organizations, and law enforcement—want to play a role in cross-border governance, the field has become a dynamic environment where each responds to the other and each seeks to exert influence over the field's units of governance—laws, regulations, processes, and procedures—in order to incorporate their interests into them.

On the sidelines, the scholarly community, too, set out to understand the paradoxical trends at the border and to study and craft new concepts to comprehend changes at the border in the twenty-first century. An important inter-

TABLE 1.1 Collective actors in the border action field and their interests within the strategic action field

	Business and corporate	Civil society and borderlanders	Criminal organizations and groups	Law enforcement and security
Interest	Open, flexible, seamless border to take advantage of cross-border labor cost differentials and minimize business transaction costs	Relatively open border with increased access and stricter adherence to due process and human rights	Understanding control of border flows to find and exploit vulnerabilities in the system to smuggle drugs and people	Closed border with tightly managed border ports of entry and strict border flows control with absolute discretion and no public accountability

pretation of the emerging border structure came from an examination of the physical transformation of the U.S.-Canadian border. It relates to the idea that the governance system on the ground is primarily influenced by the creation of secured corridors and gateways and a dramatic reinforcement of the line between gateways (Konrad and Nicol 2008). The idea behind border control strategies was to build a border that facilitated economic activity through tightly controlled corridors and gateways while attempting to fend off "undesirable" actors along the line between and at ports of entry. The literature on *rebordering* processes has since exploded along these lines. But however we conceive the border, scholars of border studies will likely have to theorize harder and appeal to many disciplines simultaneously. Thus, to understand the character and nature of governance at the U.S.-Mexico border today—thirty years after the end of the Cold War—this chapter uses key concepts from Fligstein and McAdam's (2015) strategic action field (SAF) theory. SAF, as a sociological theory, provides for: (1) the *action field* or space where all interaction among players occurs; (2) the *actors* vying for influence in the action field; (3) the *strategic behavior* of the players, who pursue their interests over those of the other players in the field; (4) the *units of governance*—laws, regulations, processes, and procedures—that all players seek to capture and by which all players must abide; and (5) the external shocks to the environment, which begins periods of contention where different players seek to defend or advance their interests. This chapter argues that by focusing on SAF actors—whom Fligstein and McAdam (2012) divide into *incumbents* and *challengers* and who interact competitively in the border space to shape the units of governance in their favor—it is possible to understand how the border is governed and who governs it today as well as the character and nature of cross-border governance.

A More Complex Framework and Methodology

An adjustment to Fligstein and McAdam's theoretical framework is merited here. Although their SAF theory is applicable to many different issue areas, borders are particularly complex SAFs because they are fields crossed by robust lines of demarcation, exclusive jurisdictions, joint policy areas with different national approaches, and institutional variation from one side to the other. All of this further complicates using the theory to understand border governance. The border is not just a policy field but a space in motion (Konrad 2015), contested (Anderson and O'Dowd 1999b), negotiable (Allmendinger et al. 2015), resisted (Bejarano 2010), but especially bifurcated by national lines. The border as a policy space is hardly ever completely settled—something it shares with other issue areas contained within a country—but its governance is the result of structures negotiated by the actors inhabiting within a national SAF and between them and actors inhabiting a different national SAF across a borderline. Thus, players seek to project their organizational and individual interests in the entire binational SAF and to act and react, operate and resist, compete and cooperate, and ultimately dominate and impose their vision of the border in a complicated space where power projection is not unidimensional or linear but complex and multilayered.

Moreover, the U.S.-Mexico border is neither a "thin" nor a "thick" border (Haselsberger 2014). Although central governments weigh heavily, the border SAF is never entirely fixed from above. On the contrary, as in any SAF, agency matters in generating various levels and degrees of competition and domination of the governance units. The skills required are even more complex because actors must navigate between two legal and institutional policy systems and must relate to other players in the field and to the masters above in the national hierarchy. Thus, power practices matter substantially as SAF actors negotiate their place in and use of the border and seek to extract its benefits for themselves and their group. In that sense, the U.S.-Mexico border has developed endogenous inertias (Medina García 2006) that have nothing to do with the central government. These inertias reflect an amalgam of lines and flows that show marked differences by and for different actors as they interact horizontally and vertically. Finally, as Fligstein and McAdam would have it, in the border SAF, the units of governance are never neutral. Instead, they are the very instruments of governance system control. The units of governance are not all the same for everyone but are always negotiated and resisted, sometimes issue by issue, flow by flow, gate by gate, and corridor by corridor. Contemplating the border SAF from above, it is easy to appreciate it as a highly dynamic field, the various actors jockeying for position within it, and ultimately to determine the character and nature of cross-border governance and who enjoys privileges and access and who suffers disadvantages and denial of access. Additionally, there is a fundamental misunderstanding about the U.S.-Mexico border. Despite increased controls, its dynamism at the micro level is more like that of a frontier because it is a zone of interpenetration between two peoples, many of whom share cultural, social, and linguistic traits and view the boundary as largely artificial, albeit real in its effect (Parker 2006). The border is thus constructed into a

complicated matrix of overlapping problems and issues, jurisdictions and interests, and desires and aspirations. And all SAF actors pursue their own vision
of themselves and the borderlands in this matrix. When confronted with power
differentials, they create their own dynamics of domination and resistance and
continuously renegotiate privileges and access.

At an empirical level, to understand governance at the U.S.-Mexico border,
this chapter relies on seventy-one interviews with key actors on the border conducted between 2013 and 2014. The interviewees come from elected officials, the
security community, the business and entrepreneurial class, and members of the
borderland's civil society. All interviews were carried out in the Paso del Norte
region and were done by members of a larger research team. The interviews
lasted from thirty minutes to an hour and a half each. The questions asked were
semistructured to allow the interviewees to explain how they view themselves
and their organizations in the border space, who they think "governs" the borderlands, and how different players have carved out spaces for themselves and
their organizations within the border SAF. Questions were also asked about
how they have pursued their interests and those of their group and how they
have had to negotiate with the dominant players and the content of the governance units on a day-to-day basis. From these interviews, this study assembles
the processes of flows to investigate the nature of governance in the SAF, how
the units of governance that prevail in the border space are defined, and the
privilege and access that various actors can negotiate for themselves. It thereby
shows how the various actors continue to negotiate governance structures to
preserve the border as a resource. Finally, the study included an open survey conducted through Survey Monkey with many of the same and additional actors.

The next section briefly examines the nature of the border SAF. The following sections then analyze each of the collective actors who interact within it
and their strategic behavior—how they interact with one another—to answer
the central question of who governs the border. Finally, the chapter draws conclusions about the nature of the governance system at the U.S.-Mexico border
as seen through an examination of the actors and their behavior in the SAF.

The Border Strategic Action Field

The strategic action field (SAF) examined here, namely, "the border," is not
easy to define—it can geographically stretch in many different directions

and reach many different proportions (Payan and Cruz 2017) and it can have different meanings for different actors (Van Houtum 2005). Indeed, the border means different things to different SAF players depending on the action, the public policy issue at hand, the actors involved, the territorial area of the intended action, and whether the action is horizontal—toward other actors in the SAF—or vertical—toward the national political actors or principals. In this sense, this chapter does not attempt to define the border territorially or to resolve the problem of its meaning to understand cross-border governance. Instead, it assumes that the best way to understand the nature of cross-border governance is to look at the border as a "strategic action field" (SAF)—a space where actors compete to become *governors* of the field, however they define it. It also assumes that by focusing on who the SAF actors are—their interests, their skills, as well as their structural advantages within the SAF—it is possible to understand the character and nature of cross-border governance. In that sense, looking at the border SAF and the actors who populate it, three features stand out: (1) players in the field navigate the tension between policies directed at maintaining an open border and policies directed at controlling the border; (2) the security paradigm that prevails today creates structural *field environment* advantages for some and disadvantages for others; and (3) the embeddedness of the border SAF within a larger political context tests the actors' skills to pursue their vision of the border by leveraging resources outside the field. Let us break down each of these features.

First, the border SAF is characterized by a fundamental tension between opening and closing. This tension provides the first layer on which the border governance system has grown for a quarter century—perhaps much longer—and it stems from two competing visions of the border, both of which emerged at the end of the Cold War. One came from the political Right in the United States, with law enforcement as its instrument, and the other from an amalgam of advocates of free trade, immigration, and human rights. The former implied increasing control of border flows and a gradual closing of the border. This group seems to have reached its apex in the policies of the Trump administration. The latter group implied a gradual, albeit orderly, opening of the border. To be sure, there were serious attempts at reconciling these visions of the border. The Security and Prosperity Partnership (SPP) of North America is an agreement that tried in fact to reconcile these two contradictory forces (Villarreal and Lake 2009), but it did not have much success in creating a political coalition to do so. The SPP initiative was practically stillborn, as its timing was not auspicious, and it faced political resistance and institutional dysfunctions in all countries (Gluszek 2014). This tension provides the background against which border actors pursue their interests.

Second, there is a growing national and international ideological context focused on security as the summum bonum. Borders have in fact become a major focus of this ideological bent. As such, the U.S.-Mexico border SAF has come increasingly under the definition of a security paradigm—with an increasingly militarized outlook. Most public policy issues came to be negotiated within a framework that prioritizes border security. All players in the borderlands (from federal bureaucracies to local businesses, corporations, governments at all levels, civil society organizations, organized criminals, and individuals) interact with governance units—laws, regulations, processes, and procedures—heavily influenced by the border security paradigm. This provides a structural advantage to actors focused on border security; they have created a virtuous cycle for themselves, arguing at every turn that the border is a "dangerous" place and placing themselves at the center of the solution to border insecurity. Moreover, U.S.-Mexico border security policies are not today confined to the borderlands. There is a deliberate policy to deploy policy instruments forward to neutralize "border threats" before they arrived at the ports of entry or the borderline by preclearing travelers and cargo and exercising denial of access well before arrival at the borderline (Purcell and Nevins 2005; Bowman 2007; Bersin 2015). To reinforce this form of governance—a heavily militarized borderline and a forward deployment of the border—initiatives were born to make the border "smarter" (U.S. Department of State 2002; Ackleson 2003) without really specifying why the border was not smart in the first place—something that suggests that "smart" is essentially a code word for far-reaching control by actors who favor security (Purcell and Nevins 2005) and the creation of a rights-free zone (Doty 2007; Salter 2008). This trend, already under way in the 1990s, was reinforced by the terrorist attacks of September 11 and the political anxiety that followed. After 9/11, the initial instinct was to close the border tightly, although in the end there emerged a debate on how to balance border security and national prosperity (Villarreal and Lake 2009; U.S. Customs and Border Protection 2015). Still, over time, it was clear that the terrorist attacks of 2001 provided additional impetus for the idea that security is primordial and additional justifications for the security-focused bureaucratic scaffolding that was already being built in the 1990s. September 11, for example, provided further rationale to reorganize border government agencies to further securitize functions that had been previously viewed as largely administrative (Brunet-Jailly 2005; Payan 2016). Moreover, the new security environment loosened the nexus between bureaucracy and democracy as agencies became less accountable for their power uses and abuses (Balla and Gormley 2017). This basic framework (controlled corridors and gateways, forward deployment of the border, and a state of exception at the borderlands) prevailed through the Obama administration. It seems poised to become even more rigid during the Trump administration. Indeed, the 2016 presidential election in the United States did away with all pretentions of balancing security and prosperity. The Trump administration appears to have resolved the tension between prosperity and security once and for all in favor of the latter. There are plans to accelerate the securitization of the border by adding thousands of U.S. Customs and Border Patrol (CBP) and U.S. Border Patrol agents, building a two-thousand-mile concrete wall, and revising NAFTA in favor of a more nationalist economic paradigm. The Trump administration's proposals seem to be a natural step in a historical trend to expand and harden border control. Although scholars over the last two decades have invested much time and energy studying and advocating for cross-border integration (CBI), geo-economic mobility, and cross-border territorial projects (Sohn 2014), all such concepts apply less and less to the U.S.-Mexico border, even if there are small successes, such as the Tijuana Airport CBX project (McCartney 2016).

Third, the border SAF remains embedded in a larger context—a politically motivated support for absolute control of the border. The political profit to be had by elected officials, many of whom ultimately determine the shape and form that the units of governance take, is enormous, and the costs for castigating the borderlands are too low. Border security agencies are ultimately implementers of a political use of the border. They have also proven extremely capable of connecting with the broader or external political environment that frames border policies. Governing the border remains in fact an activity strongly centralized in the two nations' capitals in the hands of elected officials, the principals, in sync with the ground agents, law enforcement. The principals—political actors—and their agents—law enforcement—found in fact a way of marrying their interests by building an image of the border as an insecure place. This was easy, as all actors in an SAF make their own social history, sometimes at odds and sometimes in line with the centralized political and economic powers of the nation-state (Baud 1997), but they must necessarily accommodate directives that come from above. When these interests line up, they are mutually reinforcing, as in the case of the U.S.-Mexico border. In the end, there was relatively little input from most other local SAF actors in the public policy process (Payan 2010) when it came to the border. All interaction between border actors in the SAF cut through the directives that came down from political principals beyond the borderland.

The border governance system today is largely the result of these features of the border SAF—tensions between two visions of the border, an increased dominance of the security paradigm, and the compatibility between politically motivated central directives and the priorities of border law enforcement actors. These features of the border SAF create structural advantages for certain actors in border governance—the incumbents—and place nearly all others at a disadvantage—the challengers. And although the meaning and significance of borders can change over space and time (Anderson and O'Dowd 1999a) and the issue at hand, actors negotiate their own place on the border (Wilson and Donnan 1998) and pursue their interests within these structural constraints. This environment in fact tests the skills of all challengers to negotiate their place in the SAF in the face of border security agency dominance. Interestingly, even under these conditions of near absolute dominance by one actor—law enforcement—the border is always in motion (Konrad 2015) and always being interrogated (Tripathi 2015).

To illustrate this further, we can see how trends are self-reinforcing, perpetuating the structural orientation of governance and making mounting a challenge ever more difficult. For example, while NAFTA projected the border as a valuable resource for economic actors whose agenda shifted in favor of open borders in the 1990s (Newman 2003), it became increasingly difficult for other noneconomic actors (e.g., civil society) to cross that same border to take advantage of old or new opportunities. For many, those usually at the bottom of the socioeconomic rungs, the border became in fact a militarized space with harsh consequences (Slack et al. 2016). This resulted in increasing numbers of migrant deaths (Cornelius 2001; Rubio-Goldsmith et al. 2016) and multiple violations of human rights (Staudt, Payan, and Kruszewski 2009; Simmons and Mueller 2014). What that means is that the most vulnerable of all border users saw their vulnerability compounded by the dominance of those actors who positioned themselves as the border guards. Paradoxically, even as the security scaffolding directed at migrants and border residents grew, there was no noticeable change in drug trafficking. This should not be surprising. Drug trafficking and other actors dedicated to illegal activities are also strategic players who adjust quickly and adeptly to new conditions in the border SAF. All statistics point in that direction. Thus, when it comes to the war on drugs at the border SAF, border residents were affected more than drug traffickers (Chalabi 2016). Border residents as a group will not be discussed here, but they are never absent, as they, too, are used rhetorically by the governors of the border to continue building their rhetorical advantage—the border SAF as a dangerous place—and to place themselves as the solution to the same danger.

Having surveyed the central features of the border SAF, it must now be said that all actors must be examined in their structural context if we are to understand the nature of cross-border governance. For economic actors and entrepreneurs, the border became an area of great opportunities to conduct business, to profit from important price differentials in labor and supply markets, and to take advantage of structural tax incentives—witness the still-strong border maquiladora industry (Cañas et al. 2013). But for immigrants, the border SAF became a liminal space, the difference between a bad and a better life (Fourny 2013) and sometimes the difference between life and death. For shoppers, the border SAF represented an opportunity to stretch their hard-earned family earnings (Baruca and Zolfagharian 2013), but they, too, had to put up with stricter controls in their use of the border as a resource. For security actors, however, the border became a space where they can exert their bureaucratic imperialism impulses (Roberts 1976) even as smugglers of illegal goods and humans continue finding opportunities to do business (Passas 2003). In fact, the law enforcement and criminal cat and mouse side game cannot be understood but in the context of the larger cross-border governance system and its structure. The list of players goes on depending on the granular focus of the observer. Thus, the border SAF is primarily a competitive space where actors pursue their interests, negotiate and resist, and attempt to implement their own vision of the border, ideally, by capturing the governance units.

The dynamic nature of the field is reinforced by a lack of binational institutions. Unlike Europe, North America is characterized by low and uneven levels of institutionalization with a relative absence of binational frameworks for local governments to exercise varying degrees of functionally pooled sovereignty (Payan 2010; Payan and Cruz 2018). Some areas exhibit greater degrees of institutionalized cooperation (Spalding 2000), while other issues are approached both unilaterally and largely from the great centers of power, such as Washington, D.C., or Mexico City. Areas of lesser institutionalized cooperation magnify, quantitatively and qualitatively, the areas of potential conflict among actors on the ground, providing them with more opportunities to assert their interests—witness the perverse dance between law enforcement agents and drug traffickers at the borderline (Sanderson 2004; Payan 2016). However, local actors are not powerless. They do push against the units of governance and those who would enforce them. Some negotiate spaces of privilege with the actors who govern the border space; for example, the wealthy and international corporations can use fast lanes for precleared travelers and merchandise (Sparke 2006), while other border users are excluded and even criminalized (Ackerman and Furman 2013). Thus, the border is subject to continuous motion (Konrad 2015), contestation (Anderson and O'Dowd 1999b), reinterpretation (Newman 2001), low and uneven levels of institutionalization (Payan and Cruz 2018), multiple gray areas (Vergani and Collins 2015), all making for a field of action where all players have to craft their rhetoric, exert whatever influence they can over the governance units, accommodate or resist the goals of others, and seek to position themselves to dominate the SAF.

Field domination is an existential drive, and a border SAF is no different—all actors in the space jockey to achieve dominance amid their own constraints and opportunities. Since the 1990s, the main rhetorical portrayal of the U.S.-Mexico border has been that of insecurity (Ackleson 2005), and that has given the advantage to actors who "provide" security or hold the promise of increased security in the space. That image has been constructed and reaffirmed over time by bureaucracies that would benefit materially from that image and politicians who would profit politically from the moral panic they create (Hughes 2007). This rhetoric has generated policies that give a structural or material advantage to those same actors who back a security agenda. All other actors are left to react. The next section examines each of the actors who populate the border action field, describing how each behaves and examining the final power arrangement within the field.

The Field Actors

In theory, any SAF is populated by actors who at a minimum pursue their interests or preferably seek to dominate the SAF they inhabit by capturing the units of governance—laws, regulations, processes, and procedures—and reshaping them to embody their interests and their vision of the field. Sometimes SAF actors behave cooperatively and sometimes competitively, but all strive to influence the governance units—laws, rules, regulations, procedures, and processes—because doing so is the most efficient way to survival and dominance. The alternative is a highly competitive field where no one dominates and high degrees of competition and conflicts ensue. That scenario requires too much energy and produces too much uncertainty. If a given SAF actor achieves control of the governance units, the capturing actor becomes the SAF incumbent. Those who at any one point are not considered incumbents are, essentially, challengers of the status quo in one way or another. This section examines the incumbents and the challengers of the U.S.-Mexico border field of action, as an efficient heuristic analysis to understand who governs the border SAF.

The Security Community: The Incumbents

Since the 1990s, the U.S.-Mexico border has been primarily governed by actors whose instruments to dominate the governance units have been crafted around the concept of security. They have taken the historical, rhetorical, and structural advantage for nearly three decades—since the end of the Cold War—continuously working to reinforce all three advantages and creating a cycle of dominance for them. They have shown themselves to have skills to leverage these advantages to position themselves in the border SAF. As trends in dealing with public and international affairs have become permeated by the concept of security (Buzan, Wæver, and Wilde 1998), for example, border security actors have positioned themselves to take advantage of legislative processes, regulatory benefits, and budgetary advances to be increasingly dominant, and they have expanded their discretionary power as well (Landau 2016). At key junctures, such as the events of September 11, security border SAF players have advanced the rhetorical display on security, reaffirming a historical trend and compounding their structural advantage. The U.S. Border Patrol, for example, has increased its budget steadily from 1990 through 2017 (fig. 1.2) by convincing political actors that the border SAF is lawless and overrun by criminals (Cabrera 2015). U.S. Customs and Border Protection has also grown substantially since its creation in 2002 (fig. 1.3).

Consequently, in the U.S.-Mexico border field of action, the incumbents are the security community—Customs and Border Protection (CBP), Border Patrol, Immigration and Customs Enforcement (ICE), and state and local law enforcement agencies who have been deputized as border guards (e.g., the Texas Department of Public Safety [State of Texas, Legislative Budget Board 2016]). Actors charged with "securing" the border have in effect been skillful

United States Border Patrol Budget, 1990–2017

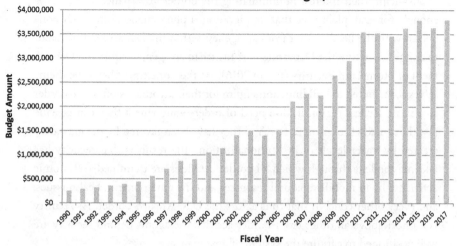

FIGURE 1.2 U.S. Border Patrol budget since 1990 (Source: US Border Patrol Fiscal Year Budget Statistics 1990–2017, https://www.cbp.gov/document/stats/us-border-patrol-fiscal-year-budget-statistics-fy-1990-fy-2017, accessed January 31, 2018 [no longer posted])

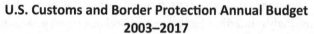

U.S. Customs and Border Protection Annual Budget 2003–2017

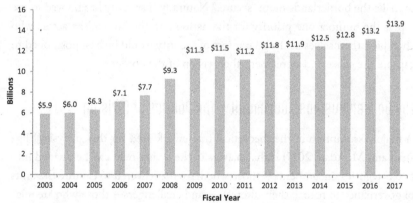

FIGURE 1.3 U.S. Customs and Border Protection budget since 2003 (Source: American Immigration Council 2017; US Department of Homeland Security, Budget-in-Brief, FY 2005–2017, https://www.americanimmigrationcouncil.org/sites/default/files/research/the_cost_of_immigration_enforcement_and_border_security.pdf and https://www.dhs.gov/dhs-budget., accessed January 31, 2018 [no longer posted])

at advancing their interest in dominating the border governance system. It is enough, for example, to see that immigration, a phenomenon intimately connected with the border, went from an agency within the Department of Labor to an agency within the Department of Justice to an agency within the Department of Homeland Security (Payan 2016). At the same time, they have themselves contributed to building momentum for their favored vision of the border space as a lawless region in dire need of order—one where they can provide just the remedy (Johnson 2011). And they have been favored by the gray areas created by lower levels of institutionalization. The result is that security has become the lens through which all border activities are examined—economic activity, human mobility, natural resources and the environment, health issues, and every other concern that runs across the U.S.-Mexico border. As security is a priori above all other cross-border activity, the agents behind security are well positioned to capture the system of governance.

Clearly, the units of governance—laws, rules, procedures, and processes—are therefore never neutral. They embody and project the interests of the so-called incumbents—the actors who have, through a combination of historical, rhetorical, and structural advantages as well as their own skills have managed to become the governors of the field. In our case, the U.S.-Mexico border space has become dominated by law enforcement agencies, all of which have acquired an increasingly militarized outlook as they seek to project power and the ability to make the borderlands more "secure." Naturally, if security has buoyed to the top as the number one priority for the nation and the border, the actors who champion themselves as the guarantors of security would be best positioned to capture the space and implement their vision of the border.

The Border Business Community: The Politics of Division

A major assumption in the theoretical framework used for this analysis (Fligstein and McAdam 2015) is that players in the action field can be divided into two categories: incumbents—those who have maneuvered to capture the units of governance to realize their interests—and challengers—those who are relatively unhappy with the action field power distribution and desire to modify the units of governance to reflect their interests. The interviews conducted for this study reveal a different picture, considerably more nuanced. Action field players who can be considered challengers possess different skills and have different resources at their disposal, and they also possess different interests, which may not necessarily coincide. Thus, not all challengers are the same and sometimes they compete among themselves. This cleavage among challengers is evident in the border governance system.

On the U.S.-Mexico border, the entrepreneurial class, propped up by their business connections with international corporations, has had both the skills and the resources to steer itself into a position of privilege in its interactions with the incumbents—a position of privilege constructed partly on the distance they keep from the working class and social activists in the border field. The interviews with several of the subjects of this study show that the entrepreneurial class in fact enjoys liberties and privileges directly related to their higher socioeconomic status. When crossing the borderline, for example, most of them make use of the designated commuter, or SENTRI (Secure Electronic Network for Travelers Rapid Inspection), lanes—a privilege predicated largely on the ability to pay (in addition to being considered a "trusted traveler"). Many of them consider themselves binational, hold dual citizenship, own real estate and businesses on both sides of the border, marry each other, and generally lament the fact that the border is largely "closed" and that it is not "what it used to be." Thus, their desire for a "more open" border makes them challengers since they would likely benefit from more open borders but are still obliged to negotiate spaces of privilege with the true incumbents—the security community. The fact that they enjoy negotiated access privileges also puts distance between them and the rest of the challengers. Indeed, they enjoy an elevated level of mobility and cross-border access that most people on the border do not. This is further exacerbated by the inequality in wealth and income along the U.S.-Mexico border, which further separates various socioeconomic classes, giving the richer groups a buoyancy in the system of governance not available to the poorer classes (Peach 1997; Esparza and Donelson 2008; Moré 2011; Anderson and Gerber 2017).

Moreover, during the dozens of hours of interviews, there were practically no manifestations of solidarity with the working class among the entrepreneurial-class interviewees. Their conception of the border is one where business is impeded by the security apparatus and the status quo is somewhat discouraging, but the burdens on the overall cross-border civil society (Payan and Vásquez 2007) are not problematic per se. Many saw the maquiladoras, for example, as the symbol of border development and prosperity despite alternative narratives that claim that workers are exploited and even pauperized by the industry (La Botz 1994; Staudt and Coronado 2002; Gibbs 2004; Wójtowicz and Winiarczyk-Raźniak 2014; and many other works) and that maquiladoras have contributed to serious violations of legal and human rights (Lusk, Staudt, and Moya 2012; Simmons and Mueller 2014). Mobilizing civil society in their view would not necessarily be to their advantage. Consequently, most of the interviewees within the entrepreneurial group viewed the border as a resource (Sohn 2014), and their ability to take full advantage of it was evident, but they did not speak to border agent treatment of border crossers or poverty or militarization of the border. One of their fundamental preoccupations, instead, was with the economic losses caused by long wait lines at the ports of entry—something directly related to their interests. For instance, the San Diego Association of Governments (2016) has commissioned several studies to quantify the losses to businesses. All along the border, the entrepreneurial class appears to be narrowly focused on their interests, and they negotiate with the incumbents accordingly. Thus, although the business class may appear to be incumbents in the governance scape, the privileges that they enjoy in the field are primarily negotiated with the true incumbents—the security community, in whose hands lie the governance units.

At the U.S.-Mexico border, market players have therefore taken advantage of the asymmetry to exploit comparative advantages on one side or the other, but they do not negotiate within their group, the challengers. Instead, they negotiate with incumbents based on their narrower interests. There is very little solidarity with the rest of the actors who could be labeled challengers. Thus, the challengers are arranged hierarchically, with civil society—workers, nongovernmental organizations, and the general population toward the bottom of the border hierarchy. This arrangement is largely propped up by the prevailing ideology, security and neoliberalism, an important structural advantage that confines each actor to its layer in the field, although this structure may be eroding with the shifts in the political landscape under the Trump administration. Clearly, the security community is best positioned to advance its interests under the new administration, and the economic actors stand to lose ground, which explains why many of them have quickly mobilized to defend NAFTA, a framework under siege by the Trump government. One such business organization is the newly formed Texas-Mexico Trade Coalition (2017), whose mission is to defend the prevailing economic structure.

Workers and Civil Society: The Governed

The U.S.-Mexico border has nearly fifteen million residents and a long history of cross-border contacts—from mass migrations (Monroy 1999) to contraband

(Díaz 2015) to protest (Hathaway 2000). The overwhelming majority of these fifteen million borderlanders belong to the working class. They fill the relatively low-paying jobs in the region and labor under enormous wage disparities (Clemens 2015). They are tethered to their territorial communities and have little or no cross-border mobility. They are generally the object of suspicion, surveillance, and control by law enforcement (Andreas 2012) even though the link between poverty and security and crime is controversial (Sharkey, Besbris, and Friedson 2016) and in spite of the fact that the U.S. side of the border remains one of the safest areas in the country according to the FBI Uniform Crime Reports. For them the border is not a readily available resource. Moreover, they bear some of the steepest costs of social, health, and environmental problems at the border (Bastida, Brown, and Pagán 2008), and they engage in a daily struggle to survive rends in the social fabric caused by stricter law enforcement and the violence inflicted by criminal groups. Most border residents enjoy few of the prerogatives of the entrepreneurial class, such as double residences and precleared traveler access, and they make up most of the individuals who cross the border on foot, exposing them to elevated levels of pollution (Galaviz et al. 2014). They undergo the harshest scrutiny of the law enforcement agents who control the borderline (Lusk, Staudt, and Moya 2012). It has also been argued that they are subject to intimidating tactics and experience constant fear as they cross the border (Correa, Garrett, and Keck 2014). These border residents are the *governed.*

This does not mean that they do not coalesce around their group interests, but it is difficult for them to do so across the borderline as cross-border contact is increasingly curtailed by securitization. A recent count of organizations active and relatively effective along the border, for example, found that many of them are related to economic activities. The Border Governors Conference, the Border Legislative Conference, the U.S.-Mexico Border Mayors Association, the Border Trade Alliance, the RGV Partnership, the Arizona-Mexico Commission, the Borderplex Alliance, the Cali-Baja Bi-National Mega-Region, the Western Maquiladora Trade Association, the Association of Maquiladoras A.C., and several other organizations, including multiple chambers of commerce, are dedicated primarily to the interests of the entrepreneurial class. Clearly, these organizations are largely created around economic interests, primarily those related to binational trade and investment, and are maintained and funded by the entrepreneurial class. Many of these organizations articulate the interests of the higher socioeconomic classes, entrepreneurs, traders, and investors, and they serve as interlocutors to negotiate with the incumbents and carve out spaces of privilege for the upper classes. They hold regular meetings, meet with elected officials, lobby in favor of an "open" border, and negotiate spaces of greater mobility for their economic activities. These groups are major clients of systems such as SENTRI and the Customs Trade Partnership Against Terrorism (CTPAT), a program secures fast access to trade lanes (Free and Security Trade program, or FAST program).

Regular borderlanders and citizens and their associations and networks are not as effective or influential because they do not organize effectively. On the U.S. side, for example, they have some of the lowest voting rates in the country. There are organizations dedicated to defending the legal and human rights of the border population, many of which are dedicated to protecting the rights of migrants. Some such organizations are the Borderlinks, Border Philanthropy Partnership, Border Network for Human Rights, Border Angels, the South Texas Human Rights Center, the Kino Border Initiative, the Southern Border Communities Coalition, and so on. Few of these organizations, however, advocate for the creation of binational communities that include merging labor markets that deal jointly with environmental issues, quality of life, and other concerns. Overall civil society organization across the border is rare and difficult to achieve (Sabet 2008). Workers and other border users are the lower rungs of the socioeconomic order and do not articulate well their interests to improve the quality of life in the borderlands. The few organizations that exist are poorly funded and often delinked from each other.

The state of cross-border civil society further demonstrates that the nature of governance in the region is hierarchical and heavily influenced by the ability of different actors to interact with each other and to use their resources and skills to navigate their relationship with the units of governance—laws, rules, procedures, and processes—and the incumbents. The border action field is not, therefore a simple tug between two groups, incumbents and challengers, but a struggle for each to individually and as an interest group defend and advance its position. Governance is, demonstrably, heavily mediated by player skills, as Fligstein and McAdam (2015) predicted, but also by their ability to galvanize resources in favor of their interests.

Political Actors and the Field Environment

It is difficult to understand the border action field and the prevailing structure of cross-border governance without dedicating some time to examining the broader *political* environment, particularly because the border is not only a multifaceted resource to its dwellers but also to nonborderlanders who would profit handsomely from a remote rhetorical construction of the borderscape. The border has in fact exhibited a high degree of vulnerability to rhetorical construction and deconstruction by outsiders, especially politicians, in state and national capitals (DeChaine 2012). Fligstein and McAdam (2015) do indeed pay attention to the embeddedness of any action field in its larger context. Thus, the border is embedded in a much larger *political* national context within the United States. Understanding this political context is fundamental to understanding the structure of border governance because governance units originate largely in the national capitals. Given the asymmetrical power position between central governments and borderland civil society (Kozák 2010), border residents are generally left to adopt and adapt to national capital-driven designs of border governance, primarily those coming from Washington D.C.

California in the 1990s under Governor Pete Wilson is one example of outsider rhetorical construction of the border for political profit (Larsen 2017). The Texas border has continuously, to this day, been used as a platform for outsiders who profit from portraying it as a lawless frontier and the source of severe threats. Dan Patrick, Texas lieutenant governor, had said that the border was being "overrun by illegal immigrants" who brought with them "Third-World diseases" (Selby 2014). Clearly, the border is vastly profitable as a way of focalizing ideologies for political rent. This has certainly been the case from the 1990s, as the border has become profitable to politicians who are adept at creating moral panic (Garland 2008) and then projecting themselves as the actors who can resolve it. There are multiple instances of politicians referring to the border as a place sieged by "invaders," drug traffickers, illegal migrants, terrorists, and others.

The border SAF incumbents—the security community—have been very adept at responding to the national political environment to advance their interests. Nearly every testimony before the U.S. Congress by the leaders of border security agencies claims that the border is "not safe." As former CBP acting deputy commissioner Vitiello put it, "The security challenges facing CBP and our Nation are considerable, particularly along the Southern border" (Vitiello 2017). Interestingly, public safety, undocumented migration, and violence numbers on the U.S. side of the border have all trended lower (figs. 1.4, 1.5). But incumbents have shown an ability to fuel moral panic around ground conditions on the border SAF and to push for higher material resources, more

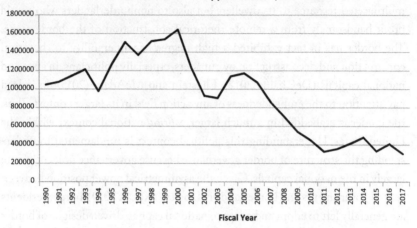

FIGURE 1.4 Annual apprehensions on the U.S.-Mexico border (Source: U.S. Customs and Border Protection, "US Border Patrol Fiscal Year Southwest Border Sector Apprehensions (FY 1960—FY 2018)," https://www.cbp.gov/newsroom/media-resources/stats)

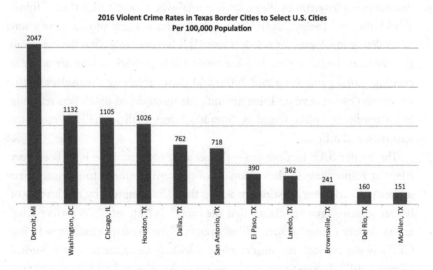

FIGURE 1.5 Violent crime composed of five offences: murder, nonnegligent manslaughter, rape, robbery, and aggravated assault—with border cities in comparison to other metropolitan areas (Source: https://ucr.fbi.gov/crime-in-the-u.s/2016/crime-in-the-US-2016/topic-pages/violent-crime, accessed February 3, 2018 [no longer posted])

jurisdictional power, and less accountability—all desirable goals for any bureau-cracy (Wilson 1989). Security agencies have positioned themselves to expand their role in border governance and have used opportunities to further their goals—including key moments such as the terrorist attacks of September 11. The ability of the incumbents to assert their dominance in the SAF in the face of trends that would be heartening to challengers testifies to their skills to use their advantages. This also illustrates that incumbents are not necessarily sat-isfied with the status quo at any one moment even if they dominate the SAF. They, despite wielding control of the governance units, seek to expand their own prerogatives. The national political context has, therefore, reinforced security agencies' historical, rhetorical, and structural advantage with little possibility of change in the future. In this context, challengers, privileged or not, are left to negotiate only on the margins of the governance units in place.

The same political context is not favorable to civil society organizations and individuals who would like to see a different governance system on the border. The ability of organizations that seek a more open border or greater human mobility and added attention to due process and human rights is limited. They are hardly ever invited to testify before the U.S. Congress or are actively con-sulted. This has been referred to as a "democratic deficit" (Payan 2010). Their weakened status in the border action field is an indication of their rhetorical, historical and structural disadvantage vis-à-vis other actors, especially incum-bents. It also signifies that border governance is a state of exception not only in terms of law enforcement but also in terms of democratic participation of borderlanders in shaping the borderscape.

Although the theoretical framework created by Fligstein and McAdam does not mention technology, a word about it is warranted here. The incumbents have used the resources acquired from political figures to expand their technological reach, further reinforcing their dominance in the border action field. They have achieved nearly full database coordination with nearly every other law enforce-ment agency in the country. They have expanded their intelligence apparatus at home and abroad. They acquire traveler information on every passenger coming to the United States the moment a plane ticket is booked. They have grown the database on border crossers and can run sophisticated algorithms to under-stand "customer" behavior. They have also deployed tactical infrastructure in the field—from cameras to sensors to unmanned aerial vehicles to gamma ray scanning equipment and so forth with the ability to detect nearly all movement along or across the borderline. These are complemented by a growing number of control centers that relay real-time information from sensing technology to agents on the ground. And border law enforcement agencies are already working on acquiring massive amounts of biometric technology, including face recognition (Owen, Luck, and Michelini 2017). In general, technology has served to consolidate their action field dominance well into the future, and in ways that no other player can match. Technology is, in a way, a force multiplier for the incumbents. Consequently, technology has become part of the field environment as it becomes increasingly integrated into border control.

Border Governance Change and Continuity

Although the central questions of this chapter are how the border action field is governed and who governs it, another key question in this essay relates to the idea of change and continuity in governance at the U.S.-Mexico border. To address the issue of change and continuity in the border action field, this essay examines the issue through the lens of the distribution of power among the actors who inhabit the action field—the borderlands. The position of the actors in the action field over time should be enough to determine whether the field has experienced changes partly based on who controls the units of governance, for how long, and how strong their hold on the units of governance is and has been. Thus, it not only asks who of them governs the border and how they do so—that is, who determines the governance units and enforces them—but also what the border action field has looked like since the end of the twentieth century—what has changed and what has remained the same—as a good way to determine whether governance in the field has been continuous or has gone undergone changes. Examining the action field players over time allows us to see change and continuity in the governance system.

At the U.S.-Mexico border, the incumbents are the security community. Continuously, for nearly three decades, law enforcement agencies have consolidated their dominance in the border action field. They have done so through policies that might rub against their dominance, such as the birth of NAFTA in 1994 accompanied by an impetus for open borders, and those that might reinforce their dominance, such as the events of September 11 accompanied by a renewed fear of open borders. They have built solid iron triangles (Adams 1981; Spar, Tobin, and Vernon 1991) by coalescing with the political community and private industry in order to capture the public's imagination, magnifying their rhetorical, historical, and structural advantages to capture and retain control of

the governance units—laws, regulations, procedures, and processes—and to enforce them on all other action field actors. Rhetorically, they have increasingly spoken of potential terrorists crossing the U.S.-Mexico border even though there is no evidence of any terrorists using the border to attack the United States. They have also changed the language, referring to what are essentially economic migrants as invaders, threats to the American way, and criminals (Ackleson 2005).

The challengers of this rhetoric have not been able to put a dent in an increasingly hostile narrative against border crossers who are constructed as potential major threats to national security. For border crossers, legal and illegal, the terrain is rhetorically shifting against them. The evolution of the words used to refer to migrants has gone from undocumented to illegal to invaders to potential terrorists—all signaling an ever more aggressive portrayal of those who move to seek a better life for themselves and their families. Tracking the rhetoric allows us to see that the trend is now historical—thirty years of increasing dominance for law enforcement. With every new fence, every new technological gadget, every new database, every new camera, every new helicopter and drone, every new agent and vehicle, and every new budget dollar, law enforcement asserts its dominance of the field, putting all other actors on the defensive. The resources have followed the rhetorical pattern outlined above—more qualitatively and quantitatively for law enforcement and less for administrative efficiency, for accountability, for human and individual rights enforcement, and for venues to manage complaints. The material resources have overtime reinforced law enforcement dominance in the action field. They allow agencies to build alliances with politicians, who can claim credit for the increased security, and with the private sector, which lobbies for additional resources as they stand to benefit from the additional resources by obtaining the contracts for goods and services to further reinforce the borderline. Through these iron triangles law enforcement agencies have further reinforced their position by acquiring and adapting modern technologies to enforce their vision of the border. If the foundational question of this essay is who governs, a question central to any governance system, the answer is law enforcement agencies govern the border. In this sense, law enforcement has had the material advantage as well, as its budgetary resources keep growing over time. And the Trump administration has further argued for an additional five thousand border agents for CBP and ICE. Clearly, the law enforcement community has built a self-reinforcing border security industrial complex.

Therefore, if a central line of inquiry in this essay is whether border governance has changed in the borderlands—the border action field—the answer is no. Vis-à-vis the dominance of the law enforcement security paradigm on the border, all other actors are at some level *challengers*, even if not all challengers are equal. The entrepreneurial and industrial community has managed to negotiate certain spaces of privilege for itself, but it has done so often at the expense of its solidarity with other community actors. In that sense, they remain challengers, but the rest of the community, borderlanders, remain *the governed*. This cleavage between the entrepreneurial class and the rest of the community, interestingly, might be by design. Dividing the challengers by opening spaces of privilege for some at the expense of solidarity throughout the border community makes it easier for incumbents to use a system of carrots and sticks to reinforce their dominance. This demonstrates, therefore, that the law enforcement and security communities have been much more skillful than the challengers not only at capturing the governance units but also at distributing certain incentives to maintain community solidarity relatively low, something that amounts to an inability to organize across many sectors to change the border landscape.

Conclusion

Who governs the U.S.-Mexico border and how do they govern it? Asking this allows us to conceive the borderlands as a SAF and the players within it as actors seeking to implement their vision of the border. Focusing on the actors' strategies allows us to discern the character and nature of the cross-border governance system. But the border space is additionally complex—dividing, lines, exclusive sovereignties, fragmented territories, variable legal rights for separate groups, market differences, institutional incompatibilities, and authorities generally accountable to only specific segments of the overall population inhabiting a region complicate the SAF. Thus, understanding governance by simply examining the SAF and the actors who inhabit it is insufficient to understand governance. The field, the actors, their position in the SAF, their strategies, their advantages, and their skills are all important, as is the broader field environment. In this sense sociological theories such as Fligstein and McAdam's SAF help glimpse how the border space is contested and controlled. In SAF, actors are not passive either; they behave strategically, seeking to ensure that their interests are embedded into the structure of governance itself, that is, the units of governance—laws, regulations, processes, and procedures—that every other actor in the space must abide by. It is understanding what actors have achieved that can then reveal the nature of field governance.

Moreover, examining the central actors operating in the border SAF and how they seek to secure control of the governance units helps us understand who ultimately governs the field—the incumbents—and who are the governed—the challengers, which in turn facilitates understanding the evolution of governance in the SAF over time. Stacking all the actors in the field and examining their strategies and their achievements in relation to the units of governance in the space can shed light on the nature of governance in that field. This is particularly important in border SAFs because of their nature. Actors do not operate under a hierarchical, traditional, and state-centric field. Instead, they operate under governance frameworks that are more akin to networks, market-based or exchange governance systems, and across sovereign spaces where the rules themselves can change radically from one geographical point to another. Actors navigate not only one set of rules but several sets of rules simultaneously. This clearly makes for a very dynamic field, and the structure of governance is more likely to reflect a high degree of competition among SAF actors for control of the governance units. This is key because it reveals that on the U.S.-Mexico border, governance is complex and multilayered. Players pull in their own direction, negotiating privileges and access for themselves and not necessarily moving in tandem toward a single vision of the border.

Finally, institutional deficiencies mean that the U.S.-Mexico border has been unable to develop effective, comprehensive mechanisms for joint and highly formalized governance, relying at a first level on hierarchical, state-centric structures of governance and secondarily on cross-border solidarity networks, privileging competing interest and visions of the border field itself and forcing all players to navigate multiple sets of rules around which different actors will prevail over others. Governance on the U.S.-Mexico border is, therefore, uneven and often burdensome on groups that do not have the resources or skills to negotiate spaces for themselves—immigrants, cross-border workers, and most border users in general. Under these circumstances, dominance by one group and a weakened solidarity among challengers, there is little room for institutional innovation. The functions of the border are intervened by different actors based on organizational and individual interests, and even powerful actors, like economic players, do it on the terms of the dominant group—law enforcement and security actors. Thus, governance in the region is more of an amalgam of actors constantly jockeying in a highly competitive space with low levels of cooperation to achieve true democratic governance.

REFERENCES

Ackerman, Alissa R., and Rich Furman. 2013. "The Criminalization of Immigration and the Privatization of the Immigration Detention: Implications for Justice." *Contemporary Justice Review* 16 (2): 251–63.

Ackleson, Jason. 2003. "Securing Through Technology? 'Smart Borders' after September 11th." *Knowledge, Technology and Policy* 16 (1): 56–74.

Ackleson, Jason. 2005. "Constructing Security on the US-Mexico Border." *Political Geography* 24:165–84.

Adams, Gordon. 1981. *The Politics of Defense Contracting: The Iron Triangle*. New York: Routledge.

Allmendinger, Phil, Graham Haughton, Jörg Knieling, and Frank Othemgrafen, eds. 2015. *Soft Spaces in Europe: Renegotiating Governance, Boundaries, and Borders*. New York: Routledge.

Anderson, James, and Liam O'Dowd. 1999a. "Borders, Border Regions and Territoriality: Contradictory Meanings, Changing Significance." *Regional Studies* 33 (7): 593–604.

Anderson, James, and Liam O'Dowd. 1999b. "Contested Borders: Globalization and Ethnonational Conflict in Ireland." *Regional Studies* 33 (7): 681–96.

Anderson, Joan B., and James Gerber. 2017. "The US-Mexico Border Human Development Index 1990–2010." *Journal of Borderlands Studies* 32 (3): 275–88.

Andreas, Peter. 2012. *Border Games: Policing the US-Mexico Divide*. Ithaca, N.Y.: Cornell University Press.

Balla, Stephen J., and William T. Gormley. 2017. *Bureaucracy and Democracy: Accountability and Performance*. Washington, D.C.: CQ Press.

Baruca, Arne, and M. Zolfagharian. 2013. "Cross-Border Shopping: Mexican Shoppers in the US and American Shoppers in Mexico." *International Journal of Consumer Studies* 37 (4): 360–66.

Bastida, Elena, H. Sheldon Brown III, and José A. Pagán. 2008. "Persistent Disparities in the Use of Health Care Along the US-Mexico Border: An Ecological Perspective." *American Journal of Public Health* 98 (11): 1987–95.

Baud, Michiel. 1997. "Toward a Comparative History of Borderlands." *Journal of World History* 8 (2): 211–42.

Bejarano, Cynthia. 2010. "Border Rootedness as Transformative Resistance: Youth Overcoming Violence and Inspection in a US-Mexico Border Region." *Children's Geographies* 8 (4): 391–99.

Bersin, Alan. 2015. "The Outer Ring of Border Security: DHS's International Security Programs." In *Hearing Before the Subcommittee on Border and Maritime Security of the Committee on Homeland Security of the House of Representatives*. Washington, D.C.: US Government Printing Office. https://www.gpo.gov/fdsys/pkg/CHRG-114hhrg 95682/html/CHRG-114hhrg95682.htm.

Bowman, Gregory W. 2007. "Thinking Outside the Border: Homeland Security and the Forward Deployment of the U.S. Border." *Houston Law Review* 44 (2). https://papers .ssrn.com/sol3/papers.cfm?abstract_id=921121.

Brunet-Jailly, Emmanuel. 2005. "Theorizing Borders: An Interdisciplinary Perspective." *Geopolitics* 10:633–49.

Brunet, Jailly, Emmanuel. 2007. *Borderlands: Comparing Border Security in North America and Europe.* Ottawa: University of Ottawa Press.

Buzan, Barry, Ole Wæver, and Jaap De Wilde. 1997. *Security: A New Framework for Analysis.* Boulder, Colo.: Lynne Riener.

Cabrera, Chris. 2015. "Testimony of Chris Cabrera Before Senate HSGAC Committee," March 17. http://www.bpunion.org/newsroom/special-reports/1771-cabrera -testimony-hsgac, accessed February 3, 2018 (no longer posted)

Cañas, Jesús, Roberto Coronado, Robert W. Gilmer, and Eduardo Saucedo. 2013. "The Impact of the Maquiladora Industry on the US Border." *Growth and Change: A Journal of Urban and Regional Growth* 44 (3): 415–42.

Chalabi, Mona. 2016. "The 'War on Drugs' in Numbers: A Systematic Failure of Policy." *Guardian,* April 19. https://www.theguardian.com/world/2016/apr/19/war-on-drugs -statistics-systematic-policy-failure-united-nations.

Chomsky, Noam. 2009. "Barack Obama and the 'Unipolar Moment.'" *In These Times,* October 6. http://inthesetimes.com/article/4990/barack_obama_and_the_unipolar _moment/.

Clemens, Michael. 2015. "The US-Mexico Wage Gap Has Grown, Not Shrunk, Under NAFTA. Awkward." Center for Global Development. https://www.cgdev.org/blog /us-mexico-wage-gap-has-grown-not-shrunk-under-nafta-awkward.

Cornelius, Wayne. 2001 "Death at the Border: Efficacy and Unintended Consequences of US Immigration Control Policy." *Population and Development Review* 27:661–85.

Correa-Cabrera, Guadalupe, Terence Garrett, and Michele Keck. 2014. "Administrative Surveillance and Fear: Implications for US-Mexico Border Relations and Governance." *European Review of Latin American and Caribbean Studies* 96:35–53.

DeChaine, D. Robert, ed. 2012. *Border Rhetorics: Citizenship and Identity on the US-Mexico Border.* Tuscaloosa: University of Alabama Press.

Díaz, George T. 2015. *Border Contraband: A History of Smuggling Across the Rio Grande.* Austin: University of Texas Press.

Doty, Roxanne L. 2007. "States of Exception on the Mexico: US Border: Security, 'Decisions,' and Civilian Border Patrols." *International Political Sociology* 1 (2): 113–37.

Dunn, Timothy. 2010. *Blockading the Border and Human Rights: The El Paso Operation That Remade Immigration Enforcement.* Austin: University of Texas Press.

Esparza, Adrián X., and Angela J. Donelson. 2008. *Colonias in Arizona and New Mexico: Border Poverty and Community Development Solutions.* Tucson: University of Arizona Press.

Fligstein, Neil, and Doug McAdam. 2015. *A Theory of Fields.* Oxford: Oxford University Press.

Flynn, Steven E. 2000. "Beyond Border Control." *Foreign Affairs* 79 (6): 57–68.

Fourny, Marie-Christine. 2007. "The Border as Liminal Space." *Journal of Alpine Research* 101–2. http://journals.openedition.org/rga/2120.

Fukuyama, Francis. 1992. *The End of History and the Last Man.* New York: The Free Press.

Galaviz, Vanessa E., Michael G. Yost, Christopher D. Simpson, J. E. Camp, M. H. Paulsen, J. P. Elder, L. Hoffman, David Flores, and Penelope J. E. Quintana. 2014. "Traffic Pollutant Exposures Experienced by Pedestrians Waiting to Enter the US at a Major US-Mexico Border Crossing." *Atmospheric Environment* 88:362–69.

Garland, David. 2008. "On the Concept of Moral Panic." *Crime, Media and Culture: An International Journal* 4 (1): 9–30.

Gibbs, Jennifer. 2004. "The Exploitation of Women in Mexico's Maquiladoras." Honors thesis, Western Kentucky University. https://digitalcommons.wku.edu/cgi/view content.cgi?article=1176&context=stu_hon_theses.

Gluszek, Alicja. 2014. "The Security and Prosperity Partnership and the Pitfalls of North American Regionalism." *Norteamérica* 9 (1): 7–54.

Haselsberger, Beatrix. 2014. "Decoding Borders: Appreciating Border Impacts on Space and People." *Planning Theory and Practice* 15 (4): 504–26.

Hathaway, Dale. 2000. *Allies Across the Border: Mexico's 'Authentic Labor Front' and Global Solidarity.* Cambridge, Mass.: South End Press.

Hughes, Bryn. 2007. "Securitizing Iraq: The Bush Administration's Social Construction of Security." *Global Change, Peace and Security* 19 (2): 83–102.

Huntington, Samuel P. 1991. *The Third Wave of Democracy: Democratization in the Late Twentieth Century.* Norman: University of Oklahoma Press.

Johnson, Kevin A. 2011. "Hegemonic Ideological Coordinates and the Rhetorical Construction of 'the Illegal Immigrant' in the United States." *American Studies in Scandinavia* 43 (1): 11–38.

Konrad, Victor. 2015. "Toward a Theory of Borders in Motion." *Journal of Borderlands Studies* 30 (1): 1–17.

Konrad, Victor, and Heather Nicol. 2008. *Beyond Walls: Reinventing the Canada-US Borderlands.* New York: Routledge.

Kozák, Kryštof. 2010. *Facing Asymmetry: Bridging the Peripheral Gap in US-Mexico Relations.* Frankfurt am Main: Peter Lang.

La Botz, Daniel. 1994. "Manufacturing Poverty: The Maquiladorization of Mexico." *International Journal of Health Services* 24 (3): 381–401.

Landau, Joseph. 2016. "Bureaucratic Administration: Experimentation and Immigration Law." *Duke Law Journal* 65:1173–1240.

Larsen, Tyler. 2017. "Proposition 187: California's Fear of Immigration." Thesis, Western Oregon University. https://digitalcommons.wou.edu/his/63/.

Lusk, Mark, Kathleen Staudt, and Eva Moya. 2012. *Social Justice in the US-Mexico Border Region.* New York: Springer.

Maril, Robert Lee. 2004. *Patrolling Chaos: The US-Border Patrol in Deep South Texas.* Lubbock: Texas Tech University Press.

McCartney, Scott. 2016. "Fliers Cross the Border to Mexico for Cheaper Fares and More Options." *Wall Street Journal*, March 9. https://www.wsj.com/articles/fliers-cross-the-border-to-mexico-for-cheaper-fares-and-more-options-1457550819.

Medina García, Eusebio. 2006. "Aportaciones para una epistemología de los estudios sobre fronteras internacionales." *Estudios Fronterizos* 7 (13): 9–27.

Monroy, Douglas. 1999. *Rebirth: Mexican Los Angeles from the Great Migration to the Great Depression*. Berkeley: University of California Press.

Moré, Íñigo. 2011. *The Borders of Inequality: Where Wealth and Poverty Collide*. Tucson: University of Arizona Press.

Newman, David. 2001. "Boundaries, Borders, and Barriers: Changing Geographic Perspectives on Territorial Lines." In *Identities, Borders and Orders: Rethinking International Relations Theory*, edited by Mathias Albert, David Jacobson, and Yosef Lapid, 137–52. Minneapolis: University of Minnesota Press.

Newman, David. 2003. "On Borders and Power: A Theoretical Framework." *Journal of Borderlands Studies* 18 (1): 13–25.

Owen, Todd, Scott Luck, and Dennis Michelini. 2017. "Testimony of CBP Office of Field Operations Executive Assistant Commission Todd Owen, CBP US Border Patrol Acting Deputy Scott Luck, and CBP Air and Marine Operations, Operations Acting Director Dennis Michelini for a House Committee on Homeland Security, Subcommittee on Maritime Security Hearing Titled 'Deter, Detect and Interdict: Technology's role in Securing the Border.'" July 25. Washington, D.C.: Customs and Border Protection. https://www.dhs.gov/news/2017/07/25/written-testimony-cbp-house-homeland-security-subcommittee-border-and-maritime.

Parker, Bradly J. 2006. "Toward an Understanding of Borderland Processes." *American Antiquity* 71 (1): 77–100.

Passas, Nikos. 2003. "Cross-Border Crime and the Interface between Legal and Illegal Actors." *Security Journal* 16 (1): 19–37.

Payan, Tony. 2010. "Crossborder Governance in a Tristate, Binational Region." In *Cities and Citizenship at the US-Mexico Border: The Paso del Norte Metropolitan Region*, edited by Kathleen Staudt, César M. Fuentes, and Julia Monárrez Fragoso, 217–44. New York: Palgrave Macmillan.

Payan, Tony. 2006. *The Three U.S.-Mexico Border Wars: Drugs, Immigration and Homeland Security*. Santa Barbara, Calif.: Praeger Security International.

Payan, Tony. 2016. *The Three US-Mexico Border Wars: Drugs, Immigration and Homeland Security*. Santa Barbara, Calif.: Praeger Security International.

Payan, Tony, and Pamela L. Cruz. 2017. "Managing the US-Mexico Border First Requires Defining It." *Issue Brief*, April 20. https://www.bakerinstitute.org/media/files/files/fc064f03/BI-Brief-042017-MEX_DefineBorder.pdf.

Payan, Tony, and Pamela L. Cruz. 2018. Binational Institutional Development and Governance at the U.S.-Mexico Border. Unpublished manuscript.

Payan, Tony, and Amanda Vásquez. 2007. "The Costs of Homeland Security." In *Borderlands: Comparing Security in North America and Europe*, edited by Emmanuel Brunet-Jailly, 231–58. Ottawa, ON: University of Ottawa Press.

Peach, Jim. 1997. "Income Distribution Along the United States Border with Mexico." *Journal of Borderlands Studies* 12 (10): 1–16.

Purcell, Mark, and Joseph Nevins. 2005. "Pushing the Boundary: State Restructuring, State Theory, and the Case of US-Mexico Border Enforcement in the 1990s." *Political Geography* 24 (2): 211–35.

Roberts, P. Craig. 1976. "The Political Economy of Bureaucratic Imperialism." *Intercollegiate Review* (Fall): 3–10.

Rubio-Goldsmith, Raquel, Celestino Fernández, Jessie K. Finch, and Araceli Masterson-Algar. 2016. *Migrant Deaths in the Arizona Desert: La vida no vale nada.* Tucson: University of Arizona Press.

Sabet, Daniel M. 2008. *Non-Profits and Their Networks: Cleaning the Waters Along Mexico's Northern Border.* Tucson: University of Arizona Press.

Salter, Mark B. 2008. "When the Exception Becomes the Rule: Borders, Sovereignty, and Citizenship." *Citizenship Studies* 12 (4): 365–80.

Sanderson, Thomas M. 2004. "Transnational Terror and Organized Crime: Blurring the Lines." *SAIS Review of International Affairs* 24 (1): 49–61.

San Diego Association of Governments. 2016. "Impacts of Border Delays at California-Baja California Ports of Entry." http://www.sandag.org/index.asp?classid=19& projectid=535&fuseaction=projects.detail.

Selby, W. Gardner. 2014. "Dan Patrick Has Called Illegal Immigration an Invasion and Said Immigrants Bring 'Third-World Diseases.'" *Politifact*, June 20. http://www .politifact.com/texas/statements/2014/jun/20/battleground-texas/dan-patrick-has -called-illegal-immigration-invasio/.

Sharkey, Patrick, Max Besbris, and Michael Friedson. 2016. "Poverty and Crime." In *The Oxford Handbook of the Social Science of Poverty*, edited by David Brady and Linda M. Burton, 623–36. Oxford: Oxford University Press.

Simmons, William Paul, and Carrol Mueller. 2014. *Binational Human Rights: The US-Mexico Experience.* Philadelphia: University of Pennsylvania Press.

Slack, Jeremy, Daniel E. Martínez, Alison Elizabeth Lee, and Scott Whiteford. 2016. *Journal of Latin American Geography* 15 (1): 7–32.

Sohn, Christophe. 2014. "Modelling Cross-Border Integration: The Role of Borders as a Resource." *Geopolitics* 19:587–608.

Spalding, Mark. 2000. "Addressing Border Environmental Problems Now and in the Future: Border XXI and Related Efforts." In *The US-Mexican Border Environment: A Road Map to a Sustainable 2020*, edited by Paul Ganster, 105–38. San Diego, Calif.: San Diego State University Press.

Spar, Deborah L., Glen Tobin, and Raymond Vernon. 1991. *Iron Triangles and Revolving Doors: Cases in US Foreign Economic Policy.* Santa Barbara, Calif.: Praeger.

Sparke, Matthew. 2006. "A Neoliberal Nexus: Citizenship, Security and the Future of the Border." *Geopolitics* 25 (2): 151–180.

State of Texas, Legislative Budget Board. 2016. "Update: State Funding for Border Security." http://www.lbb.state.tx.us/Documents/Publications/Presentation/3248 _Update_State_Funding_Border_Security.pdf.

Staudt, Kathleen, and Irasema Coronado. 2002. *Fronteras no más: Toward Social Justice at the US-Mexico Border*. New York: Palgrave Macmillan.

Staudt, Kathleen, Tony Payan, and Z. Anthony Kruszewski, eds. 2009. *Human Rights Along the US-Mexico Border: Gendered Violence and Insecurity*. Tucson: University of Arizona Press.

Texas-Mexico Trade Coalition. 2017. http://www.texasmexicotrade.com/.

Tripathi, Dhananjay. 2015. "Interrogating Linkages Between Borders, Regions, and Border Studies." *Journal of Borderland Studies* 30 (2): 189–201.

U.S. Customs and Border Protection. 2015. *Vision and Strategy 2020: U.S. Customs and Border Protection Strategic Plan 2020*. Washington, D.C.: Department of Homeland Security. https://www.cbp.gov/sites/default/files/documents/CBP-Vision-Strategy -2020.pdf.

U.S. Department of State. 2002. "Smart Border: 22 Point Agreement—US-Mexico Border Partnership Action Plan," Office of the Press Secretary, White House, March 21. https://2001-2009.state.gov/p/wha/rls/fs/8909.htm.

Van Houtum, Henk. 2005. "The Geopolitics of Borders and Boundaries." *Geopolitics* 10:672–79.

Vergani, Matteo, and Sean Collins. 2015. "Radical Criminals in the Grey Area: A Comparative Study of Mexican Religious Drug Cartels and Australian Outlaw Motorcycle Gangs." *Studies in Conflict and Terrorism* 38 (6): 414–32.

Villarreal, M. Angeles, and Jennifer E. Lake. 2009. "Security and Prosperity Partnership of North America: An Overview and Selected Issues." CRS Report for Congress, May 27. https://fas.org/sgp/crs/row/RS22701.pdf.

Vitiello, Ronald. 2017. "Written Testimony of CBP Acting Deputy Commissioner Ronald Vitiello for a Senate Committee on the Judiciary, Subcommittee on Border Security and Immigration Hearing Titled 'Building America's Trust Through Border Security: Progress on the Southern Border.'" U.S. Department of Homeland Security, May 23. https://www.dhs.gov/news/2017/05/23/written-testimony-cbp-senate -judiciary-subcommittee-border-security-and-immigration.

Wilson, James Q. 1989. *Bureaucracy: What Government Agencies Do and Why They Do It*. New York: Basic Books.

Wilson, Thomas M., and Hastings Donnan, eds. 1998. *Border Identities: Nation and State at International Frontiers*. Cambridge: Cambridge University Press.

Wójtowicz, Mirosław, and Anna Winiarczyk-Raźniak. 2014. "The Maquiladora Industry Impact on the Social and Economic Situation in Mexico in the Era of Globalization." In *Environmental and Socio-economic Transformations in Developing Areas as the Effect of Globalization*, edited by Slawomir Dorocki and Paweł Brzegowy, 93–110. Kraków: Wydawnictwo Naukowe UP.

CHAPTER 2

Reimagining the Border Between Canada and the United States

VICTOR KONRAD

When Donald Trump was elected president of the United States in late 2016, some Americans and most Canadians immediately became concerned about how this unanticipated event would affect the relationship between Canadians and Americans, particularly at the border. Trump's campaign rhetoric about building a wall between the United States and Mexico alarmed Canadians as well as Americans living along the border. Whereas most borderland residents assumed that the new president would not go as far as building a U.S.-Canada wall, they did imagine a more formidable border featuring enhanced security and longer wait times to cross. Also, Canadians feared a greater emphasis on profiling Muslims and other minorities for greater scrutiny at the border. Equally important, Canadians and their neighbors in the adjacent United States were uncertain of the economic effects of proposed American trade protectionism and "America First" policies. In essence, fears were heightened, on the one hand, concerning the extension and expansion of a border transformation already in progress since the beginning of the twenty-first century. On the other hand, anxiety increased, particularly in Canada, about how Canada's massive trade with the United States and economic reliance on America would be affected. A new image of the border emerged as a complex and multifaceted bundle of concerns about how the United States and Canada would intersect in this strangely unpredictable and potentially chilling political setting. In the first half of 2017, the pendulum of concern moved from great relief as Prime Minister Trudeau gained assurances from President Trump to trade scares related to milk products and the resurrected softwood lumber issue. In 2018, the relationship between Trump and Trudeau deteriorated substantially. In early 2019, civil interaction between the leaders has disappeared across an increasing gulf of differences. Imaginaries of how the border may materialize and possibly stabilize still vary and remain in motion. Certain, however, is the consensus among both Canadians and Americans that the border between the countries remains in a state of transformation and that this process of continual change is the hallmark of the twenty-first-century border between the United States and Canada.

The early twenty-first-century transformation of border governance was sudden and sweeping along what is ostensibly the world's "longest undefended border," the border between Canada and the United States (Andreas 2003). In the aftermath of the events of 9/11, border governance was shaken as tenets of power and influence were tested and, moreover, the capacity to order, moderate, and manage the border was questioned. The capability, prevalence, and predominance of evolved systems of border governance that had worked for most of the twentieth century were abrogated in favor of more strident security controls exercised mainly by the U.S. government through its newly established Department of Homeland Security (DHS). The DHS has sought to control flows of people and goods by reinforcing territorial control primarily through "top-down" security enhancement, but increasingly the DHS and other border governing agencies in both the United States and in Canada have acknowledged that effective border management of flows also requires devolved governance through "bottom-up" allowances. A scalar optimum in border governance remains to be achieved between federal and local levels (Alper and Hammond 2011). The deeper concern, however, is that governing the border in an era of globalization is not successful, and it is not adequate to meeting the challenge of governing the increasing and diverse flows of people, goods, and communications across borders.

Meanwhile, cross-border culture, rather than being sublimated by an incised Canada-U.S. border and virtual walls, has reemerged more sharply defined, and this cultural production has reinvented itself differentially in places along the border and spaces in the borderlands (Konrad 2012). The "thickening" of the border (Ackleson 2009) has extended and deepened the zone of cultural interaction across the border, expanded resistance to enhanced security, and broadened the borderlands. Indeed, the business of the border is populating the borderlands but also it is garnering resistance expressed in cultural production including literature, art and film (Amilhat-Szary 2012). As Alm and Burkhart (2013b) emphasize in their analysis of narratives from border communities on Lake Superior, cross-border culture as expressed in the stories of ordinary people is integral to understanding the border and theorizing how it works. Newly formed cross-border culture since 9/11 embraces imaginaries of how the border is in need of stiffer controls on the one hand and is overfortified and mismanaged on the other. These imaginaries lead to resistance as well as constructive engagement to develop remedies for governing the border. This chapter focuses on the range of imaginaries apparent among border stakeholders, why these imaginaries have emerged, and how these imaginaries are shaping multiple approaches to the border.

Border governance and border culture, then, are conceptualized as intertwined and interrelated in such a way that changes in one will affect the other. Brunet-Jailly (2005) has identified both governance and culture as among four key interactive components in the understanding of border dynamics. The governance-culture-identity relationship has been explored and elaborated by Konrad and Nicol (2011). In this chapter, I suggest that cross-border culture materializes and essentializes governance in cultural production, and in so doing, it underlines that governance of borders is ultimately less important in globalization than governance of the more extensive borderlands or cross-border dynamic and interactive zone. Furthermore, I suggest that Americans and Canadians are reimagining the border between them in various ways and that these imaginaries are guiding and shaping their views, approaches, and reactions to the border of the twenty-first century. As the border changes, imaginaries of how the border will evolve direct and lead thinking about what the border is indeed becoming. Some of this thinking ultimately affects border policy, whereas some of it washes up against the "wall" of regulations, policy, and practice at the border. This chapter focuses on reimagining the Canada-U.S. border through the lens of border culture to explore how imaginaries of the border position and code a complex, varied, and plural bordering between peoples. Border imaginaries are scrutinized and explored in the context of culture theory and emerging border theory to offer a conceptual framework for reimagining the border between Canada and the United States. Seven imaginary clusters are identified in the following discussion. They are a secured border, a biopolitical border, a border with directed flows, a managed border, an unbalanced border, a unicultural border, and finally an inadequate border. These imaginaries are then articulated in an overall reimagining of the Canada-U.S. border. Before embarking on this detailed analysis of the interplay of border and culture between the United States and Canada, however, I will begin with a brief review of how the border is reimagined through a lens of border culture and how this thinking has guided the approach and methodology in the research.

Reimagining the Border Through a Lens of Border Culture

In recent years, scholars have acknowledged the power of culture at the border and of the border (Konrad and Nicol 2011; Brambilla 2015). There is a growing recognition that powerful imaginaries of the border position and code a complex, varied, and plural bordering between peoples (Schimanski and Wolfe 2017; Rodney 2017). Consequently, the Canada-U.S. border is increasingly everywhere yet nowhere as bordering becomes more complex and universal, detached from the border, and linked to globalization tendencies (Konrad and Brunet-Jailly 2019; Konrad and Kelly, forthcoming). To comprehend this new border requires a new paradigm. Models of contemporary border interaction already include a component of culture (Brunet-Jailly 2005), but given the recent research and theorizing about border culture, it is instructive and revealing to examine how current thinking about border culture influences our understanding of how borders work in globalization.

Several directions of thought are useful in this regard. First, it is evident that border culture emerges through the intersection and engagement of imagination, affinity, and identity. This production of culture usually is most evident and materialized in the borderlands (Konrad 2012). But how does border culture emerge in this crucible? Anthropologists argue that border culture emerges at the intersection of cultural meaning; that is, human beings build themselves into the world by creating meaning. Culture gives meaning to action by situating underlying states in an interpretive system (Saleeby 1994). Part of this cultural meaning relates to and activates the boundaries of being (Shweder 1984).

Border culture is that part of meaning. Yet our theories of culture and border culture are grounded in the essentialist view of culture and caught in the "territorial trap" (Agnew 1994). Culture is viewed as a bounded system contained in a defined territory. Also, culture is expected to be homogeneous (Lugo 1997). Culture is shared by members of society. "This territory-oriented rhetoric of culture, cultural border and boundary faces a great challenge in a multicultural society because intense contacts between various cultural carriers blur the clarity of the demarcation lines" (Chang 1999). Consequently, border culture is no longer culture at the margins but rather culture at the heart of geopolitics, flows, and experience of the transnational world. Border culture may be situated away from the border: in world cities, at airports, in detention centers, and in immigrant enclaves. Border culture may be at once a manifestation and an imaginary. Border culture is an integral component of borders in motion. Border culture is experienced by more people in more circumstances than ever before.

At this point it is important to distinguish between border culture and culture at the border. Border culture is the "articulative" social science explanation of how culture inhabits borders. It explores how culture helps to constitute and reinvent borderlands, create "borderscapes" (Brambilla 2015), and establish transnational regions. The concept of border culture helps the researcher assess the transformation of the meaning of border and to map and analyze the terrain of border studies. Culture at the border is manifested in humanistic appreciation of the border and bordering. It enables the exploration of the "parallel encounters" that take place at and near borders (Roberts and Stirrup 2013). Herein we see the mobility of cultural forms and cultural stereotypes and the circulation and relationality of cultural products in association with the border. It is an exploration of the heavier presence of borders. And, in considering culture at the border, we move from analysis to appreciation of the terrain of border studies.

Consequently, to know border culture is to capture both the "essential" and the "imagined" qualities of hybridization and differentiation at borders and in borderlands (Shimoni 2006). Understanding border culture entails relating international forces operating between nations to transnational forces produced by the presence of one nation within another (Fein 2003). Also, understanding border culture acknowledges the partiality and incompleteness of cultural shells that continue to prevail in the nation-state and predominate in its territory. To comprehend border culture more fully, then, we must go beyond rationalizations to daydream about the allowances, thick margins, receptors, and interfaces that are both possible and plausible where nations meet and cultures intersect anywhere around the globe. In theory, border culture is conveyed in imaginaries and productions that are linked to identities constructed in the borderlands, and these identities underlie the enforcement of control and resistance to power that also make up border cultures. This emerging theory of border culture is based on several understandings. "The border is at the nexus of international and transnational, territorial and extraterritorial, and political and socio-cultural" (Fein 2003). The border is looming as a more important yet more poorly understood concept in globalization. Also, understanding border culture is a key component in comprehending borders in motion in an increasingly transnational world with cultures stretched, split, relocated, and reconstituted.

A Note on Methodology

The analysis of imaginaries in this chapter is grounded in ninety-eight detailed interviews, five focus group discussions, and 160 border stakeholders surveyed in the Cascadia coastal cross-border region of Washington State and British Columbia and the interior border areas on both sides of the border (Konrad 2010). To build on this base of interviews and surveys completed in 2009 and 2010 and to update the assessments, additional interviews of border stakeholders in the Cascadia region in subsequent years are complemented with border stakeholder interviews in other border regions along the Canada-U.S. border with a particular focus on the Great Lakes region and Atlantic Canada–New England. For these and the remaining border regions, imaginaries were constituted as well from the published research on views and perspectives on the border in various locales (ranging from published articles—Alm and Burkhardt 2013a, 2013b—to theses—Vandervalk 2017), a review of media stories on U.S. and Canadian perspectives on the border in 2015 and 2016 by the author, an assessment of government documents and reports on border attitudes completed by the author in 2015 and updated in 2017, and an extensive and ongoing review of the literature related to the Canada-U.S. border.

The following imaginaries are essentially clusters of consensus of how people in the borderlands between the United States and Canada "see" the border. The imaginaries are not silo-like divisions of perspective in which people have only one discrete imaginary. Indeed, some people may ascribe to multiple imaginaries simultaneously, and they may identify them in order of influence or not. Some imaginaries are constituted of subcomponent imaginaries, yet others appear to be singularly ascribed. Ultimately these imaginaries are generalized inclinations useful for understanding how border culture is constituted and how it evolves.

Border Security Canada-U.S. Style:
A Prevailing Imaginary and Evolving Reality

A central concern among most border stakeholders and the borderlands population as well is the issue of border security. The emergence of security primacy has introduced a new order in border relations between constituencies and people across the border and throughout the borderlands. Security primacy also has invaded all other cross-border functions and aligned them within a new security paradigm that now prevails in North America (Konrad 2014). This security imperative articulates as well the new cultural production of landscapes of resistance and imaginaries of governance in the post-9/11 "securityscape" (Appadurai 1996) of the Canada-U.S. borderlands. In fact, so imposing is the growing presence of security apparatus, particularly on the U.S. side of the border, that the everyday policing of threat and suspicion now targets anyone appearing "out of place" (Boyce 2018).

As security primacy came to prevail along the boundary between the United States and Canada, federal governments on both sides of the border emphasized territorial sovereignty while increasing security infrastructure and surveillance capabilities at the boundary (Alm and Burkhart 2013a). The result has been the expansion of insecurity because the achievement of total security and the complete elimination of the risk of compromising the border are avowedly impossible. Yet territorial sovereignty and security imperatives have become intertwined, and federal governance now requires this aligned commitment. Herein lies the fallacy of contemporary Canada-U.S. border governance: both the United States and Canada remain committed to aligned territorial and border control even as borders become less based on territorial demarcations. Almost 25 percent of Canadians and Americans cross the border into the neighboring country through airports.

In Canada, the entry into the United States is actually at the Canadian airport where U.S. border officials screen travelers before they board planes destined for the United States (Hiller 2010). This pattern of preinspection and preclearance has been codified by the recent Beyond the Border Accord and Action Plan (Canada, Foreign Affairs and International Trade 2011; Government of Canada 2015a, 2015b). Beyond the Border initiatives extend to control the movement of both people and goods at the border as well as away from the boundary line. In many instances, this extension of border space has moved from the border to one hundred kilometers and more away from the border. The U.S. Border Patrol has enhanced territorial jurisdiction, increased personnel, and expanded infrastructure, and in now has greater powers than ever before in its history (U.S. Customs and Border Protection 2015). Beyond the Border may take the border away from the boundary line to a certain extent, but the border continues to follow and interdict people, often in a more clandestine way than the direct intervention at the border.

Border security Canada-U.S. style is essentially securing against the outside on the inside, whether it is Canadians and Americans working together to stop unwanted or targeted people within Canada from entering the United States, joint efforts to stop the flow of illegal goods away from the actual border, Americans extending the line of defense into communities in the borderlands, or Canadian and American officials cooperating in shiprider programs to patrol the Great Lakes and coastal maritime areas (Royal Canadian Mounted Police 2015). The nonborder of the late twentieth century has emerged as the super border of the twenty-first century.

This super border is replete with the latest technological advances in identity verification, dangerous materials screening, and contraband detection. Also, the border is hardened at crossing points with extensive fortification and surveillance infrastructure and armed with sensors along the boundary including at remote and impassable locations. In this regard, the Canada-U.S. border resembles fortified boundaries around the world, although in the Canada-U.S. instance, much of the fortification is more sophisticated and subtle. The Canada-U.S. border is, however, unlike the Shengen perimeter around the European Union. Shengen is highly visible, finite, and the "in" or "out" line between the increasingly integrated members of the European Union (and their compatriots such as Switzerland) and the states that lie outside the EU, predominantly to the east and to the south (EUR-Lex 2015). Although Shengen has moved several times in recent decades with new accessions to the EU, the line remains the ultimate defining border between the EU and the outside whether it is encountered at the actual perimeter or in Europe's airports. Also, the Canada-U.S. border differs from Shengen in a fundamental way. The Canada-U.S. border has more of a filtering capacity, and it still functions to enable seasonal and permanent migrations between the countries themselves as well as between each of the countries and the rest of the world.

A Managed Border: Reimagining Border Governance

From the anachronism that Canada and the United States continue to rely on aligned territorial control (whereas borders are less based on territorial demarcations) emerge a series of imaginaries or perceived realities of border governance, each of which has an effect on how border governance is viewed by authorities and the public and how governance is then developed at the border and in the borderlands. The *first imaginary* of border governance is that control of the border assures control of the territory. Although this position was strident during most of the first decade of the twenty-first century, the position has softened somewhat as both the United States and Canada acknowledged the need for Beyond the Border strategies to enhance security.

The *second imaginary* of border governance is that borders are most effectively governed by federal authorities not the local constituencies that develop and maintain cross-border flows, relationships, and controls. This position was invoked vigorously by both the United States and Canada immediately after the events of 9/11 with the establishment of the U.S. DHS and Public Safety Canada. Both of these first two imaginaries are linked to the territorial trap: "States as fixed units of sovereign space, domestic/foreign polarity, and states as 'containers' of societies," all conceptualizations which have been eroded to various degrees in globalization (Agnew 1994, 2010). Other imaginaries of border governance extend beyond the territorial trap.

A *third imaginary* is that distance from the border calibrates with the reduction of border governance. Yet airports and ports of entry by sea and rail have long been part of the borderlands no matter what distance they are situated from the border. In Canada, U.S. preclearance of people and goods has been routine at major Canadian airports for over fifty years (Hiller 2010). The recent Beyond the Border Accord (Canada, Foreign Affairs and International Trade 2011) aims to acknowledge, construct and codify other preclearance procedures, spaces, and places at some distance from the border in both countries. Among these are container inspection at points of origin, more intensive immigration clearance at source, and the authorization of security personnel to work across the border as well as on the line.

A *fourth imaginary* is the differentiation of security and nonsecurity spaces and places. At border-crossing points this distinction remains firmly in place: a place or space is either secured or it is not secured. This is true of airports and other primary port of entry facilities as well, but degrees of security are evident in a host of other facilities related to cross-border transfer including border patrol depots, brokerage firms, and border communication facilities. Also, many sections of the Canada-U.S. border remain unsecured or partially secured.

A *fifth imaginary* of border governance describes the complication of governance resulting from the interaction of multiple agencies and the rapid introduction of technologies and new procedures. This results in confusion and uncertainty at the border and rapidly escalates into expressions of resistance such as complaints from transportation companies and associations and stories about border injustices in the media.

A *sixth imaginary* is the specter of militarization as the unifying governing principle, particularly on the U.S. side of the border. Military style uniforms, guns, military protocols, and other aspects of an overall military stance at the border build this imaginary, and ultimately it becomes portrayed in cultural productions such as the television series *The Border* and Hollywood's *Border Wars*. Undoubtedly, there are other imaginaries of cross-border governance that have emerged, but further research is required to identify these components and the cultural production and production through culture (Schimanski and Wolfe 2010) that resists these imaginaries. The goal is to evaluate both the governance imaginaries and the resistance to them as facets of cultural response to a rapidly changing border milieu between Canada and the United States.

The political geography of borders has always emphasized the predominant role of governance in the control and management of territory up to and at its edges. In this conception, governing borders becomes a show of territorial control akin to the "viral" YouTube standoff at Wagah on the Indo-Pakistani border (YouTube 2008). Most border edges are not this abrupt and raw, yet even there the border standoff is at once serious and on the other hand infused with pomp, pageantry, humor, and ultimately cultural display. Increasingly, borders in globalization, and the Canada-U.S. boundary among these, are governed with a softer touch even in an era of security primacy. Imaginaries of border governance are produced by governing authorities and by people living near and interacting with the border in order to comprehend the changes at the border and, increasingly, changes related to the border away from the border.

Border governance is not just the articulation of power and control at the border; it also engages border stakeholders in the borderlands who develop their imaginaries of how the border works and how it falls short of meeting their needs. These imaginaries lead to resistance and in some instances to dialogue among stakeholders, as in the case of the International Mobility and Trade Corridor project (International Mobility and Trade Corridor 2009) in the Cascade Gateway between Washington State and British Columbia. In this instance, border governance actually manifests in part as cross-border governance. The expression of territorial control at the border remains, yet border governance has also advanced to engage government and nongovernment stakeholders, at federal to local levels, within a cross-border region.

Rethinking border governance in globalization requires a new paradigm encompassing the role of cross-border culture and the imaginaries produced and performed by the people who inhabit the borderlands as well as those who would impose their imaginaries of how the border should work. The current paradigm of border governance focused on the border provides insufficient space for the articulation and integration of all of the constituencies that meet at and across borders in globalization.

The Biopolitical Border Is Bordering People Everywhere: Embodied Imagination

The biopolitical border is in effect taking the border to every person whether they approach the border or not. In the years since 9/11, most Canadians and Americans, as well as travelers elsewhere, have encountered the biopolitical border that is essentially bordering people everywhere (Muller 2010). Borders have approached people with new technologies, accumulated data and assessments of who they are, and whether they are admissible, whereas in previous decades people approached borders where they were obliged to identify themselves. Fingerprints, iris scans, and other forms of digitized information now confirm identities beyond the capabilities of passports and alternative forms of identification such as enhanced drivers' licenses, NEXUS lane crossing cards, and passport cards (Konrad and Nicol 2008b). In the wake of the events of 9/11, airport security was enhanced substantially in both the United States and in Canada where new U.S. standards of surveillance and security procedures were adopted (Salter 2008, 2010). Land and water borders, and the travelers who cross them, do not receive the same level of scrutiny, although since 9/11, both land and water borders have been subjected to heightened surveillance and more time-consuming interrogation of all travelers. Trusted-traveler programs have been established to expedite crossing for frequent and routine travelers, and particularly business and elite travelers (Sparke 2006). In essence, the biopolitical border is the new way of defining territory and sovereignty (Coleman and Grove 2009).

One illustration of this phenomenon may be found in the immigration detention centers located throughout the United States and Canada. Immigration detention currently engages space in centers established for this purpose and at existing detention centers for domestic incarceration. In the United States, Immigration and Customs Enforcement (ICE) operates or authorizes seventy-eight facilities and incarcerates detainees in spaces "bought" at more than one hundred other detention facilities in all regions of the country (U.S. Immigration and Customs Enforcement 2015). In 2012, over four hundred thousand people were detained in about 250 facilities at an annual cost of $1.7 billion (Detention Watch Network 2015). The Global Detention Project (2015) identifies three major centers operated by the Canada Border Services Agency in Toronto, Montreal, and Vancouver, with immigration detainees also held at forty other domestic prisons throughout Canada. Immigration detention and quarantine facilities have a long history in the United States with the establishment of facilities such Ellis Island in New York harbor and in Canada at Grosse Isles (St. Lawrence River near Quebec City) and Pier 21 (Halifax harbor). Once located at entry points, these facilities have now migrated throughout Canada and the United States (and elsewhere around the globe) to illustrate how domestic and international space, legal borders, and geopolitics have become intertwined in a biopolitical space that is neither here nor there but somewhere in between (Nethery and Silverman 2015; Coleman 2012).

Recent legislation in Canada seeks to codify this in-between space and to suspend the sovereign rights of terrorists and potential enemies of the state. Bill C-51 has now become law as the Antiterrorism Act of 2015, which enacts security information sharing, secures air travel further, and amends the criminal code, the Canadian Security Intelligence Service (CSIS) Act, the Immigration and Refugee Protection Act, and other acts of Parliament in Canada (Government of Canada 2015a, 2015b). Whereas there is acknowledgment by informed observers that it is important that these security issues are addressed by law and not extrajudicial government power, there are concerns about abuses with preventative detention, abusive interrogation, detaining the wrong people, abuse of privacy rights, and much more.

Particularly troubling are prohibitions on free and open speech and the potential for driving terrorism underground with no open and candid forum for discussion. The state may now censor the internet and seize propaganda, and CSIS gains new kinetic powers. In essence, according to critics of the law,

Canada is endangering charter rights and doing so with no review and oversight of the new draconian process and the agencies enabled under the legislation (Walrus 2015). The biopolitical border is an uncertain boundary with troubling implications for the definition and acknowledgment of sovereignty and the right to occupy territory in mobile and selectively controlled space.

Directing Border Flows and Motion: Imagining Borders on the Move

Contemporary borders are increasingly about directing flows and motion and less about defining territory and sovereign space. This observation certainly holds up well about the border between Canada and the United States. Much of the movement of goods, capital, services, and people in Canada is actually not just domestic but either linked to or expressed as cross-border flows and broader international motions and flows. The United States, with the largest economy in the world, is clearly the destination of most of these flows, although the backflow into Canada is also significant as a link in supply chains or a final destination for goods, services, capital, and people. Whereas the border of the twentieth century was focused primarily on the control of cross-border flows of goods and people, the border of the twenty-first century seeks to direct and manage all flows at all scales. Given the volume, number, and type of these flows and the continual growth and velocity in their movement, borders have been challenged to provide adequate control of the flows.

During the last decade and a half, a new geography of the Canada-U.S. border has emerged that seeks to move beyond the objective of flow control through interdiction to the alignment and management of motion through systemic change (Konrad 2015). Two major changes have emerged in the efforts to manage the system of flows. The first is the focus on alignment and development of funnel constructions to channel flows approaching the border and at the border. This focus began to gain momentum with the Free Trade Agreement (FTA) and NAFTA agreements, and it was expedited after the events of 9/11. The second change has been a rationalization of crossing points at the border into a hierarchical system of flow management that now extends into the borderlands in both countries and differentiates more clearly, both regionally and binationally, the most important crossing points and flows from those successively down the hierarchy (Konrad and Nicol 2004). The result is the definition, articulation, and enhancement of cross-border corridors, gateways, and terminals in the cross-border system of spaces and places.

The cost of this systemic change has been substantial. Billions of dollars have been spent by both governments at all levels, the private sector, and organizations created to reorganize and expedite the border-crossing system between Canada and the United States. Numerous adjustments have been required of industry, government, and people crossing the border. Although some of this reorganization was initiated in the 1980s and was further prompted in the 1990s by the FTA and NAFTA, the catalyst for rapid and thorough reorganization was clearly 9/11 and the move toward security primacy. Several outcomes are evident. The twenty-first-century border is focused more than ever on market flows and border management. The flows are decidedly regional in their geographic distribution. Transportation networks and supply chains are key to the sustenance and alignment of the flows. Human migration is linked more than ever to changing labor markets. New governance regimes are emerging to deal with cross-border flows management at regional and international levels. Whereas some of these outcomes are evident at all scales, the flow systems are in most instances still emerging as Canada and the United States both engage aggressively in globalization and maintain their own special bilateral exchange.

The Reinvented Border Is Driven by U.S. Interests over Canadian Interests: Unbalanced Border

The bilateral relationship between Canada and the United States remains unbalanced as always. The border may be reinvented to accommodate more flows and security requirements (Konrad and Nicol 2008a), yet the "elephant and mouse" relationship between the United States and Canada remains articulated at the border as it is in most facets of Canada-U.S. relations. The hegemonic power of the United States has always affected the border between the countries, but this effect has grown substantially since the events of 9/11 and the focus on securing the border. Security enhancements on both sides of the border have been shaped by U.S. policies and demands, particularly during the eight years of the Bush administration following 9/11. Yet even during the Obama administration, border policies and border politics has been driven by U.S. interests. In recent years, the Beyond the Border Accord appears to have established a more cooperative and balanced approach to border policy, but even this move toward greater emphasis on perimeter security and moving border business away from the border may be interpreted as injecting greater U.S. presence and influence in Canada.

In this sense, the border may be viewed as a Canadian sovereignty reduction strategy employed by the United States and allowed by a conservative government in Canada intent on aligning with the U.S. securitization strategy. Whether this assessment is warranted or not will require more detailed study and hindsight, but it is clear that bordering uneven states becomes more problematic in an era of security primacy. With a current liberal government in Canada and the conservative leadership in the United States, the balance is thwarted again. This unbalanced border affects other aspects of the cross-border relationship. The twenty-first-century border between Canada and the United States is arguably more heavily loaded with U.S. interest and influence because of the security agenda and the attention directed toward Canada as a potential gateway for negative forces entering the United States.

Toward a Unicultural Border: Multiculturalism Stops at the Border

Characterizations of Canada compared with the United States have emphasized traditionally the "mosaic" versus "melting pot" conceptualizations of Canadian and American societies. Although this post–World War II characterization has maintained a long shelf life, other descriptions have emerged to clarify how values and institutions maintain the divide between the United States and Canada, particularly as the two countries drew closer to each other in freer trade (Lipset 1989, 1990). Yet Canada retained and codified the multicultural society as a signature of identity whereas the United States continued to claim a more monocultural sense of identity.

During the twenty-first century, U.S. security and bordering practices have prevailed along the Canada-U.S. border to narrow the definition of admissibility to the United States and into U.S. society. Canadian multiculturalism is at odds with this sense of American identity and the continued growth of American exceptionalism that parallels it (Lipset 1997). This juxtaposition of Canadian multiculturalism and American uniculturalism and exceptionalism clearly incises the border. More significantly, in the context of day-to-day border work, the acknowledged cultural diversity of Canada and Canadians complicates and slows the process of establishing identity at the border. Moreover, some

Canadians are treated differently than others by American and even Canadian officials with alleged profiling of inadmissible persons and targeting of certain ethnicities for greater scrutiny. The result is that the border is more and more a unicultural border, and multiculturalism stops at the border. Also, a unicultural border emerges in Canadian deference to the American hegemon.

Imagining an Inadequate Border

Perhaps the most significant observation to be made about the Canada-U.S. border almost twenty years after the border was reinvented is that the border remains inadequate. A "thick" border has emerged between friends and substantial trading partners, and this security border has been enhanced progressively since 9/11 in an effort to make it even more secure and to reduce risks of any incursions by terrorists as well as to enhance border management. As the border has thickened, the discourse surrounding the border has become more negative, and criticism has mounted. "Thick" is now too much, yet it is also deemed not enough by many border stakeholders, particularly those in the burgeoning security sector (Konrad 2010).

The U.S.-Canada border is crossed annually by millions of travelers in uneven migration patterns. A recent estimate counts an annual exchange of thirty-three million tourists between the countries, but more specific statistics show that there were over thirty-nine million trips to the United States by Canadians in 2009 and more than twenty million trips to Canada by Americans in 2010. Over 15,700,000 people flew on scheduled flights between the United States and Canada in 2010. More than three hundred thousand people cross the border daily (Canadian Broadcasting Corporation 2011). These levels of cross-border travel are sustained and even increased despite setbacks in the U.S.-Canada relationship. Canadians and Americans cross in seasonal migrations with Canadian "snowbirds" flocking to states across the south in winter and Americans vacationing in Canada during all seasons (Konrad and Kelly, forthcoming). Both Canadians and Americans cross more frequently when currency exchange rates are favorable. Borderland residents exhibit regional, seasonal, and sectoral patterns of migration that vary from year to year. All of this unpredictable cross-border travel needs to be accommodated by a finite border management force operating under the weight of a larger rulebook with heightened security and more public and particularly media scrutiny (Alper and Hammond 2011). The result has been measured in excessive and sometimes growing wait times facing travelers who feel entitled to cross. Trusted-traveler programs have mitigated the situation somewhat, but these programs remain undersubscribed and sometimes problematic to operate. An increasing number of travelers are actually mistrusted and identified through data sets such as no fly lists. The cost of all of this increased security, digitization, scrutiny, and militarization has been billions of dollars with no end in sight for escalating costs for rebuilding the border and developing beyond the border initiatives. All of these components have become a magnet for criticism, and the border is deemed essentially inadequate.

Reimagining the Border Between Canada and the United States

Reimagining the border between the United States and Canada begins, as one might expect, with the border imaginaries. These need to be articulated before evaluating cultural production and the cultural identities that manifest in the borderlands and at the border. Once these imaginaries are articulated, it becomes more evident how cultures of border control and resistance operate in a world of mobile and evolving borders. Border imaginaries link with the cultural meaning of landscape, aesthetics, identities, belonging, settlement, community, migration, work, play, stories, and other forms of border experience. Canadians develop their imaginaries about the border, and Americans develop theirs, and some inhabitants of the borderlands share imaginaries. This construction of imaginaries has already been discussed in detail with regard to the governance of the Canada-U.S. border. In addition to evaluating these imaginaries in the context of themes such as border governance, flows, security and sustainability, it is also instructive to view the imaginaries as tied to levels of viability.

Life-securing imaginaries relate to survival in the borderlands. For example, a rapid drop in the value of the Canadian dollar may lead American border business owners to imagine a sharp decline in revenues. The imaginary may lead to mitigation strategies by American business owners, particularly if they have experienced such currency fluctuations previously. Other imaginaries are life sustaining; that is, the imaginaries are part of cultural views developed by borderland residents to facilitate everyday interaction across the border. These imaginaries often lead to programmed reactions such as characterizations of Americans as potentially dangerous carriers of handguns. Life-enriching imaginaries involve the mutual engagement and linkage of creative people and agencies across the border such as collaborative and interpretive border theater in border communities such as Stanstead, Quebec, and Niagara, Ontario.

These examples lead directly to cultural production (Schimanski and Wolfe 2010). Culture is on the move, and cultural productions of bordering abound in and beyond the borderlands. In assessing the interactions between Canada and the United States, it is important to acknowledge that interactions among cultural components are complex and multidimensional rather than binary as might be expected. This is due in part to multicultural realities that manifest at the border. For example, Lynden, Washington, in the Pacific Northwest, at once displays and celebrates the town's Dutch heritage, the community's American nationalism, and the extension of the Dutch heritage across the border into the Fraser Valley of British Columbia (Konrad 2010). Culture is being decolonized with transnationalism everywhere, but at borders this process is accelerated as cultures express multiple allegiances and plural meaning. Researchers are exploring this process in many contexts. In the case of the Canada-U.S. border and its numerous local and regional border situations, several questions need to be addressed. What kinds of borders encourage more cultural production? How does cultural production at borders convey and expand cultural meaning in transnationalism and globalization?

Researchers generally acknowledge that cultural identities at the border are socially constructed (Paasi 1998). Also emerging is the understanding that multiple identities converge at borders in globalization as borders become the filters and traps in the enhanced movements of people worldwide. The Canada-U.S. border is no different in this regard as the border becomes the flashpoint for identity expression by Indigenous cultures, visible minorities, and recent immigrants. Numerous questions remain to engage researchers. How do multiple identities enable and reduce belonging in contemporary borderlands? How does cultural meaning derive from transnational identities and national identities in globalization? Research at the Canada-U.S. border, with its rich interaction and juxtaposition of Indigenous, immigrant, and heritage cultures, promises substantial dividends of understanding related to such questions.

Of more urgent concern, given the polarization of views about securitization in the United States and the conservative political position on the need for more walls and barriers, are the emerging cultures of border control and resistance. The point that culture is related to and influenced by power is well developed in geopolitical writing (Mitchell 2000, Elden 2009). Also, culture is influenced increasingly by transnational regimes of knowledge, which are, in effect, power (Foucault 2007). Power at borders is border control (Newman 2006). Border control produces cultures of border control (Konrad and Nicol 2008a, 2011; Konrad 2012). In Europe, a Shengen border culture has evolved to enforce and maintain the increasingly significant and problematical border around the European Union in the face of heightened attempts by illegal immigrants and the entrepreneurs conveying them to confront the culture and cross the line.

Security primacy at the Canada-U.S. border has created two parallel yet still distinct border cultures at Homeland Security (the name says it all) in the United States and at the Canadian Border Services Agency. Although the control cultures vary in their characteristics and intensity, the orientation toward the use of barriers, fences, and ultimately walls continues to grow in both. Also, border culture affected by power resists through a variety and richness of cultural imaginaries and cultural productions. Resistance is often strident and usually symbolic. The resulting cultural expression is conveyed in protest, violence, and often artistic representation. Although cultures of border resistance between the United States and Canada are not as violent and extreme as those emerging between ISIS and Middle Eastern states or in the Afro-Mediterranean interaction zone and along the border between Mexico and the United States, expressions of protest are found in blockades at the border by Indigenous groups and occasionally labor organizations affected by border policy. Most resistance, however, is found in literature and artistic expression at or near the border (Amilhat-Szary 2012).

Reimagining the border between the United States and Canada requires more than simply engaging governments in the process of planning a new border regime between the countries. As this chapter has shown, the focus on security primacy by both Canada and the United States has evolved a border that is inadequate in many ways to deal with current requirements at the border and to prepare for a border that will serve both countries in the vanguard of globalization. Figure 2.1 illustrates the major components that have contributed to the construction of a unicultural, imbalanced, and ultimately inadequate border. Security primacy has been the guiding vision. Americans have imagined a border that is totally secure, and although authorities acknowledge that total security is not attainable, efforts have been made to reach this goal in several ways. One is to create the biopolitical border and to focus on the border between each person and the state. Another is to manage the border

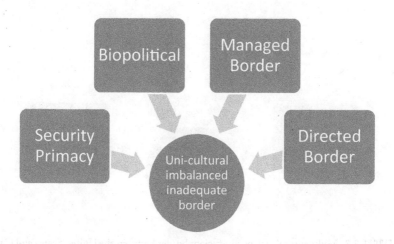

FIGURE 2.1 Unicultural, imbalanced, and inadequate border between the United States and Canada (diagram by the author)

by addressing imaginaries of governance through such avenues as digitization technologies and militarization of the borderlands. The directed border is imagined as well as a hierarchy of corridors and gateways to channel and expedite flows.

Reimagining the border between the United States and Canada is appealing because the contemporary border, despite massive investment, planning, reconstruction, and reorientation, has failed to produce a better border. In this chapter, I argue that although many of the components of a new and better border have been imagined and developed, the components for a better border need to be reimagined in concert with each other to produce a multicultural, balanced, and efficient border (fig. 2.2). Foremost among the changes required is the need to move away from security primacy and align security with other border imperatives. This alignment of security with trade, tourism, information exchange, human rights, and employment would result in a more transparent focus on the biopolitical in accordance with human rights and state charters, coordinated and scaled management, and rationalized flows. In effect, the border reimagined by the people living in the borderlands would be combined with the border required by the state authorities. In order to achieve this balanced border, it is necessary to identify and understand the imaginaries of the border before policies of border management are implemented.

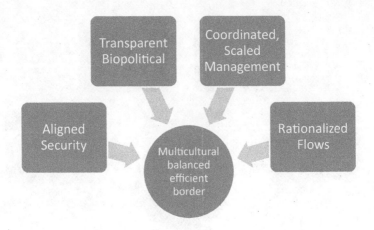

FIGURE 2.2 Multicultural, balanced, efficient border between the United States and Canada (diagram by the author)

Conclusions: Reimagining the border between Canada and the United States in the Trump Era

Whereas it is enticing to reimagine the U.S.-Canada border as a line diminished in geopolitical significance, where aligned security, transparent biopolitical screening, coordinated and scaled management, and rationalized flows mesh at a multicultural, balanced, and efficient border, this imaginary remains unrealized over two years into the Trump presidency. Indeed, prospects for such realization remain limited. On the surface, there appears to be alignment of security with sharing of information, joint enforcement measures and even arming of officers on both sides. Also, there are extensive measures to expedite flows of goods and people across the border.

Yet, a balance is not evident between concerns for security and the acknowledgment of constantly increasing flows of people, goods, and information in a myriad of interactions characteristic of globalization. Security primacy continues to prevail. Border policy and management remain directed by centralized authorities amid realizations that scaled-down borders work better. Images of a predominant American culture continue to shape border enforcement despite the evident multiculturalism of the United States. Ultimately, the border is imagined quite differently in the United States and in Canada, and this difference, instead of decreasing with the advent of globalization, is in fact increasing with the strident positions on border enhancement and enforcement advocated by the Trump administration.

This great misalignment of the United States and Canada at the border may become both a short-term difficulty and a long-term benefit for both countries as globalization continues to unfold, and North America becomes reconfigured. At first, both countries may struggle to redefine commonalities and points of juncture as they renegotiate NAFTA. Yet, hopefully, as North American considerations are contextualized globally, a more plural and multifaceted direction may become evident to benefit both the United States and Canada, in North America as well as in the global system. Despite Trump's refusal to engage the global dynamic, the United States continues to participate in it. Globalization is not a U.S. force, although the United States is among the foremost of countries engaged in its realization. Accordingly, the United States cannot halt or substantially redirect globalization. The sidelining of the United States in the G20 meeting in Germany underscored that the United States has actually become less powerful and relevant in directing world policy.

Also, Canada and Mexico are diversifying their relationships with other parts of the global community and vowing to rely less extensively on their connections to the United States. The impact of these measures may well afford opportunities to renegotiate North America, not just as envisioned by the hegemon, but also as anticipated by other North American partners with a more global outlook. Indeed, American exceptionalism and hegemony may well fade after the Trump administration's strident burst of efforts to over inflate these imaginaries. The growing discontinuity at the border between Canada and the United States, just like the even more alarming disjuncture of the Mexico-U.S. border, is a sign of upheaval and change in North America. Yet considered in the context of global adjustments and the many efforts and processes of North American integration and alignment of energy, trade, investment, environment, communication, and governance, among other facets, the border concerns are also an indicator of an overdue redefinition of North America.

REFERENCES

Ackleson, Jason. 2009. "From 'Thin' to 'Thick' (and Back Again?): The Politics and Policies of the Contemporary US-Canada Border." *American Review of Canadian Studies* 39 (4): 336–51.

Agnew, John. 1994. "The Territorial Trap: The Geographical Assumptions of International Relations Theory." *Review of International Political Economy* 1 (1): 53–80.

Agnew, John. 2010. "Still Trapped in Territory?" *Geopolitics* 15:779–84.

Alm, Les, and Ross Burkhart. 2013a. "Bridges and Barriers: The Lake Superior Borderlands." *Journal of Borderlands Studies* 28 (1): 47–60.

Alm, Les, and Ross Burkhart. 2013b. "Canada–US Border Communities: What the People Have to Say." *American Review of Canadian Studies* 43 (1): 86–106.

Alper, Donald K., and Brian Hammond. 2011. "Bordered Perspectives: Local Stakeholders' Views of Border Management in the Cascade Corridor Region." *Journal of Borderlands Studies* 26 (1): 101–14.

Amilhat-Szary, Anne-Laure. 2012. "Walls and Border Art: The Politics of Art Display." *Journal of Borderlands Studies* 27 (2): 213–28.

Andreas, Peter. 2003. "A Tale of Two Borders: The US-Canada and the US-Mexico Lines after 9/11." In *The Rebordering of North America*, edited by Peter Andreas and Thomas J. Biersteker, 1–23. New York: Routledge.

Appadurai, Arjun. 1996. *Modernity at Large: Cultural Dimensions of Globalization.* Minneapolis: University of Minnesota Press.

Boyce, Geoffrey A. 2018. "Appearing 'Out of Place': Automobility and the Everyday Policing of Threat and Suspicion on the US/Canada Frontier." *Political Geography* 64:1–12.

Brambilla, Chiara. 2015. "Exploring the Critical Potential of the Borderscapes Concept." *Geopolitics* 20 (1): 14–34.

Brunet-Jailly, Emmanuel. 2005. "Theorizing Borders: An Interdisciplinary Perspective." *Geopolitics* 10:633–49.

Canada, Foreign Affairs and International Trade. 2011. *Perimeter Security and Economic Competitiveness.* Ottawa: Queen's Printer. Accessed March 30, 2015.

Canadian Broadcasting Corporation. 2011. "The Canada-U.S. Border: By the Numbers." CBC News, December 7. http://www.cbc.ca/news/canada/the-Canada-U-S-border -by-the-numbers-1.999207.

Chang, Heewon. 1999. "Re-Examining the Rhetoric of the Cultural Border." Critical Multicultural Pavilion. http://www.edchange.org/multicultural/papers/heewon.html.

Coleman, Matthew. 2012. "Immigrant Il-legality: Geopolitical and Legal Borders in the US, 1882–Present." *Geopolitics* 17 (2): 402–22.

Coleman, Matthew, and Kevin Grove. 2009. "Biopower, Biopolitics and the Return of Sovereignty." *Environment and Planning D: Society and Space* 27 (4): 489–507.

Detention Watch Network. 2015. "About the US Detention and Deportation System." Accessed May 3, 2015. http://www.detentionwatchnetwork.org/resources.

Elden, Stuart. 2009. *Terror and Territory: The Spatial Extent of Sovereignty.* Minneapolis: University of Minnesota Press.

EUR-Lex. 2015. "The Shengen Agreement. Document 42000A0922(01)." Accessed June 4, 2015 (no longer posted). http://www.eur-lex.europa.en/legal-content/EN /ALL/?uri=CELEX:42000A0922(01).

Fein, Seth. 2003. "Culture Across Borders in the Americas." *History Compass* 1 (1): 1–6.

Foucault, Michel. 2007. *Security, Territory, Population.* New York: Palgrave.

Global Detention Project. 2015. "Canada Detention Profile." Accessed May 30, 2015 (no longer posted). http://www.globaldetentionproject.org/countries/americas/canada/introduction.html.

Government of Canada. 2015a. "Anti-Terrorism Act, May 4, 2015. Bill C-51. An Act to Enact the Security of Canada Information Sharing Act and the Secure Air Travel Act, to Amend the Criminal Code, the Canadian Security Intelligence Service Act and the Immigration and Refugee Protection Act and Make Related and Consequential Amendments to Other Acts." Accessed May 30, 2015 (no longer posted). https://laws-lois.justice.gc.ca/eng/annualstatues/2015_20/.

Government of Canada. 2015b. "Border Action Plan." Accessed April 28, 2015 (no longer posted). http://www.actionplan.gc.ca/en/content/beyond-the-border-action-plan.

Hiller, Harry. 2010. "Airports as Borderlands: American Preclearance and Transitional Spaces in Canada." *Journal of Borderlands Studies* 25 (3/4): 19–30.

International Mobility and Trade Corridor. 2009. *International Mobility and Trade Corridor Project Resource Manual.* No longer posted. http://www.wcog.org/imtc.

Konrad, Victor. 2010. "'Breaking Points' but No 'Broken' Border: Stakeholders Evaluate Border Issues in the Pacific Northwest Region." Border Policy Research Institute, Western Washington University, BPRI Publications, Research Report 10. https://cedar.wwu.edu/bpri_publications/79/.

Konrad, Victor. 2012. "Conflating Imagination, Identity and Affinity in the Social Construction of Borderlands Culture Between Canada and the United States." *American Review of Canadian Studies* 42 (4): 530–48.

Konrad, Victor. 2014. "Borders, Bordered Lands and Borderlands: Geographical States of Insecurity Between Canada and the United States and the Impacts of Security Primacy." In *Borders, Fences and Walls: State of Insecurity?*, edited by Elisabeth Vallet, 85–102. Aldershot: Ashgate.

Konrad, Victor. 2015. "Toward a Theory of Borders in Motion." *Journal of Borderlands Studies* 30 (1): 1–18.

Konrad, Victor, and Emmanuel Brunet-Jailly. 2019. "Approaching Borders, Creating Borderland Spaces, and Exploring the Evolving Borders between Canada and the United States." *Canadian Geographer/Le geographe canadien* 63 (1): 4–11.

Konrad, Victor, and Melissa Kelly. Forthcoming. "Introduction: Culture, Borders in Globalization and Canada's Borders." In *Culture, Borders in Globalization and Canada's Borders*, edited by Victor Konrad and Melissa Kelly. Ottawa: University of Ottawa Press.

Konrad, Victor, and Heather N. Nicol, 2004. *Boundaries and Corridors: Rethinking the Canada–United States Borderlands in the Post-9/11 Era.* Canadian-American Public Policy 60. Orono: Canadian-American Center, University of Maine.

Konrad, Victor, and Heather N. Nicol, 2008a. *Beyond Walls: Re-inventing the Canada–United States Borderlands.* Aldershot: Ashgate.

Konrad, Victor, and Heather N. Nicol, 2008b. *Passports for All.* Canadian-American Public Policy 74. Orono: Canadian-American Center, University of Maine.

Konrad, Victor, and Heather N. Nicol, 2011. "Border Culture, the Boundary Between Canada and the United States of America, and the Advancement of Border Theory." *Geopolitics* 16:70–90.

Lipset, Seymour M. 1989. *Continental Divide: The Values and Institutions of the United States and Canada.* Toronto: C. D. Howe Institute.

Lipset, Seymour M. 1990. *North American Cultures: Values and Institutions in Canada and the United States.* Borderlands Monograph Series 3. Orono: University of Maine Press.

Lipset, Seymour M. 1997. *American Exceptionalism: A Double-Edged Sword.* New York: W. W. Norton.

Lugo, Alejandro. 1997. "Reflections on Border Theory, Culture, and the Nation." In *Border Theory*, edited by David E. Johnson and Scott Michaelson, 43–67. Minneapolis: University of Minnesota Press.

Mitchell, Don. 2000. *Cultural Geography: A Critical Introduction.* Oxford: Blackwell.

Muller, Benjamin. 2010. *Security, Risk and the Biometric State: Governing Borders and Bodies.* New York: Routledge.

Nethery, Amy, and Stephanie J. Silverman. 2015. *Immigration Detention: The Migration of a Policy and Its Human Impact.* New York: Routledge.

Newman, David. 2006. "Borders and Bordering: Towards an Interdisciplinary Dialogue." *European Journal of Social Theory* 9 (2): 171–86.

Paasi, A. 1998. "Boundaries as Social Processes: Territoriality in a World of Flows." *Geopolitics* 3 (1): 69–88.

Roberts, Gillian, and David Stirrup. 2013. *Parallel Encounters: Culture at the Canada-US Border.* Waterloo: Wilfrid-Laurier Press.

Rodney, Lee. 2017. *Looking Beyond the Borderlines: North America's Frontier Imagination.* New York: Routledge.

Royal Canadian Mounted Police. N.d. "Canada-US Shiprider." Accessed June 18, 2015. http://www.rcmp-grc.ca/ibet-eipf/shiprider-eng.htm.

Saleeby, David. 1994. "Culture, Theory and Narrative." *Social Work* 39 (4): 351–59.

Salter, Mark B. 2008. *Politics at the Airport.* Minneapolis: University of Minnesota Press.

Salter, Mark B. 2010. *Mapping Transatlantic Security Relations: The EU, Canada, and the War on Terror.* London: Routledge.

Schimanski, Johan, and Stephen Wolfe. 2010. "Cultural Production and Negotiation of Borders: Introduction to the Dossier." *Journal of Borderlands Studies* 25 (1): 39–49.

Schimanski, Johan, and Stephen Wolfe. 2017. *Border Aesthetics: Concepts and Intersections.* Oxford: Berghahn.

Shimoni, Baruch. 2006. "Cultural Borders, Hybridization, and a Sense of Boundaries in Thailand, Mexico and Israel." *Journal of Anthropological Research* 62 (2): 217–34.

Shweder, Richard A. 1984. *Culture Theory: Essays on Mind, Self and Emotion.* Cambridge: Cambridge University Press.

Sparke, Matthew. 2006. "A Neoliberal Nexus: Citizenship, Security and the Future of the Border." *Political Geography* 25 (2): 151–80.

U.S. Customs and Border Protection. N.d. "Border Patrol Overview." Accessed May 3, 2015. http://www.cbp.gov/border-security/along-us-borders/overview.

U.S. Immigration and Customs Enforcement. N.d. "Detention Facility Locator." Accessed May 3, 2015. http://www.ice.gov/detention-facilities.

Vandervalk, Sandra. 2017. "Line Dancing." MA thesis, Carleton University.

The Walrus. 2015. "Bill C-51: the Good, the Bad . . . and the Truly Ugly." http://thewalrus.ca/bill-c-51-the-good-the-bad-and-the-truly-ugly/.

YouTube. 2008. "India-Pakistan Border Ceremony." http://www.youtube.com/watch?v=NC9NeJh1NhI.

CHAPTER 3

Twenty-First-Century North American Borders

More Fixed, Fuzzy, Flexible, Fluid, or Free?
Sovereignty Lesson from Around the Globe

RICK VAN SCHOIK

> *The future isn't what it used to be.*
> —PAUL VALERY

Borders, Integrity, and Sovereignty

The single greatest boost to economic development and especially alleviation of poverty around the planet would be found in reducing the transactional costs of and at borders. The question is, of course, confounded by the challenges of defending versus some recognition of and reconciliation of the sovereignty issues across the border. The hypothesis I hope to test herein is that borders are shaped and rebordered by modern forces leading to necessary sovereignty shifts and sharing. Borders are securitized in different and it is to be hoped more modern ways such as by use of sensors and other technologies, secondary internal checkpoints, and pushing border processes such as inspections as far away from the territorial boundary as possible.

In this chapter I further test the following subhypotheses:

- While international relations matter, sovereignty defines borders, and they are becoming either more fixed or more fluid.
- Sharing sovereignty across more flexible borders has mutual benefit not only at the borders but at far distances from the border.

- Borders with neighbors are becoming dominated by investment in security infrastructure versus trade, transportation, and tourism infrastructures that boost economic opportunity on both sides.
- Sovereignty sharing is in its infancy but taking many larger than baby steps.

First, an examination of borders today is necessary to examine their integrity and the subsequent dependent expression of sovereignty.

Context: Borders Are Not What They Used to Be

The election in the United States in 2016 and the negotiations about the exit of Britain from the European union are graphic illustrations of the rise of populist nationalism that has consequences for borders worldwide. Leaving aside the implications of renegotiating NAFTA (now ratification of the newer United States–Mexico–Canada Agreement, or USMCA), the United States apparently wants to recover a sense of sovereignty, a stricter enforcement of immigration laws, and even hardening or militarization of the border with Mexico. The construction of prototype border walls in San Diego is demonstrative of possible eventualities. They remain symbolic, if not symptomatic, and even a harbinger of things to come. Borders and securitization are back, but not always in productive and positive ways. Populists, nationalists, even isolationists are both antiglobalization and antimigration, and therefore antirealistic.

Globalization is manifest in everything we buy, wear, eat, invest in, and even talk about. North Americans (residents and citizens of all three nations) cross borders all the time with ideas, investment, and involvement even if we individually don't personally cross. Americans are permanently engaged with Canada and Mexico as we probably burn some of their petroleum and otherwise use fuels and electricity derived from up north or eat some of the multitude of produce grown in the south. The realistic ideal of a common production platform is also manifest.

Today we live in a time of upheaval that is as startling as when man lived in caves. In fact, CAVES is an apt acronym to describe the Complex and complicated nature of the world today with Ambiguous outcomes to most geopolitical decisions, Volatility in the price, cost, and value of things, Error-prone and extreme uncertainty about the future, and Stateless actors who affect and in most cases dominate world affairs as much as our formal sovereign governments. These stateless actors, multinational corporations, transnational crime organizations (TCOs), and terrorists may have a greater role in the CAVES future than even now. They certainly make the role of borders and powers of sovereignty harder to discern.

Walls are not security. In fact, they may be the opposite (i.e., false and symbolic but very expensive and relatively ineffective). The first realization about borders for serious thinkers is that walls and fences don't work. Migrants and refugees, drugs and other contraband move north across the U.S.-Mexico border while guns, cash, and ammunition move south. In some ways, the efforts by Department of Homeland Security (DHS) and Customs and Border Protection (CBP) make the pay to "coyotes" and "burros" that smuggle people and drugs much higher by making the effort more strenuous but not stemming the actual flows (prices as high as $30,000 to smuggle a person from Asia to the United States is noted).

Finally, border studies are mature enough now to be labeled border science, with testable hypotheses and methodologies to design, develop, and organize data sets. However, the current general disdain for all sciences is cause for some concern.

Introduction: Borders and Sovereignty Mattered Once and Again

Where are borders? They used to be just on land and only mattered if the nation was densely inhabited right up to the frontier hinterlands. These natural borders consisted of deep seas, high mountains, arid deserts, dense forests, and other uninhabitable spaces. Now both poles, most of all the oceans, space, and even underground are divided or contested.

Borders formally began about the same time, some say exactly the same time, as sovereignty began (with the Westphalian Peace Treaty of the late 1600s) and as sovereign rulers—known previously as lords, princes, fiefs, and so forth—needed to know where their powers began and ended. Borders were until that time natural divisions (rivers and straights, or mountains and deserts) or other forms of frontier and hinterland. Borders were born as an afterthought but just as relevantly and reverently as sovereignty after the Thirty Years' War, when the European national leaders sought to assert their voice in the otherwise winless situation that they had lived through for a generation. The pope had hitherto been the de facto ruler of many territories and determined what was worth fighting for, and they, the real rulers, sought to impose their laws, but just as importantly their own order.

It was after all global forces, at least European forces, that created sovereignty. The Little Ice Age of the medieval period was marked by floods, famine, and food shortages. The regional rulers, tired of ineffective and distance governance from the pope and church, decided to "take control." They and their diplomats met in Westphalia and agreed that they held ultimate power to decide all issues within their territory and over all its peoples. Thus, borders were borne as the mechanism to demarcate one sovereign from another. They have persisted in one form or another for centuries.

Because the study of international relations and the study of borders have not always been comfortable with one another, border studies, like borders themselves, have been marginalized. Michel Foucault wrote, "What we need is a political philosophy that isn't erected around the problem of sovereignty" (Foucault 1977). This is unfortunate, as borders today are perhaps the most dynamic component of international relations. Drives of fixedness and bolstering are perhaps more dynamic than drives toward fluidity and flexibility.

History: Borders Change as Nations Emerge and Evolve

Many of the older generation are dumbstruck when they see maps of the nations of the world just one hundred years ago, just before and after World War I, and the next generation is again struck when they consider the borders just before and after World War II. Wikipedia lists over two hundred changes to borders since World War I. New nations emerge nearly every decade, and one electorate voted for the first time a few years ago, and several are poised for the next decade.

But few of us, if any, really know how we'd redraw the world today or next year. The values and therefore the definitions of borders, nations, and sovereigns is changing, but not in the same directions or to the same degree everywhere. Witness the new argument about where the "essential" Russian border is in Ukraine. The old argument to divide Iraq and other Muslim nations into tribal zones is being reconsidered yet again.

Many border, security, and military issues are driven by access to resources and sea lanes. Where would one, for example, draw the border between Russia,

Ukraine, and Crimea and how would one accommodate Russia's understand-
ably perennial refusal to give up its access to seaports and energy pipelines
through the area?

Today some borders are being bolstered. The most contested control over
sovereignty and borders is exerted by Israel over Gaza's border with itself and
Egypt. At the same time the border between generations-old enemies of China,
Russia, North and South Korea are changing right before some unbelieving eyes
as workers, resources, and production are shared across and into industrial parks
on both sides of both the borders.

Hypotheses: Borders Imply Sovereignty Shifting and Sharing

The hypothesis to test herein is that borders are shaped and rebordered (i.e.,
second inner border as well as pushing borders away from territory) by modern
forces leading to necessary sovereignty shifts and, in some cases, sharing. As
border become more fixed or more frayed faster, the international conventions
meant to deal with them would need to, but of course cannot, react quicker or
at least as well. How are borders becoming more fixed on the one hand, and in
some cases are forced, while on the other hand, others are fraying by becoming
fuzzy, flexible, and even fluid. Only sovereignty sharing can resolve these complex international relations issues.

Borne out of war and bloodshed, borders clarified a previously chaotic world
of natural geographic frontiers. Borders enabled sovereigns to extend to their
boundaries their rules of law and order. As Kapka Kassabova writes, "It is where
power acquires a body if not a human face" (Kassabova 2017).

Economist Elinor Ostrom received the Nobel Prize for arguing that the
sharing of pooled resources that are common to many nations has more benefits
to the nations bordering the common resources than the transactional cost of
negotiating their use. In other words, sharing resources, like sovereignty, needn't
have an undue cost. The United States and Mexico recently began settlement of
the hydrocarbon resources in the maritime border zone as well as the donut hole
in the center of the Gulf of Mexico where neither nation's exclusive economic
zone reaches. Dealing with contentious issues such as transborder pollution,
research in aquifers, and preventing pathogens and exotic species from crossing
into neighbors' territories just made so much sense for the common security

and prosperity of both that these issues that were solved for the U.S.-Canadian border decades ago are being negotiated now with Mexico.

Some today believe we can share sovereignty, and such agreements as international trade, transboundary environmental protection (such as air quality), and protection during mass migration are examples. Indeed, if Japan and Russia can "share sovereignty" over the Kirill Islands, as they have recently agreed, then the rest of us should be able to articulate an America First that is not so America Alone. The controversy over the Kirill Islands now being solved has been brewing since 1855 and was renewed again soon after the Second World War. What the two nations agree to now is to "share" governance by contributing services each naturally has to offer—for Japan, this is domestic support, and for Russia, it is international military might.

The European Union, with its vast bureaucratic infrastructure, is but one example of suprasovereigns sharing authority and meeting regional needs. The European border and coast guard, however, has an increasingly difficult role in this time of migration across the Mediterranean.

The reality that Mexico would change its constitution to share sovereignty in the form of armed law enforcement by U.S. agents on Mexican land was unimaginable just a decade before. But security concerns and progress in international, at least North American, cooperation on policing issues mandated such changes. Even today, Canada is considering changes to NORAD to match U.S. suggested changes in its trilateral Northern Command to accommodate threats from Russia after Russia's behavior in Crimea, Ukraine, and Syria.

In this chapter, I review borders of the world and classify some showcase examples of how borders lie along a continuum of dynamism, I examine the forces that are driving borders to be more fixed or fluid, and I discuss implications for the world's but especially North America's borders with a focus on sovereignty.

Borders of the World: North American Borderlands Are Both Progressive and Regressive

The U.S.-Mexican and U.S.-Canadian border regions (United States Border Regions [USBR]) and international relations concerning them have served as a model for some positive collaborations—the century-old International Boundary and Water Commission (IBWC), the La Paz Environmental Cooperation Agreement, the North America Free Trade Agreement (NAFTA, which should

actually be abbreviated NATFA for North American Tariff-Free Agreement)—
have served as milestones and guides to subsequent international relations
between and among nations but have been woefully inadequate for other
challenges. The USBR could import models from other places—the Mekong
Delta model for river and water management; the Schengen Accord for labor
mobility, education, and tourism; the European Union's (EU) use of technology,
such as satellites, for border monitoring—but those experiments are fraying
quickly as well.

North American borders are a mix of bordering styles. The U.S.-Canada,
or northern, border is well regulated on both sides by all pertinent and linked
agencies—physical, ecological, agricultural (food and drug), and in terms of
human security. Canada has active immigration, border-security services, and
national intelligence agencies that correspond to U.S. agencies. Their relatively
liberal migration and refugee policies translated into several thousand tempo-
rary residents from nations the United States considers suspect, meaning an
increased threat to U.S. interests arises out of Canada even though more but different (typically poorer nations of origin) migrants arrive at the southern border.

A Continuum: Borders and Therefore Sovereignty Are Dynamic and Consequential

North American borders have been variously described after 9/11 as thicker,
stickier, and denser, but we have self-imposed costs with little if any real benefit
instead of making ourselves more secure by making the borders thinner, less
sticky, and broader (i.e., internal security checks for contraband and criminals).
Borders were established for greater order. But as we approach the end of only
the second decade of the new millennium, we find borders fraying as well.
One reason borders are so dynamic lately is the even more dynamic nature of
international relations.

A continuum is suggested as a model. Herein I describe six states of borders
as further described by sovereignty adherence. They are from failed to free.

Failed
Fractured/Forced
Fixed
Fuzzy/Frayed/Fragmented

Flexible/Fluid

Free/Open

They are further defined, and examples are given, below.

Failed

Failed states have failed or completely ineffective borders. Currently Syria and Yemen can be considered failed states and their external borders no longer operational. Syria presently has no less than five "controllers": the Syrian government, the Islamic State, Kurdish forces, the Jubhat al-Nusra, and other rebels and mixes of the above (not to mention ISIS/ISIL).

Fractured/Forced

Borders that are breached by military aggression or other blunt force become fractured. The Ukraine/Crimea-Russia border is an example. A new and highly contested Ukraine-Crimea border has been forced on the people of the region nearly seventy years after Russia gave the island to Ukraine under USSR rule.

The India-Pakistan region of Kashmir has paramilitary forces on both sides, drones from India, and earthquakes contesting an already tense region. On the other side of the country, India faces challenges from the drawing of its borders in 1947 and the designation of 162 parcels of one nation actually located in the other, a remnant of an even older treaty of the eighteenth century. It is becoming less contested as the fifty thousand residents are getting to choose both citizenship and which nation provides basic services.

Finally, on the island of Cyprus, which joins two nations (Turkey and Greece), the residents share no basic amenities such as electricity and telecommunications even though they share a territory and a future.

Fixed

Traditional borders are fixed by rigid delineation and sovereignty. Most international borders are fixed, though tensions or pressures may exist. Most borders are fixed until an internal or external force modifies its status. One might assume most of today's borders are fixed and sovereignty reigns, but regrettably that is not so. The Carolinas of the United States have agreed to reset their borders after decades of agreeing but not quite knowing what to do. North and South Carolina recently reconciled their centuries-long debate with a bistate border commission, while California recently resolved through arbitration a disagreement with the federal government over their maritime border.

Fuzzy/Frayed/Fragmented

Borders become fuzzy when sovereignty issues are not dealt with properly, leaving openings for redefining the border, a process that can be called "rebordering." Some would say steeply stepped-up migration has rebordered the Mediterranean. The African-European border is a classic fuzzy border in that people regularly cross the Mediterranean Sea (from Tunisia and Libya to Sicily and Italy, respectively) or enter enclaves on the African mainland (Ceuta and Melilla, Spain in Morocco) to gain access to Europe and its relative wealth.

Glaciers are melting because of climate change, and this is changing the borders that were previously designated as the highest elevation between nations. Today, treaties are written more diligently regularizing these borders, such as the one between Italy and Switzerland.

Emerging volcanic islands, such as in Tonga in 2015, and disappearing islands and seamounts usually present limited challenges as most new territory is recognized as belonging to the nation whose continental shelf from which it originated. The consequences of sea level rise (exacerbated by climate change) means many of those nations' affected citizens may eventually need to change nationality or become climate refugees.

Ebola spread quickly in 2014 among the Kissi-speaking people of three western African nations because the borders and health agencies there are grossly underfunded, according to a report by the *New England Journal of Medicine*. What could have been roughly a billion dollar loss of life, vitality, and economy became a tragedy triple that cost. Relations and resources available among the three nations were insufficient to limit or track travel during the early days of the disease.

The South China Sea is a classic example of effective division being confounded by a new power or presence arriving late to the game and wanting to be treated either specially or as an old-time member. China's Nine-Dash Line is less than three quarters of a century old, but just as it did when it claimed Tibet as its territory in 1949, China claims most of the sea where some estimate almost 40 percent of world trade passes through and calls its sovereignty "indisputable." Five other nations have had control of this area over the centuries. China ignores decades-old exclusive economic zones and even the more recent UN Convention of Law of the Sea rules. China has long had a gradation of control over various offshore assets such as Taiwan and Hong Kong but is now asserting itself into the South China Sea to control sea-lanes and ocean bottom resources. China bolsters its claim by dredging the ocean bottom for sands and erecting islands and placing military installations on then, challenging all other nations' free and open navigation through these waters.

Canada and the United States agree to disagree about the border between Alaska and Yukon. Resource competition there may force resolution, especially now that global climate disruption has made the Arctic Ocean more accessible. The Arctic, as the ice recedes summer by summer, is being contested not only by those who have a land stake above the Arctic Circle or bordering on the Arctic Sea but also by those interested in the sea-lanes (read: China). Russia has the most ice breakers of any national fleet (approximately forty) but the other fast-growing nations that have Arctic aspirations are building them so they can assure the northern passage as a much shorter route to their markets. Recently, the United States yielded chairmanship of the Arctic Council after a two-year post.

Flexible/Fluid

Borders can achieve a flexibility where and when the geographic border and sovereignty are maintained but certain additional flows, both economic and diplomatic, across the border are more and more accommodated. Many democracies, seeking greater integration of economy, commerce, trade, transportation, and tourism across borders are moving toward this modality. NAFTA can be considered a milestone in making North American borders more flexible. The securitization reaction to 9/11 has made them less flexible.

The Pacific Northwest Economic Region grew out of the Cascadia ideal during a transborder challenge over water governance. Today it stands as a classic case study of how to share sovereignty to meet states' and national needs.

The "donut hole" in the middle of the Gulf of Mexico was a decade-long moratorium of the lands outside both the United States and Mexico's exclusive economic zone (EEZ). When settled, it allowed each nation to develop a portion of the energy resources that exist there, again a classic study of how to agree to disagree and then agree. Unresolved for now is the remaining donut hole between the two nations and Cuba. Again, resource competition and thawing of cool relations may resolve this sooner rather than later.

The University of Texas at Brownsville (now University of Texas Rios Grande Valley, or UTRGV) campus, where the authors initially met to discuss the chapters in this book, is bisected by a security fence erected by DHS right through the campus golf course. Rather than resign more campus lands to securitization, the campus and CBP jointly developed a camera, lighting, and communications system of towers for the baseball field that afforded both access to surveillance information of interest and that was notably cheaper than the federal government doing all the heavy lifting. This collaboration remains a living example of flexibility.

Free

Borders can be considered open when the transactional costs of crossing are minimal or nothing. In other words, sovereignty has been negotiated. The Schengen zone in Europe (not always contingent with EU nations) is an open travel zone. The labor- and materials-mobile European Union and Schengen are the best examples of how nations, facing larger global threats, agreed to reconcile internal border issues collaboratively and even establish an external border agency (FRONTEX).

North America is both an integrated economy and a border challenge but less a nightmare because of the shared sovereignty among the three nations (albeit shared differently on the northern and southern borders). Cross-border securitization has been met by sharing of sovereignty on such matters as intelligence, law enforcement, frequency-matched communications, and regional surveillance.

Most borders do not fit exactly into one category but may be moving between two stages on the continuum. Examples abound. Almost all borders are one way or another compromised.

Fixedness: Drivers in Both Directions

Security, even a false sense of it, and sovereignty assertion seem the only drivers toward fixedness. Each is benefitted by firm, clear borders that are semipermeable to the things we want to allow to cross them. Unfortunately, most of the modern world works in opposition to such fixedness as xenophobia and the resource race drive nations to contest and pursue new and different borders.

Robert Green (2006, 448) closes his excellent review of war with the following:

> In the end, in a world that is intimately interlinked and dependent on open borders, there will never be perfect security. The question is how much threat are we willing to live with? Those who are strong can do with a certain acceptable level of insecurity. Feelings of panic and hysteria reveal the degree to which the enemy has triumphed as does an overly rigid attempt at defense, in which a society and culture at large remain hostage to a handful of men.

The global problem of illicit drug production, trafficking, and sales by transnational crime organizations can no longer be ignored by any nation, spurring many to suggest changes to national laws. Free-trade zones have been especially effective at establishing transportation systems that narco-traffickers take advantage of. Nations with drug problems should see the advantage of lowering their hard borders and collaborating with other nations in fighting this massive international industry ($39 billion in Mexico alone). Prohibition unilaterally no longer makes sense, as every time a packet of drugs crosses the border, it doubles or more in value. The only prescription is one of global negotiation.

Most issues, however, tend to make borders fuzzier or at least more flexible within boundaries, and efforts have been expended to accommodate the new sovereignty situation.

- Environmental issues such as air quality and pesticide drift drive cooperation as transborder transport of contaminant is inevitable. The summer of 2015 saw Canadian wildfire smoke dense enough to make people in Colorado cough.
- Natural disasters, their prevention, and preparedness for their eventuality, immediate reaction, midterm response, and ultimate recovery can be called catalysts for change. The reaction to the devastating earthquake in Mexicali–Imperial Valley that broke water supply levees was a joint agreement to open and maintain an emergency connection so the Mexican town could have safe drinking water.
- Trade, commerce, and labor mobility are part of desirable economic development. The list of cooperative and collaborative initiatives is numerous.
- Criminal activity. TCOs used to carry out mere drug trafficking across national borders until they diversified into common crime and specialized in transportation and distribution not just across the border but into U.S. cities. Sharing of intelligence and agreements on extradition of drug kingpins such

as El Chapo are examples of shifts insovereignty, and the change to the Mexican constitution to allow U.S. drug agents to carry arms in Mexico is a direct sovereignty action.

- Diseases emerge and reemerge demanding that public health systems, especially detection and classification labs, extend to where the infections and contaminant may be coming from. After 9/11 there were extraordinary efforts to develop the capacity of laboratories on both sides of both borders to detect and report contaminations.
- Food security is the manifest nexus to water, climate, and energy that assures not only a safe but a reliable supply of fresh fruits, vegetables, and other produce.
- Biodiversity, like food, knows no boundaries. Sanctuaries, in the form of natural protected areas, should and do exist on both sides so that species have room to roam and range under normal as well as under climate-change scenarios of migration.
- Ecological processes such hydrology and fires should be allowed to cross borders or not as deemed needed by both nature and humans on both sides. Now fires are prevented and fought together as part of interstate compacts (ISC; see below).

Energy Independence Through Interdependence

Perhaps the best example of an absolute driver is energy integration as each nation increasingly needs access to the forms of fuels and electricity more available and more affordable locally but across borders as well. The connection between energy and water, called "watergy," and that connection with both food and climate is undeniable.

In addition to European Union, EU could also mean "Energy Union," as even more sovereign issues yield to common interests and endeavors to share clean energy sources in the region as a strategy to become more self-sufficient and less dependent on unfriendly suppliers. California has recently passed legislation entering into a regional system of operator plans with western states, expanding its independent system operator (CalISO) across borders both state and national.

On the North American continent, energy, especially electricity, flows across borders in both directions depending on the time of year and seasonal demand.

In times of shortage, emergency connections are used to allow electrons to flow to otherwise needy areas. Texas, which operates its own grid (ERCOT), needed power during a drought that reduced its hydroelectricity supply and also during a heat wave that exploded demand.

Independent energy is the ability to recognize codependence and even interdependence as North America becomes a mass exporter of petroleum to the world, not only now but later, when Mexico develops its known and probable reserves. We already enjoy relatively cheap and readily available uranium, petroleum, natural gas, and clean renewable electricity from our friendly neighbors, and together we enjoy energy security through interdependence, not independence. Energy dominance implies a zero-sum game.

In summary, essentially all the forces of the modern world are stressing borders, some more than others and some more continuously than others.

Sovereignty Compromised or Confirmed: Traded, Bargained, or Shared?

Some would hope we can all recognize a larger sovereignty than ourselves, such as cities respecting states and states deferring to federal governments when necessary. The following questions emerge:

- Do past models of border drive and define sovereignty or the other way around?
- Do we adjust sovereignty to match the control we have at borders and the need to make borders more open to some phenomena?
- Can sovereignty be traded, bargained, or shared?

"Sovereignty is not what it used to be. It is more. And it is less. . . . No state, not even the superpower, can by itself protect its people from . . . upheavals half a world away. We all inhabit a planet on which our worst problems are shared problems. They demand cooperative solutions . . . in fluid alliances that now mark the ways we best govern" (Smith and Naim 2000, xiii). Among the challenges, they think the world should accept is comprehensive transboundary risk assessments for nations before they reach in extremis. They compute that global climate change is the permeating factors lessening the stability of any and all states.

Why would a nation voluntarily give up sovereignty and change a border? Historically, empires have returned lands to people when services and governance became too difficult and expensive or when defending far-flung property was simply too diffused and other interests competed for attention.

In some cases, in response to need or convenience, sovereignty is being traded, shared, and even compromised for mutual benefit. David Ricardo (1817), the British economist, two centuries ago wrote about complementarities of nations. Trade and other cross-border investments are a form of sovereignty sharing as public and private actors obey the rules and regulations of the host nation for the obvious benefit of sharing, for example, complementary agricultural and industrial assets. If fuels and electricity are broadly available across borders, it enhances the energy security of the neighbors even if the sending nation must meet standards of the importer or vice versa. This phenomenon has extended itself to even far-flung friends. Management of both environmental quality and ecological integrity has benefitted from shared sovereignty. When a species disappears on one side, that nation may find it beneficial to cooperate, even comingle funds that spur the recovery of the species on the other side, anticipating that the species will spread back across the border later. And finally, but hardly of least importance, disease monitoring by necessity mandates certain compromises of sovereignty. The North American experience with sudden acute respiratory diseases (SARS), several avian pandemics, and even Ebola compares well with the Asian, African, and South American experience where sovereignty got in the way of sharing precaution, diagnostic monitoring, and treatments. Sovereignty also exacerbated the limited fund expenditures that did occur.

Trade is the ultimate in sovereignty sharing as nations take advantage of complementarities in other places, as the economist David Ricardo (again) recommended. Senator and presidential candidate Elizabeth Warren is very vocal about the potential infringement on U.S. rights and rules from Trans-Pacific Partnership (TPP). For example, removing remaining trade barriers within the NAFTA bloc, a process called "regulatory cooperation," harmonizes such standards as laboratory procedures and policies so that safety inspections can be done in the nation of origin and recognized in the others.

In the Arctic, increasingly an area of border contest, several functions are shared. Canada has taken a stewardship approach to its claimed territories and conducts search and rescue, environmental protection, and oil spill monitoring and recovery. It only asks that vessels entering Canadian territory identify themselves—a huge difference from the situation in the South China Sea.

A common bottom line is that sharing or even swapping sovereignty has little cost. "Borders retained their porosity without states relinquishing their sovereignty" (Wong 2004, 31).

North America Next: Sovereignty Sharing Examples

Many of the negatives of borders and the transactional cost of them have been overcome. Free-trade agreements have removed protectionist and ruinous tariffs, and all nations are involved in several formal dialogues about how to remove other restrictions to trade. Co-location of facilities, starting logically at small and remote border crossings in the northern plains, has been resuggested only a decade after the Government Accounting Office studies revealed that sovereignty was a stumbling block to such arrangements in the past (Government Accountability Office 2007).

But borders are confounded by real sovereignty claims. The United States has different levels of sovereign engagement with Canada's ten provinces (one of which, Quebec, still talks about succession and its sovereign rights being different from the others) and its three territories (Yukon, Northwest, Nunavut). The United States, on the other hand, has several more layers of control or lack thereof over its interests. It also has twelve territories and outlying areas and three associated relationships (used to be called "protectorates"). By the way, what to do with the U.S.-Canadian border, famous for being the most democratic and least protected in the world, is still undecided since the two nations agree to disagree about the maritime border between Alaska and Yukon, especially at sea and as U.S. president Trump remains adamant in his beliefs.

Implementing both joint border securitization and transborder trade has necessitated compromises among the three North American nations. The whole concept of facilitating trade at the border by moving security away from the borders has meant, and continues to mean, inspections, clearances, and screenings in the interiors of the three (as close to the point of production, be it farm or factory), all along the trade corridor, and when cargo enters the North American external security perimeter. Ideally, the three nations will work out the steps to their shared final vision of "inspect once and accept thrice" by sharing standards, intelligence, and even operations and facilities. Regulatory cooperation is breaking down some of the last barriers to trade by enabling laboratories in other nations to assure quality of drugs, food, and other consumer products much the way the three have cooperated in the past for automobiles and aircraft (i.e., building to a common continental standard or a global specification versus merely a national regulation).

Shiprider, a program where U.S. and Canadian armed officers travel and enforce respective laws on Coast Guard and other ships of the Great Lakes and Saint Lawrence Seaway, was among the first experiments in "exchanging" sovereignty.

Finally, as elections are a manifestation of sovereignty, almost every nation and subnational entity legislates and guards against foreign influence over campaigns and the votes themselves. But as every political watcher can attest, fraud in election finance can be from some external contributor. In some cases, the gray area of political favors acts in a similar manner to influence the decisions made by those who are duly elected.

If we are concerned about terrorism and drugs, we ought to invite Canada and Mexico to join in a 3-D hemispheric security zone and join a common customs union so that imports enter the continent inspected once and accepted thrice. While the geographic location of the North American borders is fixed (though some are disputed), the flows and dynamics of them are more fluid and flexible even given the severe securitization that they have experienced.

How do the United States, Canada, and Mexico negotiate shared sovereignty? The electrical grid and security surveys of generators (including dams) and transmission, shiprider, transborder petrochemical and subsequent refinery operations (in the United States of Mexican oil!), drone flights, and smart border telemetry are a few examples. One of the positive outcomes of the hysteria of 9/12 (the reaction to 9/11) was expanding the Border Infectious Disease System to include the Early Warning Infectious Disease Surveillance, where the United States and Mexico cooperate in laboratories and clinics on noting first disease appearance. And the most amazing and recent story of sovereignty bargaining is Mexico changing its constitution to allow U.S. law enforcement agents, specifically CBP and maybe even the U.S. Drug Enforcement Administration, to carry weapons is a perfect example of how responsive nations need to be. The trial will be conducted at the border at Laredo and Otay Mesa as trade and flows at land ports of entry drive the conversion and conversation hereafter.

Technology sharing at the border is also possible as both nations now engage in exit and entry controls. There is no need for two inspections if one suffices. At one time within the past decade, CBP would not even consider a joint booth with our neighbors to the north.

Hydraulic fracturing, also known as "fracking," has consequences throughout the underground geology, meaning fracking on one side of a border can prompt tremors, pollution, and gas escape on the other side. Though transborder drought monitoring and water supply data sharing has gotten better, as other challenges emerge, such as the renegade flows from the Tijuana River into the U.S. estuary. The lining of the All-American Canal was almost totally a sovereignty issue, with the United States claiming all the water was theirs and Mexico warning of salinity issues endangering species in the wetlands on their side supplied by subsurface flows from the unlined canal. The issue was never resolved even through the canal was lined and the water saved was instead shipped to the thirsty and higher populated coast.

World Reordered: Implications for North America

Based on regular crossing of all North American borders by train, ferry, private vehicle, bus, bike, foot, and of course air, and being intimately familiar with the crossing between San Ysidro and Tijuana, I have long claimed every border is different and every port of entry is different not only from each other but from what they were yesterday. While the U.S. southern border is different from the U.S. northern border, some similarities exist. DHS and CBP has imposed a securitization that accommodates the differences but addresses the underlying common threats and risks to themselves. The Canada Border Services Agency (CBSA) acts much as the CBP and the Transportation Security Administration (TSA) do, and Mexico has strengthened its policing of both its southern border with Guatemala and internally. What perhaps is different is Immigration Customs Enforcement (ICE) and internal enforcement of immigration laws by the United States, an effort that by some estimates exceeds all other law enforcement in the United States, including that of the DEA and the FBI.

Many complain that securitization of borders by the U.S. government has been inadequate or superlative to the degree that environmental concerns place a distant third to security and economic development, industrialization, and urban development. As this is written, the sixth exemption to existing rules on environmental review are being used to waive such precautions. At least a dozen species have been identified that are at greater risk, and the decision was challenged by three international environmental and biodiversity groups.

That the United States has four conversations on regulatory cooperation (one with Canada, one with Mexico, one with Pacific trade nations, and another with Europe) versus one with opt out and opt in conditions is indicative of how many believe the two borders are forever different and irreconcilable. An external security perimeter proposed long before 9/11 and resurrected only by Canada in the 2000s is an example of how the three cannot unify over a common customs union let alone a trilateral, multidimensional, defensive space around and over North America.

The United States and Canada are closest in the "inspect once, accept thrice" goal of having a shipment arrive on either of their shores and be cleared for travel to the other nation. An interesting corollary of "test once, accept (or ban) thrice" is not being following for designation, laboratory testing, and banning of dangerous chemicals. Plasticizers, such as those in baby bottle liners, banned in Canada but allowed in the United States, are now being joined by chemicals used to make skillets and other cooking ware as potential cancer risks.

Of recent concern to some is the laundering and then influence of foreign funding for political campaigns. San Diego is still rocked by a scandal from the election in late 2013 for several candidates. Even though rules prevent such external tampering with sovereign affairs, the wave of money is large, and the conniving of the washing is nearly complete.

Conclusions: Yes, Borders and Sovereignty do Change

The critical role of subnationals—such as cities, counties, and states—cannot be encouraged enough. Because they control land use, taxes, incentives, transportation, education, and much else and because they have the constitutionally granted power of interstate compacts (ISCs) that they can use across international borders, they are slowly taking on the role they need. Traditionally ISCs are used across the U.S.-Mexico border to exchange equipment, training, and communication for firefighting, and the same mechanism is used for fire prevention. It is proposed to assist in transborder consultation on environmental review, siting, finance, and approval for energy transportation and transmission infrastructure.

California and its neighbor Baja California signed a memo of understanding on environmental and climate cooperation, and while California also has agreements with Mexico (in the absence of the U.S. federal government initiatives with Mexico), California is more likely to affect and be affected by conditions and mitigations directly across the border.

The private sector is slowly entering international relation as well. A recent binational public-private partnership (P3) illustrates. Private funds raised by the Puerto Peñasco tourism and convention agency were passed to the binational Arizona-Mexico Commission, which passed them to the Arizona Department of Transportation to build more lanes to and from the Lukeville-Sonoyta, Sonora, port of entry so more holiday traffic could use the passage on their way to and from vacation on the Sonoran gulf coast.

Are North American borders fuzzier, more fluid and flexible, or more fixed? For security issues the border itself is more fixed (i.e., no joint facilities) than ever, but sovereignty has been shared by law enforcement programs, such as shiprider with Canada, and there are still few clearing customs in Mexico like those in Canada, the European Union, and some Asian countries.

Climate-Change Leadership: Next and Necessary

Environmental governance of the North American commons is still undone as we note that the United States and Mexico still do not perform and share insights from assessing the transborder effects when conducting environmental reviews. The three North American nations, together and apart, have set the stage for negotiations toward global fixes. The Obama, Calderón, and Trudeau leadership established trilateral progress on clean energy and carbon sequestration. It will be curious to see what Trump and Lopez Obredor do. Nations, individual states/provinces, and municipalities established or entered carbon markets. In the early 1990s Ottawa and Michigan began trading emission reduction credits (ERCs) for acid rain precursors harnessing the power of states and the private sector to reduce pollution using market forces. In late 2014 California and Quebec began auctioning carbon together, a market that was later joined by several more states and provinces. Can a North American carbon offset strategy be far off?

The oceans and particularly the Arctic Ocean, now that climate change has opened it, are fraught with border issues. Fisheries, minerals, and hydrocarbons on and under the sea bottom and navigation access lanes are at the top of many other issues being contested.

Final Thoughts: North America Could Lead Again

What might this mean for the planet as borders blur, soften, and rigidify and as nations affirm or change the rules of sovereignty from what they were four hundred years ago? Leaders need to pretend we live in CAVES again. The new state-challenged and border-challenged world is Complex, with Ambiguous outcomes from any action, with Volatile costs and benefits, and an Error-prone system that has extreme uncertainty as to who or what might be an ally and reduction of risk or an enemy and hazard, of which most are Stateless actors. The emergence of stateless actors as major power players means both that more is really at stake and that no one really has any control. Terrorists, multinational corporations, and transnational criminal and cyber organizations mean national powers and territorial borders have less ability to prevent, plan, and prepare for and then react, respond, and recover from both natural and human-intended disasters. In other words, threats will be general versus targeted, risks will be across domains of defense, and hazards will multiply.

Just as early borders attempted to set standards for behavior within the bounds, today's borders stand symbolically for a set of principles that the citizens extend as an offering to those outside. In the speeches of Martin Luther King Jr. (1992) we saw first articulation of the ethos that as long as people anywhere were not free we were not free here within our borders. Some have found advice and even admonition to raise the quality of life of all nations. The three nations have cooperated on both borderlands governance and sovereignty. They will need the same spirit to demonstrate to the world such outcomes if they can host, successfully, the World Cup in 2026.

NOTE

This paper was written in the spring of 2015, when the U.S. president in office was firm and almost predictable in his treatment of borders and sovereignty as he began to wrap up his second term. But at that time, the next president hadn't quite announced his candidacy. The paper was revised in mid-2017 during the second one hundred days of the term of the U.S. president elected in 2016, again in the summer of 2018, and finally again in the fall of 2019. The new administration's foreign policy has been variously described as "negotiable," "bargaining," and "transactional," and his economic policies as "nationalistic," "antiglobalization," and "populist," even "protectionist" and "isolationist," while his attitudes toward the border, sovereignty, migrants, and the wall have become well-known.

REFERENCES

Foucault, Michel. 1977. *Discipline and Punish: The Birth of the Prison*. New York: Vintage Press.

Government Accounting Office. 2007. "Security Vulnerabilities at Unmanned Ports of Entry, GAO-07-884T." Washington, D.C.: Government Accounting Office.

Green, Robert. 2006. *33 Strategies of War*. New York: Joost Elffers.

Kassabova, Kapka. 2017. *Borders*. London: Granta.

King, Martin Luther, Jr. 1992. *The Papers of Martin Luther King, Jr*. Berkeley: University of California Press.

Ricardo, David. 1817. *On the Principles of Political Economy and Taxation*. London: John Murray.

Smith, Gordon, and Moises Naim. 2000. *Altered States*. Ottawa: IDRC Press.

Wong, Diana. 2004. *The Rumor of Trafficking: Border Controls, Illegal Migration and the Sovereignty of the Nation-State*. IKMAS Working Paper Series 10. Bangi, Malaysia: Institut Kajian Malaysia dan Antarabangsa.

PART II

Spaces, Divisions, and Connectivity in North American Borderlands

CHAPTER 4

Transborder Spaces and Regional Identity in North America

FRANCISCO LARA-VALENCIA

Introduction

Against the backdrop of the North American Free Trade Agreement (NAFTA, now United States–Mexico–Canada Agreement [USMCA]), 9/11, and Donald Trump, the idea of a North American region has trudged through an uncertain path of shifting sentiments toward cross-border integration and cooperation. In the mid-1990s NAFTA produced a milieu that de-emphasized national, centralized policy and favored narratives of interdependence and regionalism. In contrast, 9/11 generated a retrenchment toward a more fortified United States, prioritizing border control and surveillance over integration. In 2016, the triumph of Donald Trump invigorated by antiglobalization attitudes among large segments of the U.S. population ignited an unapologetic nationalism committed to erect walls and put America first and above North American integration. In the short span of two decades, cross-border governance in North America progressed swiftly toward trilateral and binational mechanisms of cooperation and cross-border localized integration efforts just to turn abruptly toward a nationalistic rescaling of the region (Ayres and Macdonald 2012).

Despite these political swings, even a casual observer will notice that efforts to build transborder spaces along the U.S.-Canada and U.S.-Mexico boundaries have remained a common occurrence in the region. Concentrated mainly in the economic-development arena and dominated by the private sector and subnational governments, these efforts reflect the inescapable power of inter-dependence, complementarity, and socioterritorial proximity over the kind of policy choices available to regional actors. The persistence of these efforts speaks volume about the resilience of existing transborder linkages as well as the strength of the cross-border social capital accumulated in the region over time (Wong-González 2005; Lara-Valencia 2011). Ultimately, the nature, scope, and evolution of these efforts are deeply embedded in a complex political field where space, identity, and governance are constantly renegotiated within a multiscalar system of interests, dispositions, and power.

As suggested by Paasi (1991), the emergence of a feasible border region, that is, a space able to sustain meaningful cross-border networks and cooperation, demands much more than mere bureaucratic structures. It requires a foundation of collective and territorial identities providing the strength and flexibility to cope with internal and external pressures and with constantly shifting national representations of borders. Consequently, the full understanding of cross-border integration—this is the politics and the "muddling through" of region building observed in the North American borderlands—requires the examination of three interconnected analytical domains. The first domain comprises the soci-oterritorial configuration of the imagined region, primarily the set of values, ideals, and symbolic elements supporting the plausibility of collective narratives of cross-border regionalism. As Klaus Eder (2006) suggests, the plausibility of regional building efforts depends on the shared stories that help people to come together around larger-than-life ideas demanding collective action. The second domain involves the networked constellation of actors performing the resultant social space. Paasi (1991) has made a useful distinction between "producers" and "reproducers" of transborder spaces, the former being activists and advocates in the economic and political arenas and the latter journalists, media organizations, artists, and all sort of intellectuals and creators. The third domain comprises the contextual elements that determine the rhythm and direction of change and correspond loosely to what Eder refers as the historically contingent context that creates continuities and discontinuities in the permanent process of region building (Eder 2006).

Certainly, one of the principal assumptions of postpositivist paradigms of regional building is that symbolism invigorates collective action by creating a sense of common understanding and providing a narrative promoting place attachment, social cohesion, and collective action. The analysis here uses this perspective to explore transborder space formation in the U.S.-Canada and U.S.-

Mexico borders from a comparative perspective. Ultimately, this exploration is motivated by an attempt to comprehend the construction of transborder spaces for development planning and cooperation in North America. Further motivation comes from the realization that the study of regional consciousness is an issue that has been neglected by border scholars, a fact with implications both for the theoretical evolution of the field of border studies in North America as well as for the advancement of border governance and cooperation at the regional scale.

This work is organized in four sections. First, I review the recent literature on region building and identity formation in order to connect this analysis with the current discussions and debates in the field. In the second section, an overview of cross-border regionalism and institutions in North America is presented as a way to contextualize the analysis. This is done by contrasting the European and North American experiences with cross-border regionalism in recent years. In the third section, I take an empirical turn by introducing an operational framework to analyze regional identity manifestations and the practice of cross-border regionalism on the ground. The framework closely follows the conceptualization provided by constructivist views of regions and regional development. I conclude with some closing thoughts about how resurgent narratives of transborder regionalism can potentially contribute to stronger transborder communities and warn about the need to translate symbolism into concrete incentives and opportunities for a broader social participation in cross-border work. In all four sections, some empirical observations are introduced based on the comparative exploration of three case studies in the Canada-U.S. border and three in the U.S.-Mexico border.

Conceptual Approach

Academic work on symbolic and discursive representations of borders and borderlands in North America and their influence on integration and cooperation is still scarce. This lack of interest contrasts with the experience of political and economic elites that for a long time have known that regional realities along borders can be produced and shaped through identity-forming narrations of exceptionality and opportunity. The power of the discursive construction of border regions for collective action is revealed by the contemporary and recurrent portrayal of U.S. borders as the source of all the national goods and bads—depending on the dominant political or economic circumstance—through all kind of media and communications. Equally illustrative of this power is the naming of border areas as "borderplexes," binational megaregions or sister cities for branding purposes and to market the real or imaginary possibilities of cross-border integration. It has also been documented by numerous studies emphasizing the notion that the construction of transborder spaces for joint planning and development is as much the result of material conditions as of subjective factors embedded in collective cognition, place attachment, and regional consciousness (Scott 2002; Jones and MacLeod 2004; Balsiger 2011).

In the case of the European Union, for example, the injection of huge amounts of government funding for regional development programs along the Union's internal borders has been effective in reducing barriers to cross-border mobility of people and goods, yet it has been observed that "despite more or less explicit attempts at a Europeanization of society and space, integration—and therefore spatial politics—remains a contested project" (Scott 2002). It is against this sort of observation that some scholars have begun to examine closely the argument that identity-forming narrations of shared experiences and expectations are an important component of consequential efforts to establish effective transborder policy making and planning (Eder 2006, Paasi 2009). Theorization and empirical analysis of the importance of the so-called regional consciousness on development and cooperation have practical ramifications as they open new ways of understanding the hurdles of regionalism and integration efforts, public or private, targeting border areas.

Drawing insights from postpositivist thinking, contemporary sociospatial analysis of regions focuses on its relational and contingent character and how discourse and symbolism may influence the process of how people "come together" to understand and define their regional space (Allen and Cochrane 2007). This view contrasts with traditional territorial perspectives mainly concerned with the relationship between sovereignty, land, and people and criticized because their bounded, static, and often ahistorical representations of space and place. As noted by Agnew (1994), this form of thinking supports the tendency to conceptualize the world as a mosaic of socially, spatially, and politically self-contained nation-states and led into the so-called territorial trap that hinders the consideration of unbounded, deterritorialized spaces. In contrast, many contemporary regional theorists prefer to think of regions as fluid, boundless, and historically contingent social constructions (Allen and Cochrane 2007; Taylor 1994; Paasi 2009).

Referring to the construction of regions, Paasi (2010) suggests that "regions are performed and made meaningful in material and discursive practices and

networks that cross borders and scales," and that through institutionalization regions they become "actors" guiding collective action and differentiation. Through this process, which can be conceptualized as a looped system of
identity production, people construct representational images of places while
the imagined place, in turn, transforms people. From this perspective, regions,
including border regions, should be examined not as static or objective realities
but as a fluid, socially constructed phenomena shaped by a dialogical interaction
between context and collective cognition and expectations. Collective cognition and expectations, two main ingredients of regional identity, are neither
static nor predefined entities but contingent representations resulting from the
cross-fertilization of place and people. As van Houtum points out (2012, 47),
"The dominant representation of places and people as separate entities" is a
misleading depiction of current territorial identities as people take clues from
the territory to define themselves while simultaneously changing territorial configurations and features, real or imagined.

An important aspect of this conceptualization is that regional identity, as
suggested by McSweeney (1999), is neither an object floating out there waiting
to be found by social scientists nor a monolithic reality. In other words, it is
simplistic to think that individuals in a community conform reflexively to a
congealed set of collective values and beliefs, resulting in practices that define—
nearly in absolute terms—the essence and contour of a collective identity. A
view such as this often results in notions that equate identity, society, and territory and set unambiguous boundaries for what belongs and what does not.
It might also derive from the naive idea that identity can be mapped out by
conducting surveys of the distribution of language, music, cuisine, and religious
practices that are conventionally associated with a human group (McSweeney
1999; Paasi 2011).

Although it is true that society restricts the ability of its members to wander
aimlessly in search of identity, it is also true that each person constructs its own
identity depending on individual experiences and preferences. Therefore, even
though certain places are powerful enough to provoke similar responses and
feelings across social groups interacting with it, there is always the potential
for divergent reactions within society. When meanings of certain places are
too divergent, such divergence could result in the entrenchment of contradictory understandings and representations, which in turn might result in tension
and even conflict. As observed by Paasi (2011), the vision of a region is not
always embedded in a spirit of solidarity or uniform sentiments across social

groups that many times coexist and compete with contrarian views and often are the source of narratives of resistance and distinction. In fact, what positivist accounts of society tend to present to us as people's identity is usually the identity of the dominant group of the political or economic elites who have succeeded in producing and projecting an image and narrative that gives the appearance of cohesion and collective purpose. Often this narrative is so forceful that tends to downplay or even wipe out alternative regional views.

It is worth noticing that recognizing and accounting for the diversity of meanings held by different community groups within a region is critical from an analytical and policy-making perspective. Diversity of values regarding regional development goals and how such values are ingrained in people's identity can lead to paralysis in terms of collective action and may thwart the ability of a region to effectively navigate a pathway of development balancing economic growth, sustainability, and equity. Identifying place-based values specifically and regional identity broadly can help to determine where the limits of a broad consensus lie and provide the foundations for a minimalist view of the region or for the renegotiation of a common vision. As put by McSweeney (1999), identity is a process of constant negotiation among interest groups who engage in a collective competition that could lead to different outcomes depending on the political capabilities and resources available to each of the players. In fact, as suggested earlier, the outcome of this negotiation is constantly contested by the evolving material context in which society exists and by the emerging ideations that social groups develop on how to approach the challenges and opportunities coming out of a constantly shifting reality. Therefore, although regional identity by itself is a legitimate object of scientific inquiry, what is really relevant is the understanding of identity-producing processes—that is, their players, their interests, their resources, and the rules shaping negotiated outcomes (McSweeney 1999).

Individual and collective consciousness are dimensions of identity that are important to differentiate because they are analytically connected to distinct sociotemporal scales. According to Paasi (1991, 249), "Individuals come and go, regions remain and are transformed." This sentence puts forward the idea that individual consciousness is not what produces a region; rather, regions are sociocultural entities engendered by institutionalized collective practices that transcend the lifespans and life experiences of any of their individual inhabitants. In other words, collective identity is "a significant element in the construction of regions as meaningful socio-political spaces," whereas individual experiences with spaces are what articulate personal senses of place. According to this, collective consciousness is an important factor for regional development strategies in general and cross-border regionalism in particular. Besides the conceptual distinction between individual and collective identity, Paasi (1991, 249) also observes that in a global and networked society, highly mobile individuals will develop a sense of place shaped by personal experiences and events of everyday life "taking place at varying localities" that together give shape to a noncontiguous, hybrid, and diasporic space.

Transborder Spaces

If a region is conceived as a space constituted by contingent networks of local and extralocal social interactions the scale and field of which do not necessarily correspond to territorial and jurisdictional limits, then they could conceivably be a sociospatial entity stretching across national borders (Allen and Cochrane 2007). From this perspective, regions can exist as transnational or transborder sociospatial entities that can be viewed as the space for unique cross-border endeavors and governance. Furthermore, as territorial and formal jurisdictional borders lose relevance for the configuration and functioning of these transborder spaces, their social and economic cohesion are likely to be more dependent on endogenous regional processes and on globalization forces, leading to a centrifugal rescaling in which national boundaries become increasingly thinner and permeable.

Nevertheless, the construction of a viable and resilient cross-border space is not guaranteed by the operation of these networks alone. First, often these networks are only the conduit for opportunistic interactions and are prone to fade once the incentives that incited their creation disappears. Second, historically the most common incentive for the engagement in cross-border regionalism is the exploitation of price-cost disparities or institutional differences, and this seldom leads to the type of holistic thinking linked to the concept of regional development. Third, the construction of cross-border spaces is inherently complex, especially if the boundary to be crossed is a place where cultural, political, and institutional differences are significant and can be a barrier for interaction. Not surprisingly, as suggested by Eder (2006), the building of a cross-border space begins with the construction of a "communicative space" in which social relations become the medium for the circulation and reproduction of the cognitive and narrative elements of regional identity.

In theorizing the importance of communication in the construction of transnational spaces in the context of the European integration framework, Eder (2006) distinguishes three basic moments. First, "well-established narrative communities" enter into contact and become exposed to communities who do not share their communicative space. In the European context, exposure is induced by EU-sponsored initiatives and cooperation programs that make spatial planning and integration a policy imperative in areas along shared internal borders. Second, political and cultural elites formulate cognitive propositions that initially are not attuned with the cognitive experience of the people but that might trigger an identity-forming process based on a shared narrative. According to Eder (2006), these cognitive propositions could be articulated in narratives emphasizing citizenship, culture ties, or shared well-being. The third moment is the creation of a regional space of communication supporting a collective identity based on narratives substituting the discursive claims of political and cultural elites.

In a more pragmatic tone, Paasi (2010) notes that regions are discursively produced and reproduced by newspapers, museums, schools, universities, and other cultural institutions with the mission of routinizing social practices embedded in regional cultural symbols. Equally important in the discursive construction of a region is the "soft work" performed by business organizations, journalists, politicians, coalitions, and governments that rely on the internet, social media, and other information and communication technologies to help people in and out of the region to make sense of it as a space of exceptionality and possibility for investors, tourists, entrepreneurs, educated workers, and eventually ordinary citizens (Paasi 2002).

Constructing Transborder North American Spaces

In order to highlight the specificities of the construction of transborder spaces in North America, I have opted for a brief comparative analysis using the European experience as sounding board. Indeed, there are a number of significant differences in the way border and border issues are approached in Europe and North America (Scott 1999; Blatter 2004). However, the most foretelling difference is the role assigned to borders in the context of the process of integration launched in Europe in 1992 with the signing of the Maastricht Treaty and in North America in 1994 with the formalization of NAFTA.

On the one hand, the creation of the EU was framed under the assumption that removal of internal barriers to economic flows as well as the reduction of regional disparities were requisites for a full-fledged integration (Deas and Lord 2006). Border regions in particular were perceived as disadvantaged and isolated territories needing special programs to develop the infrastructure and the capacities to engage and contribute to a globally competitive Europe. At the same time, it was assumed that border regions would play a central role in any successful integration process because their potential to bridge nationalistic values hindering the articulation of the vision of a unified Europe. In congruity with this perspective, European spatial policy toward border regions was not a strategy driven solely by economic objectives but also by a reevaluation of the political and cultural role that border regions could play in the construction of a new pan-European identity and community. As noted by Scott (1997), transboundary cooperation became an area of high priority for European spatial planning and development efforts because border regions were seen as anchor territories in the construction of a cohesive, competitive, and flat Europe.

In contrast, border regions in North America were dealt with using a narrower perspective emphasizing mainly their function as control tools and seeking to increase their efficiency in filtering cross-border flows. As suggested by Ayres and Macdonald (2012), NAFTA's only focus was on the facilitation of trade and capital flows under the assumption that national complementarities under market-driven policies would give North America unique competitive advantages in a globalized economy. In the context of this limited integration philosophy, North America borderlands were primarily seen as sites for the location of more maquiladoras or the emplacement of more efficient border infrastructure and not places for social cohesion, collaboration, and development (Scott et al. 1997). The nontrade provisions of NAFTA, for example, are narrow, and its side agreements on labor and the environment were introduced during negotiations mainly to appease groups in the United States and Canada that threatened to derail the highly politicized negotiation process leading to the eventual passage of the agreement. As Blatter (2004) convincingly concludes, border policy in North America is more about the borderline than the borderland as the priorities are set in expediting economic flows and not on creating identity and community.

Despite some common themes and even the suggestion that "Europeanization" is a good model for border policy in North America (Della Sala 2007), the difference between both continents are copious and conspicuous. The sources of the differences between Europe and North America are multiple and overlapping, but they depend largely on the specificities of the historical realities of each continent, including the way national self-awareness, regional identities, ideological discourses, and the strategic symbolism of the border are negotiated in the political arena. Keeping this in mind, in the rest of this section I outline some of the major elements characterizing the development of border regionalism in North America.

First, as a phenomenon embedded in the larger context of the North American integration process, border regionalism in Canada, the United States, and Mexico is constantly challenged and constrained by national imperatives and a limited and fragmented institutional border regime. We may observe this in the type, scope, composition, and permanency of the cross-border efforts that are more prevalent in the region. The most common type of partnerships are those driven by the incentives to exploit disparities, interdependences, and complementation, which creates an opportunity for extraordinary profits or benefits for those involved. Therefore, the spectrum of participants is limited and dominated by private and government actors who see cross-border action as an investment necessary to pave the way for the expansion of a particular business or the growth of a whole industry. In consequence, the scope of the cross-border activity of these actors is restricted to business promotion, regional branding, infrastructure creation, or lobbying for legislative and policy change aligned with those interests. Hence, a defining characteristic of cross-border efforts in North American borders is its ephemeral existence and its inability to create durable collaboration platforms. Also, since the possibility of exploiting border asymmetries and complementarities is territorially fixed, they tend to be constructed as a source of comparative advantages vis-à-vis nonborder regions. Therefore, in an area as highly unequal as the U.S.-Mexico border, the incentives to deal with existing gaps in regional development and not only growth are few. This is not to say that there is no exception to this pattern, but the instances of the contrary only confirm the norm. Two of such instances are the Arizona-Mexico Commission, a decades-long transborder organization with the participation of governments, entrepreneurs, academicians, and civic leaders, and the Pacific Northwest Economic Region (PNWER) partnership in the U.S.-Canada border.

Second, social interactions across borders in North America occur in a highly charged political environment in which the domestic agenda of the United States dictates the tone of its bilateral relations with Canada and Mexico and consequently the progression of the regional integration process. The politicization of the border became particularly intense after 9/11, complicating the traditional compartmentalization of bilateral relations and slowing the advance of the integration agenda. As conservative groups in the United States successfully portray the borders as a threat to national security and sovereignty, the opportunities for cross-border cooperation, and even simple coordination, dwindled in North America. The U.S.-Mexico border is particularly vulnerable to political polarization because the pervasive violence affecting Mexican border cities and the inability of the Mexican government to eliminate structural factors forcing many of its citizens to migrate irregularly to the United States is a source of constant fuel to the negative construction of the border. Peter Andreas's annotation that Washington's response in the aftermath of 9/11 was the "Mexicanization" of the U.S.-Canada border reflects both the severity of the security situation in Mexico and the dynamic of power that allows the United States to treat similarly its southern and northern borders despite significant differences (Andreas 2005). To a great extent, recent efforts of individuals and groups concerned with the promotion of border integration are focused on maintaining the cross-border agenda and on recovering cross-border regionalism from loses inflicted by political polarization in the United States. Indeed, much of the cross-border activity observed in North America recently is in a sort of recovery mode treading well-traveled roads and focusing on safe strategies such as information sharing and soft partnerships. Efforts to maintain the functionality of collaborative bodies in the U.S.-Mexico border, such as the Arizona-Mexico Commission and the Border Governors Conference, after the turmoil that followed the implementation of controversial immigration laws and programs in Arizona are an example of this.

Third, existing narratives and discourses about the border among supporters of cross-border regionalism are cautious representations of the region, using language and metaphors that reflect the border's ambivalence and the uncertainty of the moment. Public perception of loss of sovereignty, external threats, and uncontrolled movement of people is a forceful reality in the United States and can have political consequences for those challenging its validity. Hence, the "open borders" label used dismissively against cross-border integration and cooperation is counteracted with phrases such as "separating the good from the bad," "security and prosperity," and "zone of tranquility," all of them elements of a very restrained counternarrative. In any case, both narratives, dominant and resurgent, are carriers of a certain symbolism and meaning attributed to border regions by two opposing forces. They also illuminate the practice of "inventing communities" as well as the practical consequences of regional identity for social interaction and development in the North American borderlands.

Grounding Regional Identity and Cross-Border Regionalism

In this analysis, I adopt the view that border regions are "relationally constituted" spatial entities that possesses multiple and changing meanings because they result from intertwined processes of social competition, negotiation, and acquiescence (Jessop, Brenner, and Jones 2008). Accordingly, border regions are not seen as fixed, self-contained places bounded by the limits of a discrete, unique territorial unit but as an amalgamation of "*multiple geographies of affiliation, linkage and flow*" (Amin 2004, 38). However, I do not see border regions as purely social abstractions disconnected from the material support a territory provides to ongoing social relations. Instead, it is recognized that society and territory are the two parts of a mutually constitutive reality mediated by material, ideological, and symbolic systems that secure the production and reproduction of social relations. Therefore, the working definition of regional identity used in this analysis comprises two key conceptual domains: socioterritorial identity and regional consciousness. These dimensions and their components are diagrammed in figure 4.1.

Socioterritorial identity relates to people's perception and connection to the natural and built environments and their attributes, which can be subdivided into place-based cognition and place-sourced identity. Place-based cognition depends on people's awareness of the borderland's natural and environmental features and its articulation in predominantly descriptive narratives highlighting their contribution to the sustenance, wealth, and cohesion of society. In its most primary formulation, place cognition representations speak of landmarks and landscapes that provide material continuity to the region and mark its contour beyond the international boundary. Often, place cognition also results in images that highlight the exceptionality of the region as it relates to other nonborder places that can be used as a reference for differentiation. On the other hand, place-sourced identity relates to narratives linking perceived attributes of the people's character and their assumed connection with certain aspects of the border that tend to be characterized as the source of particular collective behaviors or practices. It also relates to elements of the material culture or the built environment that operate as signifiers and participate in various ways in the making of the region. This idea follows Benwell and Stokoe's (2006) proposition that

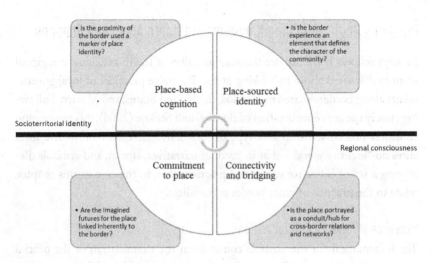

FIGURE 4.1 Border dimensions of regional identity

people's sense of who they are is shaped by the stories they make about where they are. Overall, socioterritorial representations are the result of a self-reflective process of a group of individuals who make sense of their selves via the attribution of meaning to places.

The second domain, called regional consciousness, comprises two dimensions. The first dimension is place commitment, which implies an affective relationship with the region. Individuals and social groups are proud to be part of the region and develop a strong connection with the border. Because of this connection, individuals and groups across the community grow a sense of solidarity that entails the potential of some form of collective action to enhance and safeguard those elements that are the source of the uniqueness of the region. This leads to the second dimension, connectivity and bridging, which entails cross-border actions adopting the form of activities and strategies to cope with or mitigate situations or events, real or perceived, that threaten with disrupting processes or activities deemed important for the success or progression of the region. The most sophisticated form of regional consciousness becomes apparent when individuals and groups of actors engage in institutional forms of planning, as this activity expresses a deliberate and forward-looking understanding of the development of the region. Collective active participation in regional institutions or organizations (partnerships, associations, etc.) and active commitment and engagement are vehicles for social cohesion and development.

Exploring Region-Building Narratives in North American Borders

In what follows I will explore the manifestation of the dimensions of regional identity discussed above by looking at the discursive practices of local governments along borders shared by Canada, the United States, and Mexico. Following closely the conceptualization of Benwell and Stokoe (2006), this exploration considers official websites as a type of "discursive environment" where local elites do "identity work"—that is, produce narratives, stories, and symbols displaying a set of collective values and practices that, in the case of this chapter, relate to the practice of cross-border regionalism.

Research Methods and Information

The information for the analysis comes from the examination of the official websites of six city pairs along the Canada, Mexico, and United States common borders. Three border-city pairs were selected in the U.S.-Canada boundary and three in the U.S.-Mexico boundary based on the volume of international travelers and visitors crossing through the nearest port of entry, a surrogate of the level of cross-border interaction. The six border ports of entry chosen registered the largest amount of people entering the United States by land in 2014 according to U.S. Custom and Border Protection (table 4.1). The rationale for selecting the city pairs with the largest volume of cross-border traffic is dual. First, I assumed that the number of pedestrians and passengers traveling in personal vehicles is a reasonable proxy of interlocal connections involving people engaged in place-based, quotidian activities (e.g., transborder commuting and shopping). Second, the amount of border activity is correlated with the size of the cities, which in turn correlates with the e-government capacity of the place. Several studies suggest a positive relationship between population size and local capacity to create and maintain websites for e-government and branding functions, a necessary prerequisite for this analysis (Moon 2002; Roy et al. 2015; Musso, Weare, and Hale 2000).

In this research, an official website was defined as the online platform created by the border-city government to provide information about municipal services for residents, e-government, economic promotion, tourist promotion, and place branding in general. I use the term *online platform* purposely because the examination included the main city webpage but also linked websites of agencies, commissions, corporations, and other entities supported by the city to communicate city efforts or convey services in the areas of business recruitment,

TABLE 4.1 Population Size and Cross-Border Flows in Selected Border-City Pairs, 2010

Border	City pair	Combined population (a)	Travelers/ visitors (b)	Ratio (b/c)
U.S.-Canada	Blaine, Wash.-Surrey/White Rock, BC	492,334	7,389,462	15.01
	Detroit, Mich.-Windsor, ON	924,668	7,510,751	8.12
	Niagara Falls, N.Y.-Niagara Falls, ON	133,190	12,952,831	97.25
U.S.-Mexico	El Paso, Tex.-Ciudad Juárez, Chih.	1,970,125	26,007,386	13.20
	Laredo, Tex.-Nuevo Laredo, Tamps.	609,816	15,347,298	25.17
	San Diego, Calif.-Tijuana, B.C.	2,910,900	40,041,029	13.76

Source: U.S. Census, Statistics Canada, and Instituto Nacional de Estadística y Geografía (INEGI).

tourism attraction, or cultural activation. These linked websites might operate as separate websites but were reachable through a direct link on the main city homepage.

The examination consisted in the cursory inspection of the official website with the aim of identifying content relative to the city's efforts to recruit or retain business, attract tourism and visitors, and promote the cultural, historical, and natural assets of the place. As noted above, the framework used for the analysis is based on the four dimensions involved in regional identity formation: place-based cognition, place-sourced identity, place commitment, and connectivity and bridging. The inspections and analysis of the websites focused on identifying such dimensions and their use as elements of narratives to characterize the cities in relation to the border.

Canada-U.S. Border Case Studies
Blaine, Washington-Surrey/White Rock, British Columbia
Blaine's identity is strongly connected to the border as indicated by the branding of the city as the "Peace Arch City" and the place "where America begins" (City of Blaine 2015). The Peace Arch, a monument completed in 1921 that anchors a binational park straddling the border, seems as important as Birch Bay and the Fraser River in place-based cognition of the city. As indicated in Blaine's website, the "unique relationship" between the United States and Canada that resulted in an "unguarded border" is celebrated by the Peace Arch that bears the inscription "brothers dwelling together in unity." In fact, the demarcation of the international boundary in 1817 (Rush-Bagot Agreement) is portrayed as

the foundational event for the city of Blaine and of its character as community. Local narratives identify as founders of the city settlers that came to the area when the United States Boundary Survey Commission arrived in 1856 to survey the forty-ninth parallel. The border experience is also celebrated in activities such as the International Arts Festival at Peace Arch Park that is held in Blaine and convenes artists from the greater Northwest in a symbolic event commemorating "diversity, lasting peace and exchange" between the United States and Canada.

As a border city, Blaine's economy is highly dependent on tourism and retail trade, a fact that is acknowledged in local narratives. References to the evolution of the exchange rate between the U.S. and Canadian dollar and to the natural resources and beauty of the area are prevalent features in local narratives of prosperity and quality of life. Surrey (City of Surrey 2015) and White Rock (City of White Rock 2015), on the other hand, are two cities in British Columbia whose narratives barely relate to the border. Both cities refer to their geographical location as being in the lower mainland, highlighting their proximity to Vancouver, which is the main source of visitors and business opportunity in the area. The two border crossings Surrey shares with Blaine are mentioned only in the context of the logistic advantages that comes from the location of the former city in the trading corridors of greater Vancouver and the Pacific Rim. Interestingly, the Peace Arch Park is not given the same symbolic value or used as place marker by either of the two cities at the southern Canadian border.

Detroit, Michigan–Windsor, Ontario

Windsor's connection to the border is made evident in the references to the proximity of Detroit as a "big city" that complements the "small town" feeling of the Canadian side (City of Windsor 2015). The significance of the border location as an identifying element of place is also reflected in the reference to Windsor as the "top Canadian border city." The War of 1812 and Prohibition are mentioned as historical events that shaped the personality of the city. Looking forward, the website highlights the importance of thinking of Windsor as part of the Great Lakes region and strengthening its relation with Detroit in addition to direct efforts to make the border "work for Windsor." However, narratives about cross-border interactions are basically confined to trade and tourism. Therefore, Windsor is portrayed as a gateway to Canada and a major transportation hub for international trade because of its proximity to the U.S. Midwest production and consumption centers. The city is also portrayed as a friendly place for U.S. tourists since "distance is short, language is common, and the US dollar is accepted at par with the Canadian dollar."

In open contrast, the representation of the city of Detroit as border city is negligible (City of Detroit 2015). The only insinuation of the border as a defining element of the city's identity is a reference to Detroit as an "international waterway," which is part of the Great Lakes region. Besides that, Detroit's website makes no mention of the border as an element that defines the character of the city, and it does not link its future to the development of the border or to any sort of cross-border regionalism.

Niagara Falls, New York–Niagara Falls, Ontario

Niagara Falls, Ontario, and Niagara Falls, New York, are two cities whose identity is fundamentally defined by their location on the gorge of the Niagara River. In both cases, tourism and hydropower are the two main economic engines of the local economy, and both industries depend on the existence of the river. Although the river is also the international boundary between Canada and the United States as well as the location of three bridges connecting the two countries, the river seems to be the source of multiple, scaled identities characterized by notions of autonomy from the border and attachment to a region whose centripetal forces are the big cities in their respective nations and, from there, to the rest of the world.

On the one hand, the narratives connecting Niagara Falls, Ontario, with the other side of the border are limited not only in number but also in substance (City of Niagara Falls 2015b). References include mention of the fact that the Canadian falls "carry nine times more water than its US counterparts" and that the close proximity to the United States allows businesses in Niagara Falls, Ontario, to participate of the celebration of some American holidays, such as Thanksgiving, so they invite U.S. residents to cross the border and celebrate where the American "dollar goes much further." Extensive information is provided about crossing procedures both for U.S. and Canadian travelers moving across the border. A central feature of the discourse of place formation is the narrative of the War of 1812 between the United States and England, which is portrayed as a "defining moment for the resident of Niagara and an event that has contributed to the identity of our community."

On the other hand, Niagara Falls, New York, identifies itself as an international city emplaced on "the longest, undefended border" connected by three bridges that provide "a natural link between the United States and Canada markets" (City of Niagara Falls 2015a). This city also relies on the colonial war as a source of identity, yet the significance of the War of 1812 seems less crucial than it seems to be for the Canadian side. The connection with the city on the other side of the border is minimal, indicating limited connectivity and bridging. Niagara Falls, New York, celebrates some Canadian holidays with fireworks and a light show over the waterfall. In sum, the border is still a sensitive issue in the region while competition and rivalry seem to be the dominant characteristics of the relationship between the two Niagara Falls.

U.S.-Mexico Border Case Studies

El Paso, Texas–Ciudad Juárez, Chihuahua

El Paso has built a narrative of place explicitly linked to the international border (City of El Paso 2015). Elements of this narrative include the location of the city "where Texas, New Mexico and Old Mexico meet" and being part of a "tri-state binational region that is the second largest metropolitan area in the US-Mexico border." Referred to as El Paso del Norte, this binational region is identified as being formed by the cities of El Paso, Ciudad Juárez, and Las Cruces. This location is referred to as the source of significant identifying attributes of El Paso, including a "multicultural atmosphere" where "cultures and traditions blend seamlessly" (City of El Paso 2015). It is also the source of many of El Paso's qualities—such as a "large bilingual and bicultural labor force, resources for manufacturing, and access to a consumer base of more than 2.5 million people"—that translates into important economic advantages.

The local elite's commitments toward the region is expressed in the concept that the city "stands at the forefront of communities transcending borders" (City of El Paso 2015). This narrative is reinforced with words of commitment "to regional collaboration, cooperation and integration to maintain the region's relevance in a highly competitive global economy." An expression of El Paso's cross-border regionalism includes links to Ciudad Juarez's website and information on border crossing, but most important perhaps is the endorsement of the "North American Borderplex" initiative, an economic-development effort led by the private sector to brand and promote internationally the binational area. In open contrast, Ciudad Juarez's website offers few narratives connecting the city with the border or some form of cross-border regionalism (Ayuntamiento de Ciudad Juárez 2015).

The most apparent marker of place is the Río Bravo (Río Grande), which is described as "separating the city from the US and the neighboring City of El Paso." The Rio Bravo is indeed a very important source of identity for

Ciudad Juárez, given its central role in the dispute between Mexico and the United States for the El Chamizal area, which started when the river shifted course and put on the north margin land owned by Mexican citizens. Ciudad Juárez is touted in the city's website as the "only city to which the United States has returned land without going to a war." The few elements of a transborder narrative detected include the description of Ciudad Juárez as a place functioning as a "binational link" and characterized by a "border biculturalism." The idea of a binational region or the concept of cross-border regionalism are almost completely absent in the narratives found in Ciudad Juárez's website.

Laredo, Texas–Nuevo Laredo, Tamaulipas

Laredo's identity as city is firmly connected to the international border, starting with the claim of being the southern gateway of the United States as well as being the only border city sharing ports of entry with two Mexican states (City of Laredo 2015). A concept found in the city's website reinforcing this narrative is the claim that in Laredo a person can be "in Mexico without having to cross the border." The border is also acknowledged as a source of local culture marked by a "progressive and entrepreneurial spirit" fit for the "opportunities created by an international good neighborliness" (City of Laredo 2015). The strong bonds with Mexico manifest in local traditions such as the International Bridge Ceremony, which "serves as the 'welcoming ceremony' between officials and dignitaries from Mexico and the United States by exchanging 'hugs' symbolizing the amity and understanding between two neighboring nations." Some expressions of cross-border regionalism are the Border Trade Alliance, which defines itself as the "premier authority on issues affecting the US northern and southern borders," and the monitoring of border traffic through live cameras in the four bridges connecting the city with Mexico (City of Laredo 2015).

The city of Nuevo Laredo, on the other hand, asserts an identity linked to the U.S.-Mexico War that resulted in the loss of territory and a strong allegiance to the homeland (Ayuntamiento de Nuevo Laredo 2015). As narrated in the city's website, following the signing of the Guadalupe Hidalgo Treaty in 1848, Mexicans loyal to their nation crossed the Río Bravo to found Nuevo Laredo and brought with them their dead who "were exhumed, so they could keep their Mexican citizenship." Interestingly, Nuevo Laredo calls itself the "Gateway to Mexico, the Land of Opportunities," indicating a strong connection with the border. It is claimed that the city benefits from a "strategic geographic location along the most important commercial corridor in North America, through which 40% of the trade between Mexico and the US occurs." The city also emphasizes that its "logistics capabilities, infrastructure, human resources, and telecommunications technology" for trade are not found in any other Mexican border city.

San Diego, California–Tijuana, Baja California

The City of San Diego (2015) acknowledges its geographical location in southern California as a major source of its power to attract visitors, highly skilled labor, and investors. The proximity of the border comes with this location and adds some advantages to the city's economy and culture. The city's website states that the Pacific Ocean and the U.S.-Mexico border make San Diego's location strategic for the United States and "perfect for companies interested in international markets." In tandem with the city of Tijuana, it is claimed, San Diego is part of the "largest metropolitan area on the border, making it an ideal area for taking advantage of NAFTA." The proximity of the border is particularly beneficial because companies with maquiladora plants in Tijuana maintain operations in San Diego, contributing to the "local economy and adding to the region's importance as a manufacturing area." The contiguity of Mexico is also contributing to San Diego's transformation into an "increasingly bicultural" community (City of San Diego 2015).

The narratives in the city's website clearly reflect that San Diego sees the border as a resource that enriches its own development potential. Those resources are tangible—such as the manufacturing capabilities of the maquila industry, Tijuana's airport, and the tourist attraction of Baja California—or intangible—such as language and biculturalism. Several instances of cross-border regionalism indicating a commitment to place are observable, including the promotion of Baja California as a tourist destination, the advertisement of corporate events, and the access to planning agencies and programs "with the goal to create a regional community" with Mexico.

On the other hand, Tijuana's foundation and history cannot be disconnected from the border according to the narrative presented in their city's website (Ayuntamiento de Tijuana 2015). Since its establishment in 1889, Tijuana went through several transformations driven by events such as the Great Depression and Prohibition, the two world wars, the expansion of the U.S. economy in the postwar period, the bracero program, the creation of the maquiladora program, and NAFTA, because Tijuana's border location shaped the economy, demography, and culture of the city. Tijuana's place identity derives to a large degree and explicitly from vicinity with California and particularly with San Diego, which is designated as its "sister city."

According to the narratives presented, the connection with the border has shaped the character of Tijuana's people, who are described as "open, friendly and progressive" because of the location of the city. As to underline its progressive spirit, Tijuana is paradoxically branded as the "City without Borders" by the Convention and Visitors Committee. Tijuana with San Diego, it is claimed, create the border area "with the highest number of border crossings in the world" and their "efficient port of entries," "binational airport," "leading R&D centers," "and manufacturing capabilities" are critical assets for the development of the region. The commitment to the border translates into multiple expressions of cross-border regionalism, including the promotion of San Diego as a tourist destination, the celebration of U.S. programs to expedite border travel, the joint promotion of the region, and the provision to travelers and local residents of information about crossing procedures and border waiting times.

Concluding Discussion

The cases above illustrate the different ways borders are perceived and related to in North America. In each case, similar elements of regional identity emerge to define the contours of contrasting ideas of what the border means and contributes to each community in Mexico, Canada, or the United States. It is evident that no particular contour is privative of one nation, and similarities and contrasts can be observed across and along borders.

As illustrated by the cases of Tijuana, Blaine, or Windsor, strong border attachments are observed in the three countries. In the case of Tijuana, the companion city of San Diego also displays a regionalism strongly connected to the border, while Blaine and Windsor narratives of cross-border regionalism are not mirrored by South Surrey/White Rock and Detroit, respectively. Asymmetries in border narratives were also observed at El Paso del Norte region, with Ciudad Juarez expressing a less vigorous commitment than the City of El Paso. Also, different intensities and modalities of cross-border regionalism are observable along the U.S.-Mexican border as well as the U.S.-Canadian border. San Diego and Tijuana constitute a border-city pair that is developing a strong narrative of cross-border regionalism based on elements of biculturalism, bilingualism, and complementarities. In the U.S.-Canadian border the relationship between the two Niagara Falls is based on rivalry and competition with no clear evidence of institutionalized forms of interlocal coordination or collaboration.

Though on opposite sides of the spectrum, these two city pairs exemplify levels of cross-border regionalism that contrast substantially with the levels observed in the other cases studied in their corresponding borders.

Overall, these North American case studies show that looking at border regions through elements of regional identity formation highlights the significance of the historical context for local processes of interaction as well as the risk of thinking of the U.S.-Mexico and U.S.-Canada borderlands as two completely different realities in term of cross-border identity formation and regionalism. As shown above, there are at least three aspects that should be considered in the analysis of regional identification processes and regionalism in North American borders.

First, these case studies highlight the historically contingent nature of all identity formation and cross-border regionalisms processes. The border connectedness of the City of Detroit and Ciudad Juárez offers two interesting instances of the implications of localized crisis on boundary making and narratives of place. Detroit's current positions vis-à-vis the border cannot be disconnected from its functional role of nodal economy in the Great Lakes region during most of the twentieth century and its mounting economic difficulties in recent decades. The role of Detroit as manufacturing and innovation center for most of the twentieth century gave the city its status as an autonomous space toward which other urban centers in the Great Lakes region tended to gravitate, while the processes of economic restructuring and decline that began in the 1970s forced the city to turn in on itself in order to recover and secure its viability as a community. To some extent, Ciudad Juarez also has been forced to turn in on itself as a result of the wave of violence and crime that overwhelmed local authorities and citizens in the last decade and gave the city the international reputation as being one of the "un-safest cities in the world" (Consejo Ciudadano 2011). The magnitude of the challenges faced by Ciudad Juarez demanded the intervention of Mexican federal authorities and the complete rebooting of narratives of identity to assure residents of the city's ability to overcome the crime wave and infuse the community with a new sense of hope and pride based on local values and symbols.

Second, the analysis made evident that nationalistic views of war and conflict are still playing a role in identity-forming narratives in North America. The wars that defined the borders between Canada and the United States and Mexico and the United States in the nineteenth century, for example, still echo in Niagara Falls, Canada, and Nuevo Laredo, Mexico, and have a symbolic value used by local elites to exalt the struggles of their people to overcome formidable forces and explain their attachment to the place. Based on this research, however, it is not clear what role these symbols play in cross-border interactions and regionalism.

Third, discourses of identity shift and adapt to opportunities and challenges perceived by public and private actors reflecting the political character of the region-building processes. Rescaling seems to be a strategy used by border elites as an adaptation mechanism as demonstrated by El Paso, where connection with Ciudad Juárez is circumvented in a narrative that makes reference to Mexico rather than to the border city. In this case, rescaling allows El Paso to benefit from the border location while avoiding the association with the rampant violence affecting Ciudad Juárez. McSweenney (1999) highlights the political nature of region-building process and suggests that there is not a collective identity but a discourse of identity articulated by actors such as politicians, entrepreneurs, intellectuals, activists, and many others "who engage in the process of constructing, negotiating, manipulating or affirming a response to the demand—at times urgent, mostly absent—for a collective image."

Finally, while this research proves that web platforms can be a useful tool to explore narratives of identity, it is important to highlight some of its limitations. Although the cases studied in this paper reveal significant variation in website content, municipal websites in the three countries differ substantially in the ways they provide accessibility, the type of information delivered, and their target audiences. The community's socioeconomic circumstances, the institutional environment, and e-government practices of each country can explain some of these differences. Furthermore, in a rapidly evolving technological landscape, cities with less resources available face more difficulties in crafting more complete narratives involved in branding or developing communication platforms targeting global or international audiences. Regardless, the results of this research have a number of implications for public officers, community leaders, and scholars interested in border narratives of cooperation and regionalism.

REFERENCES

Agnew, John. 1994. "The Territorial Trap: The Geographical Assumptions of International Relations Theory." *Review of International Political Economy* 1 (1): 53–80.

Allen, John, and Allan Cochrane. 2007. "Beyond the Territorial Fix: Regional Assemblages, Politics and Power." *Regional Studies* 41 (9): 1161–75. https://doi.org/10.1080/00343400701543348.

Amin, Ash. 2004. "Regions Unbound: Towards a New Politics of Place." *Geografiska Annaler: Series B, Human Geography* 86 (1): 33–44. https://doi.org/10.1111/j.0435-3684 .2004.00152.x.

Andreas, Peter. 2005. "The Mexicanization of the US-Canada Border: Asymmetric Interdependence in a Changing Security Context." *International Journal* 60 (2): 449–62. https://doi.org/10.2307/40204302.

Ayres, Jeffrey, and Laura Macdonald. 2012. *North America in Question: Regional Integration in an Era of Economic Turbulence.* Toronto: University of Toronto Press.

Ayuntamiento de Ciudad Juárez. 2015. "Heroica Ciudad Juarez, Gobierno Municipal 2013–2016." Accessed November 18 (no longer posted). http://www.juarez.gob.mx /bienvenido/.

Ayuntamiento de Nuevo Laredo. 2015. "Nuevo Laredo, Puerta de México, Tierra de Oportunidades." Accessed November 15 (no longer posted). http://www.nuevolaredo .gob.mx/.

Ayuntamiento de Tijuana. 2015. "Ayuntamiento de Tijuana." http://www.tijuana.gob .mx/index.aspx.

Balsiger, Jörg. 2011. "New Environmental Regionalism and Sustainable Development." *Procedia: Social and Behavioral Sciences* 14:44–48. http://dx.doi.org/10.1016/j.sbspro .2011.03.019.

Benwell, Bethan, and Elizabeth Stokoe. 2006. *Discourse and Identity.* Edinburgh: Edinburgh University Press.

Blatter, Joachim. 2004. "From 'Spaces of Place' to 'Spaces of Flows'? Territorial and Functional Governance in Cross-Border Regions in Europe and North America." *International Journal of Urban and Regional Research* 28:530–48.

City of Blaine. 2015. "Blaine, Washington." http://www.ci.blaine.wa.us/.

City of Detroit. 2015. "City of Detroit." http://www.detroitmi.gov/.

City of El Paso. 2015. "City of El Paso Texas." https://www.elpasotexas.gov/.

City of Laredo. 2015. "City of Laredo." http://www.ci.laredo.tx.us/.

City of Niagara Falls. 2015a. "Niagara Falls, New York." http://www.niagarafallsusa.org/.

City of Niagara Falls. 2015b. "Niagara Falls, Canada." https://www.niagarafalls.ca/.

City of San Diego. 2015. "The City of San Diego." http://www.sandiego.gov/.

City of Surrey. 2015. "The City of Surrey, the Future Lives Here." http://www.surrey.ca/.

City of White Rock. 2015. "White Rock, City by the Sea!" http://www.whiterockcity.ca/.

City of Windsor. 2015. "The City of Windsor, Ontario, Canada." http://www.citywindsor .ca/Pages/Home.aspx.

Consejo Ciudadano. 2011. *Estudio comparativo de la incidencia del homicidio doloso en ciudades y jurisdicciones sub-nacionales de los países del mundo (2010).* Mexico City: Consejo Ciudadano para la Seguridad Pública y la Justicia Penal A.C. http://editor .pbsiar.com/upload/PDF/50_ciud_mas_violentas.pdf.

Deas, Alain, and Alex Lord. 2006. "From a New Regionalism to an Unusual Regionalism? The Emergence of Non-standard Regional Spaces and Lessons for the Territorial Reorganisation of the State." *Urban Studies* 43 (10): 1847–77. https://doi.org/10 .1080/00420980600838143.

Della Sala, Vincent. 2007. "Birth of a Union: Lesson for North America from the European Union." In *Politics in North America: Redefining Continental Relations*, edited by Yasmeen Abu-Laban, Radha Jhappan, and Francois Rocher, 115–31. Toronto: University of Toronto Press.

Eder, Klaus. 2006. "Europe's Borders: The Narrative Construction of the Boundaries of Europe." *European Journal of Social Theory* 9 (2): 255–71. https://doi.org/10.1177/1368431006063345.

Jessop, Bob, Neil Brenner, and Martin Jones. 2008. "Theorizing Sociospatial Relations." *Environment and Planning D: Society and Space* 26 (3): 389–401. https://doi.org/10.1068/d9107.

Jones, Martin, and Gordon MacLeod. 2004. "Regional Spaces, Spaces of Regionalism: Territory, Insurgent Politics and the English Question." *Transactions of the Institute of British Geographers* 29 (4): 433–52. https://doi.org/10.1111/j.0020-2754.2004.00140.x.

Lara-Valencia, Francisco. 2011. "The 'Thickening' of the US–Mexico Border: Prospects for Cross-Border Networking and Cooperation." *Journal of Borderlands Studies* 26 (3): 251–64. https://doi.org/10.1080/08865655.2011.675715.

McSweeney, Bill. 1999. *Security, Identity and Interests: A Sociology of International Relations*. Cambridge: Cambridge University Press.

Moon, M. Jae. 2002. "The Evolution of E-Government Among Municipalities: Rhetoric or Reality?" *Public Administration Review* 62 (4): 424–33. https://doi.org/10.1111/0033-3352.00196.

Musso, Juliet, Christopher Weare, and Matt Hale. 2000. "Designing Web Technologies for Local Governance Reform: Good Management or Good Democracy?" *Political Communication* 17 (1): 1–19. https://doi.org/10.1080/105846000198486.

Paasi, Anssi. 1991. "Deconstructing Regions: Notes on the Scales of Spatial Life." *Environment and Planning A* 23 (2): 239–56.

Paasi, Anssi. 2002. "Bounded Spaces in the Mobile World: Deconstructing 'Regional Identity.'" *Tijdschrift voor economische en sociale geografie* 93 (2): 137–48. https://doi.org/10.1111/1467-9663.00190.

Paasi, Anssi. 2009. "The Resurgence of the 'Region' and 'Regional Identity': Theoretical Perspectives and Empirical Observations on Regional Dynamics in Europe." *Review of International Studies* 35 (S1): 121–46. https://doi.org/10.1017/S0260210509008456.

Paasi, Anssi. 2010. "Commentary." *Environment and Planning A* 42 (10):2296–301. https://doi.org/10.1068/a42232.

Paasi, Anssi. 2011. "The Region, Identity, and Power." *Procedia: Social and Behavioral Sciences* 14:9–16. http://dx.doi.org/10.1016/j.sbspro.2011.03.011.

Roy, Marie-Christine, Anne Chartier, Jean Crête, and Diane Poulin. 2015. "Factors Influencing E-government Use in Non-urban Areas." *Electronic Commerce Research* 15 (3): 349–63. https://doi.org/10.1007/s10660-015-9193-4.

Scott, James. 1997. "Dutch-German Euroregions: A Model for Transboundary Cooperation." In *Borders and Border Regions in Europe and North America*, edited by P. Gaster, A. Sweedler, J. Scott, and W. Dieter-Eberwein, 107–40. San Diego: San Diego State University Press.

Scott, James. 1999. "European and North American Contexts for Cross-Border Regionalism." *Regional Studies* 33 (7): 605–17. https://doi.org/10.1080/00343409950078657.

Scott, James. 2002. "A Networked Space of Meaning? Spatial Politics as Geostrategies of European Integration." *Space and Polity* 6 (2): 147–67. https://doi.org/10.1080/13562 57022000003608.

Scott, James, Alan Sweedler, Paul Ganster, and Wolf-Dieter Eberwen. 1997. "Dynamics of Transboundary Interaction in Comparative Perspective." In *Borders and Border Regions in Europe and North America*, edited by P. Ganster, A. Sweedler, J. Scott, and W. Dieter-Eberwein, 3–23. San Diego: San Diego State University Press.

Taylor, Peter. 1994. "The State as Container: Territoriality in the Modern World-System." *Progress in Human Geography* 18 (2): 151–62. https://doi.org/10.1177/0309 13259401800202.

van Houtum, Henk. 2012. "Remapping Borders." In *A Companion to Border Studies*, edited by Thomas M. Wilson and Hastings Donnan, 403–17. London: Blackwell.

Wong-González, Pablo. 2005. "La emergencia de regiones asociativas transfronterizas: Cooperación y conflicto en la región Sonora-Arizona." *Frontera Norte* 17 (33): 77–106.

CHAPTER 5

Territorial Divisive and Connective Spaces

Shifting Meanings of Borders in the North American Borderlands

DONALD K. ALPER

Introduction

At least two core ideas have guided much contemporary comparative analysis of borders in North America. The first is the perception that both the U.S.-Mexico and U.S.-Canada borders have been greatly thickened since the events of 9/11. The second is that the northern and southern borders are fundamentally different and therefore analysts should proceed with caution in seeking comparative and, more importantly, policy insights. Although there is much truth in both ideas, as paradigmatic guides they can limit our thinking about the true complexity of borders and how different policy sectors produce and respond to differing bordering dynamics.

While not denying border thickening or the significant differences in northern and southern borders, this chapter takes a different approach. It is framed around the idea that the U.S.-Canada and U.S.-Mexico borderlands are marked by two kinds of bordering: territorial divisive bordering and connective spatial bordering. The former reflects the *closing-off* effect of bordering resulting from territorial borders as sites of securitization that enhance physical and discursive lines of separation. The latter reflects the *opening-up* effect of bordering resulting from economic, environmental and cultural borders functioning as transaction mechanisms enabling exchanges of flows within, across, and beyond borderlands. As enhanced securitization has restricted movement and perpetuated separateness, transnational economic, environmental, and cultural activity has induced new forms of cross border-transactional and spatial connectedness. Tension inherent in these dynamics is chronic and continual; that is, central government imperatives for enhanced security run counter to natural societal and market forces that function to make easier connections across borders. This tension is not new, but with enhanced securitization at both North American borders since 9/11 and continuing political pressures in the United States for fortifying the borders (with new walls and massive increases in border patrol and immigration agents), it has become more pronounced. Reconciling these tensions is imperative for the achievement of sensible public policy on both the U.S.-Canada and U.S.-Mexico borders.

Rather than focusing solely on securitized borders in terms of their divisive and inequitable effects, especially on populations in the borderlands, my approach examines the northern and southern borders as complex social, economic, and political constructions that, borrowing from the insights of John Agnew (2008), both disable and enable various forms of individual and collective action. In this regard, in this chapter I argue that these borderlands contain multiple forms of bordering that interact in different ways. I focus specifically on three forms of borders: security, economic, and environmental.

Most prominent are security borders with barrier functions and effects that strongly influence other forms of bordering. Economic borders, increasingly blurred, facilitate exchanges of goods, services, and capital regionally and globally. Environmental borders reflect a shift of scale away from territorial perspectives to cross-border spatialized entities corresponding to natural boundaries or cross-border resources. All these forms of bordering affect cultural relationships by blurring and reinforcing cultural identities. Viewing borders in terms of their bordering dynamics presents a broader conception of borders—one that situates borders as part of a system of regional and global relationships involving transportation corridors, economic and business relationships, and ecological flows and cultural ties.

The chapter proceeds by first discussing the tensions inherent in borders as dynamic sociospatial formations. Next, it examines shifting meanings of borders—altered security borders, blurred economic borders, and rescaled environmental borders—and their significance for regional policy processes within and beyond the U.S.-Canada and U.S.-Mexico borderlands. Finally, it discusses the importance of cross-border regional political processes and initiatives that nurture transboundary interactions while also potentially mediating the effects of centrally driven security borders on borderlands' communities and populations.

Border Dynamics in Tension

As sociospatial formations, borders have contradictory meanings and functions (Balibar 2002). They mark the external limits of national territory while also representing zones of overlapping cultures, commercial activity, and ecologies. They also reflect identities, cultural orientations, and symbols. All borders are socially constructed, and the acts of creating borders and maintaining them are expressions of social and political power.

Whether borders represent lines separating political or geographical areas or everyday social practices that categorize and identify, thus validating certain perspectives while marginalizing (or blocking) others, their effects are to create dichotomies. Anderson and O'Dowd (1999) refer to this as the dual nature of borders: they can be protective and imprisoning, areas of opportunity and insecurity, zones of contact and conflict. Soja (2005) views borders as having a double power because of their potential to be oppressive and repressive as well as liberating and enhancing, whether in the context of ordinary life experience or in the realm of global politics. For Sohn (2015), borders not only mark a separation between inside and an outside but also "invite" passing and entry as well as transgression and nonadmittance. In this way, the border is a source of ambivalence summoning both feelings of desire and fear.

Inherent in bordering processes are different power dynamics. Most often analysts focus on the controlling power of central governments and how borders are constituted and used to serve state political interests. However, power relations are more complex, and their essence goes beyond the familiar hierarchical model of central governments controlling cross-border flows. For example, bordering processes exercise power by sorting groups and identities into categories. Examples include "wanted" tourists as opposed to "unwanted" migrants. At a broader level, a border "encapsulates the identity of a community" through the interaction of its members with other communities against which it is distinguished or wishes to distinguish itself (Cohen 1985, 12). Other bordering dynamics that reveal power relationships are the creation of spatial entities such as trade corridors or ecosystems.

Understanding how multiple meanings inhere in bordering processes—and the power dynamics contained within—reveals how borders can and do serve a variety of interests. In this regard borders present challenges but also opportunities for state and nonstate actors alike.

Borderlands as Places and Spaces

Borderlands in their most basic sense are areas adjacent to international boundaries and are usually characterized by considerable cross-border interaction. Border researchers have for years argued that borderlands are not merely margins of states, societies, or nations but cultural systems straddling international boundaries. As Van Schendel (2005) points out, borderlanders are aware of and are involved in transboundary processes as part of their everyday lives. In this sense, the inhabitants of borderlands represent local and global worlds simultaneously (Van Schendel 2005, 22).

Much of the literature comparing the northern and southern borders in North America focuses on cross-border relationships within adjacent regions. Historically, these studies have emphasized how border regions have developed institutions and relationships to mediate asymmetry along the border (Konrad and Nicol 2008; Ganster 1997). On both the U.S.-Mexico and U.S.-Canada borders, regional organizations have been created to deal with cross-border transportation, economic development, and ecological, public health, and emergency management problems. Following establishment of NAFTA, considerable attention has been focused on degrees of integration within cross-border regions (Policy Horizons Canada 2009; Mendoza and Dupeyron 2017). The seminal work of Oscar Martínez (1994) provides a valuable framework for comparatively assessing different kinds of cross border relations on a spectrum ranging from "alienated borderlands" to "integrated borderlands." More recently, analysts have pointed to the complexity and range of cross-border relationships that extend far away from territorially proximate border regions. Cross-border relationships increasingly connect global city regions, noncontiguous ecological spaces, economic clusters, and strategic trade axes (Paul 2013; Deas and Lord 2006; Rumford 2006). These studies highlight the changing meaning of borders—and border regions—while acknowledging that territorial boundaries remain highly resistant to change.

Borderlands are places marked by physical lines, but they are also spaces of flows and connectivity. As places, borderland communities are strongly influenced by the line—the physical border. For these communities as well as the nation, the border signifies identity and nationality, who is included and excluded, and the rules and practices that determine inclusion and exclusion. At a more basic level, the border intrudes on the everyday political, economic, and social life of inhabitants of borderland communities. Paasi (2004, 13) observes that "life on the immediate vicinity of a border differs in many ways from life elsewhere in the state because the border and the imaginaries related to it become part of the daily life practices." For example, securitization at the borderline, greatly increased since 9/11, has affected local and regional economies creating what many refer to as the "border industrial security complex."

Although border communities are shaped and often defined by their bounded nature, it is equally true that borderlands comprise relationships as well as fixed territory. Borders are situated in physical spatial settings, but they also represent interconnected sets of social, political, and economic relations stretching across space (Cochrane and Ward 2012). Economic clusters span borders, imports and exports cross multiple borders, ecological entities crisscross territorial borders, and ethnicity and cultural life defy strict boundedness. Even security controls function as much away from the physical border as at the borderline. Territorial space is bounded but it is also made up of relationships that extend over a range of geographies. Bordered space is characterized by both dynamics and the meaning of borders and how they affect communities varies depending on what functions borders serve and for whom.

Altered Security Borders

Securitized Borders: Zones and Images

Security has always been a paramount function of territorial borders. In the most basic sense, territorial borders are expected to facilitate the protection of the nation against external threats. Threats are of many kinds—invading armies, terrorists, criminal activity, epidemics, cyber threats, and many others. Territorial borders are blunt instruments of security intended to operate like a fence, or virtual fence, to keep harms outside from coming inside. To accomplish this, territorial borders consist of infrastructure—borderlines, physical buildings and structures, agents, and security technologies—that function to wall-off territorial space. With increased securitization in North America, border infrastructure has created militarized zones extending beyond the immediate territorial boundary and deep into border communities and beyond.

Border security must also be understood as discourse and symbols that convey powerful images to communities both inside and outside territorial borders. Buzan and his coauthors (Buzan, Waever, and Wilde 1998, 4) have pointed to the powerful role of discourse in securitization. In their view, security is a "discursive practice which attaches the label of security to an issue, thus presenting it and dramatizing it as a being of supreme priority." The refrain "secure the border," repeatedly heard in U.S. political circles, creates powerful images of threats lurking on the other side of the border. Schwell (2011) points out how both the existence of borders and border narratives create mental as well as material boundaries. As she notes, border controls and security are the expression of drawing a strict line around the national community and signaling that people and goods arriving at the border are potential dangers to be kept out or let in under variable conditions. When this kind of imagery becomes a rallying cry, especially from presidents and other political leaders, such claims become convincingly accepted by audiences. A 2014 CNN poll showed how U.S. public opinion concerns about the need to "secure the border" and turn back migrants, even children, had accelerated in recent years (Steinhauser 2014). Donald Trump's rhetoric in the 2016 presidential campaign exploited fear by implicating immigrants at the border as an invasion force (Ball 2016). In a 2018 CBS poll, more Americans than not supported detaining or deporting illegal aliens, including their children (Meads 2018). Greater securitization, sustained by alarmist rhetoric and threatening images, inevitably generates psychological as well as physical barriers. Such barriers are especially influential in border regions, where the flow of people, commerce, and ideas are hindered.

Shifting Meaning of Security Borders in North America After 9/11

The United States' borders with Mexico and Canada have never been without security activity. As early as the 1820s, American federal troops were sent to what was then the border between the United States and Mexican territory to "protect" American settlers and traders. From that time forward, the United States employed military operations—including cross-border attacks—to protect American citizens and property along the border from various threats. The creation of the Border Patrol in the 1920s shifted most border-security activity from the military to civilian organizations. In the 1950s, border security focused on "illegal immigration," and of course this continues to the present day. In the 1980s, federal law enforcement agencies with support from the military engaged in a war on drugs at the Mexican border, which was ramped up considerably in the 2000s. Following 9/11, immigration and illegal drugs became intertwined with the war on terror, resulting in an ever-increasing security bureaucracy militarizing much of law enforcement in the U.S.-Mexico borderlands (Payan 2016).

On the Canadian border, despite the image of tranquility evoked by the label "the longest undefended border in the world," border policing has a long history. Militarization of the Great Lakes occurred during the War of 1812 but ended with the Rush-Bagot Treaty in 1817. With the end of militarization, U.S. and Canadian border policing generally involved matters of law and order. Policing, sometimes reinforced by federal troops, was not a matter of defending a boundary line as much as it was responding to "Indian problems" and controlling criminals who exploited the border for a variety of purposes. Prohibition smuggling and other forms of contraband were prominent concerns in the first half of the twentieth century. In the 1990s, border policing was stepped up in both countries to deal with the drug trade and increased human smuggling. The events of 9/11 ushered in a new militarization of the northern border.

Following 9/11, border controls were retooled and redesigned as part of an expanding "war on terrorism" (Andreas 2003). Propelled by anxiety-ridden politicians in Washington, D.C., and U.S. media hype about broken borders, both the northern and southern borders were seen in need of increased security personnel and more effective border control technology—including a massive buildup of border fencing and a multibillion dollar "techno-fence" to be built by Boeing and other large defense contractors on the southern border. The building of a new and more expansive border wall on the southern border was a central promise in the Trump campaign for president in 2016 and remained a priority of the Trump administration.

In response to these efforts to harden both North American borders, business groups pointed out how strengthened border controls were a serious threat to cross-border trade flows and border-region-dependent businesses and communities. A solution to enhancing securitization while also facilitating trade was found by reinventing borders as "smart borders." The core idea of smart borders was to utilize information and intelligence to sort flows into high- and low-risk categories. Borders would work like a screen or filter through which goods and people deemed low risk would pass efficiently while security resources would be focused on flows most likely to pose higher levels of risk. The smart borders paradigm was officially articulated in the Smart Border Declaration signed by the United States and Canada in December 2001 and followed by a similar accord between the United States and Mexico, titled the U.S.-Mexico Partnership Agreement, signed in March 2002. The agreement with Canada was given top-level support from both the U.S. and Canadian governments, and action plans were implemented almost immediately. On the southern border, alignment of U.S. and Mexican border agendas was weak at best, making cooperation more difficult. For one thing, antiterrorism and perceived threats from migration became interwoven as the focus of border security. Another problem was that the idea of smart borders was less applicable on the U.S.-Mexico border because there was little binational agreement on what constituted border security. For Mexicans, salient border-security issues were less about countering terrorists and more about deteriorating conditions at the border, such as gang violence, public health issues, and treatment of migrants.

In the United States, borders had come to be seen by politicians and the public in simple security terms. In essence, borders were viewed as vital instruments for controlling dangerous flows—both material and human—emanating from the outside world. Smart borders, intended to strike a better balance between providing security and facilitating movement of legitimate people and goods, continued to prioritize border security by placing emphasis on risk management strategies and deployment of new technologies. By the time of the ascendancy of Michael Chertoff as secretary of the Department of Homeland Security in 2005, the smart borders paradigm, according to Edward Alden (2008), had been reformulated in accordance with the United States policy goal of exercising total control over borders, north and south.

The emergent post–9/11 border-security paradigm was more layered and continental in scope. While the northern and southern land borders would continue to be the prime theaters for security efforts, borders would also be pushed outward to form a widened security perimeter. In addition to smart border technological fixes that focused on border infrastructure and sophisticated risk assessment, the idea of an enlarged zone of security based on North American perimeter borders worked its way into border-security language. Perimeter security focuses on the screening of goods and people "away from the border." *Perimeter* did not refer to a particular geographical designation but a process of checking flows of goods and people transiting into the United States (Bersin 2011).

Acceptance of the idea of perimeter security as a new framework for U.S.-Canada border governance was made official with the unveiling of the Beyond the Border (BtB) accord by President Obama and Prime Minister Harper in 2011. The bilateral accord set out specific and general policy objectives to be jointly pursued by Canada and the United States over several years. Notably, the accord was not extended to Mexico, setting the stage for a dual bilateral approach to border security and, perhaps more important, detaching Mexico from a broader North American goal of linking smarter borders with strengthened economic competitiveness (Golob 2012).

The organizing principle underlying BtB was that borders were as much about the securitization of flows as defending physical lines. This view of the border stressed the need to implement controls on flows away from the border, thus relieving security pressure on the border line. The BtB plan set out security-tightening initiatives, including increased integration of law enforcement operations (such as expansion of joint patrols on sea and land), new data-sharing protocols, deployment of an entry-exit system that tracks entries and exits in and out of each country, and alignment of Canadian and U.S. practices for prescreening travelers and cargo shipments.

The shifting conception of border security as "securing flows" has had the effect of both reinforcing and detaching border security from the North American borderlands. Yet securitization at territorial border lines has not been lessened. If anything, it has been strengthened. At the same time, the process of securitizing flows across continental and global domains has had the effect of globalizing border security. Indeed, as former assistant secretary of Homeland Security Alan Bersin (2011, 9) argued, "Homeland security has evolved into a species of national security, with border protection part of a larger effort of mission integration."

The post–9/11 U.S. security border underwent significant changes in meaning. No longer fully anchored to the frontier, it became a far-reaching continental and global system for securitizing flows of which the highly securitized U.S.-Canadian and Mexican frontiers are intricate parts. These changes have affected the functioning of border regions as spaces of cross-border integration and social cohesion. The North American borderlands have always been characterized by a relatively high degree of openness and easy back-and-forth movement (recognizing of course that the degree of openness has varied considerably between the northern and southern borders). New securitization processes on both borders are in contradiction to this state of affairs. The major approach to reconciling this incongruity on the U.S.-Canadian border has been smart borders premised on using technology to sort border crossers into low- and high-risk categories coupled with greater securitization of flows at the perimeter. On the southern border, the high degree of social and economic interdependence in borderlands has been overwhelmed by militarization, walls, and fear. As 9/11 receded into history, border regions on both the northern and southern frontiers remained fully securitized with continuing adverse economic and social consequences.

Blurred Economic Borders

Economic activity works at odds with a territorially bordered world (Agnew 2008). This is not to say that territorial borders are eroding, a common view proclaimed in the years following the end of the Cold War. On the contrary, borders in North America and in most parts of the world remain very much protective security zones designed to filter "wanted" from "unwanted" flows entering or exiting nation-states. Despite this, economic borders are being reshaped and playing new roles. Increasingly, economic borders defy territorial lines and are shaped by economic configurations such as clusters and corridors as well as distant bordering processes diffused throughout the continent and world.

Although much economic activity is more or less "contained" within borders (e.g., regulatory actions, certain forms of taxation, income support programs), the form and reach of economic activity extending across territorial geographies has had the effect of blurring neat economic boundaries. Castells, in his classic *The Rise of the Network Society*, observed that the bordered nation-state has been overlaid by a range of flows that follow other principles of interaction (Castells work cited in Yndigegn 2011). The traditional focus on territorial borders as mechanisms to contain, constrain, and facilitate economic flows has given way to what Werlen (2005) calls a shift from a geography of things to a geography of actions. Amin (2004), in his critique of place-based geography, advances the idea that economies are not territorially grounded but consist of multiple components that tie producers, intermediaries, and consumers in patterns of mutual and dependent actions across spatial geographies. Although borderlands as spatial entities confer location and market opportunities for economic activity, it is the outward and inward flows that form spaces of economic connectivity.

The Growing Importance of Regional Transborder Clusters

Cluster-based cross-border economic activity linking agglomerations of industry activity on either side of a border have configured new regional economic actors in North America and across the globe. As spatial entities produced by business, technological, and labor factors, economic clusters represent an important form of rebordering. Amin and Cohendet (2003) point out that clusters can be seen as "ecologies of knowledge" where the components (firms, research institutes, entrepreneurs, capital, and economic-development agencies) closely interact. Clusters display a complex relationship to place and space. Amin and Cohendet (2003, 12) refer to clustered economies as "geographies of circulation" producing knowledge and supported by mobile workers, global transportation, instant communications, and related resources. Boundedness, to the extent that it exists, is a "feature of . . . the nodal position of knowledge within specific actor networks . . . and not a feature of local confinement." As spatial formations hinged to national economies through networks of relations, clusters are inevitably conflicted with traditional borders.

On the U.S.-Mexico border, the San Diego–Baja California region and the Cali Baja Bi-National Mega-Region are emblematic of the growing significance of cross-border clusters. As nonterritorial economic formations, the clusters emphasize synergies provided by the region's access to the California and North American markets and connections to the Pacific Rim and gateway to Latin America. The North American Research Partnership organization has identified five regional cross-border hubs along the U.S.-Mexico border (see Wilson and Lee 2014). One of the most important is the Texas-Mexico Automotive Super Cluster (TMASC), a binational regional unit that consists of Texas, Tamaulipas, Nuevo León, Coahuila, and San Luis Potosí. The economic region is home to twenty-seven automotive assembly and parts assembly plants and includes over 230 supplier plants with strong clusters in Dallas–Fort Worth, San Antonio, along the Monterrey-Saltillo corridor, and straddling the border in the Lower Rio Grande Valley. The North American borderplex cross-border region, encompassing Juarez, El Paso, Santa Teresa, and Las Cruces, has embraced the binational cluster strategy in diverse industry sectors such as life sciences, defense, tourism, and advanced logistics (González 2016).

On the Canadian border, the Detroit-Windsor cross-border region is a hub for auto manufacturing and the core area of what has become known as the "auto belt," an area encompassing several Midwest states and southern Ontario where auto production has been historically centered. Other clusters straddling the U.S.-Canada border include Quebec–New England hydro development projects, the oil patch in Alberta coupled with affiliated energy industries in Colorado and Texas, and an emerging technology and digital media-based cluster linking economic activity in British Columbia with the Pacific Northwest states.

Cross-border clusters differ in scope. Most definitions of what constitutes geographical concentration of clusters vary—from interdependencies involving cities or states and provinces to several countries. The power of proximity stems from both physical closeness (as well as the quality of institutional and scientific relationships) and sociocultural factors such as trust and social ties (Royer 2007). Storer, Davidson, and Trautman (2015, 6) describe a Washington State–Canada aerospace trade cluster in which the Boeing corporation, with hundreds of suppliers in both countries, essentially builds airplane components together with its Canadian affiliates. One example is landing gear built in Ontario, Canada, for Boeing planes manufactured in Washington State. In turn, the landing gear may later return to Canada as part of a 737 jet purchased by the airline WestJet. A similar circular trade occurs in fossil fuels. For example, crude oil from Alberta is exported to Washington State, some of the refined products of which then are exported back to Canada. The scope of clusters is often continental and global. Queretaro State in central Mexico hosts one of the most advanced manufacturing clusters in the country (Ketels, Ramírez, and Porter 2015). The cluster produces landing gear systems, engine parts and propulsion systems. Among the industry partners are global corporations such as Canada-based Bombardier, GE, Michelin, and IBM. Interestingly, the cluster competes with emerging cross-border clusters with comparative cost advantages centered in Baja California, Sonora, Chihuahua, and Nuevo Leon (Ketels, Ramírez, and Porter 2015).

Cross-border clusters have proven to be efficient tools for regional development and enhancing competitiveness (Konstantynova 2013; Porter 1998). Clusters flourish in environments of flexibility and openness, qualities that are hindered if not compromised by the barrier effect of thick territorial borders.

Bordering as Trade Corridors

Growing intracontinental trade in North America has reshaped the functioning of borders. Although borderland regions have strong historical antecedents as cultural and commercial crossroads (Konrad and Nicol 2008), they have in recent years become major transit points for transportation and trade traversing the continent. In their work on Canada-U.S. borderlands, Konrad and Nicol (2008) discuss changes in borderlands as a result of rapidly increased economic integration and the new security environment. They argue that on the Canada--U.S. border there is a "continuum of crossings" that form a "hierarchy with three major corridor complexes prevailing in the cores of two regions: Pacific Highway in the far west, and Michigan/Ontario and Niagara Frontier in the Great Lakes" (Konrad and Nicol 2008, 107). Similarly on the U.S.-Mexico border, Van Schoik, Lee, and Wilson (2014) depict four major border regions that serve as major gateways for U.S.-Mexico trade: California–Baja California, Arizona-Sonora, West Texas–New Mexico–Chihuahua, and South Texas–Tamaulipas–Nuevo León–Coahuila. These subnational areas have become externally oriented and highly integrated into the transportation infrastructure and supply chains of continental and global trade corridors.

Trade corridors represent an emerging transnational economic space characterized by border regions interacting with the broader flows of North American and global commerce and people. As Biersteker (2003, 159) writes, referencing the work of sociologist Saskia Sassen, the important issue is not that transactions occur on territorial space but that the precise location of those transactions is increasingly ambiguous, and they tend to be located in different spaces for different purposes.

Borderlands in all three North American countries are connected by busy trade corridors that are aligned with major north–south transportation routes. A close analysis of freight flows reveals a set of "corridor regions" that drive commerce across the continent and provide critical economic benefits to borderland cities and the states and provinces in which they are located. Research by Davidson and Rose (2011) shows a midcontinent region heavily associated with manufacturing, with integrated manufacturing supply chains extending from Ontario and Quebec in Canada through the U.S. Midwest to industrial and manufacturing zones in the Mexican borderlands. The large border cities of Detroit and Laredo serve as "bookends" for this important corridor. Large border states—Michigan, Pennsylvania, New York, and Texas—account for a very large proportion of exports and imports traversing the northern and southern borders. A similar pattern is found on the West Coast, where north-south trade flows through key ports on the California-Mexico border (Otay Mesa) and the Washington-Canada border (Blaine). All three countries have a strong stake in the maintenance of efficient north-south corridors and the land ports of entry that serve as gateways to them.

The paramount role of key states in anchoring North American trade corridors cannot be overlooked. Detailed research by Davidson and Rose (2011) points out that on the southern border, California and Texas serve as major trip beginning points and endpoints for cross-border trade. Texas is the origin of 82 percent of the exports moving south through El Paso and 86 percent of the exports moving south through Hidalgo. California is the origin of 92 percent of exports and the destination of 86 percent of imports flowing through Otay Mesa.

On the northern border, no one state plays such a commanding position in sourcing or receiving cross-border trade. However, Michigan, Pennsylvania, and New York all are major source and destination states for freight crossing at ports of entry to Canada in Detroit, Buffalo, and Champlain. Similarly, California and Washington State are highly significant beginning and end points for trade spanning the West Coast corridor and traversing the northern border at Blaine. Ports of entry are closely linked to the economies of the cross-border regions—and especially the states and provinces—in which they are located. Given the ways regions interconnect economically across North America and the resulting effects played out in subnational governmental and local border communities' contexts, regionalist strategies built on emergent "corridor regions" are vital. Such corridor regions depend heavily on the resources of the states and provinces in which they are located.

Further reinforcing borderlands' interconnectedness to distant economic relationships is the fact that imports and exports traversing North America cross many borders. Research reported by Storer, Davidson, and Trautman (2015) indicates that a large proportion of American states' trade with Canada crosses borders at various entry points across the continent. An example from Washington State makes the point. The researchers found that in 2014, five of the top ten land crossing points for Washington's exports to Canada were located away from the Washington-Canada border. The five ports extended from Eastside, Idaho, to Buffalo–Niagara Falls, New York. What this shows is that "actual" borders for much of the trade emanating from states and provinces in North America are diffused throughout the continent. Thus, borders that matter most to Washington State trade with Canada and Mexico may not be adjacent to the state but located far to the east or to the southern border, as is the case with Washington agricultural products exported to Mexico. An important conclusion is that development of markets for exports and imports is affected by both nearby locational factors and border conditions at distant frontiers. Thus, economic borders are blurred across several locations.

Retail Rebordering

Cross-border shopping, common in border communities on the northern and southern borders, has resulted in what might be called retail rebordering. The dynamics of cross-border shopping are most often asymmetrical; one side of the border is typically the more attractive destination depending on factors such as currency values, availability of goods, ease of travel, and overall economic and safety conditions. In northern border communities such as Bellingham, Washington, shoppers from the Lower Mainland of southwest British Columbia make up a large percentage of routine customers. The spending by British Columbia is large, estimated by one 2013 study to be between C\$1.0 and C\$1.6 billion on goods purchased in the United States during trips lasting less than forty-eight hours (cited in Storer, Davidson, and Trautman 2015, 23). Thus, marketing efforts in the form of billboards, newspaper ads, and regular internet and radio "updates" on border wait times are plentiful in Vancouver, British Columbia, and its surrounding communities and have served to create a cross-border retail "market zone" that extends well into British Columbia. This zone also relates to air travel. In the case of Bellingham and Plattsburg, New York (located about seventy miles from Montreal), their airports depend heavily on Canadian travelers and are often called "cross-border airports." As for regional tourism, the Whistler resort, located about 170 miles north of Seattle, draws heavily on American tourists who are within a four-to-five-hour drive.

Similar dynamics exist in border communities along the U.S.-Mexico border, although the flow of shoppers is predominantly from south to north. A study by Nivin (2013, 6) on Mexican visitors to the Texas border regions cited the importance of Mexican shoppers. The Mexican share of Texas border-city retail sales ranged from 40 to 45 percent in Laredo, 35 to 40 percent in McAllen, 30 to 35 percent in Brownsville, and 10 to 15 percent in El Paso. Kutchera (2009) and Guerrero (2017) reported that Tijuana shoppers not only frequent retail outlets in communities immediately across the border but that they also are big contributors to the retail and entertainment sectors throughout San Diego County. In 2017, Guerrero reported on a study that found Baja California cross-border shoppers spend more than \$4.5 billion a year in the San Diego area (2017).

Interestingly, the blurring of national borders for shopping and other forms of tourism in border regions has actually been helped by policy actions. The NEXUS and SENTRI passes for preapproved travelers were initiated and expanded mostly to ease crossings for frequent travelers. The enhanced drivers' license (EDL) used in several states and provinces on the northern border was invented by policy leaders in Washington State and British Columbia. Border infrastructure has seen significant improvements to facilitate local cross-border travelers and workers as well as the promotion of broader trade and business interests. In 2015, there were fifty-five automobile inspection booths northbound and southbound serving the Cascade Gateway (the four ports linking the I-5 corridor and the Lower Mainland of British Columbia), which is a 28 percent increase from the number in 2001 (Storer, Davidson, and Trautman 2015, 45). Such policy actions have helped to enliven cross-border retail economies and have served as policy laboratories for business groups, research institutes, and national and regional actors to come together to connect and in some cases reconnect spaces divided by territorial borders.

Rescaled Environmental Borders

Borders interact with environments in complex ways. Water systems, airsheds, landscapes, and wildlife span and crisscross territorial borders. Political jurisdictions overlie shared waterways and landscapes. Borders often frustrate efforts to mitigate ecosystem damage where the activity causing damage occurs on one side of the border and the environmental costs fall on the other. This asymmetric distribution of costs and benefits is typical of many transboundary environmental controversies and explains why these conflicts arise and why so many are intractable (Caldwell 1985, 213). Even in cases where there is desire to work cooperatively across political jurisdictions to resolve environmental problems, borders complicate cooperative efforts because of different legal and regulatory systems and political cultures.

However, borders also present opportunities for cooperation over shared resources. For example, watershed approaches to transboundary environmental governance can be traced at least in part to frustration about the mismatch of political boundaries and natural landscapes. Some of the most ingenious outcomes to transboundary environmental problems have been motivated by the need to overcome nationcentric thinking and interest politics incentivized by political borders. Further, cross-border regional conceptualizations can create new forms of environmental policy space. Spatial formations corresponding to biophysical processes such as bioregions, airsheds, and wilderness areas represent a form of environmental bordering that can be used to mobilize resources and people for specific purposes. Cooperative linkages among West Coast states, provinces, and Indigenous communities focused on climate policy are examples of leveraging borders to strengthen regional climate efforts and inspire action on climate in the rest of North America and globally. Viewing environmental borders this way challenges the idea that borders are always impediments because they impede ecosystem flows (Noe 2010). Contemporary approaches to environmental borders acknowledge that the drawing of borders is fundamentally a political act to achieve a myriad of goals.

Coexistence of Multiple Borders

Emma Norman (2015) has pointed to the tension between fixed political borders, fluid natural resources, and cultural landscapes. This tension highlights critical questions about the nature and construction of borders: Whose borders? For what purposes? With what consequences? These questions are key to recognizing that environmental borders reflect complex and often changing power relationships and vary in terms of form and function. In short, there are multiple environmental borders with a variety of functions.

Ecological landscapes are composed of overlapping ecosystems. Landscapes have "natural" (biological) as well as human and cultural dimensions. Biological and human processes do not stop at boundaries based on property rights or territorial sovereignty. Streams flow across different ownerships and political boundaries. Wildlife migrates across jurisdictions. Contiguous forest lands straddle private and public lands as well as communities. Landscapes in all their dimensions are essentially transboundary in composition and as resources.

Although all transboundary landscapes display borders at odds with political boundaries, it is the pervasiveness and size of border-straddling watersheds on both North American borders that have made them central issues in transboundary environmental politics. On the Canada-Alaska Northwest coast, several large transboundary watersheds drain across the border from northwestern British Columbia into Alaska. These watersheds have classic upstream-downstream pollution issues, mostly resulting from the release of toxic wastes from mining activity in British Columbia that flow into salmon-producing rivers that straddle the international boundary and empty into Alaska waters. The Columbia River Basin forms perhaps the largest transboundary watershed in North America, involving two Canadian provinces (British Columbia and Alberta) and parts of seven American states (Washington, Oregon, Idaho, Montana, Nevada, Utah, and Wyoming).

On the southern border, the Tijuana River Watershed, lying between the United States and Mexico, is one of the fastest-growing regions along the border. With approximately six million people within its boundaries—mostly in San Diego and Tijuana—it mixes a large, diverse, urban environment with a natural environment recognized globally for its unique biodiversity. Another important transboundary watershed is the Upper–Santa Cruz Basin located along the Arizona-Sonora section of the border that includes the twin cities of Nogales, Arizona, and Nogales, Sonora.

Many other transboundary watersheds could be mentioned. What is common to all of them is the mixing of territorially based governance with evolving forms of environmental governance that revolve around nonterritorial boundaries and natural and cultural resources.

Increasingly, watersheds are viewed as having legal status. Rachael Stoeve (2015), a Seattle environmental journalist, noted the significance of a 2012 agreement between the New Zealand government and Maori tribal groups that recognized the Whanganui River as an "indivisible and living whole, from the mountains to the sea," with "rights and legal standing" (Stoeve 2015, 1). The river was conferred "legal personhood" by the New Zealand parliament in 2017 (Roy 2017). Stoeve suggested the New Zealand action as potential guidance for the 2012 agreement between the United States and Mexico that affirmed an ecosystem approach to U.S.-Mexico comanagement of the Colorado River. That agreement included a critical provision to reconnect the river to the Gulf of California (Lovett 2012) and create what one naturalist called a "sacred reunion" by returning the Colorado to the sea (Postel 2014).

In both the New Zealand and Colorado River cases, considerable consultation with tribes occurred, and Indigenous beliefs and lifeways figured prominently in the language of the Maori agreement. As Stoeve stated, these agreements reflect "bioregionalism at work" where the river is seen "not as a natural resource to be apportioned among its various users, but as an integral part of both the cultural and material life of the communities that interact with it" (Stoeve 2015, 1). Many similar examples could be given, including the struggle of Northwest Indigenous people to restore the health of marine and freshwater resources to preserve native salmon and orca whales. From this perspective, transboundary watersheds involve people and nature in a relationship of equality as opposed to hierarchy, thus flattening notions of borders as territorially and jurisdictionally based. Norman (2015, 100) put it this way: "The goal should be to treat the transboundary watershed as a unified political-cultural space."

Another kind of environmental bordering conforms to new regionalist ideas driven by environmental or economic interests. Perhaps the best representation of this kind of bordering is the idea of Cascadia, which ties together in various ways and degrees ecological values with consumer lifestyle economies on the U.S.-Canada West Coast (Alper 2005). First conceived by the sociologist Robert McCloskey, Cascadia was characterized as "a land rooted in the very bones of the earth, and animated by the turnings of sea and sky, the mid-latitude wash of winds and waters." Viewed as a distinct region, McCloskey's Cascadia "arises from both a natural integrity (e.g. landforms and earth-plates, weather patterns and ocean currents, flora, fauna, watersheds, etc.) and a sociocultural unity (e.g. native cultures, a shared history and destiny)" (see Abbott 2015, chap. 6, "Cascadian Dreams: Imagining a Region over Four Decades").

Cascadia has had many representations, ranging from McCloskey's bioregional Cascadia extending from Cape Mendocino in Northern California to Yukutat Bay in Southeast Alaska to the notion of a Cascadia mega-urban region unified by high-tech, green economies and anchored by the three largest Pacific Northwest cities—Portland, Oregon; Seattle, Washington; and Vancouver, British Columbia (see Abbott 2009). Perhaps the title of Douglas Todd's book, *Cascadia: The Elusive Utopia* (2008), best reflects the intangible nature of Cascadia's borders as relationships between place, culture, and spirituality.

The spatial entity of the Salish Sea is an example of rebordering based on ecosystem boundaries and traditional cultural ties among aboriginal people. The Salish Sea is a network of coastal waters spanning southwest British Columbia and coastal Washington. Before 2009, when Washington State and British Columbia officially adopted the name Salish Sea, the cross-border marine area was known as the Georgia Basin–Puget Sound. Naming this region the Salish Sea was meant to pay tribute to the Coast Salish peoples who have inhabited the area for thousands of years as well as to reinforce the idea that this network of waterways formed an ecologically and culturally unified transboundary region and should be managed as such.

As in the Pacific Northwest, the use of naming to evoke geographical, hydrological, and human unification across transboundary water basins is common in the U.S.-Mexico borderlands. One example is the transboundary collaboration in the Upper San Pedro River Basin that crosses the Sonora-Arizona border. This cross-border basin was the first congressionally designated natural riparian conservation area. Although numerous issues continue to be viewed through national lenses—particularly water quality and source—the region as a whole has developed thriving scientific relationships and works together fairly harmoniously (*Sonoran News* 2016).

Rescaled Environmental "Soft Spaces" and Governance

The idea of "soft spaces" has been introduced by scholars and planners to reflect new forms of spatial entities that relate to flows and relationships but that do not conform to traditional territorial borders. Haughton et al. (2010) characterize soft spaces as multiarea subregions in which strategy is made between or alongside formal institutions and processes. The soft spaces of governance, where normative policy aims are emphasized, are often contrasted with what are termed "hard" spaces of government jurisdictions represented by legally defined territorial boundaries linked to administrative structures of government (Haughton et al. 2010). Soft spaces, according to Allmendinger and Haughton (2009), tend to be overlapping, composed of fuzzy boundaries, and pragmatic.

The soft spaces concept is an attempt to move away from "state-centric metageographies" (see Taylor 2000). Soft spaces fill in gap areas that do not fit with traditional concepts of representation and domestic constituencies in politically bordered jurisdictions. As new domains of governance, they are spaces of planning outside of what Haughton and Allmendinger (2007, 307) call the "frictions of formalized processes and institutionalized histories." Although separate from formal governments, soft spaces of planning are not autonomous from these same traditional governmental processes (Haughton and Allmendinger 2007). Examples include the Great Lakes Water Resources Compact, the Baltic Sea Plan Vision 2030, and the Border 2020 Program (the U.S.-Mexico environmental program implemented under the 1983 La Paz Agreement).

In transboundary ecological contexts, soft spaces often are carefully built around and scaled to governance processes aimed at resource protection and restoration. Such processes can be led by NGOs, officials from different levels of government, aboriginal groups, or quasi-private entities such as cross-border business alliances. Karkkainen (2002) suggests that soft spaces fit within a family of transboundary governance frameworks that have potential to create normative regimes without international laws and contracts. Such regimes, generally more flexible and inclusive than formal legal governance and anchored within civil society, can be better tailored to the diverse social, sustainability, and economic needs of a river basin, marine commons, or wilderness area (Jay

2018). As potential governance forms, soft spaces should not be thought of as replacements for territorial governments; instead, they coexist with them.

Bordering and Energy Politics

In recent years the battle over climate change has been played out over infrastructure projects. Nowhere is the climate and fossil-fuel fight more intense than in the Pacific Northwest and Western Canada. Battle lines have formed around every new fossil-fuel development, including West Coast coal ports, LNG terminals, and bitumen pipelines.

Similar concerns have arisen over fossil-fuel projects in the U.S.-Mexico borderlands, but the nature of the issues is different. Much of the Southwest-Mexico borderlands, with increasing population and manufacturing plants, is remote from the major gas and oil pipelines originating in central Mexico, and thus new infrastructure is generally welcomed. Large discoveries of shale oil and gas in northeastern Mexico extracted through fracking have evoked relatively minor protests from environmental justice groups (Smallteacher 2015). These energy developments are widely viewed as an important contributor to Mexican economic growth in the border regions, although much of this production is slated for international markets (Payan and Correa-Cabrera 2014). Energy pipelines from the United States have fueled power plants in the Mexican borderlands, which in turn serve consumers north of the border. LNG projects on the Baja California coast are controversial because those large facilities are viewed as posing threats to the natural ecology.

British Columbia, Oregon, and Washington have seen proposals for new coal terminals, additional oil and natural gas pipelines, increased oil and coal trains, and plans for several LNG terminals and oil-by-rail facilities. This uptick in energy projects motivated by the growing Asian market has been spurred by the availability of huge oil supplies from the Alberta oil-sands developments and the surge of coal and oil sourced from the northern interior of the United States. These projects have significant border-crossing effects because tankers ply transboundary inland waters, trains move Montana- and Wyoming-sourced coal through Washington State across the border to Vancouver, and Alberta and British Columbia oil and gas moves south to Washington, Oregon, and California. In addition, proponents and opponents of these projects do not operate in country-bounded political or economic arenas. Energy and climate politics increasingly straddles national political borders. Indigenous communities find common cause throughout traditional territories and across national borders, NGOs engage in transnational environmental campaigns, and resource companies are global in their business operations and political lobbying.

North American energy politics has produced new kinds of bordering in subtle ways. The controversy over carbon infrastructure in many parts of North America but especially in British Columbia, Washington State, and Oregon has been manifested by the emergence of a transboundary movement to prevent the coastal area from Oregon to northwest British Columbia from becoming a major continental hub for global energy export. Both pro- and anticarbon forces view the cross-border region as a spatial context for achieving certain development opportunities. The energy companies view the cross-border region as a potential major export hub, well networked by rail and pipelines to the interior of the continent and strategically positioned to feed the growing energy appetite of Asia. The opponents view the region as a focal point for a new kind of green economy. The Sightline Institute in Seattle has referred to "The Thin Green Line" as a metaphor for a "David and Goliath" kind of battle between a Pacific Northwest clean energy regional vision and that of global energy corporations (Roberts 2015).

A second rebordering dynamic is the growth of subnational regional arrangements focusing on climate and sustainability. The absence of serious federal action to address climate change in all three North American countries has spurred subnational governments to fill the void. The result has been the formations of subnational regional clusters on both northern and southern borders but with more prominence in the north. As incipient new regions, they are characterized by epistemic communities of like-minded government officials, NGOs, and scientific and technical people who have been instrumental in depicting (and mapping) things such as greenhouse gas emissions, pollution deposition patterns, and power grid structures (Selin and Vandeveer 2011). Healy and his coauthors (Healy, Van Hijnatten, and López Vallejo 2014, 48–49) refer to these arrangements as new sites of governance where policy actors create networks that form "a dense web of relations" usually dominated by subnational governmental officials. Without sovereign authority, the influence of such regional arrangements is based on deliberation and persuasion, or what is referred to as "soft power" (49). These interactions—especially related to fossil fuels—have produced identifiable regionalist policy actors who have been articulating, and moving forward on, a wide range of policy actions related to climate change (VanNijnatten 2011). Subnational governments in British Columbia and Washington State have taken strong stands against pipeline expansion because of the risks of oil spills and broader climate effects associated with expanded production of oil-sands crude (Bernton 2018).

In the Pacific Northwest, the Pacific Coast Collaborative (PCC), created in 2008, links Alaska, British Columbia, Washington, and Oregon. The PCC's overarching priority is to promote innovation to mitigate climate effects on marine and terrestrial environments and foster a green transformation of the economies in British Columbia and the Pacific states extending from California to Washington. In 2013, the states of California, Oregon, and Washington and the province of British Columbia signed the Pacific Coast Action Plan on Climate and Energy, committing the jurisdictions to a set of common goals and timetables for carbon reduction. In 2016, the climate accord was expanded to include the mayors of six major West Coast cities (Inslee 2016). Tribes and First Nations have made their voices heard through such organizations as the Pacific Northwest Tribal Climate Change Network and the Climate Change and Pacific Rim Indigenous Nations Project (2017). Such regional agreements are built around setting a shared agenda with the goal of coordinating policy actions (VanNijnatten 2011). Mobilizing political action at the subnational level is viewed all the more important as the Trump administration will not abide by the Paris climate accord and has prioritized reductions of federal regulations and scientific study pertaining to climate change.

Although the focus in the previous section has been primarily on the Pacific coastal region, environmental cross-border regions focused on climate action are well developed on other parts of the U.S.-Canada border. VanNijnatten (2011) identifies three distinct clusters of subnational jurisdictions: the Pacific Northwest, the Great Lakes region, and the New England–Atlantic provinces region. In the Northeast, the New England Governors/Eastern Canadian Premiers' Climate Change Plan joins six states and five provinces. The Regional Greenhouse Gas initiative, which links nine states—Connecticut, Delaware, Maine, Maryland, Massachusetts, New Hampshire, New York, Rhode Island, and Vermont—is the nation's first mandatory cap-and-trade program for greenhouse gas emissions (Ramseur 2015).

A somewhat different pattern of environmental regionalism is found on the southern border. Partly because of institutional factors related to government structure and a slower pace of developing state-to-state cross-border relationships, climate initiatives on the U.S.-Mexico border have been largely led by the two federal governments (see Border 2020). Moreover, climate narratives and policy have taken on a different form in the Southwest-Mexico region. Faced with chronic shortages of clean water resulting from lack of infrastructure, droughts, and age-old conflicts among user groups as well as air issues and toxins, the focus has been more on sustainability in the border region. For example, the stated mission of the U.S.-Mexico Border 2020 Program is to "protect the environment and public health in the U.S.-Mexico border region, consistent with the principles of sustainable development."

With the support of the two federal governments, environmental interactions between U.S. border states and their Mexican counterparts have increased dramatically in recent years (Farias and Lucas 2017). Texas has bilateral agreements with all four adjacent Mexican states. California has several agreements with Baja California, including an innovative local climate issues information exchange partnership between the San Diego Association of Governments and its counterpart in Baja California (Wilder et al. 2013). In 2005 the governments of Arizona and Sonora created the Arizona-Sonora Regional Climate Change Initiative that, among other things, coordinates the identification of emission reduction opportunities in the cross-border region. (Healy, VanNijnatten, and López Vallejo 2014).

Conclusion

Two tendencies in the U.S.-Canada and U.S.-Mexico borderlands are in contradiction. First is the "closing-off" effect that results from increased fortification and militarization of the borders. This tendency is strengthened by anti-immigration and border-wall narratives and serves to deepen dividing lines between the three countries. The second tendency is the "opening-up" effect of bordering resulting from economic, environmental, and cultural borders functioning as transaction mechanisms enabling exchanges of flows within and across borderlands.

The argument developed in this chapter is not an attempt to debate or resolve the incongruity between closing-off and opening-up effects of borders. Securing borders is a core function of sovereign states. The forms of securitization will change (as they have in the past) in response to political conditions and unforeseen events. As both northern and southern boundaries become more fortified, the fabric of North America will be further strained, but more so at the U.S.-Mexico borderlands. Yet border-security policies will continue to garner high levels of public support because such policies respond to numerous missions including crime prevention, maintaining safety around borders, ensuring confidence in the movement of goods and people, and protecting natural resources. At the same time, connectiveness displayed in borderland economies, ecologies, and overlapping cultures has not lessened, nor is it likely to, despite the uptick in divisive rhetoric and policy pronouncements from nationalist constituencies in the United States and elsewhere.

The argument here is that a new scenario is possible based on recognition of the changing meanings of borders, one that posits multiple spatial arenas of activity that both connect and divide simultaneously. Haselsberger (2014) helps us think about what a new scenario might look like conceptually. She describes how borders and the relational geographies that they project demarcate different types of spaces with particular functional dynamics. In her words, "The challenge is to work in hard, soft and fuzzy spaces in parallel" (Haselsberger 2014, 523). While recognizing that sovereignty-related border narratives and actions reinforce strong territorial meanings of borders, we must also recognize that the meaning of boundaries at different spatial scales involve relational geographies that have logics representative of soft or fuzzy spaces that defy strict territorial perspectives. Different, overlapping spatial formations with different dynamics are highly interconnected. For one thing, actors operating in one space—sometimes quite autonomously—inevitably interact with actors in other spaces. Interspatial interaction is likely only to increase as the pace of people and goods' mobilities accelerate and environmental agendas increasingly become linked with cultural and social perspectives of global scope. Border regions where the intensity of cross border interactions flows is the greatest are focal points for these networks of intertwined spaces that encompass borderline security structures, border-spanning ecosystems, and transnational economic relationships. It is important to note that these spatial entities do not displace one another but coexist. It is the coexistence that should be our focus going forward.

From a policy perspective, the goal should be to nurture cross-border regional political processes and initiatives that improve awareness and understanding of the different spatial bordering processes while also mediating the effects of centrally driven security policies on borderlands' communities and populations. Creative institutions that operate across different functional spaces and that may or may not align with traditional jurisdictional boundaries are needed to do this work. Working within and across spatial bordering processes offers new possibilities for "reducing the oppressive burden of borders while maximizing their enabling, connecting and transcending powers" (Soja 2005, 44). One can imagine a future where actors situated within different bordering processes engage one another in a healthy dialogue about optimizing policy for assuring prosperity, safety, and sustainable living in the borderlands and beyond.

Boundaries and borders in North America have been restructured with new meanings and configurations partly in response to altered conceptions of security borders but also because of globalization and localization processes that have shaken up traditional territorial control functions of borders and stimulated the emergence of new and different forms of bounded economies, ecologies, and cultures at every geographical scale (Soja 2005). What is missing is better understanding of the complex nature of emerging spatial connectedness and, more important, the development of more robust regional institutions to inject borderland-level actors and agendas (both governmental and civil society) more directly into border politics at both the local and national levels.

Many institutions already exist. The Pacific Northwest Economic Region (PNWER) in links five Canadian provinces and territories and five northwest states. Its mission is to articulate common issues in the cross-border region and to project their concerns to the federal capitals and ultimately facilitate problem solving. In the Northeast, the New England Governors–Eastern Canadian Premiers Conference performs a similar function, but its effectiveness is reduced by its formalized structure and lack of strong representation from the private sector characteristic of PNWER. Subnational legislatures are active in regional associations such as the Western Governors Association (on both borders). At the executive level, Washington State governors and British Columbia premiers meet regularly. On the U.S.-Mexico border, there are many initiatives linking local groups and municipalities in state-to-state linkages. Most of these exist in urban "twin cities" and must deal with the hard issues related to public health, the effects of rigid border security, and economic development. The Border Governors' Conference links four U.S. states and six Mexican states, although it has been criticized as more of a "feel-good" photo op for the attending political officials. The point is not building institutions for the sake of making new institutions. Institutions should be viewed as mechanisms through which actors at various scales shape collective action across border spatial domains, and institutions perhaps most importantly project outward to North American citizens and their leaders the vital workings and functions of U.S.-Canada and U.S.-Mexico borderlands in the future health and prosperity of North America.

REFERENCES

Abbott, Carl. 2015. *Imagined Frontiers: Contemporary America and Beyond*. Norman: University of Oklahoma Press.

Agnew, John. 2008. "Borders on the Mind: Reframing Border Thinking." *Ethics and Global Politics* 1 (4): 175–91.

Alden, Edward. 2008. *The Closing of the American Border: Terrorism, Immigration and Security since 9/11*. New York: HarperCollins.

Allmendinger, Phil, and Graham Haughton. 2009. "Soft Spaces, Fuzzy Boundaries and Metagovernance: The New Spatial Planning in the Thames Gateway." *Environment and Planning A: Economy and Space* 41 (3): 617–33.

Alper, Donald K. 2005. "Conflicting Transborder Visions and Agendas: Economic and Environmental Cascadians." In *Holding the Line: Borders in a Global World*, edited by Heather N. Nicol and Ian Townsend-Gault, 222–37. Vancouver, BC: University of British Columbia Press.

Amin, Ash. 2004. "Regions Unbound: Toward a New Politics of Place." *Geografiska Annaler: Series B, Human Geography* 86 (1): 33–44. https://doi.org/10.1111/j.0435-3684 .2004.00152.x.

Amin, Ash, and Patrick Cohendet. 2003. "Geographies of Knowledge Formation in Firms." Paper presented at DRUID summer conference Creating, Sharing and Transferring Knowledge: The Role of Geography, Institutions and Organizations, Copenhagen, June 12–14. Accessed July 30, 2015 (no longer posted). https://.druid .dk/conference/summer2003/papers/amin_cohendet.pdf.

Anderson, James, and Liam O'Dowd. 1999. "Borders, Border Regions, and Territoriality: Contradictory Meanings, Changing Significance." *Regional Studies* 33 (7): 593–604.

Andreas, Peter. 2003. "A Tale of Two Borders: The US-Mexico and US-Canada Lines After 9/11." Working Paper no. 77. La Jolla, Calif.: Center for Comparative Immigration Studies, University of California, San Diego. https://escholarship.org/uc/item /6d09j0n2.

Balibar, Etienne. 2002. *Politics and the Other Scene*. London: Verso.

Ball, Molly. 2016. "Donald Trump and the Politics of Fear." *Atlantic*, September 2. https://www.theatlantic.com/politics/archive/2016/09/donald-trump-and-the-politics -of-fear/498116/.

Bernton, Hal. 2018. "Canadian Government Acquires Key Pipeline to Washington Refineries." *Seattle Times*, June 10.

Bersin, Alan. 2011. "Lines and Flows: The Beginning and End of Borders." Paper presented at the Ira M. Belfer Lecture, Brooklyn Law School, October 6, 2011. https:// www.law.berkeley.edu/files/Lines_and_Flows_final100611(1).pdf.

Biersteker, Thomas J. 2003. "The Rebordering of North America? Implications for Conceptualizing Borders After September 11." In *The Rebordering of North America*, edited by Peter Andreas and Thomas J. Biersteker, 153–65. New York: Routledge.

Border 2020. Bi-National Policy Fora. United States Environmental Protection Agency. https://www.epa.gov/border2020/bi-national-policy-fora.

Buzan, Barry, Ole Waever, and Jaap de Wilde. 1998. *Security: A New Framework for Analysis*. Boulder, Colo.: Lynne Rienner.

Caldwell, Lynton K. 1985. "Binational Responsibilities for a Shared Environment." In *Canada and the United States: Enduring Friendship, Persistent Stress*, edited by Charles F. Doran and John H. Sigler, 203–30. New York: American Assembly.

Cochrane, A., and K. Ward. 2012. "Researching the Geographies of Policy Mobility: Confronting the Methodological Challenges." *Environment and Planning A* 44:5–12.

Cohen, Anthony C. 1985. *The Symbolic Construction of Community*. New York: Travistock.

Davidson, David, and Austin Rose. 2011. "Cross Border Freight Flows at Two Land Borders." *Border Policy Research Institute Publications* 24. https://cedar.wwu.edu/bpri_publications/24/.

Deas, Iain, and Alex Lord. 2006. "From a New Regionalism to an Unusual Regionalism? The Emergence of Non-standard Regional Spaces and Lessons for the Territorial Reorganization of the State." *Urban Studies* 43 (10): 1847–77.

Farias, Ivan, and Scott Lucas. 2017. "Can the US-Mexico Relationship Be Saved from Trump?" EA Worldview, July 20. http://eaworldview.com/2017/07/us-mexico-relationship-saved-trump/.

Ganster, Paul. 1997. "On the Road to Interdependence? The United States-Mexico Border Region." In *Borders and Border Regions in Europe and North America*, edited by Paul Ganster, Alan Sweedler, James Scott, and Wolf-Dieter Eberwein, 237–66. San Diego, Calif.: San Diego State University Press.

Golob, Stephanie R. 2012. "Barriers to Entry: The Canada-US Beyond the Border Perimeter Initiative and the Democratic Deficit(s) in North American Governance." Paper presented at the XXII World Congress of Political Science of the International Political Science Association, Madrid, Spain, July 8–12.

González, Nancy J. 2016. "Binational Cluster Strategy Would Boost the US-Mexico Border Economy." *Mexico Now*, April 29. https://mexico-now.com/index.php/18-magazine/articles/93-binational-clusters-strategy-would-boost-the-u-s-mexico-border-economy.

Guerrero, Jean. 2017. "Tijuana Retail Reaping Profits That Once Flowed to San Diego." KPBJ News, May 17. https://www.kpbs.org/news/2017/may/17/tijuana-retail-reaps-profits-once-flowed-san-diego/.

Haselsberger, Beatrix. 2014. "De-coding Borders: Appreciating Border Impacts on Space and People." *Planning Theory and Practice* 15 (4): 505–26.

Haughton, Graham, and Phil Allmendinger. 2007. "Soft Spaces in Planning: The Emergence of Soft Space of Governance Within Which Planning Increasingly Has to Work." *Town and Country Planning* (September). Accessed September 5, 2015 (no longer posted). https://www.academia.edu/12412401/Soft_spaces_in_planning_The_emergingsoft_spaces_of_governance_within_which_planning_increasingly_has_to_work.

Haughton, Graham, Phil Allmendinger, David Counsell, and Geoff Vigar. 2010. *The New Spatial Planning: Territorial Management with Soft Spaces and Fuzzy Boundaries*. London: Routledge.

Healy, Robert G., Debora L. VanNijnatten, and M. Lopez Vallejo. 2014. *Environmental Policy in North America: Approaches, Capacity, and the Management of Transboundary Issues*. Toronto: University of Toronto Press.

Inslee, Jay. 2016. "West Coast Leaders' Climate Change 'Resolve is Strong' as COP22 Concludes." Washington Governor Jay Inslee, November 18. http://www.governor.wa.gov/news-media/west-coast-leaders'-climate-change-"resolve-strong"-cop22-concludes.

Jay, Stephen. 2018. "The Shifting Sea: From Soft Spaces to Lively Space." *Journal of Environmental Policy and Planning* 20 (4): 450–67.

Johnson, Corey. 2009. "Cross Border Regions and Territorial Restructuring in Central Europe." *European Urban and Regional Studies* 16 (2): 191–206.

Karkkainen, Bradley C. 2002. "Collaborative Ecosystem Governance: Scale, Complexity and Dynamism." *Virginia Environmental Law Journal* 21:189–243.

Ketels, Christian, Jorge Ramírez, and Michael Porter. 2015. "Aerospace Cluster in Queretaro, Mexico." Microeconomics for Competitiveness, Harvard Business School. www.isc.hbs.edu/resources/courses/moc-course-at-harvard/documents/pdf/student-projects/queretaro_aerospace_cluster_2015.pdf.

Konrad, Victor, and Heather N. Nicol. 2008. *Beyond Walls: Re-inventing the Canada–United States Borderlands.* Aldershot: Ashgate.

Konstantynova, Anastasiia. 2013. "Supporting Cross-Border Inter-clustering, Why Matter?" Orkestra, Basque Institute of Competitiveness. https://www.orkestra.deusto.es/en/latest-news/news-events/beyondcompetitiveness/1376-supporting-cross-border-inter-clustering-why-matter.

Kutchera, Joe. 2009. "40 Billion Dollars in Cross-Border Latino Retail Revenue." MediaPost, September 24. https://www.mediapost.com/publications/article/113819/40b-in-cross-border-latino-retail-revenue.html.

Lovett, Ian. 2012. "US and Mexico Sign a Deal on Sharing the Colorado River." *New York Times*, November 20.

Martínez, Oscar. 1994. *Border People: Life and Society in the US-Mexico Borderland.* Tucson: University of Arizona Press.

Meads, Timothy. 2018. "CBS Poll: Most Americans Want Illegal Alien Families Either Deported or Detained." Townhall, June 24. https://townhall.com/tipsheet/timothymeads/2018/06/24/untitled-n2493996.

Mendoza, Jorge Eduardo, and Bruno Dupeyron. 2017. "Economic Integration, Emerging Fields and Cross Border Governance: The Case of San Diego–Tijuana." *Journal of Borderlands Studies*, September 8. https://doi.org/10.1080/08865655.2017.1367711.

Nivin, Stephen. 2013. *The Spending Patterns and Economic Impacts of Mexican Nationals in a Twenty-County Region of South and Central Texas.* San Antonio, Tex.: SABÉR Research Institute, St. Mary's University. https://www.sahcc.org/wp-content/uploads/Presentation-on-Mexican-Nationals-Impact-4-12-13.pdf.

Noe, Christine. 2010. "Spatialities and Borderlessness in Transfrontier Conservation Areas." *South African Geographical Journal* 92 (2): 144–59.

Norman, Emma. 2015. *Governing Transboundary Waters: Canada, the United States and Indigenous Communities.* New York: Routledge.

Paasi, Anssi. 2014. "The Shifting Landscape of Border Studies and the Challenge of Relational Thinking." In *The New European Frontiers: Social and Spatial (Re)integration Issues in Multicultural and Border Regions*, edited by M. Bufon, J. Minghi, and A. Paasi, 361–79. Cambridge: Cambridge University Press.

Paul, T.V. 2013. *International Relations Theory and Regional Transformation.* Cambridge: Cambridge University Press.

Payan, Tony. 2016. *The Three US-Mexico Border Wars: Drugs, Immigration and Homeland Security.* 2nd ed. Santa Barbara, Calif.: Praeger.

Payan, Tony, and Guadalupe Correa-Cabrera. 2014. "Energy Reform and Security in Northeastern Mexico." Issue Brief 05.0614, Baker Institute, Rice University. https://www.bakerinstitute.org/media/files/files/21e1a8c8/BI-Brief-050614-Mexico_Energy Security.pdf.2015.

Policy Horizons Canada. 2009. "The Emergence of Cross-Border Regions Between Canada and the United States." Briefing Note. Government of Canada. Accessed August 27, 2015 (no longer posted). http://www.horizons.gc.ca/sites/default/files/Publication-alt-format/2009-0001-eng.pdf.

Porter, Michael. 1998. "Clusters and the New Economics of Competition." *Harvard Business Review*, November-December.

Postel, Sandra. 2014. "A Sacred Reunion: The Colorado River Returns to the Sea." *National Geographic*, May 19. https://blog.nationalgeographic.org/2014/05/19/a-sacred -reunion-the-colorado-river-returns-to-the-sea/.

Ramseur, Jonathan L. 2015. *The Regional Greenhouse Gas Initiative: Lessons Learned and Issues for Congress*. Washington, D.C.: Congressional Research Service. https://fas .org/sgp/crs/misc/R41836.pdf.

Roberts, David. 2015. "The Thin Green Line: Fighting Fossil Fuel Exports in the Pacific Northwest." *Vox: Energy and Environment*, August 16. https://www.vox.com/2015/8 /16/9155849/cascadia-activism-billionaire.

Roy, Eleanor Ainge. 2017. "New Zealand River Granted Same Legal Rights as Human Being." *Guardian*, March 16. https://www.theguardian.com/world/2017/mar/16/new -zealand-river-granted-same-legal-rights-as-human-being.

Royer, Susanne. 2007. *Crossing Borders: International Clusters: An Analysis of Medicon Valley Based on Value-Adding Web*. Distance Learning Project. Flensburg: Universität Flensburg. http://www.wz.uni.lodz.pl/kpipp/dlp/Crossing-border-group %201.pdf.

Rumford, Chris. 2006. "Rethinking European Spaces: Territories, Borders, Governance." *Comparative European Politics* 4:127–40.

Schwell, Alexandra. 2011. "No Borders!? The Symbolic Meaning of Border Controls and the Body Politic." https://sharedoc.us/view-doc.html?utm_source=schwell-alexandra -no-borders-the-symbolic-meaning-of-border-controls-and-the-body-politic.

Selin, Henry, and Stacy C. Vandeveer. 2011. "Canadian-US Environmental Cooperation: Climate Change Regionalism in North America." *Review of Policy Research* 28 (3): 295–304.

Smallteacher, Richard. 2015. "Pemex Secretly Expanding Fracking in Mexico Say Activists." *CorpWatch* (blog), June 26. https://corpwatch.org/article/pemex-secretly -expanding-fracking-mexico-say-activists.

Sohn, Christoph. 2015. "Navigating Borders' Multiplicity: The Critical Potential of Assemblage." ResearchGate. https://www.researchgate.net/publication/286231854 _Navigating_borders%27_multiplicity_The_critical_potential_of_assemblage.

Soja, Edward W. 2005. "Borders Unbound: Globalization, Regionalism, and Postmetropolitan Transformation." In *B/ordering Space*, edited by Henk van Houtum, Oliver Kramsch, and Wolfgang Zierhover, 33–46. Aldershot: Ashgate.

Sonoran News. 2016. "Crossing Borders for a Secure Water Future: US-Mexico San Pedro River Aquifer Report." December 23. http://sonorannews.com/2016/12/23/crossing-borders-secure-water-future-us-mexico-san-pedro-river-aquifer-report/.

Steinhauser, Paul. 2014. "CNN Poll: Border Crisis Impacting Public Opinion on Immigration," CNN Politics, July 24. http://politicalticker.blogs.cnn.com/2014/07/24/cnn-poll-border-crisis-impacting-public-opinion-on-immigration/.

Stoeve, Rachael. 2015. "From Watersheds to Mountains, What If We Based Our Borders on Nature?" *Yes!*, Spring. https://www.yesmagazine.org/issues/together-with-earth/from-watersheds-to-mountains-what-if-we-based-our-borders-on-nature.

Storer, Paul, David Davidson, and Laurie Trautman. 2015. *Washington State's Economy in Relation to the Border: Special Report*. Bellingham, Wash.: Border Policy Research Institute.

Taylor, Peter J. 2000. "World Cities and Territorial States Under Conditions of Contemporary Globalization II. Looking Forward, Looking Ahead." *GeoJournal* 52 (2): 157–62.

Todd, Douglas. 2008. *Cascadia: The Illusive Utopia, Exploring the Spirit of the Pacific Northwest*. Vancouver, BC: Ronsdale Press.

VanNijnatten, Debora L. 2011. "The North American Case: Multi-Level, Bottom-Heavy and Policy-Led." In *Comparative Environmental Regionalism*, edited by Lorraine Elliott and Shaun Breslin, 147–62. London: Routledge.

Van Schendel, Willem. 2005. *The Bengal Borderland: Beyond State and Nation in South Asia*. London: Anthem Press.

Van Schoik, Rick, Erik Lee, and Christopher Wilson. 2014. "US-Mexico Border Corridor: Borders into Bridges." *Site Selection Magazine*, July. https://siteselection.com/issues/2014/jul/us-mex-border.cfm.

Werlin, B. 2005. "Regions and Everyday Regionalizations: From a Space-Centered Toward an Action-Centered Human Geography." In *Bordering Space*, edited by Houton van Houtum, O. Kramasch, and W. Zierhofer, 47–60. Aldershot: Ashgate.

Wilder, M., et al. 2013. "Climate Change in the US-Mexico Border Communities." In *Assessment of Climate Change in the Southwest United States, Report prepared for the National Climate Assessment*, edited by G. Garfin et al., 340–84. Washington, D.C.: Island Press.

Wilson, Christopher, and Erik Lee, eds. 2014. *The US-Mexico Border Economy in Transition*. Washington, D.C.: Woodrow Wilson International Center for Scholars. https://www.wilsoncenter.org/sites/default/files/Border_Economy_Transition_Wilson_Lee.pdf.

Yndigegn, Carsten, 2011. "Between Debordering and Rebordering Europe: Cross Border Cooperation in the Oresund Region of the Danish-Swedish Border." *Eurasia Border Review: Border Challenges in Europe* 2 (1): 47–59.

CHAPTER 6

Lines and Flows 2

The Beginning and End of Borders in North America

ALAN D. BERSIN

Introduction

More than a generation ago, in *The Structure of Scientific Revolutions*, Thomas Kuhn introduced the notion of "paradigm" to refer to a distinctive manner of viewing the world, a characteristic sense that is shaped by the larger forces at work in an era.[1] This way of seeing organizes all of the data that is around us—all surrounding sensations—into patterns that we can conceptualize and interpret and then act on. Epochal shifts in paradigms catalyze enormous alterations in how we do business and conduct operations at a point in time.[2] This chapter addresses the massive paradigm change that has taken place since 9/11 in our perception of borders not only as lines but also as movements—flows of people and goods on a global scale both legally and illegally.

The chapter proceeds in five parts. First, I present the traditional understanding and role of borders as boundary lines in a world whose basic geopolitical unit, beginning in the seventeenth century, has been the nation-state. I then show how, as the process of globalization expands, the concept of "borders" is enlarged to encompass the unprecedented flows of all kinds that cross border lines continuously on a 24/7/365 basis. These include the manifold varieties of dark commerce managed by transnational criminal organizations that operate in the nether world of globalization.[3] Next, I discuss the challenges confronted in the aftermath of Al Qaeda's 9/11 attack on the United States and the adjustments made in border management to reconcile global commerce with the requirements of heightened security. I conclude by exploring the implications of the foregoing discussion for the countries of North America, a region construed as extending from Colombia to the Arctic and from Bermuda to Hawaii.

Border Lines

The purpose and function of borders in world history has been and remains to delineate and demarcate—that is, to differentiate—one sovereignty from another. They are the lines in the sand and on a map indicating the geographical place where imperial and/or national dominion begins and ends. These shift over time because of political and military developments, usually followed by legal recognition or acknowledgment expressed in one form or another. Border lines matter but rarely account by themselves for the changes they flag. History tells the tale of these developments and shifts. Like laws, borders embody and reflect history's results with the narrative left out.

The importance of borders has been highlighted since the Peace of Westphalia in 1648, which is commonly considered the origin of the modern international system of nation-states. The Treaty of Westphalia ended the Thirty Years' War and gave rise to a new approach to sovereignty.[4] The revised concept of national authority linked respect for the nation-state and the scope of government dominion and control over a subject population to a specific territory defined by formal boundaries. Principles of mutual recognition, jurisdiction, equality, and noninterference became established tenets of the international system.[5] From the seventeenth century onward, nationalism became a central driving force of political history, in each case tied to very specific notions of border boundaries and place demarcating the edges of sovereign states according to the Westphalian system.

Border lines define a homeland. They are the primary reference points for national defense strategy and homeland security policy. Throughout history, borders have been the sites of fortification, intended variously to shut in or keep out people or things. China's Great Wall in the second century BCE, France's pre–World War II Maginot Line, the Soviets' Berlin Wall in the twentieth century, and Europe's (post-)Schengen and America's Southwest border barriers in the twenty-first century all serve to illustrate the point. It was made more poetic and timeless by Robert Frost in "Mending Wall" where he wrote, "Good fences make good neighbors."[6]

The spaces of borders, corresponding to their boundary lines, are marked by air, land, and seaports of entry and exit. It is here where cross-border transactions of people and goods are processed through the exercise of immigration and customs authorities[7]. Typically, the scope of these border inspection authorities is most broad regardless of the legal system under which they operate. Sovereignty asserts itself aggressively at the border threshold to determine who and what has the right or privilege of entrance (inbound) and exit (outbound). The levying of customs fees and duties has generated critical revenue streams for governments since biblical times.[8]

Border as Flows

The vast volumes and growing speed in the movement of people and goods toward and across border lines in the contemporary globalized world are staggering. Global air travel has increased at an average 4–5 percent rate annually since 1980.[9] International migration has risen continuously since 1990, when 154 million people resided outside of their countries of origin to 244 million (or 3.3 percent of the world's population) similarly placed (or displaced) in 2018.[10] The flow of goods across international borders has expanded dramatically as well, with international trade growing over the past quarter century by an average of 5.1 percent annually.[11] Containerized maritime trade rose 34 percent between 2005 and 2013, while air cargo grew at an average annual rate of 5.4 percent between 1993 and 2008.[12] Each and every day in 2018, an average of 1,133,914 passengers and pedestrians; 81,438 truck, rail, and sea containers; and 285,925 privately owned vehicles entered the United States. Roughly $2.4 trillion in imports and $1.6 trillion in exports crossed U.S. borders that same year.[13] And these were only the recorded *physical* flows. The remainder—an unknown but not insignificant fraction of this official total—occurred in undocumented fashion by criminal design or administrative incompetence or did not enter into official trade statistics for some other reason.

Cross-border flows, moreover, as often as not today are *virtual*. The growth of internet connectivity and information technology mark key trends of the last twenty-five years. Between 2000 and 2012, the number of global internet users increased from 360 million to 24 billion. The number of devices connected online to the internet is expected to double to 40 billion by 2020, and the number of digital transactions is expected to rise correspondingly.[14] These include the electronic movement of money and other stores of value across licit and illicit global financial systems as well as the dissemination of (lawful and unlawful) content through online media platforms and other forms of communication. U.S. exports of digitally delivered services totaled $357.4 billion in 2011, while imports amounted to $221.9 billion.[15] The advent and spread of 3-D printing procedures will operate over time to blunt the difference in the distinction between virtual and physical flows. Additive manufacturing through 3-D printing makes goods available cross-border without the goods physically crossing a border line themselves. 3-D printer use grew 59 percent a year through 2017, and the additive manufacturing market, measured by sales equipment and services, reached (an estimated) $16.2 billion in 2018, a sixfold increase over five years.[16]

Global flows nonetheless are not new. These have occurred since ancient times and are chronicled in the ages of discovery and exploration as seafaring matters and much earlier in the movement of goods and people along the Silk and Tea Horse Roads into China and the caravan paths across Arabia.[17] These flows have increased exponentially century after century, spurred by colonial empires and trading companies, activities multiplied throughout by the growing logic of comparative advantage.[18]

The intensity, volume, and speed of commercial and migratory flows accelerated mightily with the Industrial Revolution[19] and then again more recently by the invention of the jet engine and the internet. Cyberspace embodies the most recent culmination of these trends predicated on technological advance.[20] The cumulative effect is what we refer to as *globalization*: extraordinary cross-border flows of capital, goods, people, ideas, images, data, and electrons occurring daily and facilitated by a digitalization of data that has created the reality of instantaneous communication and transaction. As the process of globalization expands, the concept of borders is enlarged to encompass the unprecedented flows that cross border lines continuously on a 24/7/365 basis. Borders then are channels and points of flow as much as lines marking national sovereignty.[21]

Border Lines and Global Flows

The new border paradigm links jurisdictional lines to the flows toward and across them. Points of entry (airports, seaports, and land ports) from this perspective are the last line, not the first line, of defense for national sovereignties.

Since 9/11, we have learned that the border begins where airplanes take off and where cargo is loaded into the hold, not at the destination boundaries themselves. Homeland security and internal defense from this point of view is inherently transnational; there is virtually no adverse effect on the homeland today that does not have a cause or effect generated abroad.

Within ten years of 9/11, three terrorist plots targeting the United States involved cross-border movements of people or goods. Each event powerfully made the case for the new border paradigm that links jurisdictional lines to flows toward them.

The first, on Christmas Day in 2009, involved the so-called underwear bomber, Nigerian citizen Umar Farouk Abdulmutallab, who boarded a plane in Africa and transited in the Netherlands intending to ignite PETN explosive material and blow up a Northwest Airlines flight over Detroit.[22] Based on its targeting capabilities, U.S. Customs and Border Protection (CBP) identified Abdulmutallab as a "person of interest" after the flight departed the Netherlands.[23] When the plane arrived in the United States and he presented himself for admission, officers would have referred Abdulmutallab to secondary inspection for significant interrogation. This obviously would have been too late, because had he succeeded, he would have completed the terrorist act by blowing up the plane before it landed. Border security in this context requires that Abdulmutallab be prevented from boarding the plane in the first place. For these purposes, the border became Schipol Airport in Amsterdam, and the goal changed to the identification and preemption of high-risk individuals in the flow of passengers from their last point of departure toward the United States.

The second case was in April 2010 and involved Faisal Shahzad, the Times Square Bomber, a naturalized U.S. citizen born in Pakistan who went abroad to receive training from the Taliban in the tribal borderlands between Afghanistan and Pakistan.[24] Shahzad received support and resources in the New York metropolitan area from abroad to construct an explosive device he intended to detonate in Times Square. Foiled by an alert security guard, Shahzad attempted to flee the country on board an Emirates airline plane. Advance passenger manifest information regarding the outbound flight coupled with significant travel history data available concerning Shahzad facilitated his identification and apprehension on the tarmac at JFK airport in New York moments before takeoff.

The third terrorist plot was the shipment in October 2010 of parcel bombs by Al Qaeda operatives in the Arabian Peninsula via UPS and Federal Express.[25] Sent from Yemen and addressed to locations in Chicago, the improvised explosive devices passed into airports in London and Dubai after having been concealed in printer cartridges and timed to detonate over the United States. Because of intelligence sharing by Saudi authorities, the U.S. government was able to deploy public- and private-sector resources to locate the packages in the global supply chain before they reached their intended destinations. As in the other cases, the key lay in the collection, analysis, and sharing of data regarding the transnational origin, route, and flow, in this instance, of express carrier packages.[26]

In the years since these events, time and time again we have seen the transnational nature of homeland security demonstrated in the context of threats to internal safety entirely apart from terrorism. These can be man-made, as in the case of migrant surges into Europe and North America and the cartel-fueled fentanyl scourge in the United States, or they can be entirely natural in origin in the manner of Hurricanes Katrina and Sandy; the earthquakes in Haiti, Mexico City, and off the island of Honshu in 2011; or the 2010 floods in Pakistan. Or they can be attributed to some combination of the two as in the pandemic challenges posed by Ebola, SARS, and H1N1 diseases.[27]

The causes and effects of these harmful events do not respect Westphalian borderlines. Nor are they controlled by nation-states. On the contrary, they increasingly are the products of nonstate actors including transnational criminal organizations, terrorist groups, and multinational corporations as well as Mother Nature. For this reason, they often are referred to as borderless in nature.

The starkest exemplar of a borderless world in the traditional sense is presented by cyberspace, which also illustrates the contemporary notion of borders as encompassing flows. The new fifth domain of cyberspace may dispense altogether with the border as a line except to situate a point of transit and damage or the arc of a censor's official reach. We are at the threshold of inventing the means and methods of cyber security let alone implementing them comprehensively and updating them continuously.[28] What does seem likely, however, is that national borders may become increasingly a less relevant defining line or point in the cyber sphere while highlighting the usefulness of flows as an analytical concept.[29]

Homeland Security and National Security

The goal of border security is keeping dangerous people and dangerous things away from the homeland. In a transnational setting, homeland security and internal defense requires securing the movement of goods and people, among other flows, heading toward the border line. Borders are "pushed out" and "externalized."[30] Time and space are enlisted as allies to enhance security as far away geographically from the border boundary as possible and as early as practicable before arrival at the port of entry.

Authorities are exercised and resources are utilized to identify, intercept, and neutralize threats to the homeland well before they arrive at a port of entry on the border line. This altered paradigm regarding the border security mission has fundamental implications for a border-management agency's strategic and tactical approach to organization and function as well as to its relationships with other agencies both within and outside the government.

Fragmented border management within and between nations is a Westphalian artifact of history that globalization requires revisiting. The focus of the new border-management paradigm is to collect and analyze information on the flows that move toward sovereign borders rather than merely interacting with people and goods at the lines that divide nations. The perimeter security paradigm operating with advance information is much more effective than trying to screen everything and everyone at ports of entry at the border line. Implicit in this arrangement is the movement from bilateral border relations to binational relationships transnationally. Borders can no longer be managed satisfactorily on a unilateral basis from one side or the other.

Organizationally, networks are the key to effective border management. The relevant partnerships must be forged within the government, with the private (stakeholder) sector, and with foreign nations. New forms of governance will emerge to facilitate cooperation through "transgovernmental" mechanisms and public and private partnerships.[31]

In this context, the old dichotomies—national security and homeland security, domestic affairs and foreign affairs, law enforcement and border security— begin to dissolve under the lens of a homeland security viewed transnationally. Traditional legal reconciliation of and accommodations between and among "domestic" and "foreign" categories of action no longer always serve as reliable guides by which we can navigate unquestionably through difficult issues.[32]

United States military activities in Afghanistan, Syria, and Iraq, for example, seem less concerned with obtaining classical geopolitical advantage than with assuring that no country provides a base from which dangerous people and dangerous things can be launched against the homeland. Although means and methods differ, this focus is similar to the border protection mission of securing flows of people and goods toward the homeland. There remain distinctions here with a real difference, to be sure. The intellectual engineering—principally legal but not entirely—necessary to create a revised theory that properly aligns these functions and clearly delineates homeland security as a species of national security remains in its infancy.[33] But the need to revisit and reanalyze carefully these foundations for judgment and decision making appears pronounced in a borderless world marked by continuum and flows rather than by bright lines.

Risk Management: Making Data into Useable Information

If borders are flows of people and goods and electrons, then those charged with securing and regulating those flows must confront the reality that an estimated 98 percent of the traffic appears composed of lawful and compliant trade and travel.[34] The objective to identify and interdict dangerous passengers and cargo (and cyber-malware) from among an otherwise entirely legitimate mass generates a requirement to distinguish between high-risk and low-risk subjects.

Risk assessment and management thereby emerge as the keystone of border management. Information, in turn, becomes central to the evaluation of risk, while data are the building blocks of timely and actionable information. The logic in this environment of information data sharing and access is highlighted. In the modern age, what we learned as children remains true as ever: information is power. However, the traditional moral of the story has been upended entirely. Those who hoard information today, expecting their power to grow by forcing others to ask for it at a price, soon find themselves isolated and over time ignored. The abundance of data and the proliferation online of alternative sources of information place a premium on sharing; one's information becomes more valuable—that is, useful and actionable, by leveraging it off other information and data embodying and reflecting additional reference points that facilitate a connecting of dots. The amount of data that is stored and is available for analysis has expanded exponentially. In 2000, one quarter of global information was stored digitally while today, more than 98 percent is cloud based. Approximately 90 percent of the digital data available today was generated within the past two years. The amount of data is expected to increase by a factor of ten by 2020.[35]

Two propositions concerning big data in this context are central: The first is that the use of big data is not just desirable but also necessary in border management given the other far less attractive options available to secure global flows. Sophisticated rule searches utilizing complex algorithms—enhanced by application of artificial intelligence and machine learning—scan fused available data for signals pointing to both known and unknown threats. These search engines are based on potential risks identified by law enforcement and intelligence communities or derived from computer-trained models themselves. Targeting in this fashion increases our capacity to generate signals and discover the dangerous people and dangerous things for which we are on the lookout at the border without slowing down each border-related transaction to inspect it.[36]

The second proposition is that access to big data or metadata can be accomplished in a manner consistent with reasonable notions of privacy and personal data protection. Modern information sharing compacts are predicated on concepts of *federated search* and anonymization that avoid an actual *exchange* of data in favor of carefully tailored techniques of *access*. The only information that is "shared" derives from matches or "hits" that are returned from a masked federated search.[37] These in turn are subject to negotiated protocols that treat the matches further to eliminate false positives and otherwise enhance both security and privacy. On closer scrutiny, these values turn out not to be necessarily in conflict. Nor are security and trade facilitation mutually exclusive, as shown below.

Expediting Legitimate Trade and Travel as a Security Regime

The long-held view posited that security and trade are independent variables competing in a zero-sum game. According to conventional wisdom, trade facilitation, the expedited movement of commerce, and security ensuring the safety of that commerce must be balanced to an optimal equilibrium. The concept of "so much security" in exchange for "so much delay" in the processing of trade has governed traditional border operations for generations. Risk management comprehensively applied, however, reveals this notion not only to be theoretically false but also practically counterproductive and self-defeating.[38]

Identifying illicit trade and travel in the midst of lawful commerce is like searching for a needle in the proverbial haystack. Short of examining every piece of straw separately or burning down the haystack, there are only two ways one can find the needle. The first is to have very specific intelligence about where the needle is so that one can reach into the middle of the haystack and pluck it out. Occasionally, but with increasing frequency, we have access to that kind of granulated intelligence. That is what occurred in the Al Qaeda-Arabian

Peninsula (AQAP) cargo plot involving UPS and Federal Express parcels from Yemen. We received very concrete information and were able to reach into the global flow of millions of packages then in transit and locate the precise two packages laden with explosives. Specific intelligence, today a function primarily of informants and human intelligence (HUMINT) sources, over time increasingly will be generated by big data technology operations.

But we cannot always count on particular actionable intelligence. So, the only other way regularly to find the needle in the haystack is to make the haystack smaller. And the way to make the stack smaller is to differentiate routinely between high- and low-risk subjects and expedite movement of the latter through the global supply-chain system.

In fact, segmenting traffic flows according to risk is a necessary condition of heightening border security at any level of resource allocation. We expedite lawful trade and travel through border controls so that we may focus our scarce regulatory and inspectional resources on that traffic about which we have derogatory information or about which we lack sufficient information to make a sound judgment regarding its legitimacy. Moving ordinary travelers and regular cargo quickly through ports of entry, therefore, is not only good for the economy, but given the volumes we confront, it is essential to the security function itself.[39]

Expediting trade and heightened security, accordingly, are neither antithetical to one another nor mutually exclusive matters requiring balance. On the contrary, they are part and parcel of a single process. This approach to managing flows through the collection and analysis of advance information regarding them has become the cornerstone of modern border management. The dynamic here highlights the crucial importance of genuine partnerships with the public and private sectors as well as with other countries. What is required, however, is not only the intensification of partnership but a change in the quality and nature of the interaction. Yesterday's prevailing mode—government mandate and private-sector compliance—must give way to the model of a cocreated regulatory regime that embodies the "grand bargain" from the outset in reacting to evolving threats from transnational criminal organizations, including terrorist groups.[40]

Security as the Organizing Principle: The Searing Impact of 9/11 on the United States

The trauma of 9/11 inflicted by Al Qaeda on the world through the United States assured that we would never view cross-border movements in quite the

same way.[41] Transnational terrorism exploited the relative openness of Westphalian borders and the laxness of border regulatory regimes to inflict significant
damage in the continental United States for the first time since the British
burned government buildings in Washington during the War of 1812.[42] In one
vicious fell swoop that was actual and deadly, and unlike the potential threat
Americans had grown accustomed to during the Cold War, the events of 9/11
altered America's view of security forever.

The terrorist invasion of 9/11 gave rise to a preoccupation with the safety of
the American homeland. The sense of insecurity stemmed from the fact that
U.S. borders had been violated. The reflexive response was to hunker down
behind traditional concepts of borders as lines of defense. All planes were
grounded, and the maritime and aviation borders were closed in the immediate
aftermath of 9/11. Similarly, land borders virtually shut down as each entering
vehicle from Mexico and Canada was inspected thoroughly. In other less visible
ways, America closed its borders through restrictions on the issuance of visas
and other immigration benefits.[43]

But all the emergency measures taken immediately after 9/11 collided head-on
with the realities of travel and commerce through transit zones and supply chains
in a globalized world. The unacceptable economic and political consequences of
shutting down the border coupled with the new security imperative forced a fundamental change in border-management perspective. In order to forge practical
arrangements to accommodate travel and trade security requirements, borders
needed to be viewed and managed according to the new paradigm as flows as
much as lines in the sand, on the water, and through the air. This new focus
generated the creation of the Department of Homeland Security (DHS) in the
United States, a merger by legislative fiat in 2003 of twenty-two agencies spread
previously across the landscape of American government.[44] This included all
the agencies responsible for inspection and security at the maritime (U.S. Coast
Guard) and land (Immigration and Customs) borders and the creation of a new
agency, the Transportation Security Agency, charged with travel security.[45]

The previous scheme of divided border management, in place since the eighteenth century, was not efficient to say the least. But it had been responsive
to history. Mission success was limited by the structure of separate stovepipe
agencies zealously guarded by bureaucratic rivalries and an unending competition for resources. These tensions were swept aside in the crucible of 9/11,
and unified border management was created for the first time in American or
world history. Immigration, customs, and agricultural inspection authorities

exercised by the same officer working for a single agency defined by an overarching security mission implemented the institution of joint border management and the science and art of modern border protection. It sounds so sensible, and in practice it has turned out to be so. But it would not have come to pass in the absence of crisis, and the United States remains in North America and, along with Australia, among the Five Eye nations virtually alone in implementing it comprehensively.[46]

Border Management and Security in North America: An Intermestic Canada, Mexico, and the United States

The new border paradigm and method of management has had special implications—and holds out particular promise—for U.S. land border neighbors to the north and south and downstream in history for a broader North American region. The situation is unique because of the physical proximity of the geography. The United States shares 1,900 border miles with Mexico and 5,400 miles of border with Canada (including those between Alaska and the Yukon). A second dimension of uniqueness stems from history. Following armed conflicts by the United States with each of its neighbors in the nineteenth century, treaties and subsequent peaceful territorial adjustments have blessed North America with the longest demilitarized land borders in the world.[47]

These developments in space and over time have created a relationship between the United States and both Mexico and Canada that is equally unique. It is a relationship that is neither international in the traditional sense nor domestic, given the existence of separate sovereignties. Instead, to use a phrase coined by Bayless Manning in the 1970s, the relationship is "intermestic."[48]

Notwithstanding all of this, the fact remains that U.S. borders with Mexico and Canada historically were largely ineffective before 9/11 from the standpoint of managing flows of people and cargo efficiently. The principal reason for this was the asymmetry between the United States and its neighbors and the suspicion and fear that this generated.[49] Only at the border line are nation-states equal as a matter of juridical power as nowhere else in their bilateral relationship. At the border, therefore, Mexico and Canada jealously guarded the prerogatives of sovereignty to reinforce their national pride and identity and to avoid political, economic, and cultural domination by the "colossus" on their doorstep. Porfirio Díaz, Mexico's president between 1877 and 1880 and again between 1884 and 1911, summarized the sentiment: "Poor Mexico, so far from God and so near to the United States."[50] Particularly pronounced in Mexico, the same sense existed among Canadians, albeit expressed on different issues and in different ways.[51] As a result, demilitarized borders far from federal centers of power in the three countries were not coordinated operationally, and routine cooperation was conspicuous by its absence.[52] The events of 9/11 brought this state of affairs to a head.

By close of business on September 11, 2001, truck and automobile queues stretched miles and miles north into Canada and south into Mexico. Wait times became measured not in hours but by fractions of days. Long porous border communities became divided by physical barriers. Vibrant cross-border commerce slowed to a crawl when it did not grind to a halt. Within days, it appeared that the hunker-down security approach could turn into a self-inflicted wound for the United States more fatal than the Al-Qaeda attack itself. The CEO of General Motors telephoned President George Bush to advise that the border security regime put into effect had so thoroughly disrupted GM's cross-border supply chain and crippled its production platform that absent immediate relief, the company would be "bankrupt within a week."[53] Reimagining and then reinventing the borders with Mexico and Canada in the context of trade flows and the flows of people accordingly became a strategic necessity for the United States on both security and economic grounds in the aftermath of 9/11.[54]

Regarding commerce, the massive growth in trade among the United States, Mexico, and Canada to a combined total exceeding $1.2 trillion since the North American Free Trade Agreement (NAFTA) was enacted in 1994 required an operational recognition of the three countries' de facto economic integration. Looking ahead as well, the emergence of global trading blocs highlights the imperative of viewing U.S. economic prosperity from the perspective of enhancing North American competitiveness as a whole. To compete successfully over the next half century with East Asia, the Indian subcontinent, and Brazil, NAFTA needed to be taken to the next level.[55] One critical path to this end was increasing significantly border efficiency to reduce current cross-border transactional costs by 10–20 percent or more on the "North America Highway." The recent renegotiation and rebranding of NAFTA as the United States–Mexico–Canada Agreement in the Trump era, notwithstanding all the negative and inflammatory rhetoric that preceded it, is consistent with this end.[56]

With respect to security, the focus has shifted from an exclusive one on land border lines running east to west to one more concerned with north-south flows of goods and people and the necessity for "continental perimeter security."[57] This approach results in Canada, the United States, and Mexico jointly identifying and intercepting dangerous people and things (and eventually electrons) as they move in global flows toward and within the North American continent. The length of our land borders, coupled with the economic need to avoid "thickening" them (in the Canadian phrase), commends this course. The model here is the North American Air Defense (NORAD) command that enables Canada and the United States jointly to track and defend their shared northern continental airspace from aviation threats to it.[58] Mexico, currently an observer at NORAD headquarters in Colorado Springs, participates more each year in its activities.

During the past fifteen years, there has been considerable progress to report on both the economic and security fronts in terms of reinventing U.S. borders with both Mexico and Canada. Following the Smart Border Accords and the Mérida and Security and Prosperity Initiatives between 2002 and 2006, in May 2010,[59] U.S. president Barack Obama, together with Mexican president Felipe Calderón, issued the Twenty-First Century Border Management Declaration.[60] Substantially recasting the strategic alliance, the declaration decisively moved the bilateral relationship away from the accusatory conversations of the past concerning migration and narcotics.[61] Acknowledging the U.S. national security stake in Mexico's historic struggle against organized crime, the two presidents reaffirmed and applied generally the Mérida doctrine of "co-responsibility" for both legal and illegal flows across the border. Viewing drugs and migrant smuggling coming north and firearms and bulk cash going south as a single vicious cycle of criminality has created the conditions for binational law enforcement cooperation that was unthinkable in the past.[62]

"Beyond the Border: A Shared Vision of Perimeter Security and Economic Competitiveness Declaration" (Beyond the Border Declaration), announced in February 2011 by U.S. president Obama and Canadian prime minister Stephen Harper, represented an equally stunning departure in the context of U.S.-Canada relations.[63] Building on a longer standing and deeper foundation of trust, the Beyond the Border Declaration has generated a staggeringly ambitious action plan that encompasses the entire breadth of the U.S.-Canada security and economic competitiveness agendas. It forthrightly addresses matters that had been deferred politely in the past, ranging from information sharing on known or suspected terrorists to the preinspection of cargo and the reciprocal carrying of weapons by law enforcement personnel stationed in each other's countries.[64]

These course corrections and strides in U.S. policy have been navigated in parallel processes with its neighbors, respecting sensitivities of sovereignty on both ends as well as the differences and the difficulties inherent in the respective negotiations. Nonetheless, the stage has been set for an increasingly trilateral discussion over the next generation that holds out enormous promise for the three countries and the North America they share. Adjustments made initially on an ad hoc basis have been refined and have then matured with time into a comprehensive and entirely new philosophy and practice of binational border management that continue in spite of the populist politics that are more prevalent nowadays both in North America and elsewhere in the world.

DHS works with its counterpart agencies in Mexico and Canada to target high-risk trade and travel for interdiction and investigation. The unlawful activity targeted includes narcotics, human trafficking, terrorism, counterfeit goods, illicit finance, unauthorized migration, export of firearms, child pornography, and restricted wildlife and agricultural products as well as national security technologies and goods. Information, particularly advance information, remains central to the evaluation of risk and will become even more so with the increasing "virtualization" of border realities. To fulfill its mission, CBP has developed the U.S. government's largest collection, storage, and dissemination functions with respect to unclassified data. On a typical day, CBP exchanges more than 2.5 billion electronic messages with other government agencies, transportation carriers, customs brokers, and the plethora of additional participants in global travel networks and supply chains.[65] Given the volume and intensity of cross-border trade and travel among Canada, the United States, and Mexico, a major portion of these messages pertain to North America.

In addition, DHS has addressed the challenge through international partnerships, forward deployment of personnel and assets, and risk-based segmentation of lawful flows. The Twenty-First Century Border Management Declaration and the Beyond the Border Declaration officially established a collaborative bilateral border regimen respectively between the United States and Mexico and Canada and the United States. By "pushing borders out" in concert with its neighbors, the United States has initiated processes to minimize the inspection of people and goods at the bottleneck of the border line. Moreover, joint adoption of a North American continental perspective by the United States with both Canada and Mexico has enabled the emergence of common doctrines of border management to secure land, sea, and air corridors; prevented exploitation of lawful flows by criminals and terrorists; safeguarded key trade nodes and corridors to manage goods and people in transit; and cooperated in the investigation, disruption, and dismantling of criminal organizations.[66]

As a result, "borders" have come to be viewed by Canadian, U.S., and Mexican officials as opportunities for cooperation and coordination rather than occasions for conflict and division. These include operational coordination to reduce transaction costs and heighten security; preinspections and preclearance operations conducted in each other's countries; commercial data harmonization through the electronic single window; collaborative collection, analysis, and dissemination of biometric identity data; and joint consultation and construction of capital infrastructure. The three governments focus as well on identifying low-risk trade and travel to expedite lawful throughput in the system and across the border.[67] This is accomplished by extensive utilization of mutually recognized trusted-traveler and trader programs that facilitate expedited segmentation and clearance of preapproved lower-risk goods and travelers. These programs involving travelers include Global Entry, TSA Pre-Check, and Northern Exchange with U.S. (NEXUS [Canada]) and Secure Electronic Network for Travelers' Rapid Inspection (SENTRI [Mexico]).[68] Regarding cargo and goods, coordinated risk management at, between, and away from ports of entry takes place routinely through cooperative targeting, data exchange, and mutual recognition of their respective authorized economic operator (AEO) programs: C-T-PAT,[69] Canada's Partners in Prosperity (PIP), and Mexico's AEO program.[70]

The Future of North America

Populist challenges to the norms and practices of North America have been articulated again recently, notably, and in particularly virulent fashion by President Donald Trump. Despite these challenges, however, the ground truths of deep economic integration and security cooperation have thus far resisted the centrifugal force of populist rhetoric and fortified the cooperative trends that have reshaped North American borders during the past generation.[71] The enormous competitive advantages these changes have conferred on the region are undeniable.

While centered in Mexico, Canada, and the United States, the broader North American Region stretches from Colombia to the Arctic and from Bermuda to Hawaii. Collectively this continental and maritime bloc is endowed with unparalleled comparative advantages taken as a whole and focused at the U.S., Canadian, and Mexican core: a half billion people with distinctly favorable demographic features; robust economies that generate in the aggregate nearly thirty percent of the gross global product of goods and services; shared manufacturing and production platforms with annual commercial flows constituting nearly 20 percent of world trade; peaceful, demilitarized borders cooperatively managed by collaborative sovereign authorities; a shared commitment to democracy and the rule of law; complete energy independence within sight; a huge natural resource base (beyond hydrocarbons), including enormous navigable rivers and copious amounts of arable land; and unobstructed access to the Atlantic, Pacific, and Arctic Oceans. These represent a staggering array of precious strategic assets. Coupled with a determination to incorporate Central America and the Caribbean into North America's emerging security and economic region and the border-management regime central to it, the future presages an even greater North American presence and influence in the world. The American Century may in fact be ending, but it appears to be doing so in the context of a North American Century that is just beginning.[72]

Conclusion

The French poet Paul Valery has observed, "The [challenge of] our times is that the future is not what it used to be."[73] The themes explored here will remain the subjects of security and economic developments over the next decades as we experience their domestic, international, and intermestic effects. Through the lens of lines and flows, we discern both the old end and a new beginning of borders, commencing first in North America.

NOTES

An earlier version of this article was published as Alan Bersin, "Lines and Flows: The Beginning and End of Borders," originally presented at the Ira M. Belfer Lecture, Brooklyn Law School, October 6, 2011, and published in *Brooklyn Journal of International Law* 37, no. 2 (2012): 389–406, and republished in *World Customs Journal* 6, no. 1 (2012).

1. Thomas S. Kuhn, *The Structure of Scientific Revolutions* (Chicago: University of Chicago Press, 1962), 10–13.

2. In Kuhn's context these shifts marked the transition, for instance, from a Ptolemaic or pretentious way of seeing—the earth anchors the universe—to the materially more modest Copernican one—the sun centers the solar system—and so on through a mechanical Newtonian model to the uncertainties inherent in the relativist paradigm captured by Einstein and Heisenberg; see Kuhn, *Structure of Scientific Revolutions*, 66–91.

3. Louise Shelley, *Dark Commerce: How a New Illicit Economy Is Threatening Our Future* (Princeton, N.J.: Princeton University Press, 2018).

4. Ash, R. G., "Thirty Years War (1618–1648)," *Europe, 1450 to 1789*, vol. 3 of *Encyclopedia of the Early Modern World, 2004* (New York: Charles Scribner's Sons, 2004).

5. Austen D. Givens, Nathan E. Busch, and Alan D. Bersin, "Going Global: The International Dimensions of U.S. Homeland Security Policy," *Journal of Strategic Security* 11, no. 3 (2018): 1–34 (https://doi.org/10.5038/1944-0472.11.3.1689).

6. Robert Frost, "Mending Wall," in *The Poetry of Robert Frost: The Collected Poems, Complete and Unabridged* ed. Edward Connery Lathem (New York: Holt Rinehart and Winston, 1969), 33.

7. Michael Pezzullo, "Sovereignty in an Age of Global Interdependency: The Role of Borders," paper presented at the Australian Strategic Policy Institute, December 2014.

8. The U.S. Customs Service was established by the Fifth Act of the First Congress on July 31, 1789. "1789: First Congress Provides for Customs Administration." U.S. Customs and Border Protection (https://www.cbp.gov/about/history/1789-first-congress-provides-customs-administration).

9. Boeing, *Current Market Outlook, 2014–2033* (Seattle: Boeing, 2014), 2, 14–15 (http://i2.cdn.turner.com/cnn/2015/images/09/02/boeing_current_market_outlook_2014.pdf); International Air Transport Association, "New IATA Passenger Forecast Reveals Fast-Growing Markets for the Future," press release no. 57, October 16, 2014 (http://www.iata.org/pressroom/pr/pages/2014-10-16-01.aspx); see also Oxford Economics, *Shaping the Future of Travel: Macro Trends Driving Industry Growth over the Next Decade*, 6 (https://amadeus.com/documents/en/airlines/research-report/oxford-economics-shaping-the-future-of-travel.pdf). These data, as well as those in the text below, are drawn from work done by the Department of Homeland Security Office of Policy in connection with preparing for the Quadrennial Homeland Security Review for 2018.

10. Organization for Economic Cooperation and Development, *International Migration Outlook 2018* (Paris: OECD, 2018) (https://doi.org/10.1787/migr_outlook-2018-en); *International Migration Outlook 2014* (Paris: OECD, 2014), 19–20; International Organization for Migration, *World Migration Report 2018* (https://www.iom.int/wmr/world-migration-report-2018).

11. World Trade Organization, "Trade Statistics and Outlook," Press Release 739, April 14, 2015, 1.

12. United Nations, *Review of Maritime Transport, 2014* (Geneva: United Nations, 2014), 5; World Bank, "Container Port Traffic" (http://data.worldbank.org/indicator/IS.SHP.GOOD.TU/countries?display=graph); see also Boeing, *Current Market Outlook, 2014–2033*, 5.

13. U.S. Customs and Border Protection, "On a Typical Day in Fiscal Year 2018, CBP . . . ," March 7, 2019 (https://www.cbp.gov/newsroom/stats/typical-day-fy2018).

14. KPMG International, *Future State 2030: The Global Megatrends Shaping Government* (2013), 22 (https://wedocs.unep.org/bitstream/handle/20.500.11822/19009/Future_State_2030_The_Global_Megatrends_Shapi.pdf?sequence=1&isAllowed=y): see also

Ministry of Defense, *Global Strategic Trends—Out to 2043*, 57 (https://espas.secure.euro parl.europa.eu/orbis/sites/default/files/generated/document/en/MinofDef_Global%20 Strategic%20Trends%20-%202045.pdf).

15. See, for example, Enrique Canon, "The Future of Customs," *World Customs Organization Policy Commission Report* (December 2018); Jessica R. Nicholson and Ryan Noonan, *Digital Economy and Cross-Border Trade: The Value of Digitally-Deliverable Services*, Economics and Statistics Administration, U.S. Department of Commerce, ESA Issue Brief 01–14, January 27, 2014, 7.

16. Connor M. McNulty, Neyla Arnas, and Thomas A. Campbell, "Towards the Printed World: Additive Manufacturing and Implications for National Security," *Defense Horizons* 73 (September 2012) (https://ndupress.ndu.edu/Portals/68/Documents/defense horizon/DH-73.pdf?ver=2014-03-06-114915-097); Andrea Chang, "3-D Printing Market to Grow to US$16.2 Billion in 2018," *Los Angeles Times*, March 31, 2014 (https:// www.latimes.com/business/technology/la-fi-tn-3d-printing-20140331-story.html); Robert Parker and Keith Kmetz, "3D Printing A Transformative Opportunity for Print and Manufacturing," briefing at IDC Directions 2014 Conference, Santa Clara, Calif., March 11, 2014, 10.

17. See Mark Jenkins, "Tea Horse Road: The Forgotten Road," *National Geographic*, May 2010, (http://ngm.nationalgeographic.com/2010/05/tea-horse-road/jenkins-text).

18. Adam Smith (1723–1790), *The Wealth of Nations*, introduction by Robert Reich, ed. Edwin Cannan (New York: Modern Library, 2000).

19. Charles Hirschman and Elizabeth Mogford, "Immigration and the American Industrial Revolution from 1880 to 1920," *Social Science Research* 38, no. 4 (2009): 897–920.

20. Henry Adams, *The Education of Henry Adams* (London: Penguin Classics, 1995).

21. See Givens, Busch, and Bersin, "Going Global;" 3.

22. Kenneth Chang, "Explosive on Flight 253 Is Among Most Powerful," *New York Times*, December 27, 2009 (http://www.nytimes.com/2009/12/28/us/28explosives.html).

23. *Ten Years after 9/11: Can Terrorists Still Exploit Our Visa System? Hearing Before the H. Comm. On Homeland Sec. Subcomm. On Border & Mar. Sec*, 112th Cong. 2 (2011) (statement of Edward J. Ramotowski, Acting Assistant Sec'y for Visa Services, Department of State).

24. Mark Mazzetti and Scott Shane, "Evidence Mounts for Taliban Role in Bomb Plot," *New York Times*, May 5, 2010.

25. Erika Solomon and Phil Stewart, "Al Qaeda Yemen Wing Claims Parcel Plot, UPS Crash," *Reuters*, November 5, 2010 (http://www.reuters.com/article/2010/11/05/us -usa-yemen-bomb-idUSTRE6A44PU20101105).

26. Two additional illustrative cases involve the arrest and conviction of U.S. lawful permanent resident Najibullah Zazi and U.S. born citizen David Coleman Headley, formerly known as Daood Sayed Gilani. See United States v. Zazi, no. 09-CR-663, 2010 WL 2710605 (E.D.N.Y. June 30, 2010); United States v. Kashmiri, no. 09 CR 830–4, 2011 WL 1326373, at *1–5 (N.D. Ill. Apr. 1, 2011). Zazi was recruited by Al Qaeda to conduct suicide attacks using explosives against the New York City subway system. See *Zazi*, 2010 WL 2710605, at *1. Headley helped plan the November 2008 attacks in Mumbai in

concert with Al Qaeda and Pakistan-based terrorist organization Lashkar-e-Taiba. See *Kashmiri*, 2011 WL 1326373, at *1–2; Sebastian Rotella, "The American Behind India's 9/11—And How U.S. Botched Chances to Stop Him," *Pro Publica*, November 22, 2011 (http://www.propublica.org/article/david-headley-homegrown-terrorist).

27. Tiffany Cooks, "Factors Affecting Emerging Manager, First Responder, and Citizen Disaster Preparedness" (PhD diss., Walden University, 2015).

28. John Carlin and Sophia Brill, "Cybersecurity," in *Beyond 9/11: Building A Homeland Security Enterprise for the 21st Century*, ed. Chappell Lawson, Alan Bersin, and Juliette Kayyem (Cambridge, Mass.: MIT Press, forthcoming).

29. Fred Kaplan, *Dark Territory: The Secret History of Cyber War* (New York: Simon & Schuster, 2016).

30. David Danelo, *Policy Note: For Protection or Profit? Free Trade, Human Smuggling and International Border Management* (Geneva: Global Initiative Against Transnational Organized Crime, 2018), 12–13 (http://globalinitiative.net/wp-content/uploads/2018/03/For-Protection-or-Profit-Intl-Border-Management-March-2018-web.pdf).

31. Jason Ackleson, "From 'Thin to Thick' (and Back Again?): The Politics and Policies of the Contemporary US-Canada Border," *American Review of Canadian Studies* 39, no. 4 (December 2009): 336–51.

32. Philip Zelikow, "The Transformation of National Security," *National Interest*, March 1, 2003 (http://nationalinterest.org/article/the-transformation-of-national-security-491).

33. See Nathan Canestaro, "Homeland Defense: Another Nail in the Coffin for Posse Comitatus," *Washington University Journal of Law and Policy* 12, no. 99 (January 2003): 99–144.

34. U.S. Customs and Border Protection, *Import Trade Trends: Fiscal Year 2010 Year-End Report* (2010) (http://www.cbp.gov/linkhandler/cgov/trade/trade_programs/trade_trends/itt.ctt/itt.pdf; no longer posted).

35. Ministry of Defense, *Global Strategic Trends*, 56; KPMG International, *Future State 2030*, 22.

36. Chappell Lawson, "The Trusted and the Targeted: Segmenting Flows by Risk," in Lawson, Bersin, and Kayyem, *Beyond 9/11*.

37. Stevan Bunnell, "Increasing Security While Protecting Privacy," in Lawson, Bersin, and Kayyem, *Beyond 9/11*.

38. Alan D. Bersin and Michael D. Huston, "Homeland Security as a Theory of Action: The Impact on U.S./Mexico Border Management," in *The Anatomy of a Relationship: A Collection of Essays on the Evolution of U.S.-Mexico Cooperation on Border Management* (Washington, D.C.: Wilson Center, Mexico Institute, 2016) (https://www.wilsoncenter.org/publication/homeland-security-theory-action-the-impact-usmexico-border-management).

39. Seth M. M. Stodder, "Rethinking Borders: Securing the Flows of Lawful Travel and Commerce in the 21st Century," in Lawson, Bersin, and Kayyem, *Beyond 9/11*.

40. International Air Transport Association, "Cargo Security: Advance Electronic Information & Screening," October 2011 (http://www.org/whatwedo/cargo/tracker/october-2011/pages/security.aspx; no longer posted).

41. See Lawrence Wright, *The Looming Tower: Al-Qaeda and the Road to 9/11* (New York: Vintage, 2006).

42. American territory, of course, was again invaded in 1941 by Japan's sneak attack at Pearl Harbor. Organized cross-border raids from Mexico also occurred in the interim. Brownsville, Texas, was attacked in 1859 during the Cortina Wars, and Columbus, New Mexico, was "invaded" by Pancho Villa in 1916 during the Mexican Revolution.

43. Edward Alden, *The Closing of the American Border* (New York: Harper Perennial, 2008).

44. The Homeland Security Act of 2002, (Pub. L, no. 197–296, 116 Stat. 2135) establishing DHS, involved the largest reorganization of executive branch operations since formation of the National Military Establishment in 1947, subsequently renamed the Department of Defense (DOD) in 1949. Composed of 230,000 employees, DHS is the third largest cabinet agency after DOD and the Department of Veterans Affairs.

45. CBP itself was formed through the merger of four separate organizations from three separate cabinet departments into one new agency—the U.S. Border Patrol and Immigration and Naturalization service from the Department of Justice, dealing with people seeking to enter the country legally and illegally; the U.S. Customs Service from the Treasury Department, dealing with cargo and goods; and the Agriculture Inspection Service from the Department of Agriculture, dealing with agricultural pests and potential infestation of our crop lands. The Coast Guard became part of the Department of Homeland Security in 2003. See "U.S. Coast Guard History Program," Historian's Office, United States Coast Guard (https://www.history.uscg.mil/home/history -program/).

46. See Matthew Longo, *The Politics of Borders: Sovereignty, Security and the Citizen After 9/11* (Cambridge: Cambridge University Press, 2018). The "Five Eye" group—made up of the United States, Canada, the United Kingdom, Australia, and New Zealand— was formed for the purposes of security and intelligence sharing in the context of World War II. The relationship has been sustained and even strengthened since that time. Canada and the United Kingdom have partially moved toward unified border management. Australia alone, through the creation of the Department of Home Affairs in 2015, has proceeded to a full merger of border-related responsibilities in the manner of customs and border protection and aviation and maritime security in the United States.

47. The Rush-Bagot Treaty in 1817 with Canada (through Britain following the War of 1812) and the Treaty of Guadalupe Hidalgo in 1848, concluding the U.S.-Mexico War, established lasting peace. Additional boundary agreements were reached amicably with Canada (British North America) through the Webster-Ashburton Treaty (1842) and the Oregon Treaty (1846) and with Mexico through the Gadsden Purchase (1853). See "Milestones in the History of U.S. Foreign Relations," Office of the Historian, United States Department of State (https://history.state.gov/milestones).

48. Bayless Manning, "The Congress, the Executive and Intermestic Affairs: Three Proposals," *Foreign Affairs* 55 (January 1977): 306–9.

49. The populations of the United States, Canada, and Mexico are 313 million, 34 million, and 113 million, respectively. See "Country Comparison: Population," World Fact-

book, Central Intelligence Agency (https://www.cia.gov/library/publications/the-world-factbook/rankorder/2119rank.html). Economically, their gross domestic products are $19.49 trillion (U.S.), $1.77 trillion (Canada), and $2.46 trillion (Mexico). See "Country Comparison: GDP (Purchasing Power Parity)," World Factbook, Central Intelligence Agency (https://www.cia.gov/library/publications/the-world-factbook/fields/208rank.html).

50. Robert I. Fitzhenry, ed., *The Harper Book of Quotations*, 3rd ed. (New York: Collins Reference, 1993), 451, Randolph Wellford Smith, 31n25; "Chronology of Leading Historical Events in Mexico," in *Benighted Mexico* (New York: John Lane, 1916), 383.

51. See, for example, Meg Bortin, "Global Poll Shows Wide Distrust of United States," *New York Times*, June 27, 2007 (https://www.nytimes.com/2007/06/27/news/27iht-pew.4.6365578.html).

52. Alan D. Bersin, "Threshold Order: Bilateral Law Enforcement and Regional Public Safety on the U.S./Mexico Border," *San Diego Law Review* 35, no. 3 (Summer 1998): 715–26.

53. Danelo, *Policy Note*, 24.

54. Stodder. "Rethinking Borders," 32.

55. Known as Tratado de Libre Comercio (TLC) in Mexico, NAFTA dramatically expanded annual U.S. trade flows (imports and exports) with Canada ($525.3 billion in 2010) and Mexico ($393 billion in 2010), making them our first and third largest commercial partners. The second, fourth, and fifth rankings belonged, respectively, to China ($456.8 billion in 2010), Japan ($180.9 billion in 2010) and Germany ($130.9 billion in 2010). See "Top Trading Partners," Foreign Trade Statistics, U.S. Census Bureau, last updated July 12, 2011 (http://www.census.gov/foreign-trade/statistics/highlights/top/top1012yr.html).

56. Heather Long, "U.S., Canada and Mexico Just Reached a Sweeping New NAFTA Deal: Here's What's in It," *Washington Post*, October 18, 2018 (https://www.washingtonpost.com/business/2018/10/01/us-canada-mexico-just-reached-sweeping-new-nafta-deal-heres-whats-it/?utm_term=.4fc54f612c87).

57. See, for example, John Noble, "Fortress America or Fortress North America," *Law and Business Review of the Americas* 11, no. 3, (2005): 461–526.

58. Canadian and U.S. military forces rotate NORAD command responsibilities. On 9/11, for example, General Ralph Everhart of the U.S. Air Force was the military officer in charge of leading NORAD's response to the terrorist attack, and his deputy commander was Lieutenant General Kenneth Pennie of the Canadian Forces Air Command. See Adam J. Hebert, "The Return of NORAD," *Air Force Magazine* 85, no. 2 (February 2002): 50 (http://www.airforce-magazine.com/MagazineArchive/Documents/2002/February%202002/0202norad.pdf).

59. See Ackleson, "From 'Thin to Thick,'" 336–51.

60. "Declaration by the United States of America and the United Mexican States Concerning Twenty-First Century Border Management," Pub. Papers 2010, 682–684 (May 19, 2010).

61. Alan D. Bersin, "El Tercer Pais: Reinventing the U.S./Mexico Border," *Stanford Law Review* 48, no. 5 (May 1996): 1413–20.

62. Guadalupe Correa-Cabrera and Evan D. McCormick, "U.S.-Mexico Law Enforcement and Border Security Cooperation: An Institutional Historical Perspective" (unpublished manuscript, 2018)

63. "Joint Declaration by President Barack Obama and Prime Minister Stephen J. Harper of Canada: Beyond the Border: A Shared Vision for Perimeter Security and Economic Competitiveness," Pub. Papers 2011, 84–87 (February 4, 2011).

64. Julian Aguilar, "Mexico Loosening Rules for Armed U.S. Agents," *Texas Tribune*, June 9, 2015; U.S. Department of Homeland Security, "United States and Canada Sign Preclearance Agreement," March 16, 2015 (https://www.dhs.gov/news/2015/03/16 /united-states-and-canada-sign-preclearance-agreement).

65. These analytical communications in the security context are managed by CBP's National Targeting Centers for Passengers and Cargo, located in Virginia. They permit access, respectively, to records of every traveler and cargo shipment—land, sea, and air— that has crossed a U.S. border through a port of entry. Mexican and Canadian border officials collaborate closely in this process. Data in the trade and commerce arena is managed through the Automated Commercial Environment (ACE) system.

66. Eric L. Olson, "The Merida Initiative and Shared Responsibility in U.S.-Mexico Security Relations," *Wilson Quarterly* (Winter 2017); Department of Homeland Security, "Beyond the Border 2012–2016 Progress Report," Beyond the Border Action Plan Report Card, February 21, 2019.

67. See U.S. Customs and Border Protection, Trusted Traveler Programs (http://www .cbp.gov/xp/cgov/travel/trusted_traveler/; no longer posted).

68. Commencing in December 2010, CBP has integrated its trusted-traveler programs by extending global entry benefits to NEXUS and SENTRI members and vice versa. *Global Entry Expansion Federal Notice Published*, December 29, 2010 (no longer posted) (http://www.cbp.gov/xp/cgov/travel/travel_news/global_published.xml). There are 2.4 million participants enrolled directly in Global Entry and over 1.3 million members of NEXUS and SENTRI that also receive Global Entry benefits. "Trusted Traveler Programs Fact Sheet," 2015, Pub. #: 2118–1115 (https://www.cbp.gov/sites/default/files /assets/documents/2018-Jan/fieldops-trusted-traveler-fact-sheet-201510.pdf). More than ten thousand companies are validated in the C-TPAT cargo security program. "C-TPAT Reaches 10,000 Members," *Frontline Magazine* 4, no. 1 (Winter 2011): 5 (https://www.cbp .gov/sites/default/files/documents/frontline_vol4_issue1.pdf). On the international front, CBP has developed and continues to strengthen supply-chain security through "mutual recognition agreements" with trusted partners in cargo to include Canada, the European Union, Japan, Jordan, Korea, and New Zealand. CBP has nonbinding trusted-traveler agreements with Brazil, Canada, Germany, Korea, Mexico, the Netherlands, Qatar, and the United Kingdom. See Susan Holliday, "Global Entry Takes Off: Private-Sector Support Fuels Boost in Frequent Flier Program," *Frontline Magazine* 4, no. 1 (Winter 2011): 11 (https://www.cbp.gov/sites/default/files/documents/frontline_vol4_issue1.pdf).

69. See U.S. Customs and Border Protection, "C-TPAT: Overview," accessed February 26, 2012 (no longer posted) (http://www.cbp.gov/xp/cgov/trade/cargo_security/ctpat /what_ctpata/ctpata_overview.xml).

70. Other species of these trusted-partner programs include Free and Secure Trade (FAST) and Importer Self-Assessment employed by Centers of Excellence and Expertise (CEE).

71. Alan Bersin, "Trump Just Might Be Giving Us the Opportunity to Make NAFTA Even Stronger," *Dallas Morning News*, June 7, 2017 (https://www.dallasnews.com/opinion /commentary/2017/06/07/trump-just-might-giving-us-opportunity-make-nafta-even -stronger).

72. Alan D. Bersin, "Cross Border Economies: A Blueprint for North American Competitiveness," in *Regional Insights—William J. Perry Center for Hemispheric Defense Studies*, 3rd. ed. (Washington D.C.: National Defense University, 2013).

73. Anthony St. Peter, ed., *The Greatest Quotations of All Time* (Bloomington, Ind.: Xlibris, 2010), 264.

Border Governance in North America

PART III

Border Governance in North America

CHAPTER 7

Borders in Globalization

The Twenty-First-Century Globalization and Border Governance

EMMANUEL BRUNET-JAILLY

Introduction

In this era of global trade and connectivity at the beginning of the twenty-first century, the geopolitical governance of borders is shifting from territorial bordering to regional and possibly global bordering through functional connectivity. New border governance forms have appeared that have yet to be entirely understood by the literature on border studies. While much of the recent literature suggests that "borderscaping" is the leading concept to understand borders, borderlands, and cross-border cooperation, others focus on Ōmae's ideas of a borderless world of trade, Chen's bending border because of timescale transformation (Ōmae 1990; Chen 2005), Balibar's (2002, 217–18) suggestion of vacillating borders, Amilhat Szary's concept of mobile borders (Amilhat Szary and Giraud 2015), and Konrad's (2015) views on mobile borders, the governance of which remain somewhat unexplored. The borders, discussed in this chapter, organize the connectivity of noncontiguous territories between countries' chains of production, good and services, and labor markets with the rest of the world. These borders connect resources countries, countries of origin, to industrial centers, which turn raw material into goods that are then destined for other countries' markets, such as Western European or North America consumer markets, among others. China's Road and Belt Initiative (RBI) is such an extraordinary example today because of the size of the investments, nearly one trillion dollars, and the number of countries involved worldwide, nearly seventy. Indeed, China's RBI is particularly interesting because it is so ambitious and so controversial, but also because of the sheer size of the connectivity infrastructure developments necessary for the completion of this worldwide program linking seaports to railways, highways, and airports but also connecting production sites to Chinese custom warehouses and in the process developing connectivity infrastructures between noncontiguous countries. Hence, China's borders will be extended beyond China's territoriality. Some have argued that a new *connectography* is at the dawn of the future of global civilization (Khanna 2016). Khanna suggests it may be driven by a globalizing economy or simply by the globalizing world of information and communication. For instance, Facebook has nearly three billion friends, and there are more cell phones than humans in the world today!

This short chapter is organized in four sections: the first section is a history that emphasizes the territoriality of border governance. The second part examines center-periphery questions, suggesting that border issues mirror culture and nationalism in their construction of the sovereign nation-state. Contemporary views on borders and frontiers are discussed in the third part, which underscores the border as a territorial container rooted in territoriality, sovereign culture, and politics. In the final section, I reflect on China's current RBI to illustrate my central argument: in the twenty-first-century, borders are either territorial or they are functional. When they are functional, then they are aterritorial as detailed below. Hence, in the twenty-first century, the governance of borders can be individual, local, and cross-border at the level of a region, a state, or a vast territory encompassing many states—these remain power containers. They have the nature of premodern "castle walls." Borders, and border governance, can also be worldwide. In such an instance, they are often highly focused on one single area, industry, or sector, as is the case in North America, where industrial regulatory mechanisms straddle international boundaries and organize trade flows and human mobility according to exceptions to the territorial trap assumption. The borders of those industries are inscribed in their production process, which both contain and allow their flows and mobility.

Looking at China's strategy in the construction of the RBI, I ask whether it is the first time in the history of the modern era of states that a modern state, such as China at the beginning of the twenty-first century, is investing around the world to secure not just its territorial and maritime borders but also the construction and governance of its own infrastructures of globalization.

These are infrastructures and borders of its own connectivity with the rest of the world; they are the borders of noncontiguous states. Indeed, what we are witnessing is the progressive development of China's own bordering infrastructures across the world that organize the entry and exit of every port of entry into the global Chinese nexus. These are not territorialized borders. These are functional borders with small territorial anchorages. This chapter documents this new geopolitical object and discusses how, in their various manifestations, the borders of globalization are affecting China's One Road, One Belt (OROB) or Belt and Road Initiative (BRI), and thus other borders, for instance, in North America.

History of Borders

The history of humanity is only a few thousand years old. Humans similar to twenty-first-century humans appeared only about ten thousand years ago at a time, known as the agrarian revolution, when technological changes allowed foraging societies to settle. Anthropologists suggest that when humans planted seeds, they also became agrarian; seeding and harvesting follow seasons, and they require a sedentary lifestyle (Schmidt 2011, 917; Vigne 2000). Our very first known cities only appear about 4,500–6,500 years ago (Urukm, Erida, Jericho). The first walled city may have been Jericho in 6500 BC. Borders are human creations and an expression of humans' deep-seated desire to control and exploit their environment (Charpin 1995; Parker 2003). The idea of a boundary line is possibly as old as the first walled city, some of which may have appeared about 12,000 years ago (Göbekli Tepe is tenth century BC), when humanity very progressively started to become less migratory and more sedentary.

Early civilizations, for instance the Mesopotamian Sumer civilization, a primary mathematical civilization (like the Mayans), had detailed records of seeding and harvesting that numbered exactly seeding procedures as well as watering and also recorded harvesting. Although rare, records of territorial disputes appear during this early civilization. For instance, the first ever Sumerian record of a settled dispute between two cities, the *Stele of Vulture* (held in parts at the British Museum, London, and the Louvre, Paris), discusses a peace treaty signed by the cities Lagash and Umma about 3,700 years ago specifically over water and territorial possession at a time when Sumerian cities had been so effective at irrigating and harvesting their land possessions (Winter 1985).

Excessive erosion, unfortunately, progressively increased the levels of salinity in the ground, which affected harvest negatively and finally undermined the existence of the whole civilization over a period of two hundred years around 2000 BC.

From our perspective, borders appeared with the walls of this city-based civilization. Indeed, it is during the Sumer civilization that human settlements are built into cities and inside fortified walls. Also, what may be surprising is that such an early civilization had developed technologies and knowledges to identify and record their territorial possessions. Particularly notable is that walls were not always the appropriate technology to control territorial possessions at the peripheries of their cities; as illustrated by the *Stele of Vulture*, international treaties became the chosen technology to settle a territorial difference after a lost war. The specific case of Lagash and Umma is notable because the rule of law seems to be the first technology available to go beyond walls; to identify, record, and attribute a disputed territory; to establish a boundary line and transfer this knowledge on a stele (1.8 m. high, 1.3 m. wide, and about 11 cm thick). Clearly, as early as nearly 4,000 years ago, as the *Stele of Vulture* demonstrates to us, the rule of law was, as it remains to our day, the prime mechanism to identify, record, and attribute possession of land. Today, the same applies to sea and air boundaries as well; the United Nations keeps a repertory of hundreds of boundary treaties to this effect.

However, to this day, walls, such as Hadrian's Wall in northern England (built by the Roman emperor Hadrian, starting in AD 122) or the Great Wall of China (started about 2,700 years ago but rebuilt about 900 years ago), and maps, such as Ptolemy's map, made by a Grecque philosopher of the second century, also contributed greatly to the identification of land and then to both land and ownership. It is remarkable, though, that privatization of land in England, for instance, is only about 800 years old. In England and Wales the earliest, so-called *Greatest Survey* of land ownership was published as part of the Domesday Book of 1086 (Giles and Ingram 1996). It details who the landowners are, how land is distributed, and who pays taxes to the crown; lords, Norman conquerors, are the rightful tenants of the crown so they pay taxes to the crown. Private ownership then does not exist yet. The second "modern" Domesday Book, published in 1873, which is also called *Return of Owners of Land*, presents a very different picture of crown and of public and private ownership of land. Thus, until recently, land is the possession of the crown, and borders delineate crown land. What is particularly interesting to us is that at the time, delineation for the purpose of records remains difficult because of technological challenges; maps are approximate and drafted thanks to astronomy, and treaties walk the reader along the boundary line and do not make reference to maps.

Two technological innovations affected this situation. One can be found with a legal conceptual change. Indeed, most specialists point to the two Treaties of Westphalia of 1648, which settled peace between the Spanish crown and Dutch republics and their mutual allies, as the generally accepted turning point in the history of international relations and the beginning of our modern era of states. Those treaties settled the Hundred Years' Wars but also established the basis for the mutual recognition of powers (empires, kingdoms, duchies, and republics), whereby they were able to impose their will, including violence, onto their people and their land and territories including their conquests, yet they were not to interfere within each other's internal affairs. This is understood as sovereignty and noninterference (i.e., no interference or intrusion in internal affairs) but also as respect of territorial integrity and borders. Indeed, historians and lawyers go back to Westphalia to document the first international agreements because the modern era of states marks the emergence and recognition of the international community of states as the prime actors of the international system. This modern era also witnesses the generalization of the use of treaties between formally warring nations to negotiate peace and the idea that foes can become friends in peace periods.

At the time of Westphalia, most treaties, as they established the territory of powers, also literally described the boundary line. The treaty texts walk the reader along the boundary line because at the time, treaties were not yet able to use cartographic technology to precisely map out the location of the line that detailed the exact location of the boundary line. Often, treaties made references to the specific aspects of human or physical geography to ensure that the boundary line is refereed in the treaty. It is only after the development of the clock (and then the GPS in the 1950s) that boundary lines became particularly precise because they did not rely only on the compass, the chain, the transit, or theodolite on land, and the compass, the sextant, and the Harrison chronometer at sea, the latter of which allowed for a measurement of both latitude and longitude with a level of precision never known before in the history of humanity. Indeed, in the late 1700s, British, French, and Spanish kings had offered awards to whoever would find out how to calculate longitude at sea. Ships had used dead reckoning for centuries, a process by which one relied on the previous position to determine the current one. This led to many inexact calculations, in particular with bad weather. Navigators would sail along coasts using their sextant and compass to locate the appropriate latitude and then would, for instance, cross the Atlantic Ocean by "running a westing," or going westbound. But finding both latitude and longitude was very difficult. These techniques had issues with time and winds that made traveling all the more slow and dangerous.

The second technological change is the invention of the Harrison clock, which made the calculation of the longitude precise, made navigation much safer, but also led to much more exact territorial and maritime maps (Sobel 1995). By the end of the First World War, maps are precise enough that the Paris Peace Convention and the subsequent Treaty of Versailles are turning points because maps then become references for negotiations and a part of the treaty process. In her book *Paris 1919*, Margaret McMillan documents how "aggrandized" maps were use during the convention negotiation and how the convention had to send ambassadors and geographers to review submitted documents (McMillan 2001). Indeed, some of the powers attempted to aggrandize their own possessions and have them recorded in the treaty.

Versailles led to a generalization of the precise documentation of the worldly possessions of the winning parties; for the study of borders, this is an important historical turning point because with Versailles, maps become a second technology used by humans to systematically survey boundary lines. Versailles also marks the beginning of the worldwide documentation of territorial possessions, which then expands the usage both of treaties and maps in the delineation of worldly territorial possessions. Indeed, thanks to colonization, territories around the world that were possessions of Western European kingdoms or empires were documented both in law and in maps.

Similarly, China's territorial borders are extensively documented in historical works that underscore the power of unitary force and the role of the military in containing and expanding its borderlands over the centuries. Indeed, China's borderlands were still in flux until very recently (Howland 1996). In particular, China's borderlands were always in flux along with the fifty-five minorities that lived at the periphery of historical empires (Harrell 1995; Endymion 2000). During the early Qin and the Han eras (Tang, Song, Ming, and Quing dynasties), the borderlands of China remained borderlands and frontiers (Howland 1996). Indeed, the Qin era unifies territory and the centrality of power, law, and the military. The Han period never really undermined those foundations. In *The Chinese State at the Borders*, for instance, Diana Lary questions the current view that China's borders have always been, since about the third century BC, as they are today. Her collection carefully documents how "most of the current borderlands were not fully incorporated into the Chinese state until the eighteenth century, in a process that stretched the center to its limits—a process usefully described as 'imperial overreach'" (Lary 2007). The Vietnam-Indochina border was settled in 1894. Interestingly, confusions about this border have led China into armed conflict with Russia as recently as 1969. Indeed, the thalweg dispute regarding the northeastern Heilongjiang-Amur River was born from a misunderstanding that it divided a region when in winter it freezes over and becomes a major trade flow throughway; this was not resolved until ratification in April and May 2005.

When Japan's specialist of the Chinese Russian border, Akihiro Iwashita, published *A 4000 Kilometer Journey Along the Sino-Russian Border* in 2004, he documented increased activities on the Chinese side of the border, including along the Heilongjian River. He notes that China does not represent a threat anymore but that China is also emerging out of a long period of humiliation, which for Iwashita (contrary to Clancy's [2000] claims in *The Bear and the Dragon*) clarifies that it is nationalism that explains China's claims regarding land and seas borders, the restoration of Hong Kong and Macau, and China's position regarding Taiwan and a number of islands in the north and south China Sea (Iwashita 2004).

Clearly, historical disputes about borderlands become boundary disputes with time. That was also the case with China and Russia concerning the islands of Zhenbao and Tarabarov. Only 50 percent of Bolshoy Ussuriysky Island (Heixiazi Island) became Chinese. The 2005 peace agreement led to the creation of the Sino-Russian Border Line Agreement and the detailed demarcation of the boundary, but an agreement about the eastern boundary line was only signed in July 2008.

In sum, over the centuries, humans settled and harnessed control over land, space, and territories very progressively. In China, borderlands have been contested for centuries by numerous populations indigenous to those peripheral regions of the successive Chinese empires. Indeed, despite technological advances and general knowledge about the location and sometime demarcation of borders, borderlands become boundary lines very progressively. In China it is only very recently that contested land borders have been settled thanks to international agreements. Clearly such slow progress in the demarcation and delineation of borders has implication for our understanding of the governance of borders. Most border experts make references to concepts that acknowledge the spatiality and territory of the borderland. In North America, historians and political geographers point to this shift from border and boundary delineation; the Alaska Boundary, the Beaufort Sea, the Dixon Entrance, the Machias Seal Island and North Rock, and the Portland Canal remain unresolved positional disputes. In all cases the contention is the exact location of the boundary line, which in the treaties and maps is unclear. The next section further explores this spatially bound governance.

Center-Periphery Culture, Nationalism, and Politics of Place of Cross-Border Cooperation

As illustrated above, a geopolitics of borders leads us to focus on where the boundary line is precisely. But borders are not just about bordering at the margins of territoriality; they are also mechanisms of social differentiation as well as borders of hybridity or liminalities. The questions they raise are also part of the academic debate. Those are the borders of "us and others" whereby marginality is also understood as privileged and as constitutive of the center. Hybridity is another idea that underlines the transformative nature of the border as culture or territory of multiplicity; it is Bhabha's (1994) hybrid cultural borderlands of the postcolonial condition.

For Bhabha, as suggested elsewhere (Brunet-Jailly 2017b), essentialist historically homogeneous cultural traditions disregard the hybrid confrontational discussions necessary to the formation of cultural narratives as they produce singular cultural narratives. The border as liminality is a condition in between two others. An idea first explored in the anthropological studies of rites of passage, it was then expanded to include senses that identity could also emerge out of liminal experiences. Today, it is important to also understand social change (Van Gennep 1977; Turner 1967; Rumelili 2012; Malksoo 2012). For Bhabha (1994, 3), there is a distinction between hybridity and liminality, "the interrogatory, interstitial space." He writes, "The liminal figure of the nation-space would ensure that no political ideologies could claim transcendent or metaphysical authority for themselves. This is because the subject of cultural discourse—the agency of people—is split in the discursive ambivalences that emerge in the contest of narrative authority" (Bhabha 1994, 148). In other words, we need to understand the *cultural in-betweenness* of the postorientalist and postcolonialist world. The agency of communities depends on translational and transnational processes of production of meanings whereby borders are human territorial interfaces, marginal spaces of human consciousness and hybridity (Xie 1996). They are spaces of cooperation and confrontation of social and economic relations and where great environmental issues, such as natural reserves and peace parks, exemplify the liminality of postmodern borderlands.

Borders are also understood as socially and culturally charged forms of differentiations. Borders then may be individual or collective and vary in time while being spatial by exception; this is the process by which bordering is not only "ordering" but is also "othering" (Van Houtum, Kramsch, and Zierhofer, 2005).

Much literature focuses on the daily lives of borderlanders to illustrate both ordering and othering and their reverse processes. In many instances this is within and across territories, but it is also in cultural and literary studies focusing on ethnicity, religious belonging, age, gender, sense of belonging, and how the liminalities of cultures foster such changes across time and also sometimes across spaces. Doreen Massey discusses power geometries to question how unequal individuals are in the face of the movement and flows of the current era of globalization, and her work premises ideas by Walters and Rumford that borders are like computer firewalls—filtering movements with intelligence (Massey 1993, 1994a, 1994b; Walters 2006; Rumford 2008).

Thus, the literature engages in rather broad debates about borders as cultural praxis, everyday life constructions of the self and others, as well as various forms of regional and national bordering weaving of the emotions participating in the tapestry of identity and meaning formation. Hence, there are many narratives: historical yet changing, fluid, contextual, and sometimes spatial. Narratives of bordering are multiple, Janus-faced, real in the daily practices of borderlanders, but also real in the souvenirs, or imagined representation of borders. Some focus on borders as power containers allowing for homogenization to take place territorially, while for others bordering takes place in liminal, yet nonterritorial, spaces whereby hybridity and homogeneity are negotiated. For political scientist Benedict Anderson, these phenomena take place within imagined communities and across processes of deterritorialization and reterritorialization (Anderson 1983); today this work remains fundamental to our understanding of nationalisms, yet work on virtual communities is also pointing to the absence of territoriality of some of the contemporary movements of nationalism (Hodge 2018).

States as power containers and containers of national identities remain another important strand in border studies. In the post-Westphalia order, the modern states system inscribes itself within political philosophies that justify states' territorial formations and humanities' allegiance to rulers or religions as God's will. Nation building and state development go hand in hand with borders, along with principles of sovereignty, noninterference, and exclusive exercise of violence over one's own people. During the 1980s, ideas of borderlessness occupied the center stage of discussion on the globalizing world and the further fragmentation of some large and postdecolonialized states such as various regions of the Soviet Union and the Eastern Bloc. The literature on state border disputes focuses on two of three categories of disputes, positional and functional disputes, that have nearly completely disappeared thanks to case law developments since the Second World War that grounds dispute resolutions in international treaties and principles of fairness. But overall this literature misses the point that territorial disputes are the most relevant explanation of territorial fragmentation worldwide and of the proliferation of wars; both of these phenomena are documented today (Brunet-Jailly 2017a). Territorial disputes as a demography of states also point to John Agnew's idea of the territorial trap and to the idea of rarefication of territory. States' territories—thanks to fragmentation and further subdivision, and thanks to decentralization of states' powers and functions to lower-level governments and political communities—are further fragmenting. The increasing linkages from local to global are also challenges to states as social containers in particular because of virtual communities such as found on the web, including such virtual platforms as Facebook or Twitter (Agnew 1994).

For instance, this literature addresses issues current to the postcolonial era of the previous century, a period of decolonization and of vast expansion of the membership in the international community. Indeed, between 1950 and 2000, the United Nations membership tripled, snowballing the total number of members of the international community from about 50 to about 190 in a period of much uncertainty and negotiation and renegotiation of both states and nations. It was a period that affected both the postcolonial and the formerly colonizing world. Illustrations abound. The European Union is a good example, in particular regarding comments and criticisms of it as being a *non-imperial-empire* in which twenty-eight countries willingly pooled their sovereignties (Barros 2007; Mahony 2007; Zielonka 2006), while in 1991 the former Soviet Union disintegrated into Russia and fourteen other countries (Armenia, Azerbaijan, Belorussia, Estonia, Georgia, Kazakhstan, Kyrgyzstan, Latvia, Lithuania, Moldova, Tajikistan, Turkmenistan, Ukraine, and Uzbekistan).

As this brief review of the literature illustrates, besides a geopolitics of borders, border studies have traditionally focused on their territorial stasis—in particular on the cultural, political, and social "territoriality" of borders—as the spatial, territorialized outcomes of those manifestation, that shapes, subdivides, fragments, privatizes, and settles territories. Certainly this is evident in the reappearance of border barriers outside of and around Israel since the 1990s and standing at about 16.4 percent of all borders worldwide (with 32,891 km of walls built worldwide since 9/11). This is about twice as many kilometers of borders as had been estimated by Michel Foucher in 2007 (Foucher 2007; Vallet 2014).

In China, one exemplary manifestation of such studies focuses on the situation of peripheral ethnolinguistic minorities: the Indonesian, Tungusic, Mongolian, Turkic, Korean, Mon-Kmer, Tajik, Miao-Yao, Tibeto-Burman, Tai, and Hui, minorities, for example. To this day, about 80 percent of the Uyghurs live in the northwestern part of Southwest China across the Tarin Basin, which is nested into the Tien Shan mountain range and borders with Kazakhstan, Kyrgyzstan, Pakistan, and India and Tibet in the south. Significant numbers of Uyghurs have settled internationally but in particular in Kazakhstan, Kyrgyzstan, Uzbekistan, and Turkey (Shichor 2009). In China, fears of Islamic terrorism have led to now well-documented policies of monitoring the Uyghurs. Reeducation camps, DNA and biometric capture, and general policing access to cities in the region have led to diplomatic concerns being voiced by both the European Union and the United States. China stands by policies of reeducation necessary to reeducate possibly hundreds of thousands Uyghurs because of extremism. The policy of *de-extremification* started in 2014; it was mentioned for the first time by Xinjiang Province former party secretary Zhang Chunxian in 2012 (Zenz 2018). In North America, such research also documents the rise of border policies that wall and divide the Spanish-speaking people who live in the borderlands of the southern United States and northern Mexico; the borders of hybridity turn into borders of exclusion. The following section, focusing on the territoriality versus functionality duality of borders, further discusses this contemporary literature.

Frontiers: Today's Spatially Bound Governance

Over the last fifty years, scholarly production in border studies has followed an upward trend with a peak in the 1970s and again a much greater interest since September 11, 2001. Today, about two thousand academics study borders worldwide, and there are three overlapping networks that regroup them:

African Border Network (ABORNE),[1] Border Regions In Transition (BRIT),[2] and the Association for Borderlands Studies (ABS).[3] ABORNE network brings together Africanists. BRIT regroups primarily political geographers with interests in borderlands and border regions in Europe, but the network's biennial conferences have traveled to Latin America, Asia, Africa, and North America. ABS is by far the largest of the three networks, with quadrennial conference peaks of 550 members, regional groups in Europe and Japan, a traditional group in North America, and a publication with Routledge, the *Journal of Borderlands Studies*. These networks bring together scholars from about seventy countries.

This community of scholars generally agrees that the study of borders, boundaries, borderlands, border regions, and frontiers in our post–World War II era primarily focuses on a broadly defined understanding that borders are primarily cultural manifestations of human activities that fuel issues of nationalism and cosmopolitanisms, therefore of a geopolitical nature and continually in construction in a process that has been described as being from borders to bordering. These research views continually assess the role of states as containers of human activities against other such forces as the multiple manifestations of border-scaping communities.[4]

During the 1970s through the 1990s, border studies focused primarily on discussing the idea that the globalized world was also becoming borderless (Ōmae 1990), while at the same time much practical work focused on boundary delineation and disputes resolution. The International Borders Research Unit (IBRU) at Durham University remains the point of reference for border delineation training and boundary dispute resolution. The work of the IBRU founder Gerald Blake and a small team have helped resolve and document dozens of dispute cases. In Asia, the great specialist on China's boundary lines, Akihiro Iwashita, wrote his PhD dissertation on the resolution of delineation of all the Chinese dyads. His core argument was that China's view was that clean, noncontroversial lines dividing contested territories equally were a necessary trade-off for peace. Interestingly, this is also one of the International Court of Justice principles: *infra-legem*—that is, to apply strict equity in the division of land or sea across any kind of disputes of delineation cases.

These point to the assertive role of states as sovereign members of the international community and underline the never-ending bordering processes that make and unravel borders. For instance, in his latest book on Japanese borders, Iwashita (2016) reasserts "realism" as the only explanation for border policy, but his argument is that local borderland communities may also have a say in what are geopolitical border disputes between China, Korea, Japan, and Russia. Iwashita's argument underscores that history, in particular the post–Cold War period, should not be the frame of reference for those disputes. On the contrary, Iwashita reasons, the core determinants of those dispute resolutions should be found away from a nationalist framing regarding, for instance, the case of Okinawa (the Futenma issue). In brief, it is the well-being of local island communities and their immediate natural environment that should drive dispute resolution discussions.

Maritime disputes further illustrate those difficulties. The Nine-Dash Line in the South China Sea has been and remains, despite a decision by the Permanent Court of Arbitration,[5] an important reminder that the territorial and maritime borders of China are a work in progress. As land boundary delineation has been settled for the most part, maritime border delineations are not nearly as close to resolutions. All in all, the whole issue of the Nine-Dash Line is a concern in the South China Sea for six members of the international community (Brunei, Indonesia, Malaysia, Philippines, Taiwan, Vietnam) in a number of areas including islands and rocks but also shoals, a strait, and a gulf: the Spratly, Paracel, Natura, Patras, and Woody Islands; the Luzon strait; the Scarborough and James Shoals; the Sabah area; and the Tonkin Gulf. Similarly, in the northeast seas, the East China Sea is also an area where China has maritime delineation disputes with both South Korea and Japan. These are concerns regarding Exclusive Economic Zones that expand up to two hundred miles off the coast of each member of the international community. They include the Okinawa Trough and the Chunxiao gas field with Japan (shared exploitation since 2008) and the Socotra Rock with South Korea.

During the same period, however, border studies literature explored new ways to conceptualize bordering not only as a realist geopolitical endeavor but as a cultural process. Cultural geographers are at the forefront here as border studies is enriched by new interdisciplinary knowledge and perspectives from anthropology, sociology, culture, literature, and media studies.[6] An early attempt by Brunet-Jailly (2005a) suggested a need to look at borders from four interdisciplinary perspectives as lenses of analysis to understand cross-border relations and integration across borderlands. These, together, view borders as resulting from overlapping processes and tensions between structural and agent-led factors; they point to cultural (linguistic, ethnic, religious) and political factors but also geopolitical and institutional or economic forces as determinants of bordering processes and cross-border relations. They question past understandings of what borders are and how bordering as a process may lead to boundary lines. One important contribution in this regard is the publication of *The Ashgate Research Companion to Border Studies* (Wastl-Walter 2016), which underscores the importance of comparative social science enquiry in border studies. The subsequent publication by Chiara Brambilla (2015), "Exploring the Critical Potential of the Borderscapes Concept," asserts the conceptual proposition that "borderscapes" is an ideal way to free geopolitical imagination from the burden of "territorialist imperatives." The borderscapes concept has been at the core of the EUBorderscapes research program, led by Finnish scholar James Scott and his research team, which includes Brambilla. Borderscapes are understood as *social/political panoramas*—similar to Appadurai's ethnoscapes, technoscapes, or mediascapes—that are assumed to be part of our "global cultural flows" and the "imagined worlds." In other words, Brambilla and Scott's interpretation is that borderscapes are not necessarily territorialized but are in parts deterritorialized and thus not forced by states' sovereign and bounded spaces or by states' territoriality. As Chiara Brambilla and Johan Schimanski (2017, 52) suggest in the final report of EUBorderscape, the concept "adds to bordering the spatial and sensible components of power."

Hence, the literature on borders today defends an epistemology whereby *territorial logic* is making inroads that underscore the complexity of the cultural, social, and political *scapes* that are taking place, that overlap, and that challenge (or not) states' scapes. These are relatively stable yet always unstable manifestations of our imaginaries and cultural, social, and political scapes. They are grounded in territorial, or spatial, logic that is foundational to human communities and their many and diverse cultural, social, and political expressions, but they are not specifically bound to states' territorialities. The governance of borderscapes may result and expand from territorially bound cross-border cooperation, but it can also result from numerous other human cultural activities. Thus, they are not so much about movement, mobility or flows, as they are always being renegotiated across territories, overlapping and superimposing each other, and hence their national, or the opposite, their cosmopolitan manifestations. Hence, the form "scapes" take within single bounded states or more complex borderlands and border regions, but also possibly across larger regions across many states and spaces and territories. They express the power of nations within states and across states' boundaries, and they are also as many challenges to states as they are the "scapes' expression" of the various manifestations of their many nations.

What those researchers are not doing is looking at the role of flows in and out of states or the role of flows, mobility, and connectivity in fashioning and transforming States scapes and including local (border, land, and island) communities as points of entry or exit. They do not really account for sea or land ports—as areas of negotiation between trade flows and their mobile communities (e.g., truck drivers)—or virtual communities—as points of mediation of information and cell phone users/laborers—to question the transformation taking place at the juncture of the mobile and the territorial worlds.

Earlier attempts to size up the role of borders in spaces of flows versus spaces of places suggest borders are "vacillating" (Balibar 2002) because they are not at the border anymore, because they are demultiplied in both their localization and their functions or in "motion" because they accommodate the opening and closing of territory in particular because space of places have become spaces of flows (Konrad 2015, 4), or because they are "mobile" because of their new "portativity and a change focus toward the individual and his/her personalization of a mobile device" (Amilhat-Szary 2015, 1). In brief, those scholars suggest that borders are demultiplied, they accommodate spatial motion, and they have become portable.

None of those research dimensions and theorizations, however, document and explain the role of borders between the local and the global, the noncontiguous connectivities, the instrumentalization of points of entry and exit, while at the same time there is much evidence of a hardening of all territorial borders as well (Vallet 2014, 1–4). These occurrences suggest a paradigmatic change that underscores the rise of functional aterritorial borders and border governance.

China's Twenty-First-Century Overarching Governance of Borders

Obviously, these "new" borders of globalization are progressively being established. This is happening now, in our post–information-communication revolution era of increased but partial globalization. Like a puzzle in the making, the infrastructures and institutions of the borders of globalization are appearing in various geographies around world, and they are not apparent everywhere.

The Belt and Road Initiative (BRI), also known as One Belt One Road, symbolizes land routes as the "Belt" and maritime sea routes as the "Road." The initiative has been criticized for being a China-centered network of trade.

The official Chinese position is that it is Chinese style multilateralism, whereby infrastructures of connectivity will streamline an already very integrated economy into the rest of the world. The BRI takes stock of the level of integration of China's economy in Asia and other multilateral cooperation around the world. For instance President Xi Jinping acknowledged that BRI would lead to "economic connectivity and a new-type of industrialization in the Asia Pacific area, and promote the common development of all countries as well as people's joint enjoyment of development fruits" (Wang Huning 2015) Indeed, on the one hand, China's total trade with the countries involved in the BRI exceeds three trillion annually while contributing nearly two million jobs and over one billion in revenues to its many partners (XinhuaNet 2019). Its strategy seems to be coherent with past Chinese initiatives responsible for the oversizing of infrastructures to bolster economic development. However, such strategies are known to help development, as is the case with the European Union Regional Development Funds or, in China, with the development of long-term investment in transportation infrastructures to enhance the country's attractiveness (*Economist* Intelligence Unit 2017). RBI is particularly well set to promote three areas of cooperation—trade, energy, and information communication technologies—with the goal of creating seamless connectivity across all three infrastructure sectors. Three types of financing are available—grants, interest free loans, and concession loans—that have services backed by natural resources such as oil or coal backed loans. The unusual strength of such worldwide infrastructural development is that it creates complex and insulated trading corridors connecting resource extraction sites with industrial plants in China, and out of China, it links finished products to destination markets in Europe or North America, among others. All in all, sixty thousand kilometers of roads; dozens of container-ship harbors; and rail lines, mines, and transportation platforms have been expanded and modernized in at least seventy countries according to Chinese standards.[7]

To advance its positions, critics have argued, China is also reviewing the rule systems and tribunals in place to adjudicate disputes.[8] The Schengen Court of International Arbitration and Hong Kong Mediation Center have agreed to cooperate mediation processes while at the same time relying on preexisting enforcement mechanisms set by the Hague Convention on the Recognition of Foreign Judgements ("Comments on China's International Commercial Courts" 2018). Also, it seems the ambition goes beyond trade, for instance, for Jonathan Hillman of the Reconnecting Asia project at CSIS, the extension to a military presence is very real. Similarly, the European Union notes the importance of advising and working with EU partners to implement connectivity and security together. The EU Joint Communication of September 2018 notes "transportation security" matters in a document that details the EU strategy with regard to the flow of goods with European destinations (European Commission 2018, 4).

In sum, China is implementing noncontiguous borders across a worldwide network of infrastructures of connectivity that link trade, transportation, information communication, and security matters, and it is not the only world power with this ambition. It is, however, by far the most visible one thanks to the size and scope of investments. Similar ambitions also exist in Europe and North America but at smaller scales.

Where are these borders of globalization visible? The borders of globalization are noticeable in a variety of spaces but not just in borderlands because they instrumentalize power relations between the very diverse actors of the international community and local communities. They can be found in traditional borderlands and border regions, at the limits of those territories, but they are also apparent in the confines of states territories, in airports or seaports, or simply within the production plants or along the production chains of industries that seek to maximize economies of scale thanks to alignment with regulatory and free-trade regimes. Hence, they also take the form of product or service standards. Their limits are rarely aligned with the international boundaries of states, which they straddle and sometime overlap and encompass. They follow the functional logics of the products or services they differentiate, include, and shield beyond states' territorialities. They have understudied spatial logics.[9]

Although the debate goes on, it is not the first time in history that scholars have defended the idea that periods of globalization follow periods of technological change. The current period may be facing its own dawn with the rise of various forms of nativism and nationalism in the Western world, but since the beginning of the Industrial Revolution in the early nineteenth century, major technological changes have led to much economic growth as well as the expansion of global exchanges. Also, the current nativist and nationalist debates are not found around the same rhetoric concerning Asia. China's Belt and Road Initiative and its Belt and Road Forum for International Cooperation, for instance, have resulted in expanding and privatizing numerous transportation corridors—roads, rail lines, and seaports—around the word to implement infrastructures of connectivity that match the Venetian maritime silk road thanks to one to two trillion dollars of investments across the world that result in the superimposition of regional and international infrastructures of air, sea, and land mobility for the transportation of goods and people on traditional national infrastructures across seventy countries.[10]

In one of his very first international presentations of the program at the World Economic Forum in Davos, January 17, 2017, H. E. Xi Jinping (2017), president of the People's Republic of China, made it clear that his goal was to connect the "developing world where 80% of the world growth was taking place as a result of economic globalization, . . . growing social productivity, and . . . natural outcome of scientific and technological progress" was not the result of individuals or specific countries but of multiple scientific, social, and capitalistic advances. Hence, BRI worldwide partnership with a goal of about one hundred countries and organizations (of which forty had then already signed forty cooperation agreements in 2017). The RBI organizes trade and trade facilitation along six major economic corridors connecting China to the rest of Asia, the Middle East, Africa, and finally Europe (Ramasamy et al. 2017). The estimated cost of $1 trillion per year is in line with the estimates of the Asian Development Bank of $1.7 trillion per year suggested to maintain growth, tackle poverty and address climate change (Perlez and Huang 2017). Ultimately the BRI is about cutting transportation costs between China and the rest of the world. It is about reducing the costs of mobility. It is about aligning standards and erasing regulatory barriers to trade. It is to connect China to the rest of the world thanks to global infrastructures dismantling regulatory standards and transportation borders: it is about implementing globalizing infrastructures that connect China to the rest of the world, from primary markets to tertiary markets, connecting production chains across territories, and to markets worldwide. Other states, such as the United States, and political unions, such as the European Union, are also implementing the new requirements of the global world with new regulatory systems and ports of entry and exit connecting territories with the rest of the world. The vectors of this transformation are found in trade relations and migrations.

Obviously, as suggested in this chapter, China is implementing these instruments of globalization across the world. Indeed, China's $2 trillion Belt and Road Initiative has multiplied public-private partnerships in more than seventy countries today. It results in various forms of privatization of harbors, train lines, roads, and airports, but also in the construction of new cities, multimodal transportation platforms that link and connect Chinese trade with the rest of the world and connect the world to China. It extends from mines to industries and industrial plants to markets while also implementing new legal regimes and relying on information communication technologies with important implementation implications, in particular with regard to monitoring and surveillance.

Conclusion: New Borders, New Governance Forms

There are very few scholars who have studied from the perspective of border studies or who have raised questions regarding the implications of mobility and flows on border functions that result from market and human activities globally. Indeed, the great majority of publications are about issues of border territoriality. The works of Kenishi Ōmae, for instance, in particular the suggestion of a borderless world or of the end of the nation-state, or similarly, the work of Xianming Chen on border bending because of timescale transformation, remain viewed as farfetched. The literature points to the relative stability of migrations and trade flows and the strength of national sentiments, but it is with unease that the literature admits that boundary lines are no longer "the only lines of delimitating the territory of a state and its territorial waters" (Kolossov 2012). Indeed, there is growing literature and debate concerning the nature of borders that broach illustrations of rebordering in the post–Cold War era (Andreas and Biersteker 2003; Andreas and Snyder 2000) and ideas that borders are vacillating (Balibar 1998) or are mobile or in motion at the dawn of the twenty-first century (Szary and Giraut 2015). Much of that literature focuses on mobility and security but does not look at the phenomena of mobility and flows or of security as leading to an epistemological alteration of our understanding of what borders are, changes that have fraught consequences for human mobility.

There is of course another side to this argument: the *mobile logic*, which does not mean that borders are mobile or in motion or vacillating but that the borders of globalization, the borders of flows and of mobility, are now primarily functional. In that sense, they remain spatial but are not as territorial as borderscapes because their services are primarily to delineate mobile function: a trading or migratory function, a product or service function, the functions of multiple service providers, ultimately a mobility right of entry and exit between primary origin and final destination. The territoriality of border remains but is superimposed by diverse, invisible, aterritorial functions such as legal regime changes.

These borders of globalization are much less stable than territorially grounded borderscapes because their essence is to serve the functions of multiple forms of flows and mobility: trade flows, human movements, and their infrastructure of connectivity. Thus, they demarcate mobile goods, ascertaining their rights to movement. Also, although there are spatial attachments to those mobile rights, they are aterritorial because they are dependent on global nexus policy makers but with local and individual implications. Indeed, their complex status result from negotiation across multiple states' territorialities and multiple policy makers, states, and private and nonprofit policy actors of the global nexus.

Indeed, these borders of globalization superimpose, overlap, and straddle the borders of states territorialities and other borderscapes. They do not contribute, to use Brambilla's own words, "to bordering the spatial and sensible components of power" (Brambilla and Schimanski 2017, 152). They disregard the spatial and sensible dimensions of power to simply instrumentalize mobility as power. In that sense, they contribute to the closing of cultural, special, and political scapes, and by superimposing a logic of global mobility and flow, they harden borders and add a layer of security and control that contributes to further closing territorialities and territories as containers, hence, controlling human activities. Their governance is articulated by overarching local-global policy networks fostering functional cross-border relations.

NOTES

1. http://www.aborne.org.
2. https://ipss.ui.edu.ng/brit-2018-conference.
3. https://absborderlands.org.
4. See Brambilla (2015). This is my own summary and emphasis of the literature. (1) Borders as containers of social and cultural activities and territoriality of members of the international community: J. Agnew (1994, 2008). (2) Borders as policies: Newman and Paasi (1998). (3) Borders as interdisciplinary subjects of social science studies: Newman (2006). (4) Borders as spatial dividing and ordering principles: Van Houtum, Kramsch, and Zierhofer (2005). (5) Borders in comparative politics: Kolosov (2005). (6) Borders as comparative and multidisciplinary lens of analysis: Brunet-Jailly (2005b). (7) Borders as limited tools of the international community: Vaughan-Williams (2009); Paasi Anssi (2009). (8) Borders as objects of multidisciplinary perspectives: Wastl-Walter (2016); Rumford (2012). (9) Borders as social science objects in motion—continually articulated and rearticulated: Konrad (2015). (10) Borders as competitive advantage: Sohn (2016). (11) Borders as real and unreal, physical and metaphorical walls: Van Houtum and Pijpers (2007). (12) Borders as spatial suture points and frontiers: Salter (2012). (13) Borders as multiple spatial objects and at multiple levels continually reassessing

and inventing and reinventing border regions: Brambilla (2017, 2015). (14) Borders are mobiles: Amilhat-Szary and Giraud (2015).

5. https://pca-cpa.org/wp-content/uploads/sites/175/2016/07/PH-CN-20160712-Press-Release-No-11-English.pdf.

6. On the processual shift from borders to bordering as suggested by Brambilla (2015), see, among others, Paasi (1998), 69–88; van Houtum and van Naerssen, (2002): 125–36; and Newman (2006): 171–86.

7. Merics, Mercator Institute for China Studies (https://www.merics.org/en).

8. Hillman and Goodman (2018).

9. The works published by Geoffrey Hale and others as part of Borders in Globalization illustrates those elements well for the Canadian province of Alberta—but much more work is needed to fully understand those new borders: Anderson and Hale (2019).

10. The Second Belt and Road Forum for International Cooperation (2019). This short document explains why so many roads to sixty countries around the world are necessary.

REFERENCES

Agnew, John. 1994. "The Territorial Trap: The Geographical Assumptions of International Relations Theory." *Review of International Political Economy* 1:53–80.

Agnew, John. 2008. "Borders on the Mind: Re-framing Border Thinking." *Ethics and Global Politics* 1 (4): 175–19.

Amilhat-Szary, Anne-Laure, and F. Giraud, eds. 2015. *Borderities: The Politics of Contemporary Mobile Borders*. Basingstoke: Palgrave Macmillan.

Anderson, Benedict. 1983. *Imagined Communities: Reflections on the Origin and Spread of Nationalism*. London: Verso.

Anderson, Greg, and Geoffrey Hale. 2019. "Borders in Globalization: Alberta in a BiG Context." *Journal of Borderlands Studies* 34 (2): 149–56.

Andreas, Peter, and Thomas Biersteker. 2003. *The Rebordering of North America*. New York: Routledge.

Andreas, Peter, and Thimothy Snyder. 2000. *The Wall Around the West: State Borders and Immigration Controls in North America*. Lanham, Md.: Rowand and Littlefield.

Balibar, Etienne. 1998. "The Borders of Europe." Translated by J. Swenson. In *Cosmopolitics: Thinking and Feeling Beyond the Nation*, edited by P. Cheah and B. Robbins, 16–32. Minneapolis: University of Minneapolis Press.

Balibar, Etienne. 2002. *Politics and the Other Scene*. New York: Verso.

Barros, Jose Manuel. 2007. "European Union Is 'Non-imperial Empire.'" EUX.TV. Strasbourg, July 10, 2007. https://www.youtube.com/watch?v=-I8M1T-GgRU.

Belt and Road Forum for International Cooperation. 2017. "Vision and Actions on Jointly Building Belt and Road." http://www.beltandroadforum.org/english/n100/2017/0410/c22-45.html.

Bhabha, Homi K. 1994. *The Location of Culture*. London: Routledge.

Brambilla, Chiara. 2015. "Exploring the Critical Potential of the Borderscapes Concept."
    Geopolitics 20 (1): 14–34.
Brambilla, Chiara. 2017. "Between Crises and Borders: Interventions on Mediterranean
    Neighborhood and the Salience of Special Imaginaries." *Political Geography* 36 (3):
    174–84.
Brambilla, Chiara, and Johan Schimanski. 2017. *Bordering, Political Landscapes and
    Social Arenas: Potentials and Challenges of Evolving Border Concepts in a Post-Cold
    War World*. EUBorderscapes Final Report WP 1. http://www.euborderscapes.eu/file
    admin/user_upload/Working_Papers/final_report/D_1_50_EUBORDERSCAPES
    _Final_Report.pdf.
Brunet-Jailly, Emmanuel. 2005a. "Theorizing Borders: An Interdisciplinary Perspective."
    Geopolitics 10 (4): 633–49.
Brunet-Jailly, Emmanuel. 2005b. "Understanding Borders: A Model of Border Studies."
    Geopolitics 10 (4): 633–49.
Brunet-Jailly, Emmanuel. 2017a. "Les disputes frontalières: Territoriales, positionelles
    et fonctionelles." *L'espace politique* 33 (3). https://journals.openedition.org/espace
    politique/4488.
Brunet-Jailly, Emmanuel. 2017b. "On the Agency of Borderlands." In *The Social Ecology
    of Border Landscapes*, edited by Anna Grichtin and Michele Zebich Knos, 19–36.
    London: Anthem Press.
Charpin, D. 1995. "The History of Ancient Mesopotamia: An Overview, History and
    Culture." In *Civilizations and the Ancient Near East* vol. 2, *Part 5: History and Culture*,
    edited by J. M. Sasson, 807–829. New York: Charles Scribner's Sons.
Chen, Xianming. 2005. *As Borders Bend: Transnational Spaces on the Pacific Rim*. Lanham,
    Md.: Rowman and Littlefield.
Clancy, T. 2000. *The Bear and the Dragon*. New York: Berkley Books.
"Comments on China's International Commercial Courts." 2018. *Supreme People's Court
    Monitor*, July 9. https://supremepeoplescourtmonitor.com/2018/07/09/comments-on
    -chinas-international-commercial-courts/.
Economist Intelligence Unit. 2017. "China Going Global Investment Index 2017." *Econo-
    mist*. http://pages.eiu.com/rs/753-RIQ-438/images/ODI_in_China_2017_English.pdf.
Endymion, W. 2000. *Chinese History: A Manual*. Cambridge, Mass.: Harvard University
    Press.
European Commission. 2018. "Joint Communication to the European Parliament, the
    Council, the European Economic and Social Committee, the Committee of the
    Regions and the European Investment Bank." Brussels: European Commission.
    https://eeas.europa.eu/sites/eeas/files/joint_communication_-_connecting_europe
    _and_asia_-_building_blocks_for_an_eu_strategy_2018-09-19_.pdf.
Foucher, Michel. 2007. *L'obsession des frontiers*. Paris: Perrin.
Giles, J. A. and J. Ingram. 1996. *The Anglosaxon Chronicles*. Project Gutenberg. http://
    www.gutenberg.org/ebooks/657.
Harrell, S. 1995. *Cultural Encounters on China's Ethnic Frontiers*. Seattle: University of
    Washington Press.

Hillman, Jonathan E., and Matthew P. Goodman. 2018. "All Rise? Belt and Road Court Is in Session," Center for Strategic and International Studies, Reconnecting Asia, July 26. https://reconnectingasia.csis.org/analysis/entries/all-rise-belt-and-road-court -session/.

Hodge, Edwin G. 2018. "Grievance and Responsibility: Emotional and Conceptual Motivators Within the Men's Rights and Pro-feminist Men's Movements in Canada and the United States." PhD diss., University of Victoria.

Howland, D. R. 1996. *Borders of Chinese Civilization*. Durham, N.C.: Duke University Press.

Iwashita, Akihiro. 2004. *A 4000 Kilometer Journey Along the Sino-Russian Border*. Slavic Research Center, Slavic Eurasian Studies 3. Sapporo: Hokkaido University.

Iwashita, Akihiro. 2016. *Japan's Border Issues: Pitfalls and Prospects*. London: Routledge.

Khanna, Parag. 2016. *Connectography: Mapping the Future of Global Civilization*. New York: Random House.

Kolossov, Vladimir. 2005. "Border Studies: Changing Perspectives and Theoretical Approaches." *Geopolitics* 10 (4): 606–32.

Kolossov, Vladimir. 2012. "State of the Debate Report 1." EUBorderscapes. http://www.euborderscapes.eu/fileadmin/user_upload/EUBORDERSCAPES_State_of _Debate_Report_1.pdf.

Konrad, V. 2015. "Toward a Theory of Border in Motion." *Journal of Borderlands Studies* 30 (2): 1–17.

Lary, Diana. *The Chinese State at the Borders*. Vancouver: University of British Columbia Press, 2007.

Mahony, Honor. 2007. "Barroso Says EU Is an Empire" *EUobserver*, July 11. https://euob server.com/institutional/24458.

Malksoo, Maria. 2012. "The Challenge of Liminality in International Relations Theory." *Review of International Studies* 38 (2): 481–94.

Massey, Doreen. 1993. "Power Geometry and Progressive Sense of Place." In *Mapping Futures: Local Cultures, Global Change*, edited by John Bird, Barry Curtis, Tim Put-nam, and Lisa Tickner, 60–71. London: Routledge 1993.

Massey, Doreen. 1994a. *Space, Place and Gender*. Minnesota: University of Minnesota Press.

Massey, Doreen. 1994b. "Double Articulation: A Place in the World." In *Displacements: Cultural Identities in Question*, edited by Angelika Bammer, 110–22. Bloomington: Indiana University Press.

McMillan, M. 2001. *Paris 1919: Six Months That Changed the World*. New York: Random House.

Newman, D. 2006. "Borders and Bordering: Towards an Interdisciplinary Dialogue." *European Journal of Social Theory* 9 (2): 171–86.

Newman, David, and Anssi Paasi. 1998. "Fences and Neighbours in the Postmodern World: Boundary Narratives in Political Geography." *Progress in Human Geography* 22 (2): 186–207.

Ōmae, Ken'ichi. 1990. *The Borderless World: Power and Strategy in the Interlinked Economy*. New York: HarperCollins.

Paasi, A. 1998. "Boundaries as Social Processes: Territoriality in the World of Flows." *Geopolitics* 3 (1): 69–88.

Paasi, Anssi. 2009. "Regions and Regional Dynamics." In *The Sage Handbook of European Studies*, edited by Chris Rumford, 464–84. Sage, London.

Parker, B. J. 2003. "Archeological Manifestations of Empire: Assyria's Imprint on South Eastern Anatolia." *American Journal of Archaeology* 107 (4): 525–57.

Perlez, Jane, and Yufan Huang. 2017. "Behind China's 1 Trillion Plan to Shake Up the Economic Order." *New York Times*, May 13. https://www.nytimes.com/2017/05/13/business/china-railway-one-belt-one-road-1-trillion-plan.html.

Ramasamy, Bala, Matthew Yeung, Chorthip Utoktham, and Yann Duval. 2017. "Trade and Trade Facilitation along the Belt and Road Initiative Corridors." ARTNeT Working Paper Series no. 172. Bangkok: ARTNeT. https://www.econstor.eu/bitstream/10419/172051/1/1006745505.pdf.

Rumelili, Bahar. 2012. "Liminal Identities and Processes of Domestication and Subversion in International Relations." *Review of International Studies* 38 (2): 495–508.

Rumford, Chris. 2008. "Introduction: Citizens and Borderwork in Europe." *Space and Polity* 12 (1): 1–12.

Rumford, Chris. 2012. "Towards a Multiperspectival Study of Borders." *Geopolitics* 17 (4): 887–902.

Salter, M. B. 2012. "Theory of the /: The Suture and Critical Border Studies." *Geopolitics* 17 (4): 734–55.

Schmidt, Klaus. 2011. "Göbekli Tepe: A Neolithic Site in Southwestern Anatolia." In *Handbook of Ancient Anatolia*, edited by Sharon R. Steadman and Gregory McMahon, 1–16. Oxford: Oxford University Press.

Second Belt and Road Forum for International Cooperation. 2019. "Yang Jiechi on the Belt and Road Initiative and Preparation for the Second Belt and Road Forum for International Cooperation." http://www.beltandroadforum.org/english/n100/2019/0417/c22-1086.html.

Shichor, Yitzak. 2009. *Ethno-Diplomacy: The Uyghur in Sino Turkish Relations*. Policy Studies 53. Honolulu: East-West Center.

Sobel, D. 1995. *Longitude: The True Story of a Lone Genius Who Solved the Greatest Scientific Problem of His Time*. New York: Walker, 1995.

Sohn, C. 2016. "Navigating Borders' Multiplicity: The Critical Potential of Assemblage." *Area* 48 (2): 183–89.

Turner, Victor. 1967. "Betwixt and Between: The Liminal Period in Rites of Passage." In *The Forest of Symbols*. Ithaca, N.Y.: Cornell University Press.

Vallet, Elisabeth. 2014. *Borders, Fences and Walls: State of Insecurity?* Farnham: Ashgate.

Van Gennep, Arnold. 1977. *The Rites of Passage*. London: Routledge and Kegan Paul.

Van Houtum, Henk, Olivier Thomas Kramsch, and Wolfgang Zierhofer. 2005. *B/Ordering Space*. London: Ashgate.

Van Houtum, H., and T. van Naerssen. 2002. "Bordering, Ordering and Othering." *Tijdschrift voor Economische en Sociale Geografie* 93 (2): 125–36.

Van Houtum, Henk, and Roos Pijpers. 2007. "European Union as a Gated Community: The Two-Faced Border and Immigration Regime of the EU." *Antipode* 39 (2): 291–309. https://doi.org/10.1111/j.1467-8330.2007.00522.x.

Vaughan-Williams, N. 2009. *Border Politics: The Limits of Sovereign Power.* Edinburgh: Edinburgh University Press.

Vigne, J. D. 2000. "Les débuts néolitiques de l'élevage des ongules au proche orient et en méditérranée: Acquis récents et question." In *Premiers paysans du monde*, edited by J. Guilaine, 143–68. Paris: Editions Errance.

Walters, William. 2006. "Rethinking Borders Beyond the State." *Comparative European Politics* 4:141–59.

Wang Huning et al. 2015. "Xi Jinping Holds Talks with Representatives of Chinese and Foreign Entrepreneurs Attending BFA Annual Conference." Embassy of the People's Republic of China in the United States of America, March 3. http://www.china-embassy.org/eng/zgyw/t1250585.htm..

Wastl-Walter, Doris, ed. 2016. *The Ashgate Research Companion to Border Studies.* London: Routledge.

Winter, Irene J. 1985. "After the Battle Is Over: The 'Stele of the Vultures' and the Beginning of Historical Narrative in the Art of the Ancient Near East." In *Pictorial Narrative in Antiquity and the Middle Ages*, edited by Herbert L. Kessler and Marianna Shreve Simpson, 11–32. Studies in the History of Art 16, Symposium Series 4. Washington D.C.: National Gallery of Art.

Xi, Jinping, H. E. 2017. "Jointly Shoulder Responsibility of Our Time, Promote Global Growth." Belt and Road Forum for International Cooperation, April 17. http://www.beltandroadforum.org/english/n100/2017/0417/c25-194.html.

Xie, Shaobo. 1996. "Writing on Boundaries: Homi Bhabha's Recent Essays." *ARIEL: A Review of International English Literature* 27: 155–66.

XinhuaNet. 2019. "BRI Brings New Opportunities to SCO Members." June 14. http://www.xinhuanet.com/english/2019-06/14/c_138143932.htm.

Zenz, Adrian. 2018. "Thoroughly Reforming Them Toward a Healthy Heart Attitude: China's Political Re-Education Campaign in Xinjiang." *Central Asian Survey* 38:102–28. https://doi.org/10.1080/02634937.2018.1507997.

Zielonka, Jan. 2006. *Europe as Empire: The Nature of the Enlarged European Union.* Oxford: Oxford University Press, 2006.

CHAPTER 8

Border Narratives in a Neoliberal Era

The Central U.S.-Mexico Borderlands

KATHLEEN STAUDT

Introduction

The year 2018 closed in political flux and economic uncertainty, much of it linked to the U.S.-Mexico borderlands and trade and migration policy transitions in both countries. Two presidents relied on nationalist rhetoric but accommodated themselves to a warmed-over, modernized version of the North American Free Trade Agreement (NAFTA), negotiated and retitled the United States–Mexico–Canada Agreement (USMCA), that resonated with the global neoliberal agenda to limit government and maximize market forces. While Mexico ratified the USMCA in June 2019, the United States has not yet moved on the process, and Canada's elections in October 2019 may well determine whether it will grant (probable) approval.

Narratives offer framing perspectives for people to make sense of reality. Narratives are produced and performed in both written and visual ways, from policies, speeches, and official practices to films, memes, and carefully planned conferences that can transform old narratives into new and/or counternarratives. Like the exercise of power and the reaction to it, narratives also provoke reactions. Who defines border narratives, and to which audiences are they targeted? Politicians, their bureaucratic handmaidens, and business constituencies have long prevailed in developing and sustaining border narratives, including contradictory narratives across different cabinet-level agencies such as commerce and security. In the past, *fronterizxs* rarely had opportunities to articulate their own narratives as communicated to the North American mainstream. Borderlanders' narratives, once muted, began to be heard with two central borderlands U.S. congressmen in the twenty-first century, one with a national security narrative and the other a binational trade narrative.

In this chapter, I argue that border people developed multiple border narratives in reaction to national narratives imposed on them. However, border people's narratives tended to reinforce and legitimize the dominant security and trade voices emanating from on high in capital cities and corporate headquarters while also eventually countering excess security hyperbole and xenophobia emanating from the mainstream. The U.S. presidential election campaign and Republican victory in 2016 inaugurated yet another national border narrative on the borderlands, setting back the border congressional and business voices in ways from which recovery will be difficult. This narrative involves demagogic slogans and rhetoric about dangerous immigrant "invasions," Mexico's supposed advantage over the United States in NAFTA, and Trump's call to "Finish the Wall" in the central borderlands after retreating from his ludicrous promise to make Mexico pay.

This chapter begins with two U.S. border congressmen and their border theater performances in central borderlands conferences that drew national and binational attention. The first series of annual conferences offered architecture for militarized border national security solutions, while the second series shifted toward a binational border trade agenda that celebrated business stakes in a neoliberal trade model built on extremely unequal wages in Mexico compared with the United States. However, the second conference series also provided space for nongovernmental organizations (NGOs) and journalists to celebrate the binational borderlands community and make human rights a priority for border crossers. I then describe the ebb and flow of binational border business voices along with their increasing anxieties about presidential disregard for their interests to the extent of threatening "no deal." Contrary to their expectation of renewed business leverage under Republican leadership, their expectations clashed with the reality of an eclectic and erratic president who sought to disrupt a trade model that benefitted U.S. growth more than Mexico for a quarter century under NAFTA, as I will discuss in that section. In part 3, I conclude with strategies for border voices to be heard more broadly and border benefits to prevail rather than the corporate interests that are advantaged in the current status quo.

Part I. The Changing Border Narrative: Border Conference Theater

Grand narratives about place deeply influence the perceptions of those distant from and those inside that place. Narratives emerge from Hollywood and Mexico City films (Staudt 2014, 2017), headlines, journalism, and to a lesser extent, scholarly publications, given their limited readership outside of academia. More recently, social media such as Facebook and Twitter offer opportunities for rapidly disseminating messages and images about places like the borderlands. The U.S.-Mexico border has long been "framed" as a place of violence, chaos, sexuality, drugs, poverty, and unauthorized immigration.[1]

This first part of the chapter focuses on large-scale, multiday annual conferences organized by El Paso congressional representatives that until recently were cohosted at and with leadership from the University of Texas at El Paso (UTEP). Conference programs, speakers, and agendas—developed carefully by their organizers—are staged performances and worthy of attention for their narrative-reinforcing and narrative-changing dimensions. One might refer to them as political spectacles for their stand-alone drama, massaged for reporting to local and national media. Presentations, media reports thereof, visual images, and relational network activities have consequences beyond the conferences themselves. Below I compare two such iconic narratives in central borderlands conferences for the voices featured and the priorities emphasized.[2] In ethnographic style, I attended these conferences and took copious notes. I also highlighted the few overlapping voices in conferences I attended in the years in between from a national political appointee and a local businessman.

Presenters, then and now, can be grouped into four categories with local and national subgroup voices: (1) business, (2) political appointees and officials, (3) academics, and (4) NGO leaders, although no NGOs were invited to present at the 2007 conference. Additionally, I analyze the demographics of gender, nationality, and ethnicity for the extent of balance in public voices articulated at the conferences themselves, the media, and the instant streaming on the internet that political staff arranged.

Border Conference Security Themes 2007

At the first conference I observed, Congressman Silvestre Reyes reinforced the imprint of his background and priorities. On August 13–14, 2007, Reyes and the university president cohosted the fourth annual "Border Security Conference: Securing and Managing our Nation's Borders." Reyes, elected in 1996, was the former Border Patrol chief for the El Paso sector. He acquired local fame with the Border Blockade of September 1993, later renamed Operation Hold the Line (Dunn 2009). With a massing of agents along the borderline, his aim was to prevent unauthorized people from crossing apart from the official ports of entry in this large urban metropolitan region of 2.5 million people partly in response to a lawsuit filed by Bowie High School students who experienced street-level harassment along with many others who "looked Mexican" in an 80 percent Hispanic majority city but an even stronger majority in south and south-central El Paso near the border. One consequence of this blockade, like the one in the San Diego area, was to channel unauthorized crossers into less populated areas of the desert southwest, where hundreds of bodily remains are found annually.

The Border Security Conference audience consisted of approximately four hundred attendees, primarily political appointees from Washington, D.C., involved in military, intelligence, and homeland security agencies of the national government. The Washington attendees included ten from security, drug-control, and intelligence agencies (and one Congressional Intelligence Committee staff member) with titles such as secretary, undersecretary, and admiral. At this event, Michael Chertoff, secretary of Homeland Security, made remarks reminiscent of the Vietnam era: "We don't want to destroy the border in order to save it" (quoted in the *Washington Post* and cited in Staudt 2009). The conference also had its comic moment when an admiral, aiming to please many bilinguals in the audience, confused his opening remarks in Spanish: rather than the hospitable phrase *mi casa es su casa* (my house is your house), he said, "Su casa es mi casa" (your house is my house). Only one local government functionary spoke: the Border Patrol chief for the large El Paso sector (that stretches from Hudspeth County, Texas [Fort Hancock Station] through southern New Mexico). Four business leaders from government contractor corporations (Lockheed Martin, SAIC [Scientific Applications International Corporation], Boeing, and CSC [Computer Sciences Corporation]) spoke at the conference. Given their obvious stake in networking with officials and gaining government security contracts, these corporate sponsors also hosted two receptions, a luncheon, and a breakfast event. The lobby of the university's Undergraduate Learning Center was transformed into an exhibition hall for commercial products named, as mapped in the program, "Exhibitors' Row." Mostly businesses displayed their wares, such as technology, defense and security equipment (including a desert-camouflage jeep parked on a major university street), and computer software.

Four speakers based in academia spoke on panels, three of them ex-military with titles such as retired brigadier general.[3] Just one woman, an academic in computer science, and only one Mexican, the ambassador, plus four Spanish-surnamed men were included in the twenty-three speakers.

The tone of the conference, as dramatized in its title, was national security rather than human security, two highly contrasting paradigms with divergent policy agendas (Staudt 2009). The business community, hardly a monolithic group, tilted toward representatives and sponsors from the military-industrial complex—renamed the border-security industrial complex by some (Staudt, Payan, and Dunn 2009)—given the corporate-congressional-bureaucratic agency triangular alliance. The high-profile speaker lineup gave testimony to the influence of Congressman Reyes, who served on the House Permanent Select Committee on Intelligence since 2001 but was appointed a committee chair by House Speaker Nancy Pelosi in late 2006. Reyes did not speak at this and his other conferences except to welcome attendees. He and his invitees valued national rather than local border voices.

To be sure, 2007 marked a buildup of transnational crime associated with drug trafficking. As Tony Payan (2016) analyzes the now-familiar narrative, the diminishing drug trafficking by sea from South America to Florida led to land trafficking from and through Mexico and transnationally organized criminals who competed over spaces and gateways into the large and profitable U.S. drug market. In 2008, Mexican president Felipe Calderón expanded his own war on drug trafficking to the north, reinforced with support from the U.S. Mérida Initiative and its promise of a multiyear, more than one billion dollars of technical assistance to the Mexican government to fight this war. Calderón sent his army and federal police to Ciudad Juárez in March 2008, making the city seem like occupied territory, though murders escalated and peaked in 2010, with many convinced that the armed forces aligned with the regional politicians and crime organizations competing for control over space (see selections in Payan, Staudt, and Kruszewski 2013). To the extent that alignments occurred between government and criminals, U.S. support for the government became part of this complicity—a perception that U.S. political appointees sought to minimize in future border-security conferences.

Border Conference Trade Themes, 2015

The "U.S.-Mexico Summit: A View from the Border" conference, held August 6–8, 2015, bore the imprint and influence of Congressman Beto O'Rourke, who challenged and beat the incumbent representative Reyes in 2012. O'Rouke, a fully bilingual former two-term El Paso city council representative, was and is a technology businessman who is well networked with the binational business community, and he ran for higher office in 2018 and beyond. He acquired fame on the city council with his cosponsored resolution calling for a debate on the forty-year-old U.S. war on drugs, given the havoc and outlier murder rates that the ruthless drug supply chains created in Mexico. He helped coordinate the first ever campus–binational community Global Public Policy Forum on the War on Drugs conference in 2009.[4] With another council representative, he coauthored the book *Dealing Death and Drugs: The Big Business of Dope in the U.S. and Mexico*, advocating the legal regulation of rather than prohibition of marijuana (O'Rourke and Byrd 2011). His vocal border leadership widened the scope of change rationales in the major drug reform group, the Drug Policy Alliance. Defeating Reyes in the Democratic primary, O'Rourke's priority issues focused on stimulating economic development and on reforming the problematic Veterans' Administration and its service centers.[5]

The U.S.-Mexico Summit, with approximately 650 registered attendees, had a very different lineup of speakers, most all of them speaking in moderated conversation panels. The categorization of speakers by affiliation, gender, ethnicity, and nationality contrasted greatly to the earlier conference. Four distant political appointee panelists spoke: two from Mexico City and two nonmilitary/nonsecurity people from Washington, D.C. The high-profile secretaries of the economy (Mexico) and of commerce (United States) spoke on a panel in Ciudad Juárez (day two), as did the Customs and Border Protection (CBP) commissioner in the United States (day one), who mainly focused on trade congestion and wait times at the border. Ten political representatives spoke, including four U.S. national representatives, two local representatives, and two women elected to the Mexican Senate. Six local business people participated from the binational border region. Academics served on panels, including a panel moderator from a think tank in Washington, D.C. At an NGO panel moderated by Alfredo Corchado, El Pasoan *Dallas Morning News* bureau chief for Mexico, four community leaders spoke about immigration, human rights, health, and youth, the latter from Ciudad Juárez. The summit ended with a U.S.-Mexico 10K run to the borderline from both sides, cohosted by the chief political executives from each city. The diversity of program speakers was a stark contrast to the earlier security-oriented conference: eight women spoke, and of seventeen speakers with Spanish surnames, based in Mexico, eight were U.S.-based, participating out of twenty-six total on the program.[6]

Overlapping Speakers at In-Between Conferences

As an ethnographic observer and note taker at multiple border conferences, it was interesting for me to hear an official who spoke at multiple meetings, whether a Reyes or O'Rourke invitee, and how his discourse changed over time. Gil Kerlikowske, the career political appointee who spoke at the Reyes Border Security sixth annual conference in 2009, had recently been appointed by President Obama director of the Office of National Drug Control Policy, also known as the "Nation's Drug Czar." In 2009, Kerlikowske spoke on the panel titled "The Mérida Initiative: A Shared Responsibility to Confront Illicit Narcotics Trafficking." He joked that as former Seattle police chief, he served a community of "overcaffinated liberals" (all such quotes from my ethnographic notes). At the 2009 conference, he framed the border in dangerous terms, especially for law enforcement. On several occasions in one speech, he said, "I cannot believe" the "courageousness of President Calderón" and mentioned his "admiration of President Calderón." No doubt the frequently alleged complicity of government and organized crime spurred such attempts to reassure the audience and media. He praised Mexico for hiring thousands of college graduates in its federal Secretariat for Public Security (dissolved in 2013). Like other speakers, he evoked the language and imagery of the 9/11 terrorist attack on the United States. Kerlikowske criticized drug cartels for "moving drugs into our country . . . without care" about their effect on our community. In response to a question, he said he hoped to look "at drug problems in a more holistic way," to break down the silos in the distribution of the budget. In 2010, Kerlikowske developed a white paper on drug policy that emphasized prevention and treatment of addiction as well as interdiction, but budgetary silos maintained an interdiction approach.

Another person who spoke at both Reyes and O'Rourke conferences was local businessman Woody Hunt, CEO of Hunt Companies. Hunt has long assumed a binational business perspective, including the founding of the Paso del Norte Group, predecessor to the rebranded and expanded Borderplex Alliance (discussed below). He donated a large sum to UTEP to establish the Hunt Institute of Global Competitiveness, a concept based on low-cost Mexican labor and traffic across the borderline. At the seventh annual Border Security Conference in 2010, he spoke on a panel titled "Human Capital Development: Building on Innovation and Entrepreneurship." Hunt advocated enhanced educational opportunities on both sides of the border, as he still does today. Other panels focused on binational health care, including the long-articulated local border business vision to foster U.S. health tourism just across the border to Ciudad Juárez through a security corridor, building on the region's competitive advantage. Still, three panels from the 2010 conference retained the language and focus of the past drug war and national security emphasis: "Effective Security: Disrupting the Operational Capacity of Organized Crime," "Reducing Demand and Consumption of Narcotics," and a panel featuring the border-security industry speakers from SAIC, Boeing, Raytheon, and ManTech, who focused on technology and innovation in "smart bordering" for an ongoing national discourse.[7] By the 2010 conference, as evinced in the program itself, which began to shift toward more trade topics, many had begun to tire of messaging from the office of Congressman Reyes and were fatigued with a drug war that many U.S. states successfully fought through electoral participation to regulate marijuana for medical and leisurely use (and thereby reduce costs for prisons and the unequal protection of the law for their inhabitants).

By 2015, we can see the difference that a congressman makes, as with shifting alliances and priorities in the final two years of a second term Obama presidency. And the old public administration axiom, "Where you stand depends on where you sit," was evident as well. In 2015, commissioner for CBP Kerlikowske championed a new kind of security that he called "economic security." He called for expanded funding in staff and infrastructure, citing wait-time reductions at the San Ysidro port of entry (near a community south of San Diego proper). CBP reports showed that "every minute of additional delay at ports of entry costs the US economy about $166 million" (cited in Gray 2015, 12A). Here we see dollarized cost-benefit terms down to the minute. Kerlikowske said nothing about drugs, though much of his discussion about preclearance to ease congestion at the border through customs perhaps hinted at the hidden import of illegal substances among otherwise legitimate goods in the continuing drug prohibition-interdiction strategy of U.S. policy. The U.S.-Mexico Border Summit was devoid of singular attention on how an end to drug interdiction might reduce congestion and wait times at the border. However, businessman Woody Hunt said that drug interdiction efforts affected cross-border trade and also created a "tremendous amount of complexity in the financial system" that hurt competitiveness in the region (cited in Gray 2015, 12A).[8]

At the 2015 conference, in response to a tweeted question about the role of Fort Bliss at the border, Kerlikowske adamantly claimed that the military had no role and should have no role at the border. While many viewed former President Bush's, President Obama's, and Reyes's approach to the border as militarization (Staudt and Méndez 2015), Kerlikowske did not consider a fivefold increase in Border Patrol agents, over seven hundred miles of border fence ("wall" to its opponents), the Mérida Initiative, and massive spending in technology control of the border to be militarization. Meanwhile, the Texas Legislature in 2015 passed a bill to fund $800 million to Texas State Troopers to enhance "border security." The year before, Governor Perry appeared for photo opportunities at the border with Fox media star Sean Hannity in full masculine display: aviator glasses and an assault weapon across the chest.[9] Washington, D.C., had retreated slightly from the past militarization discourse, but the State of Texas embraced it with enthusiasm.

The tone of the 2015 U.S.-Mexico Summit focused on trade in wide array of businesses (not only security-oriented businesses, as in 2007) and on cooperation with Mexico. The 10K run at the close generated upbeat, youthful photo opportunities in local and national media. The inclusion of NGO leaders, Spanish-surnamed experts from the United States and Mexico, and women gave attention to a wider range of voices. Drugs were absent from the agenda, but immigration reform was featured several times, including from New Mexico Republican governor Susana Martínez. No Republican politicians from statewide Texas positions spoke, although high-profile local U.S. business people have donated generously to those officials, as documented in campaign reports. Yet as one speaker stated, "The border is not and should not be a partisan issue."

On conversation panels himself, Congressman O'Rourke spoke about the endless calls to establish more border security before embarking on immigration reform given the already-secure border. Besides noting how non-Mexican apprehensions at the border exceeded apprehensions of Mexicans, O'Rourke discussed the tragedies of separated families and of immigrant deaths at the border. And rather than folding to and affiliating with bureaucratic ambitions in U.S. government, O'Rourke criticized the State Department warnings about travel to Ciudad Juárez and quipped, "Why no warnings to visit high-murder-count U.S. cities like Detroit and New Orleans?" Congressman O'Rourke also emphasized waste in excessive staffing at the border, citing how in the "El Paso sector, the average Border Patrol agent made 4.5 apprehensions last year. . . . That's not a week, not a month, but for the entire year" (in Gray 2015, 12A). In contrast, as noted, former congressman Reyes never spoke on panels at his border security conferences except to welcome the audience as a cohost. Reyes appeared to align with bureaucratic agencies, while O'Rourke seemed to exercise oversight. These demonstrate noteworthy contrasts in their approaches to governance. Though both shared a neoliberal economic agenda, the former tilted toward security and militarization, no doubt sending fears to potential business investors who in more recent years the local and wider business lobbies have mobilized to counteract fears.

During his three terms in the U.S. House of Representatives, until he ran his near-victorious race against U.S. senator Ted Cruz in 2018, O'Rourke interacted with other congressional representatives about their stakes in trade with Mexico and job creation therefrom. His website contained a state-by-state breakdown with the numerical stakes, showing big-state beneficiaries such as Texas, California, Michigan, Illinois, New York, Arizona, and others (see the list reprinted in Staudt 2017, app.).

No U.S. state was excluded from trade and job-creation benefits with Mexico, yet the rhetoric emanating from the 2015–2016 campaign, the Trump presidency, and the actions of the Texas legislature, including both past and present governors, painted Mexico and Mexicans as the enemy. The New Mexico State government hosts a border agency, and Republican governor Susana Martínez attended annual meetings with her Chihuahua counterpart César Duarte along with state cabinet secretaries, as she stated on her panel at the 2015 summit. The political leadership in the State of Texas did nothing of this kind despite the $93 billion in exports and trade surplus with Mexico, perhaps assuming that in the asymmetrical relationship between Mexico and the United States, Texas can count on acquiescence from its national neighbor to the south. The Nebraska-based $500 million Union Pacific investment in the Santa Teresa facility in southern New Mexico—creating three thousand jobs in construction and six hundred permanent jobs—(I attended its inaugural day and took ethnographic notes) became a wake-up call to Texas businesses and their associations distant from the border to understand—finally—their stakes in border prosperity. After Trump assumed power in January 2017, his threat to NAFTA became not just a call but a blast, generating anxieties and shifts toward wider business lobbying and alliances. Let us look at the central borderlands business community in gradually expansive mode.

Part 2. Organized Business in the Central Borderlands

Business people have long been well organized in the central borderlands. They organize on a binational basis in the Borderplex Alliance, successor to the Paso del Norte Group. As in many cities, local governments tend to be handmaidens to the business community in order to be able to tout job creation and growth even though local officials attract new business with grants of tax abatements, such as delaying property tax responsibilities for years, thereby shifting higher tax burdens onto residential property tax payers. This part of the chapter provides a snapshot of binational business people from in-depth interviews. It also covers the way NAFTA expanded both the U.S. and Mexico economies over a quarter century, but with greater benefits to the U.S. overall economy, not necessarily workers. Ultimately, NAFTA widened inequalities between both countries yet saved some jobs in the United States while shifting more to Mexico. Such is the neoliberal "stubborn reality: plenty of work, not enough pay" in both the global north and the global south.[10] The third part of this chapter shows what reforms may be possible given the disconnect between global neoliberalism and democracy.

Pamela Cruz and I have identified themes from forty-four stakeholders' voices on both sides of the border about security and trade narratives (Staudt and Cruz 2014), as analyzed in part 1 of this chapter. The cross-border cases utilized a framework that tapped what theorists called "incumbents" and "challengers" in dynamic and changing contexts of threats and opportunities. At the time of the interviews (2013), border business stakeholders and their local government allies posed minimal threats as "challengers" to the border control machinery and achieved only weak gains in a long-term U.S. national state-security environment where official incumbents' implementation of capital-city policies presented obstacles to efficient cross-border trade. The local business people had little influence on dominant Texas party politicians and little apparent connection to the state and national business lobbies that had grown comfortable with most existing NAFTA rules until the 2016 presidential campaign and very real 2017 threats to their interests given Trump's rhetoric about the so-called NAFTA disaster. Before Trump, the narrative shift in border conferences from security to trade seemed to strengthen business hands, with a supportive congressional representative, vis-à-vis the official security machinery. However, Trump's election in 2016 changed all that.

In our 2013 interviews, Cruz and I found an overwhelming sentiment that too many barriers existed to trade in the binational region because of the Washington, D.C., agenda. To further unpack the interview content, we identified four common themes in interviews: (1) solidarity with the Paso del Norte region, (2) frustrations with security machinery, (3) celebrations of small victories, and (4) hopes and visions that decision makers in national and state capitols would better understand the border and make spaces for border voices to be heard. From our interviews, we also learned that local binational business' policy gains and visions had been meager and that gains required subsidies from local taxpayers—many of whom may not realize that they are paying for federal government responsibilities with increased property tax payments. An example is the pilot project to hire more federal staff and pay them overtime, borne by local taxpayers, for benefits that the entire United States enjoys.

To our surprise, interviewees articulated no concern for the depressed and artificially low wages on the Mexico side of the border despite the cross-border shopping on which El Paso's retail sales sector depends. The stagnant wages of the quarter million assembly-line workers in the approximately three hundred export-processing factories (maquiladoras) amounted to net pay of approximately US$40–$50 per week (one minimum wage), wages that are far less than the legal minimum wage U.S. workers make in a day (approximately US$60). Half the population in Ciudad Juárez falls below the Mexican poverty line. (While Mexico's new president doubled the legal minimum wage in early 2019, improving workers' lives, Mexico's poverty line is considered the equivalent of three minimum wages, with the change thus perpetuating the high rate of poverty.)

Since Mexico's Border Industrialization Program of the mid-1960s and NAFTA, business leaders, along with the current congressional and local political representatives, had engaged in soft lobbying efforts with other members of Congress and with the U.S. Department of Commerce and of Homeland Security, particularly CBP, to enhance trade through reducing wait times at the congested border ports of entry. However, increasing controls after the tragedy of 9/11 (September 11, 2001) lengthened delays even more. One continually hears that "time is money" in public and private discourse. Border business leaders expressed pride over achievements such as the Dedicated Commuter Lane passes, preclearance fees before border crossing, and better infrastructure, but these do not benefit the wider borderlands public except as a pass-through location to get semiprocessed goods quicker to their mainstream U.S. destination.

Before the anti-Mexico, anti-NAFTA U.S. presidential campaign rhetoric of 2016, several changes occurred on both sides of the central borders. First, Mexican border businesses, though perceived to be influential with their capital-city stakeholders, lost a border tax advantage in 2015 once granted to them. Second, the departure of the founding CEO of the Borderplex Alliance, the binational regional business NGO, paved the way for stronger, more effective advocacy with a new CEO, Jon Barela, the former New Mexico secretary of economic development who had worked closely with Governor Martínez and in the Border Industrial Association to build the huge Union Pacific Santa Teresa Intermodal Ramp at the U.S.-Mexico border that opened in 2014 in the New Mexico–Mexico borderlands.

The contrasting local-state relationships and personalities between Republican governors Perry (2000–2015) and then current Abbott of Texas compared to New Mexico's previous Democratic governor Richardson and El Paso-born Republican Susana Martínez (2011–2019) could not be greater. Texas either ignores the border or treats it as a security problem worth nearly $1 billion of taxpayer funding since 2015 to expand its Department of Public Safety as noted earlier. In other words, Texas takes trade with Mexico for granted. In the central borderlands, the Borderplex Alliance hired Barela as its CEO in 2016. He widened business advocacy beyond the binational borderlands. His leadership strengthened Borderplex and tapped wider business constituencies in other parts of the United States.

Borderplex Alliance and Trade Think Tanks

Umbrella organizations—high-functioning, well-endowed binational NGOs— have been created along the border of individual and member institutions that represent business interests such as chambers of commerce, economic development, and industrial organizations. The primary example in the central borderlands is the Borderplex Alliance, a binational, tristate, regional business organization that seeks to represent the larger Paso del Norte region of Ciudad Juárez, El Paso, and southern New Mexico. Borderplex's CEO and El Paso's mayor have visited other cities to develop interest in the region. Selected business leaders have contacted nearly a fourth of U.S. congressional representatives to visit the region and experience its safety and current tranquility (one hundred visits reported in Gray 2015, 12A).

In the Borderplex Alliance, individuals' and member institutions' annual dues (called "investments") are relatively expensive, ranging from $1,000 ("contributing") to $100,000 ("cornerstone") and $250,000 ("capstone"). In dues-paying institutions such as this, representation, leadership, and accountability reflect a less than democratic "pay-to-play" system. The Borderplex Alliance announced some repackaging to solicit more voices from a commission organized into task forces (Washington Valdez 2015). Time will tell whether or if the task forces embrace topics such as management standards, environmental sustainability, living wages for assembly-line workers, and burdens on local taxpayers for pilot programs that augment federal personnel and overtime expenses for customs officers. By 2019, this has not happened. The real challenge for the region involves the development of public regional, all-issue institutions that tap the voices of comprehensive border people and connect them to decision makers in state and national capital cities.

After the January 2017 threat of U.S. withdrawal from NAFTA and stronger leadership in the Borderplex Alliance, border business voices joined those of invigorated statewide organizations such as the Texas Association of Business, the Texas Association of Manufacturers, and the newly created Texas-Mexico Trade Coalition, organized in May 2017 concerned about the threat of NAFTA's demise. Moreover, neoliberal think tanks such as the Americas Society/American Council of the Americas (AS/AOS) organized several border and web-streamed Washington, D.C., panels to tap voices with the theme "Indivisible: A Special Issue of the Ties that Bind" (*Americas Quarterly* 11, no. 2 [2017]). Clearly, the transformation of border narratives elevated trade narratives and connected them with mainstream voices after Trump's threat to withdraw from NAFTA.

Besides AS/AOS, the Mexico Institute of the Woodrow Wilson International Center for Scholars promotes a neoliberal trade agenda with efficient ports of entry and institution-building architecture at the border (Lee and Wilson 2015, chap. 1). The institute's discourse is one of "economic competitiveness" at the border, a familiar ring with "global competitiveness," both euphemisms that denote low-cost labor, especially on the Mexico side. To its credit, the Mexico Institute also emphasizes "human capital" in Lee and Wilson, chapter 4, but mainly for high-skill, university-degreed employees produced in institutions on both sides of the border. Assembly-line work that pays the minimum wages in Mexico (approximately US$4.50–9.00 per day) will long be a large category of workers in Ciudad Juárez and part of the reason for investors seeking global competitiveness. The Wilson Center's Mexico Institute says nothing in its 141-page monograph about improving wages for assembly-line workers, work that is often quite complex, such as harness manufacturing (i.e., the internal electrical system of automobiles; Miker Palafox 2010). In fact, of the institute's twenty-seven specific recommendations developed in its monograph (Lee and Wilson 2015, 19–20), nothing is said about the largest category of workers on assembly lines. Although Corporate Social Responsibility standards may be decorative rhetoric, serious commitment to them would not tolerate the sort of impoverishment in wages and living standards as what currently exists in the central borderlands.

Mexican Perspectives

In early 2017, Trump's anti-Mexico posture, and his seeming determination to eliminate NAFTA and to tax "imports" (of jointly produced products, normalized under NAFTA), instilled a nationalist, defensive posture among some Mexican leaders in the lame-duck year of Enrique Peña Nieto's presidency. Mexico quietly sought other trading partners and alliances to reduce its dependence on the United States. Voters' fatigue with corruption and inequality gave MORENA (Movimiento Regeneración Nacional [National Regeneration Movement]) candidate Andrés Manuel López Obrador (AMLO) a distinct advantage over the multiple candidates in the presidential election. Once he took office in December 2018, AMLO delivered on promises to double the legal minimum wage in northern Mexico, as noted earlier, and restore tax advantages for businesses to compete more equitably with the U.S. side of the borderlands. A higher legal minimum wage for all Mexican workers was never in the offing during NAFTA renegotiation (except for auto workers). Mexico is in a much better bargaining position than it was in the early to mid-1990s, when NAFTA took effect.

Even in speeches before the official campaign, such as one in El Paso in early 2017 in my ethnographic note-taking mode, AMLO did not mention NAFTA but instead emphasized migrants' human rights and proposed plans to strengthen prosperity on the Mexican side of the borderlands with higher wages and tax reduction. Surprisingly, AMLO has acquiesced to the negotiated USMCA and cooperated with Trump's Remain in Mexico policy against migrant caravans in early 2019 despite the U.S. failure to comply with its own laws and signed international protocols on asylum seekers. AMLO cooperates with the United States, but also has negotiated U.S. commitments for economic-development assistance to the violent triangle of Central American countries that pushes migrants seeking safety northward.

Since NAFTA was established, dramatic economic growth occurred in all three countries as measured by GDP per capita, one of many indicators, along with job creation (some middle-class jobs, but more lower-wage categories). However, growth and expansion selectively benefit and burden people in a population, often leaving inequalities to fester. Focusing on the United States and Mexico alone with figures from the World Bank, the 2017 U.S. GDP skyrocketed with $19,391 trillion compared with 1996 figures of $8 trillion; Mexico's GDP also grew to $1.151 trillion from $397.4 billion. Mexico's annual growth rate has been jagged, ranging from –5.75 percent in 1995 to 5.8 percent in 1966 to no growth and shrinkage of –4.7 percent in 2009 and more recently 2.04 percent (2017), while U.S. rates have also been volatile, stabilizing at 2.27 percent in 2017. A comparison of the Mexico-U.S. pair of Border Inequality Ratios, based on GDP per capita purchasing power parity (constant dollar figures) over the quarter century of NAFTA, shows a slight increase in inequality rather than a decrease (Staudt 2017, chap. 4). Mexico's *internal* inequality rates remain constant, with a Gini measure of inequality among the highest in the world, including higher than the United States. Over 50 million Mexicans live under the Mexican government's definition of poverty, and millions of Mexicans migrate to escape poverty and low wages, albeit with more jobs available since NAFTA.

Obviously, both the United States and Mexico share a long-term alliance. In Europe, former enemies during World War II have become allies that work together to invest in border regions and to reduce inequalities between communities on both sides of the border (see Staudt 2017, chap. 6; Moré 2011). Albeit, European Union investment in infrastructure and poverty reduction retain a top-down orientation, but investment has also been made in bottom-up institutions in Euro-Regions (EuRegios; Llera Pacheco and López-Nórez 2012). The United States and Canada, a pair that enjoys more economic equality, reflect reinforcing integrating features as outlined in border-spanning theory— common language, ethnicity, and socioeconomic backgrounds reinforced with cross-border political NGOs and individuals further reinforced with market forces and trade flows (Staudt 2017, chap. 3; Brunet-Jailly 2007, 10)—all of which engender more political trust locally, regionally, and nationally. At the U.S.-Mexico border, trade flows are extensive, but the other elements are limited.

Part 3. What Is to Be Done for North American Prosperity?

While tension exists between the security and trade narratives and agendas, business leaders and local government officials in the borderlands tend to echo the national agendas and leave out the interests of working people and concerns about environmental health. What is to be done? Can coexistence occur in a future neoliberal agenda coupled with social democracy in the borderlands? Is proactive government doomed in a neoliberal agenda? Perhaps not, depending on the underlying framework. Neoliberal practices embrace various policy perspectives (Ban 2016, chap. 1), ranging, for example, from the more socially democratic Spain to the harsh neoliberalism of Romania. In North America, Canada is perhaps the most proactive socially democratic system, and the United States and Mexico the least—at least until AMLO's election. I pose several strategic policy interventions below but warn about their impotency if unbridled neoliberalism reigns without democratic binational local governance institutions and strong civil society activism and transnational activism, including independent unions that go beyond business interests and policy interventions to reduce wage inequalities. Why would anyone expect that elite-negotiated trade agreements would induce prosperity for more than the few?

At the U.S.-Mexico border, there are no transparent and comprehensive cross-border governance institutions wherein a broad variety of border voices can be regularly heard beyond those of business and their government handmaidens. While cooperation exists in environment and water management[11] and NGO collaboration over high-risk diseases such TB and AIDS (Moya, Loza, and Lusk 2012; Homedes 2012; Staudt and Coronado 2002), the borderlands commons are not governed as a region where border people from each side express their interests and visions to their own sovereign governments along with state, city, municipal, and county authorities. NAFTA prioritizes trade and commerce, but the idea and structure of North American governance never took hold (Pastor 2001), including the Bush-era Security and Prosperity Partnership (SPP), which focused entirely on security first, then trade (the security and trade narratives, writ large), with meetings of the Canadian, U.S., and Mexican chief executives and a business advisory council. The absence of regionalism offers a stark contrast to Europe and its Euro-Regions that have emerged with financial support from above—the European Union—and neighbor or twin-city relationality from below as noted above.

Little hope exists for local binational governance mechanisms. At the U.S.-Mexico border, local government council representatives occasionally interact at symbolic events. In the central borderlands, mayors and municipal presidents may meet one or more times annually, depending on the motivations and language skills of each incumbent. Executive terms differ markedly and asynchronically from a four-year (El Paso) to a three-year term (Ciudad Juárez). El Paso's city council seats nonpartisan representatives elected for four-year terms in low-turnout elections, while in Juárez, the *regidores* in the *cabildo* are elected from partisan lists in higher-turnout elections.[12] Since the mid-1990s, the PRI (Partido Revolucionario Institucional [Institutional Revolutionary Party]) has dominated the municipal presidency, and his party retains the majority in a strong party loyalty voting system. The border region is far from democratic. Indeed, with the heavy surveillance of federal, state, and local law enforcement in El Paso's persistent "safest big city" designation, Payan asserts a "democratic deficit" at the border (2010). National security agency personnel from both countries collaborate but in less than transparent ways.

New Policy Strategies

What policy strategies might address this complex dynamic in the borderlands—a borderlands with stakes in all or most states of Mexico and the United States? In my mind, the most important intervention is one that would reduce wage inequalities between both countries and in the borderlands for greater shared prosperity. Policy opportunities exist within each nation to raise minimum wages, but trade agreements remain no substitute for vigorous action at the national level, where NGOs and unions can counter business elites whose influence predominates in trade deals. With vigorous transnational civil society, perhaps dents could be made to supply an opportunity for leveraging shared prosperity through targeted goals and timetables.[13] After all, the extreme inequalities between the United States and Mexico—a 13 to 1 legal minimum-wage differential until 2019 and a 5.44 Border Inequality Ratio (Staudt 2017, chap. 4)—will continue to incentivize U.S. firms to shift their labor-intensive manufacturing to Mexico, thus undermining the national protectionist promises made to the political base of Trump supporters.

With stagnant and extremely low minimum-wage levels, Mexican workers work hard but reap little take-home pay, situated as they are in precarious and vulnerable living standards. Border retailers on the U.S. side surely recognize the increased or renewed consumer demand that greater prosperity would bring to cross-border shopping, but their voices are virtually invisible in state and national lobbies. In Mexico, centrist and right-of-center political parties have heretofore refused to tackle the inequality problem within the country and

between North American countries perhaps for fear of deterring foreign investment and the evocatively phrased supply "chains" of production.[14] However,
Mexico's mid-2018 presidential election produced victories for the left that will
likely address wage policy rather than a trade agreement, however "modernized," to satisfy Trump.

With a neoliberal mind-set, politicians and free-trade negotiators would no
doubt defer to the marketplace for wage adjustments, whether adjusted through
limited labor supplies or collective bargaining.[15] Greater demand for labor could
drive up wages as firms compete with one another. However, in Ciudad Juárez,
maquiladora labor shortages of up to thirty thousand unfilled positions from
2014 onward generated a different strategy: corporate labor recruiters sought
a new supply of fresh labor in the country's interior, in the central states of
Mexico, from where people then migrated northward and realized—along with
municipal governments—the costs of housing, transportation, and infrastructure and the meager pay available. In several binational regions (Tijuana, McAllen), businesses have suggested that Central American migrants be hired—a
potentially huge labor pool—though such suggestions have fallen on deaf ears.
Another route toward higher wages is theoretically available through collective
bargaining and labor unions. Besides the low 10 percent unionized labor force in
Mexico reported by the OECD, existing unions rarely defend members' interests, operate independently of politics and management, or exist beyond paper
agreements. High-visibility work stoppages at several plants in Ciudad Juárez
in 2014 and 2015 and wildcat strikes in Matamoros in 2019 resulted either
in firings or for some, lawyer-negotiated settlements and rehiring—neither of
which systemically influenced the wage structure for the hundreds of thousands
of workers in each locale. The Matamoros efforts emerged because business
tried to get around AMLO's doubled minimum wage by removing incentive
bonuses (for things such as no absenteeism, no tardiness) and thus avoid extra
compensation, but workers prevailed to maintain the new legal minimum plus
former incentive bonuses.

Another possible strategy involves voluntary standards that corporations
might adopt. In South Africa during apartheid, U.S. reverend Leon Sullivan
called for voluntary racialized desegregation and eliminating wage differences
in the 1980s (the Sullivan Principles). Alone, however, they were ineffective for
reform, as profiteering appeared to trump ethical fairness principles. Of course,
the globalized economic apartheid-like wage differences in North America are

based on geography and nationality constructions, not on racialized constructions as in South Africa. Corporate Social Responsibility (CSR) is defined as
"the firm's consideration of, and response to, issues beyond the narrow economic, technical, and legal requirements of the firm" (Keith Davis cited in
Kleine 2014, 196) and how it can create better wage standards for the entire
region. If the Borderplex Alliance Commission and its task forces move toward
a CSR model, standards could be set for decent, living wages. Currently, no CSR
reporting structure is in place, though sporadic businesses such as the Hunt
Companies report "Corporate Sustainability" on websites. Price Waterhouse
Coopers (PWC), a global accounting firm, promotes CSR training, reporting,
and practicing as good for business management, employees, and corporate
images. In PWC annual reports containing responses from large numbers of
big firms by world region, European companies stand out with double the rates
of CSR reporting (81 percent) of those in North America (40 percent; Kleine
2014, 198, citing a PWC 2010 report). The neoliberalism of Europe operates
differently from the stark neoliberalism of the United States and Mexico.

Conversely, corporations with a despicable record of low standards might be
made visible by NGOs through shaming strategies. In the cross-border worker
support efforts mentioned above, one U.S.-based corporation rehired workers
who had mobilized visible campaigns (public relations disasters one might call
them), including communications with members of the corporate board and the
U.S. media. Although the outcome of legal settlement is confidential, perhaps
the corporation granted the thirty-five cents per day that workers had sought.
However, no independent union was achieved in the face of both corporate and
Mexican establishment government-labor councils that authorize recognition.
Lawyer-led strategies with workers in individual plants do not achieve systemic
policy changes in the manufacturing sector.

In the North American neoliberal model, such voluntary practices are not
likely to gain traction except for corporations that seek to improve their public
image. No such ethical standards have been negotiated into the USMCA. Other
standards efforts exist (e.g., the International Organization for Standardiza-
tion [ISO]) that could incorporate best practices for sound management. In
NAFTA's first iteration of 1994, negotiations resulted in labor and environmental amendments, although the legalistic former strategy did little to protect
workers except for "displacement" monies to retrain workers who lost their
jobs.[16] The environmental amendment gained more traction with the creation

of and funding for the Commission on Environmental Cooperation based in Montreal (see chap. 13 of this volume).

Currently, the business debates address freer movement for trade in goods, not freer movement for people. Yet another policy strategy would involve opening borders for the movement of people and labor. Such a policy tool will not likely be adopted in this polarizing political atmosphere wherein many politicians use anti-Mexican (and in the parlance of Border Patrol and CBP officials, anti-OTM—Other Than Mexicans) rhetoric to instill fear and hate. Such polarization is absent in the long histories of border crossings for family, shopping, friends, and work in the fourteen twin cities and towns of the borderlands. An even more militarized and controlled border adds expensive public costs to the security machinery and federal officers who police the borders. Ultimately, the beauty of trade agreements for U.S. businesses relies on controlled borders and segregated national wage economies to achieve "global competitiveness" in the borderlands. In the global neoliberal era, the freedom for and profitability of capital movement do not resonate with labor mobility in borderlands. With this profound dilemma, there is the need for regional democratic institutions that include more voices than businesses and articulate their interests in NGOs and other public settings.

So what is the future of governance in our borderlands commons? The interdependent border cities and towns rely on separate, segregated, public institutions to address their "side" of the border rather than the commons of the borderlands—both sides of the border. For decades, public choice theorists and environmentalists have raised questions about who governs the commons so that all can share its resources rather than deplete them based on self-interested gain for some. Such questions need to be addressed in the borderlands as well.

Institution-building at the border must embrace border people and their local legislative council/*cabildo* representatives in a public format. Businesses alone cannot speak for employees, consumers, and the underemployed or unemployed. Local elected officials should interact regularly through border relations committees with appointed members of the public from all walks of life. Democracies cannot rely on "pay-to-play" systems, whether through expensive membership fees or through large campaign donations to politicians seeking office at local, state, and national levels. Once an intriguing idea, the Border Mayors' meetings, five of them from 2011 to 2017, seem unable to draw enough city and municipal leaders to act on their agendas, including their support for trade agreements.

Concluding Reflections

This chapter analyzed the changing narratives over the last decade in border trade and security rhetoric using central borderlands conference programs from two U.S. Congressman, speakers, presentation titles, and ethnographic notes. The congressional representatives' border voices echoed rather than defied the narratives emanating from the national level. Although the trade narrative transitioned into a more complex discussion—celebrating the border-lands and respecting human rights of migrants and the NGOs that work with crossers—the ultimate effect was to strengthen the hand of organized business constituencies.

Drawing on interviews with binational business people and their handmaid-ens in local government, the paper also revealed their concerns about congestion and transit time but not about the low wages of northern Mexican export-processing factory workers. This indicates a shallow commitment to long-term prosperity in the central borderlands of El Paso and Ciudad Juárez, particularly the low minimum wages in the latter, a large city with approximately half its residents under Mexico's poverty line. The paper takes issue with the neoliberal discourse of global competitiveness and the way it leads to the perpetuation of low-cost labor in the border region.

Finally, the chapter offers a conceptual handle around which future-oriented thinking might occur, namely, policy and capital investments to reduce bina-tional inequality, a stronger transnational civil society agenda to incorporate the interests of working people and migrants into trade agreements, and Corporate Social Responsibility (CSR), reported and practiced far more among European than North American firms. In the end, it was the election of Mexico's new president, Andrés Manuel López Obrador (AMLO), that doubled the legal minimum wage for workers at the northern border and restored a lower tax to benefit northern border businesses and make them more competitive with business on the U.S. side of the border. AMLO's national policies achieved these goals, not the former NAFTA or the possible new deal, the USMCA. In so doing, AMLO reduced the legal minimum-wage inequality from 13 to 1 to 6 to 1 (with the constant U.S. minimum wage of $7.25 hour, or approximately $60 per day, vis-à-vis Mexico's US$4.50 per day to US$9 per day). Well-organized working people in Matamoros unions took heed when maquiladoras attempted to remove incentive bonuses; now net wages can approach three times the min-imum wage for those workers with perfect attendance and no tardiness.

Public institutions should consider it a major priority to reduce inequalities at the border, particularly in the net wages their workers take home. Wages should be based on the complexity, skills, and value added to tasks, especially in assembly-line work, rather than to the education levels workers bring or to the lowest value that markets will bear. Working people require a stable currency for their wages, not one that fluctuates with political winds. Once better wages become identified as a priority, coalitions and alliance-building between business NGOs, environmental stewards, and other organizations will be all the more possible. And alliances among and across many sectors of border people must communicate with legislators and their executives in state and national capitols, working together for their region.

My final remarks address the conundrum of neoliberalism and democracy. Neoliberalism can embrace fairer wage policies, inequality reduction, and proactive programs at multiple levels of government, as evinced in a few among many countries around the world. The United States and Mexico should move to embrace these policies so that some semblance of democracy can survive.

NOTES

1. The verb *frame* has a double meaning: one academic, from sociology and communications; the other, a criminal or nefarious "set up" designed for damage.

2. I attended both conferences and conferences in between, and I took detailed notes, ethnographic style. I spoke at three of the conferences.

3. Grants from both the U.S. Department of Defense and the Department of Homeland Security gave southwestern university recipients the incentive to hire people with such credentials.

4. http://warondrugsconference.utep.edu.

5. The border region is home to military installations such as Fort Bliss and to military veteran retirees.

6. In neither conference do I count the master/mistress of ceremonies.

7. Tijuana–San Diego—claiming a 4.7 million region of "one people, one region, one economy"—is home to the Smart Border Coalition and its twenty-one person, all-male board of directors, mostly from business and government (https:// smartborder coalition.com). San Diego's city boundaries have changed to cling to the border, though once-autonomous San Ysidro and large bedroom communities sit between San Diego proper and the border.

8. He was referring to burdens on the banking industry, with the government's anti-money-laundering strategies affecting banks primarily in southern California, *ambos* Nogales, and the Rio Grande Valley in south Texas (http://www.wsj.com/articles/big-banks-shut-border-branches-in-effort-to-avoid-dirty-money-1432598865).

9. His picture was perhaps a more menacing physical image and symbol than Republican presidential candidate Donald Trump's hateful assertions about Mexicans in 2015, 2016, and ongoing.

10. Peter S. Goodman and Jonathan Soble, "Global Economy's Stubborn Reality: Plenty of Work, Not Enough Pay," *New York Times*, October 7, 2017 (https://www .nytimes.com/2017/10/07/business/unemployment-wages-economy.html?action=click &module=RelatedCoverage&pgtype=Article&region=Footer).

11. These range from the historic but narrow agendas of river management (International Boundary and Water Commission [IBWC]/Comision Internacional de Limites y Agua [CILA]) to the NAFTA-linked institutions like the Commission for Environmental Cooperation (CEC) and the North American Development Bank (NADBank, which incorporated the Border Environment Cooperation Commission [BECC]).

12. Manuel Gutiérrez and Kathleen Staudt, "Governing our Borderlands Commons," in *Binational Commons: Institutional Development and Governance on the U.S.-Mexico Border*, ed. Tony Payan and Pamela L. Cruz, forthcoming.

13. I follow U.S. trade debates closely, from the Trans-Pacific Partnership [TPP] (defunct by 2017) for the U.S.-Mexico borderlands to what the U.S. trade representative calls "NAFTA Modernization" and to national alliances affiliated with Global Trade Watch/Public Citizen both through conference calls and border events. I submitted formal comment to the three-month U.S. Trade Representative (USTR) process (one of over twelve thousand!) and joined two events with the Americas Society/Council/ Council of the Americas (AS/COA), one via two-hour webinar. Business voices heavily dominated these think-tank events. In the three days of testimony that the USTR hosted, over 90 percent of those who testified represented specific business sectors (textiles, agriculture, etc.). In the short summary USTR issued, wage issues never emerged, yet the rhetoric of "fair and free trade" was utilized, thus co-opting a concept (fair trade) for U.S. business interests. For perspectives on Mexican voices in trade debates, I organized a panel of experts in February 2014 (see El Paso Social Justice Reflections/Blog, http://www.epsocialjustice.org/new-blog) and attended and blogged about an event of the MORENA (National Regeneration Movement) presidential precandidate (in a blog site that is no longer operative).

14. The Gini index is a measure of inequality (with higher numbers denoting greater internal inequality) that suffers from some of the same problems as central-tendency measures of national income absent figures from the informal economy and hidden wealth stashed abroad. Moreover, annual figures are unavailable for all countries, making comparisons difficult. However, the World Bank estimates a higher Gini figure (43.4) for Mexico (2016) than for the U.S. (41.5) (2016) (https://data.worldbank.org/indicator/SI.POV.GINI). The source also reports that 53.2 million of Mexico's 127.5 million people (2014) live in poverty compared with 49 million people in 2008. Many millions of Mexicans live outside the country.

15. Information comes from participation in cross-border labor support groups involving workers, their lawyers, and legal experts about the challenges to independent unions in Mexico.

16. In 1997, El Paso was named the city with the highest number of NAFTA-displaced workers. Most workers never recovered, and the low-quality training programs did little to retool the displaced. See Staudt and Coronado (2002), chap. 5.

REFERENCES

Ban, Cornel. 2016. *Ruling Ideas: How Global Neoliberalism Goes Local*. New York: Oxford University Press.

Brunet-Jailly, Emmanuel, ed. 2007. *Borderlands: Comparing Border Security in North America and Europe*. Ottawa: University of Ottawa Press.

Dunn, Timothy. 2009. *Blockading the Border and Human Rights*. Austin: University of Texas Press.

Gray, Robert. 2015. "Border Leaders Say Progress Is Being Made: US-Mexico Summit Brings National Leaders, Media to Region." *El Paso Inc.*, August 9–15, 12A.

Homedes, Nuria. 2012. "Achieving Health Equity and Social Justice in the US-Mexico Border Region." In *Social Justice in the US-Mexico Border Region*, edited by Mark Lusk, Kathleen Staudt, and Eva M. Moya, 127–44. Dordrecht, Netherlands: Springer.

Kleine, Dorothea. 2014. "Corporate Social Responsibility and Development." In *The Companion to Development Studies*, 3rd ed., edited by Vandana Desai and Robert B. Potter, 195–99. London: Routledge.

Lee, Erik, and Christopher Wilson, eds. 2015. *The US-Mexico Border Economy in Transition*. Washington, D.C.: Woodrow Wilson International Center for Scholars.

Llera Pacheco, Francisco, and Angeles López-Nórez. 2012. *Cross-Border Collaboration in Border Twin Cities: Lessons and Challenges for the Ciudad Juárez-El Paso and the Frankfurt (Oder)/Slubice*. Ciudad Juárez: Universidad Autónoma de Ciudad Juárez.

Miker Palafox, Martha. 2010. "World-Class Automotive Harnesses and the Precariousness of Employment in Juárez." In *Cities and Citizenship at the US-Mexico Border: The Paso del Norte Metropolitan Region*, edited by Kathleen Staudt, César Fuentes, and Julia Monárrez Fragoso, 119–143. New York: Palgrave.

Moré, Iñigo. 2011. *The Borders of Inequality: Where Wealth and Poverty Collide*. Translated from Spanish by Lynn Domínguez. Tucson: University of Arizona Press.

Moya, Eva M., Oralia Loza, and Mark Lusk. 2012. "Border Health: Inequities, Social Determinants, and the Case of Tuberculosis and HIV." In *Social Justice in the US-Mexico Border Region*, edited by Mark Lusk, Kathleen Staudt, and Eva M. Moya, 161–78. Dordrecht, Netherlands: Springer.

O'Rourke, Beto, and Susie Byrd. 2011. *Dealing Death and Drugs: The Big Business of Dope in the U.S. and Mexico*. El Paso, Tex.: Cinco Puntos Press.

Pastor, Robert. 2001. *Toward a North American Community: Lessons from the Old World for the New*. Washington, D.C.: Institute for International Economics.

Payan, Tony. 2010. "Crossborder Governance in a Tristate, Binational Region." In *Cities and Citizenship at the US-Mexico Border: The Paso del Norte Metropolitan Region*, edited by Kathleen Staudt, César Fuentes, and Julia Monárrez Fragoso, 217–44. New York: Palgrave.

Payan, Tony. 2016. *The Three US-Mexico Border Wars: Drugs, Immigration, and Homeland Security*. 2nd ed. New York: Praeger.

Payan, Tony, Kathleen Staudt, and Z. Anthony Kruszewski, eds. 2013. *A War That Can't Be Won: US-Mexico Perspectives on the War on Drugs*. Tucson: University of Arizona Press.

Staudt, Kathleen. 2009. "Violence at the Border: Broadening the Discourse to Include Feminism, Human Security, and Deeper Democracy." In *Human Rights Along the US-Mexico Border: Gendered Violence and Insecurity*, edited by Kathleen Staudt, Tony Payan, and Z. Anthony Kruszewski, 1–27. Tucson: University of Arizona Press.

Staudt, Kathleen. 2014. "The Border, Performed in Film: Produced in Mexico and the US to 'Bring Out the Worst in a Country.'" *Journal of Borderlands Studies* 29 (4): 464–80.

Staudt, Kathleen. 2017. *Border Politics in a Global Era: Comparative Perspectives*. Lanham, Md.: Rowman and Littlefield.

Staudt, Kathleen, and Irasema Coronado. 2002. *Fronteras no Más: Toward Social Justice at the US-Mexico Border*. New York: Palgrave.

Staudt, Kathleen, and Pamela Cruz. 2014. "Getting It: Business NGOs and Political Actors Talk About the US-Mexico Border Region." Paper presented at the Association of Borderlands Studies, Albuquerque (revised several times in subsequent years for possible publication).

Staudt, Kathleen, and Zulma Méndez. 2015. *Courage, Resistance, and Women in Ciudad Juárez: Challenges to Militarization*. Austin: University of Texas Press.

Staudt, Kathleen, Tony Payan, and Timothy Dunn. 2009. "Closing Reflections: Bordering Human Rights, Social Democratic Feminism, and Broad-Based Security." In *Human Rights Along the US-Mexico Border: Gendered Violence and Insecurity*, edited by Kathleen Staudt, Tony Payan, and Z. Anthony Kruszewski, 185–202. Tucson: University of Arizona Press.

Washington Valdez, Diana. 2015. "Economic Push Set to Begin." *El Paso Times*, August 10, 1A, 6A.

CHAPTER 9

Empowering Borderlands

Lessons from Cascadia and the Pacific Northwest

BRUCE AGNEW

> *The 2014 North American Leadership Summit in Toluca, Mexico*
> *encourages entrepreneurship, research and innovation for better border*
> *management and economic development in . . . highly integrated regions*
> *like the Pacific Northwest Economic Region and CaliBaja mega region.*
> —WHITE HOUSE PRESS STATEMENT, FEBRUARY 19, 2014

> *The challenge of the border leadership in the next 10 years is actually*
> *to create joint border management that respects sovereignty, but recognizes*
> *that the flows are more important than the lines in the world we live in.*
> —ALAN BERSIN, FORMER ASSISTANT SECRETARY FOR POLICY AND
> INTERNATIONAL AFFAIRS, DEPARTMENT OF HOMELAND SECURITY,

Introduction

North America borderlands differ in their cultures, values, resources, and political leadership. The most successful borderlands share a common vision for the protection of the environment and promotion of regional mobility, business, and international trade. That common vision can be successfully achieved in the context of federal sovereignty if the right subnational policy and the proper technical and financial institutions exist in the border region.

In the Pacific Northwest, we have four successful bilateral initiatives that have developed within the policy framework of federal laws, treaties, and accords. Collectively, they have advanced major infrastructure, technology, and border clearance research as well as operational projects, and they serve as test beds for greater North American border integration.

In this chapter, I will highlight the International Mobility and Trade Corridor (IMTC) project and the Border Policy Research Institute (BPRI) and expand a review of several initiatives of the Pacific Northwest Economic Region (PNWER). I will also trace the evolution of one of the initiatives—Cascadia—from academic research on sustainability in the early 1990s by urban visionary F. J. Artibise to the current high-tech Cascadia Innovation Corridor initiative led by Microsoft.

The primary lesson from the Northwest border initiatives is the importance of long-term binational and regional border institutions and the personal public and private-sector relationships they foster. Their work transcends the constant changing of the guard of political leaders (whose interest in the border will always vary) as highlighted by the new challenge from the policies of U.S. president Donald Trump, who has upended the North American integration orthodoxy.

In general, the federal governments of the three nations have not been able to keep up with the port of entry infrastructure needs, staffing, and the remarkably accelerated supply-chain and e-commerce technologies of the private sector. As we look to the future of globalization, how will ports of entry deal with the advent of autonomous trucks and drones crossing borders with time-sensitive goods and business leaders in a hurry?

The answer lies in decentralization of federal authority to the best level of decision making. National governments should focus on security and global competitiveness counseled by companies whose business it is to efficiently transport goods and people with an advanced degree of security based on technology. Binational and regional institutions should be given the flexibility to customize border operations to account for local workforce needs, trade flows, and environmental considerations.

The case for sorting out the best level of government for cross-border initiatives is referred to as "subsidiarity" in the Canadian Council of Chief Executives report "Made in North America: A New Agenda to Sharpen Our Competitive Edge":

> While national governments and their leaders must be in the vanguard of building a more competitive North America, we see considerable scope for regional and sub-national collaboration involving premiers and governors, provinces and states, as well as municipalities in all three countries.
>
> These sub-national relationships make up much of the hidden wiring that connects our 10 provinces, three territories, 81 states and two federal districts.

On issues such as automotive emission standards and the introduction of "smart" drivers' licenses, sub-national jurisdictions are often incubators and test-beds for innovations that are eventually applied nationally and across borders.

The principle of subsidiarity appears to offer the best path towards a competitive future and a functional North American architecture. In other words, the three countries should address the issues in a manner and at the level, whether trilateral, bilateral, or regional—at the level that makes the most sense.[1]

Many of the major border infrastructure deficits can also be tackled with cross-border private capital and technical talent as we have seen in the Northwest, Detroit-Windsor, and Laredo. The federal governments of Mexico, Canada, and the United States should reward success at the subnational level and accelerate distribution of resources and responsibilities.

Exporting Northwest Border Lessons

Since 1997, the International Mobility and Trade Corridor Project (IMTC) has been directed by the Whatcom Council of Governments as a regional, binational planning coalition of over fifty public and private agencies, organizations, and interests. IMTC collaboratively plans and implements improvements in mobility and security through projects totaling US$40 million at the Cascade Gateway—the four border crossings that connect Whatcom County and the Lower Mainland of British Columbia.

The IMTC leadership team of Hugh Conroy and Melissa Fanucci also shares best practices with other regions through the U.S.-Canada Transportation Border Working Group, Canadian/American Border Trade Alliance, and the North America Strategy for Competitiveness (NASCO). In twenty-two years of operation, IMTC has earned high praise from successive national leaders in Ottawa and Washington, D.C., as the model for North America border gateway planning and project funding, technical deployment, and operational innovation.

The success of IMTC is based on the ability to gather data concerning border flows of people and goods to help guide the operational and technical deployment decisions of inspection agencies. IMTC also reaches out beyond the local crossings through state, provincial, and industry partnerships to develop regional transportation models that can be benchmarked to seasonal traffic, enrollment in NEXUS, trade flows, and surface transportation mode.

One recent example of empowering local flexibility in border operations is the U.S. inbound Free and Secure Trade (FAST) lane at the Pacific Highway crossing. The IMTC engaged with private industry in supporting the U.S. Customs and Border Protection (CBP) reallocation of commercial processing infrastructure to better serve the commercial community and those traveling by bus for cruise ships and other recreational experiences. CBP removed the FAST-only booth and opened it to all traffic, reducing all truck waits from an average of forty-five minutes to no more than fifteen minutes.

As part of the pilot, trucks were rerouted behind duty free shops, and buses were able to use the previously FAST-designated lane to bypass lengthy automobile queues. Results mirrored the model, and the process remains in effect today. Further modification resulted in the FAST lane reinstatement behind the duty free shops to give them priority access to all commercial booths. Now, a "FAST First" lane allows FAST trucks to queue up for a booth faster, giving them an advantage over non-FAST trucks.

Western Washington University has managed the Border Policy Research Institute (BPRI) since 2005 as a multidisciplinary program that conducts research and publishes papers for policy makers on matters related to the Canada-U.S. border, particularly in northwest Washington. The priority areas include human mobility, border security, binational regional economies, international trade, and transportation.

BPRI was originally directed by long time Canada-U.S. scholar Don Alper, who recognized the unique border gateway/corridor between the major metropolitan and trade centers of Vancouver and Seattle/Tacoma and the need for policy direction in global trade, security procedures, tourism, and binational cooperation for the 2010 Winter Olympics in Vancouver and Whistler, British Columbia.

Laurie Trautman is now the director of BPRI and has advanced the institute's work in emerging topics with a recent report on the effects of cannabis laws in border regions. In October 2018, she hosted other binational regional-planning leaders in a program comparing practices in their respective regions.

Through a grant from the Canadian Consulate General of Seattle, the University of Windsor Cross-Border Institute, the University at Buffalo, the State University of New York, and BPRI have jointly published the Border Barometer[2] and used the October session to highlight the report. The Barometer highlighted performance metrics at each border crossing in terms of the movement of people and goods, including an analysis of regional policy and binational networks.

Session participants suggested that binational regions have three critical components: (1) political leadership from all levels of government, (2) a "culture of cooperation" between community leaders and agencies, and (3) sufficient financial resources to build infrastructure and integrate new technologies.

Political leadership comes in a variety of ways. Bill Anderson from the Cross Border Institute highlighted the government of Canada partnership with Michigan state leaders over the course of several election cycles to begin construction of the Gordie Howe International Bridge despite legal and political opposition from the incumbent, privately owned Ambassador Bridge.

Lack of political leadership can undercut cross-border initiatives too. Kathryn Friedman, from the University of Buffalo, lamented the absence of focus from state and provincial leaders in border initiatives along the Niagara frontier and turf battles among regional leaders as barriers to consistent progress in cross-border initiatives.

PNWER is a statutory, public-private nonprofit organization created in 1991 by the U.S. states of Washington, Oregon, Idaho, Alaska, and Montana and the Canadian provinces of British Columbia, Alberta, Saskatchewan Yukon, and the Northwest Territories. As former U.S. ambassador to Canada, David Jacobsen stated at several PNWER summits, "As I have travelled throughout both the United States and Canada, I have heard from leaders everywhere that PNWER is the 'Gold Standard' in advancing cross-border regional issues."[3]

Longtime director Matt Morrison manages twenty working groups that align public, private, academic, and nonprofit stakeholders on challenges ranging from broadly inconsistent agriculture inspections to operating challenges for public and private transportation providers resulting from new federal preclearance procedures.

The consistent and personal connections PNWER fosters between private-sector leaders, elected officials, and government agencies led to successful implementation of cross-border security coordination during the Vancouver/Whistler 2010 Winter Olympics. Enhanced cooperation resulted in programs such as the Olympic Shiprider project permitting the United States Coast Guard and Royal Canadian Mounted Police to conduct cross-border integrated law enforcement operations in shared waterways.

Before the 2010 Olympics, another successful binational project was pioneered by Washington State and supported by the Province of British Columbia and PNWER—the Enhanced Driver's License (EDL) program. EDL was designed to meet the requirements of the Western Hemisphere Travel Initiative using an RFID chip and accessing data bases in both countries.

At the BPRI Barometer Forum, former Washington State governor Christine Gregoire recalled when Department of Homeland Security secretary Michael Chertoff informed her that the EDL would never be able to make it through the complicated federal approval process. She persevered, and with the support of British Columbia premier Gordon Campbell and PNWER tourism leaders, the special license was approved by the U.S. government in March 2007.

EDL-type programs are also available for U.S. citizens in Michigan, Minnesota, New York, and Vermont and Canadian citizens in Manitoba, Ontario, and formerly Quebec. As noted in parliamentary proceedings in Ottawa:

> Washington and British Columbia have worked to forge what is arguably the most successful formalized cross-border partnership network in North America, both multilateral and bilateral, with partners across our borders.
>
> The Enhanced Driver's License project is not only an innovative response to a significant and potentially damaging federal policy change, it is also a paradigm of action by sub-national jurisdictions that can drive a national agenda through bilateral and multilateral cooperation and advocacy.
>
> This project was driven by the changing nature of our international border; conceived in a bilateral, cross-border forum; advocated and advanced in a cross-border partnership; and will benefit citizens by helping make our border more effective and efficient for them as they cross it.[4]

Since 2015, PNWER has supported maximum flexibility at the border gateways for implementation of preclearance through the Agreement on Land, Rail, Marine, and Air Transport Preclearance, which was signed by the United States and Canada as part of the 2011 Beyond the Border Action Plan. Preclearance exists at eight major Canadian airports, and the agreement will extend the service to trains, ferries, and cruise ships, with the first pilot projects set for train stations in Vancouver and Montreal.

Preclearance will enhance our region's US$55 billion travel and tourism sector by making cross-border transit more efficient for business travelers, tour operators, and independent leisure travelers. However, implementation of the agreement is facing several challenges, including coordination with participating carriers on facilities and technology requirements, testing technology, utilizing data, and managing personnel.

PNWER established a preclearance task force to coordinate with agencies on both sides of the border before and during the implementation of the agreement. The task force has regular conference calls with congressional staff, CBP, the U.S. Department of State, the U.S. Department of Homeland Security, the Canadian Border Services Agency (CBSA), Public Safety Canada, Transport Canada, and dozens of private-sector carriers and trade associations across the northern border to review the challenges, process, timeline, and implementation of preclearance.

Washington and British Columbia share the common waters of the Salish Sea and present a perfect international test bed of cross-border seaplanes, cruise ships, high-speed ferries, intercity bus and tour coaches, and Amtrak Cascades and Rocky Mountaineer passenger rail services. This binational regional and multimodal transportation system is connected to international gateways through major airports in Vancouver and Seattle/Tacoma.

Looking at the next generation of technology (think facial recognition and avoidance of long TSA lines), PNWER is a cochair of the Beyond Preclearance Coalition, which released the Next Generation Canada-U.S. Border report on October 5, 2018.[5] The coalition was formed to develop a long-term vision for trade and travel with the United States–Mexico–Canada Agreement (USMCA) emerging as the successor to the North American Free Trade Agreement (NAFTA). The technology-driven border-management system envisioned by Alan Bersin at the beginning of this chapter is embedded in the report and is particularly applicable to the recent increasing migration of technology talent to the Northwest.

Cascadia: From an Urban Vision to a High-Tech Corridor

The Cascadia region of British Columbia, Washington, and Oregon has been the historic focus of nearly thirty years of binational cooperation on the environment, international trade, and the "Two Nation Vacation" tourism economy. Cascadia advocates are deeply committed to the conservation of nature, a point recently highlighted by cross-border and multilevel government cooperation with tribal nations to save several starving southern resident orca whales in the boundary waters of the Salish Sea. The Cascadia Center of Discovery Institute issued a 1993 report that highlighted the economic rationale for a new strategic regionalism: "In the new global economy, metropolitan regions even more than states, and perhaps more than nations are the key entities that compete in world markets. These regions simply must cooperate and coordinate their efforts more closely to be competitive in the new global economy."[6]

Cascadia advocates included Charles Kelly, publisher of the *New Pacific*, who viewed Cascadia in geographical terms as a new regional order in need of political reorganization, greater cooperation to compete in international markets, and harmonization of contradictory regulations. Paul Schell, former Seattle mayor and Port of Seattle commissioner early on envisioned high-speed rail connecting the Seattle, Vancouver, and Portland metro areas and international airports, and he developed a preliminary bid to bring the Summer Olympic Games to the Cascadia region in 2008.

Alan F. J. Artibise, a professor from the University of British Columbia and founding executive director of the International Centre for Sustainable Cities, was a recognized leader in promoting the Cascadia concept beginning in 1990. He understood that real cross-border cooperation to address common challenges, such as sustainable population growth, required a blending of commerce, conservation, and community goals deployed through political networks.

In 1997, Artibise collaborated with academic land-use planner Ethan Seltzer and urban-design leader Anne Moudon in a case study titled "Cascadia: An Emerging Regional Model" in urbanist Robert Geddes's edited volume *Cities in Our Future*. As the editor's introduction states:

> Cascadia is both an economic idea integrating the emerging settlements along
> a regional corridor (a main street called Interstate 5), and an ecological idea,
> informed by the geology, vegetation, natural species, climate (the "rain coast")
> and movements of water in and through the settlements.[7]

Highlighting the grassroots nature of Cascadia, local governments, tourism, and trade interests worked with Artibise's Cascadia Planning Group and Discovery's Cascadia Center. Elected leaders in the Greater Vancouver Regional District, Puget Sound Regional Council, and Portland Metro Council shared best regional practices at Cascadia Metropolitan and Mayors Forums for several years.

In 1999, the Cascadia Planning Group advocated formation of a Cascadia Corridor Corporation—a binational public-private partnership that would oversee a US$100 billion twenty-year rebuild and expansion of border crossings, roads, bridges, and high-speed rail along the Interstate 5–Highway 99 border. "Cooperation in a corridor context has numerous, clear advantages," the Planning Group noted under the heading "Cooperating Regionally to Compete Globally."[8]

The terrorist attacks of September 11, 2001, resulted in the hardening of the Canada-U.S. border, formation of the giant Department of Homeland Security, and some loss of political energy for Cascadia. At Western Washington University, Don Alper outlined in numerous publications how exclusionary border policies ("thickening of the border") post 9/11 have had a negative effect on host societies and have undercut technological advances to binational cooperation and "smarter borders."

Corridor infrastructure ideas were revived when Cascadia was named as one of ten "Mega Regions" identified by the Regional Planning Association of New York in their America 2050 report. In 2010, the Cascadia Center cosponsored the America 2050 forum through a grant from the Bill and Melinda Gates Foundation at Portland's Metro Center on "Cascadia High Speed Rail." Much of the data on land use, environmental sustainability, and urban-transport systems in Portland, Seattle/Tacoma, and Vancouver used in the seminar came from the University of Washington, Portland State University, and the Cascadia Planning Group.

Cascadia Innovative Corridor

With the filing of several executive orders by the Trump administration restricting immigration, high-tech companies in the Seattle area, including Amazon and Microsoft, are locating more employees in Vancouver and other Canadian locations. While the administration promises to overhaul and restrict the H-1B visa program (which allows U.S. employers to temporarily employ foreign workers in specialty occupations), Canada has introduced the Global Skills Visa, which enables companies to bring in skilled employees to the country in two weeks.

The surge of high-tech employment in Vancouver and cross-border interest from private-sector companies led by Microsoft and several universities helped launch the Cascadia Innovation Corridor in 2017. Greg D'Avignon, president and CEO of the Business Council of British Columbia and co-chair of the Innovation Corridor steering committee said the goal of the corridor is to create a region that "acts as a magnet for the world's top talent and capital resources."[9]

Supported by the council and Challenge Seattle, the Innovation Corridor has reenergized the previous Cascadia "new regional order" concept and incubated several cross-border mobility and research initiatives. "Harbor to Harbour" seaplane service was resumed between Coal Harbour, Vancouver, and South Lake Union in Seattle, and Washington governor Jay Inslee and British

Columbia premier John Horgan supported the Cascadia High Speed Rail study with a mix of state, provincial, and private financing in 2018 and 2019.

In a related initiative, the Madrona Venture Group in Seattle has published two reports calling for deployment of autonomous vehicles on Interstate 5 and British Columbia Highway 99. Madrona cofounder and CEO Tom Alberg and INRIX CEO Bryan Mistele have formed the ACES NW Network to pursue testing electric and autonomous vehicles in the Cascadia corridor, including a potentially autonomous truck border-crossing pilot project at the Cascade Gateway's newly expanded Lynden Aldergrove commercial crossing.

Who Will Build North American Border Infrastructure?

At the 2014 North America Summit in Toluca, former U.S. president Barack Obama joined former Mexico president Enrique Peña Nieto and former Canadian prime minister Stephen Harper in heralding a twenty-first-century North American competitive work plan with a proposed trilateral transportation plan as one of the foundational building blocks. In March 2016, bilateral relations between Canada and the United States reached a higher level when Obama and newly elected prime minister Justin Trudeau announced new immigration procedures to make the Canada-U.S. border more open and secure through preclearance and pledged a commitment to joint climate-change programs, clean energy innovation, and Arctic leadership.

The past year of the Trump administration had been tumultuous, with "national security"–based tariff wars and ever-evolving immigration procedures bringing uncertainty to regional economic markets, workforce mobility, and border operations. The hyperpolitical dialogue between the North American leaders on border security and trade imbalances contrasted sharply with the commitment to cooperative investments and private-sector innovation at Toluca.

In 2019, with the USMCA now pending legislative approval, a better opportunity to foster federal partnerships for infrastructure has emerged. Regional, binational initiatives can engage private-sector interest, equity capital, and industry leadership to build projects and update border processing in ways the federal governments envisioned in Toluca. In his book *The North America Idea: A Vison for a Continental Future*, Robert Pastor points out that the North American Development Bank (NADB) has funded environmental projects near the Mexico-U.S.

border and suggests an expansion of the NADB mandate to include transportation projects, access to domestic capital markets, and new technologies.[10] With consistent federal leadership, provincial partnerships and private capital, long-discussed critical North American infrastructure projects can move forward.

The most significant cross-border infrastructure project (estimated at US$4.4 billion) is underway through the perseverance by the government of Canada and the province of Ontario with the new Gordie Howe International Bridge at Detroit/Windsor Gateway, the busiest commercial crossing on the northern border. The Canadian government is financing the bridge, which will be owned jointly by the governments of Canada and Michigan.

The project faced serious political and legal opposition from the private owners of the existing Ambassador Bridge, who want to build their own new span. They filed several lawsuits and urged President Trump to force the Gordie Howe Bridge to use more U.S. steel by removing a waiver granted by former president Obama.

On the southern border, despite the continuing media coverage of separated families and immigrant caravans of asylum seekers from Central America, cross-border trade is robust and growing. At a recent NASCO Reunion in Vancouver, Mario Maldonado, executive director of transportation, Laredo International Bridge and City of Laredo, highlighted a successful strategy of cross-border investments and multigovernmental incentives to investors for trade infrastructure in spite of tariff and immigration uncertainties.

Laredo is the largest U.S. land port of entry by volume, with more than US$200 billion in trade flows. Roughly half of U.S.-Mexico trade passes over the commercial Laredo Colombia Solidarity and World Trade Bridges. The bridge system secured funding for a Free and Secure Trade (FAST) lanes relocating project, while Mexico improved Highway 40, and the state of Texas pursues funding for upgrades on Interstate 35 and Loop 20.

Conclusion

North America borderlands can be successful if they are empowered by the federal governments of North America to become "innovative and entrepreneurial" as called for by national leaders in the 2014 Toluca summit. While political sovereignty is sacrosanct, successful border management—ten years from now—will also revolve around embracing industry technology that secures and tracks the globalized flow of goods and people seamlessly in a safer world.

The Pacific Northwest has developed the "Gold Standard" of binational, regional institutions through a combination of several factors beginning with border data and modeling partnerships to measure border performance. Our long-term, cross-border institutions showcase the power of personal relationships among federal agencies; state, provincial, and local governments; universities; and private industry that lead to successful joint project planning and financing, introduction of technologies, and customization of border operations to local conditions.

Political leadership from the governor of Washington, premier of British Columbia, and private industry overcame federal agency resistance, resulting in adoption of the much lauded Enhanced Driver's License program, which expanded nationally. The "subsidiarity" business model of border issues triaged through a trilateral/bilateral/regional governance lens would have rewarded the innovation quickly and avoided a lot of political wrangling and wasted time.

Finally, successful borderlands have found ways to expand binational funding of infrastructure and leverage private equity, as we learned from the Laredo and Gordie Howe Bridge and trade corridor projects. The expansion of NADB's mission can accelerate that joint investment to support trade and North American economic integration.

Canada, Mexico, and the United States should accelerate the public-private partnership finance and risk-sharing model to the construction and operation of traditional cross-border infrastructure in light of federal budget constraints. They should also embrace and incorporate the creative, emerging technology advances in moving people and goods safely and efficiently that industry offers.

Empowerment of North America borderlands will ultimately enhance our global competitiveness while improving the daily crossing experience of our citizens.

NOTES

1. Eric Miller, John Dillon, Colin Robertson, Canadian Council of Chief Executives report, "Made in North America: A New Agenda to Sharpen Our Competitive Edge," December 2014, 8.

2. "WWU's Border Policy Research Institute Begins Work on New 'Border Barometer' Project," Western Washington University, Westerntoday (https://westerntoday.wwu.edu /news/releases/wwu-s-border-policy-research-institute-begins-work-on-new-border -barometer-project).

3. http://www.pnwer.org.

4. From the *Canadian Parliamentary Review* 31, no. 1 (2008).

5. Next Generation Canada U.S. Border report by InterVISTAS Consulting with contributions from Coalition members and insights gathered at the Woodrow Wilson Center and Public Policy Forum roundtables held between March and August 2018 (https://www.beyondpreclearance.org/white-paper).

6. John Hamer and Bruce Chapman, "Lead, Follow or Get Out of the Way," *New Pacific* (1993): 52–55.

7. Robert Geddes, ed., *Cities in Our Future: Growth and Form, Environmental Health and Social Equity* (Washington, D.C.: Island Press, 1997), 148.

8. Cascadia Planning Group, "British Columbia–Washington Corridor Task Force Memorandum," 1999, 3–4.

9. *Seattle Times*, "Cascadia Innovation Corridor: From Vision to Reality," October 8, 2018.

10. Robert A. Pastor, *The North American Idea: A Vision of a Continental Future* (New York: Oxford University Press, 2011).

PART IV

Integration and Border Policy Directions in North America

CHAPTER 10

North American Energy Ties Across Unequal Borders

Canada-U.S.-Mexico Energy Integration in Times of Border Disruption

GUADALUPE CORREA-CABRERA AND MICHELLE KECK

Abstract

This chapter presents a comparative analysis of energy developments on both the U.S.-Canada and U.S.-Mexico borders regarding economic integration for the purpose of energy production. It examines advances toward energy integration in both border regions and highlights the differences and limitations of these processes. The primary areas of concern are potential environmental issues that affect the entire region, a more nationalistic energy approach in Mexico, and security and corruption problems that might jeopardize a future inclusion of Mexico in a successfully integrated North American energy region.

Introduction

North American borders have experienced two contradictory dynamics in the last quarter century. On the one hand, the U.S.-Mexico and U.S.-Canada borders had been erased in response to commercial and energy integration from 1994. On the other hand, the two borders, especially the U.S.-Mexico border, have been more demarcated and visible because of U.S. Department of Homeland Security initiatives following the attacks of September 11, 2001, and the election of President Donald Trump in 2016. This analysis focuses on those events and topic areas where the borders began to be eliminated rather than on the issues that continue to reinforce the concept and existence of physical borders in North America. Even so, recent times have witnessed the attempt to redraw many of these borders, including commercial ones. This new dynamic originated with the 2016 U.S. presidential election and continued with the election of Andrés Manuel López Obrador as president of Mexico in 2018. Despite the sound and the fury the respective presidential elections concerning North American borders, the energy sector appears to remain as expected, and there is still a case of rapid North American integration in almost every area but environmental regulation.

Since 1994, Canada, the United States, and Mexico have become integrated through the North American Free Trade Agreement (NAFTA) to allow free trade and the reduction of tariffs. However, this integration has not been fully completed in the region and might now face further limitations following U.S. president Donald Trump's call for a renegotiation of the free-trade agreement. North American integration in the energy sector has been particularly slow for Mexico, as the Mexican constitution did not allow private-sector participation in hydrocarbon and electricity production. The commercial borders of the United States and Canada experienced integration decades before the 1994 signing of NAFTA. However, Mexico's full integration lagged behind because of the persistence of a state monopoly in its energy production.

In December 2013, the Mexican Congress passed a historic constitutional reform that opened Mexico's energy sector for the participation of further private investment, thus drawing new commercial boundaries. The new boundaries could be under threat from López Obrador, who has been opposed to foreign investment in the energy sector in the past and has spoken of revitalizing PEMEX. Although there is little fear that the energy reforms will be reversed, concerns among U.S. energy companies are that the new Mexican administration could disrupt future integration in several ways including an end to new oil licensing, passage of new environmental regulations and land-access laws that could stifle existing projects, and extension of special privileges to PEMEX (Flannery 2018).

The following analysis describes and compares the progress of energy integration between the U.S.-Canada and U.S.-Mexico regions. Analysis begins with a brief description of bilateral energy developments in the two regions of interest followed by a detailed description of recent cross-border infrastructure projects and the recent formation of bilateral alliances for energy development aimed to achieve North American energy independence in the current world energy markets. The conclusion highlights actual and potential limitations for achieving this goal, especially in light of U.S. and Mexico policy developments following the presidential elections of Donald Trump and Andrés Manuel López Obrador. Questions surrounding the new United States–Mexico–Canada Agreement (USMCA), as well as trilateral cooperation on climate change and clean energy initiatives are major issues that affect future energy cooperation among the three countries.

U.S.-Canada Energy Integration

The United States and Canada have a long history of energy trade in oil and natural gas shipped across their borders since the 1800s. The first recorded international electricity interconnection crossed the U.S.-Canada border near Niagara Falls in 1909, and the two countries have continued to operate an integrated electricity grid under jointly developed reliability standards. Oil discoveries in 1947 in the Western Canadian Sedimentary Basin—extending from the Canadian Shield to the Rocky Mountains through Manitoba, Saskatchewan, Alberta, and northeastern British Columbia—accelerated energy cooperation by providing the United States access to secure overland oil supplies, resulting in U.S. investment in the Canadian energy industry, including the purchase of Canadian oil and gas companies by major U.S. corporations. The event also marked an increase in the construction of oil and natural gas pipelines between the two countries. Currently there are approximately seventy operating oil and natural gas pipelines that cross the U.S.-Canada border (Natural Resources Canada 2015).

The U.S.-Canada energy relationship has been characterized as market based because of the following features: joint deregulation of the oil and gas sectors in the late 1970s/early 1980s, private-sector orientations of national energy sectors, liberalized trade in energy through provisions in the 1987 Free Trade Agreement, the 1994 North American Free Trade Agreement (NAFTA) and the proposed USMCA, and the cooperation in the electricity sector. Gattinger (2012) notes that while the U.S. and Canadian governments have affected business decisions in the energy sector through joint efforts to fight climate change and promote renewable energy, bilateral energy relations—to include investment, trade flows, and energy prices—are driven by market forces. Relations in natural gas and petroleum in particular are so integrated through shared cooperation in development, production, transportation, marketing, and joint ventures between U.S. and Canadian corporations that they operate as a single market (Parfomak and Ratner 2011).

Private industry's cooperation and its substantial involvement have driven Canada and the United States to have the most integrated and interdependent energy markets in the world (Dukert 2005). The importance of their energy trade relationship has continued to grow. In 2010, oil and natural gas trade between the two countries was around US$100 billion (Parfomak and Ratner 2011). Canada is the largest overall supplier of energy to the United States and is its single largest foreign supplier of petroleum products and natural gas energy, providing 33 percent of U.S. crude oil imports and 85 percent of U.S. natural gas imports (Rosner and McKee 2014). The relationship is reciprocally important to U.S. producers; for example, in 2010 the United States exported US$13.5 billion worth of energy commodities to Canada (Parfomak and Ratner 2011).

U.S.-Mexico Energy Integration and Mexico's Energy Reform

United States and Mexico's energy relations developed more slowly because of Mexico's constitutional mandate that Mexico be the exclusive entity to develop and produce hydrocarbons. Although the 1993 ratification of NAFTA opened the door to major constitutional reforms in a number of Mexican economic sectors, hydrocarbons remained under state control. Even so, chapter 6 of NAFTA contained language that allowed for the gradual liberalization of Mexico's energy sector. Morales (2011) notes that modest reforms came as a result, including a gradual privatization of the petrochemical industry as well as liberalized cross-border trade and limited private-sector involvement in the electricity and natural gas sectors.

While elements discussed in chapter 6 of NAFTA resulted in narrow liberalization of the energy sector, significant change finally occurred on December 21, 2013, when Mexico's Congress passed far-reaching constitutional reforms to open the energy sector to private participation and worldwide investment after seventy-six years of state monopoly.[1] Subsequently, Mexico's lawmakers passed a series of new laws and amendments that created the legal and regulatory framework under which foreign energy companies can operate in Mexico. The overall reform, which will fundamentally reshape Mexico's energy landscape, includes twelve amended laws and nine new secondary laws with changes governing the upstream, midstream, and downstream hydrocarbon sectors. The enabling or secondary legislation was approved in August 2014 (Government of Mexico 2014a, 2014b, 1958/2008).

Through this reform, domestic and foreign private investors are now allowed "to participate in activities like refining, transport, storage and distribution of oil, natural gas, fuels and other oil products" (O'Neil and Taylor 2014, para. 6). At the same time, the private sector can participate in exploration and production of oil and gas in three new ways, specifically, through licenses, profit sharing, and production-sharing agreements.[2] The private sector can also participate in the generation of electricity. This reform includes a new regulatory framework that divides oversight of the oil and gas sectors among a group of entities, including the Secretariat of Energy, the National Hydrocarbons Commission (Comisión Nacional de Hidrocarburos [CNH]), the Energy Regulatory Commission (Comisión Reguladora de Energía [CRE]), the National Agency of Industrial Safety and Environmental Protection of the Secretariat of Environment and Natural Resources (Secretaría del Medio Ambiente y Recurso Naturales [SEMARNAT]), the Secretariat of Finance and Public Credit (Secretaría de Hacienda y Crédito Público [SHCP]),[3] and two new centers called the National Natural Gas Control Center (Centro Nacional de Control del Gas Natural [CENAGAS]) and the National Electricity Control Center (Centro Nacional de Control de Energía [CENACE]).[4] What is more, with the new legislation, PEMEX and the Federal Electricity Commission (Comisión Federal de Electricidad [CFE]) have transitioned from monopoly status to state-owned productive enterprises (O'Neil and Taylor 2014).

Mexico's new economic reality under energy reform also required a number of fundamental changes in the legislation of land ownership and use. The changes were made in anticipation of potential land-related conflicts associated with hydrocarbon exploration and production as well as with the creation of new energy-related infrastructure projects. To prevent land-related conflicts, the new energy legislation was passed. Through the implementation of energy reform, landowners and users might be affected by some specific investment projects targeted to develop this strategic sector, but they do not have the right of refusal (Correa-Cabrera 2019; Payan and Correa-Cabrera 2014b, 3). In fact, "the law precludes the landowner's ability to say no and halt operations by denying access to the property" (Payan and Correa-Cabrera 2014b, 3).

The Mexican government's approach to promoting growth and economic development based on the energy sector has been supported by the private sector, especially its transnational energy corporations. For example, when referring to energy reform, ConocoPhillips CEO Ryan Lance said it "represents an interesting opportunity for the industry." He sees Mexico as "a resource-rich country" that can do and "is doing today interesting things to attract investment." Thus, he is "looking forward to the opportunity to go participate there" (McCumber Hearst 2015, para. 31). Actually, there appeared to be a consensus among the Mexican government and the business community—national and transnational—that "energy reform [would] eventually boost oil production, increase the country's natural-gas supply, and lower the cost of electricity generation" (Haahr 2015, 6). Mexico's energy reform was reinforced by the recent passage of fiscal, labor, and education reforms as well. Overall, the changes were designed to improve "the ease with which companies can do business in Mexico, removing legal obstacles and furthering labor flexibility" (Paley 2014, 90). U.S. energy companies are in line to become the biggest beneficiaries of Mexico's new energy regime.

Indeed, the new context opened unique areas of opportunity for foreign companies in Mexico. The changes that ended state-owned PEMEX's monopoly over the nation's vast energy resources and allowed foreign direct investment in Mexico's energy industry for the first time in seventy-six years were well received by the international community, who referred to a new era of Mexico's development and stability after a period of intense security and energy crises. The reform allows private international energy companies to develop unexplored oil and gas resources, creating at least four areas of opportunity: (1) shale oil and gas resources, (2) the generation of additional pipeline infrastructure and opportunities to invest in midstream infrastructure, (3) partnerships between PEMEX and private investors, and (4) opening electricity generation to private investment (O'Neil and Taylor 2014, paras. 19–21).[5]

Notwithstanding the last point and the commitment of the past Mexican administration with energy reform and the promotion of foreign investments in the energy sector, the situation may change slightly under the presidency of Andrés Manuel López Obrador. While the newer reforms cannot be reverted, their pace of change might slow down considerably.

Recent U.S.-Canada Energy Infrastructure Projects

The United States and Canada have a long history of pursuing joint energy projects dating back to the first oil pipeline constructed between the countries in 1941. That pipeline carried oil from Maine to refineries in Montreal. Recent energy infrastructure projects between the United States and Canada have involved such enterprises as the transportation of crude from oil sands located in the Western Canadian Sedimentary Basin in Alberta to the United States, the transportation of natural gas from the Marcellus and Utica shale basins in the northeastern United States to Canada, a proposed electricity transmission line project from hydroelectric plants in Canada to the New England region of the United States, and development of natural gas resources in the Artic. All of these developments have provided new opportunities and challenges to the close energy relationship between the countries.

The United States has become increasingly reliant on Canadian oil sands. In 2005, U.S. imports of Canadian oil sands were roughly 0.6 million barrels per day; however, as of 2013, these imports have doubled to 1.2 million barrels per day (Rosner and McKee 2014). In response to increased demand, the Trans-Canada Corporation proposed the development of the Keystone pipeline in 2005. The National Energy Board of Canada approved the pipeline in 2007, followed by approval from the Obama administration a year later. The Keystone pipeline was commissioned in 2010 and was built in four phases, with the first phase stretching 2,219 kilometers from Alberta to Illinois; phase two was completed in 2011, extending 468 kilometers from Nebraska to Oklahoma; and the final phase completed in late 2015, spanning 860 kilometers from Oklahoma to refineries along the Texas Gulf Coast.

While the Canadian and U.S. governments approved the Keystone pipeline with little fanfare, the Keystone XL expansion, proposed by TransCanada in 2008, received a decidedly different response. The National Energy Board of Canada acted quickly to approve the project, starting hearings on the pipeline in September 2009 and approving the project in March 2010. However, the reception of the pipeline in the United States was much more contentious, breaking down along partisan lines with Democrats and environmentalists against Republicans and the oil and gas industry supporters. Critics of the pipeline complained about lowered safety standards, the lack of specific plans to deal with potential spills, the negative environmental effects from oil sand extraction, and the addition of greenhouse gas emissions resulting from continued reliance on fossil fuels instead of cleaner alternatives. There were also issues of crossing Native American land and objections to that by both Native American and environmental activists. On the other hand, proponents argued that the pipeline would provide the United States access to oil from a safe and stable ally, create high-wage jobs, and stimulate economic growth.

Former Canadian prime minister Stephen Harper, head of the Conservative government from 2006 to 2015, repeatedly heralded the benefits of the pipeline and urged Obama administration approval. After seven years of debate, former U.S. president Obama, citing his efforts to make the United States a leader in fighting climate change and seeking to add to his legacy on climate-change initiatives, rejected the plan in November 2015.

Although the government of Canada was on the record as supporting the pipeline, the newly elected Liberal government, headed by Prime Minister Justin Trudeau, publicly voiced support for Keystone XL. However, public statements were accompanied by private relief that the project was not approved so that the Trudeau administration could better focus on improving Canada's record on combatting climate change (Austen 2015). Regardless of the private sentiments of the Trudeau administration, TransCanada indicated that it would sue the Obama administration for US$15 billion through NAFTA. TransCanada also filed a lawsuit in Houston asking for the decision to be overturned.

The surprising election of Donald Trump in the 2016 U.S. presidential election altered the fate of the Keystone XL pipeline. Throughout the 2016 election, Trump campaigned on reversing the Obama decision, vowing to approve the pipeline if elected to create jobs and promote U.S. energy independence. President Trump kept his campaign promise: in March 2017, the U.S. State Department approved TransCanada's permit to allow the company to complete construction on the pipeline to carry oil from Canada to the U.S. Gulf Coast. Although the federal government has approved the project, the Keystone XL pipeline still faces obstacles because of the need for approval from regulators in U.S. states through which the pipeline will pass. Strong opposition to the pipeline is expected, raising new concerns about the future of the project in spite of federal approval (Mufson 2018).

Technological advances in hydrological fracking have led to large discoveries of shale gas in the Marcellus and Utica basins located in the northeastern United States. Production has steadily increased from less than two billion cubic feet per day to 19 billion cubic feet per day in 2015, thereby exceeding Canadian natural gas production (Hussain 2015). While these discoveries benefit U.S. producers, they have also raised concerns among Canadian natural gas producers. In recent years, the U.S. has relied on Canada for 88 percent of its natural gas imports. However, as U.S. production has increased, U.S. imports from Canada have declined (Parfomak and Ratner 2011). In addition, in 2010, the U.S. Federal Energy Regulatory Commission (FERC) approved a new pipeline from the Marcellus shale to eastern Canada, thereby undermining western Canadian producers, eroding their market share in the Midwest and eastern markets of the United States and Canada.

A final energy project currently in approval stages is the Northern Pass project, a 309-kilometer transmission line to bring 1,090 megawatts of clean energy from hydroelectric plants in Quebec, Canada, to the New Hampshire and New England electric grid. Project officers submitted their presidential permit application to the U.S. Department of Energy in 2010, and the project's Transmission Service Agreement was accepted by FERC in 2011. Unlike the Keystone XL project, the Northern Pass relies on clean energy. Even so, concerns emerged about overhead lines affecting key scenic locations in New Hampshire, including the White Mountain National Forest and areas along the Appalachian Trail. In order to address these concerns, the project amended their presidential permit in 2013 to include information about a new route in which 84 kilometers would now be underground to eliminate its visual effect on park vistas and habitats.

Future energy cooperation between the United States and Canada involves the development of resource-rich regions in the Artic. A U.S. Geological Survey assessment estimates that the Artic region held by the United States and Canada holds approximately 1,600 trillion cubic feet of undiscovered conventional natural gas resources (Parfomak and Ratner 2011). Both countries are actively exploring the construction of pipelines to carry Artic natural gas to markets in the continental United States and Canada. In 2008, Alaska gave TransCanada a license to build an Alaska natural gas pipeline to the lower forty-eight U.S. states. A competing all Canadian pipeline was proposed at roughly the same time. Increased climate-change initiatives appeared set to boost the demand for natural-gas-fueled electricity generation, prompting much optimism regarding the development of Artic resources; however, increased production from U.S. shale has undercut natural gas prices, making Artic projects less profitable for the near future.

Mexico's New Energy Infrastructure

The new energy reforms in Mexico have resulted in significant investments in infrastructure intended to promote cross-border trade and energy development in the hydrocarbon-rich areas between Mexico and the United States to include markets abroad. These developments have been reinforced through investment projects (highways, roads, bridges, hydroelectric power stations, and a variety of energy infrastructure projects) that have connected important centers of development in strategic hydrocarbon-rich areas between the two countries (Correa-Cabrera 2019; Payan and Correa-Cabrera 2016).[6]

The construction of border and port infrastructure for international trade was a priority for Mexico's past two administrations. Key examples include the creation of major border crossings. In January 2010, for example, one of the biggest and most modern international bridges between Mexico and its northern neighbor was inaugurated: the Anzaldúas International Bridge, also known as the Reynosa-McAllen Bridge. This border crossing has facilitated the speedy transit of people and commercial products by spanning the Rio Grande / Río Bravo and connecting Mexico's border city of Reynosa to the U.S. towns of Mission and McAllen in Texas. Economically, the region is highly dynamic and very important to energy production. As well, in August 2015, the United States and Mexico launched the West Rail Bypass Bridge, the first rail crossing built between the two nations. The bridge was constructed between Matamoros, Tamaulipas, and Brownsville, Texas, and it will "move rail traffic currently flowing through the downtown area of the two cities to the outskirts of the metropolitan area" (Embassy of the United States in Mexico 2014, para. 1). In addition, the area is key to energy production and transportation—consider, for example, the proposals to build liquefied natural gas (LNG) export terminals at the Port of Brownsville (Clark 2018).

The recent construction of highways on both sides of the border better link the two nations, particularly the hydrocarbon-rich regions, where the energy sector will experience additional development in the near future. Strategic ports located along the Gulf coast—including those in New Orleans, Houston, Tampico, Veracruz, and Coatzacoalcos—will be better connected. Important efforts have been made to connect these centers of energy development.[7] For example, in September 2014, the Mexico-Tuxpan highway, which connects Mexico's capital city with the oil-rich state of Veracruz, was inaugurated.

On the U.S. side of the border, advances in highway construction have connected important areas of energy development in both countries, particularly in the U.S.-Mexico border region. The construction of the I-69 highway is exemplary. Related works include the lengthening of Highway 281—which connects Pharr and San Antonio, Texas, and crosses the country reaching the border with Canada—and U.S. Highway 77—which connects Brownsville, Texas, and Dakota City. Highway I-69, also known as "NAFTA's commercial corridor," crosses the United States through Texas, Arkansas, Mississippi, Tennessee, Kentucky, Indiana, and Michigan, and then reaches the border with Canada. Additionally, I-69 is connected with the center of Mexico and its Pacific coast through the Mazatlán-Matamoros superhighway.[8]

In recent years, Mexico enacted a series of major reforms and initiatives, including the National Infrastructure Program 2014–2018, that outline major programs and projects in the areas of energy, water, telecommunications, transportation, urban and rural development, health, and tourism. It is worth noting that many of the projects in the National Infrastructure Program (Programa Nacional de Infraestructura [PNI]) were directly linked to hydrocarbons exploration and production. Researcher Francisco Cravioto—who specializes in public policies related to extractive industries at the NGO Fundar Center for Research and Analysis and who is also member of the Mexican Alliance Against Fracking (Alianza Mexicana contra el Fracking)—notes that most of the PNI projects, including aqueducts, gas pipelines, highways, and construction of cable networks, were designed to strengthen and complete energy reform (Ramírez 2014, para. 21). For example, plans to complete the storage and distribution terminal in Tuxpan, Veracruz, were supposed to augment five-hundred-fold the nominal capacity to store gasoline, diesel, and petrol additives in the key port of Tuxpan with an aim of satisfying demand for these products in the short, medium, and long terms (Ramírez 2014, para. 23).

Mexico's energy reforms have created a new reality, perhaps a new development model, based on the projected development of the country's oil sector. Additionally, such reforms were "being used to generate new sources of electricity and to add hundreds of miles of new natural gas pipelines and power lines" in Mexico (Chapa 2015, para. 1).[9] Billions of dollars were recently allocated to build power plants, electrical distribution facilities, and natural gas pipelines. U.S. pipeline companies and gas producers have been the main beneficiaries of these developments (Black 2015, para. 1) (see map 7, fig. 10.1). Recently,

Mexico's CFE opened up a significant number of new energy projects for bidding starting in the summer of 2015 (Chapa 2015b, para. 2). The bids for the construction of gas pipelines are of particular importance because of Mexico's attempts to increase its domestic supplies of natural gas. Over the course of a few years, Mexico's natural gas use has been at its highest levels (U.S. Energy Information Administration 2013, para. 6). However, the future of its reforms and the further expansion of projects such as this are uncertain under Andrés Manuel López Obrador's new administration.

Today, Mexico must import large amounts of natural gas to meet the growing demand,[10] with U.S. natural gas exports to Mexico projected to significantly increase in the coming years. Mexico's natural gas imports now account for over 30 percent of its total supply (U.S. Energy Information Administration 2013, para. 6). Yet ironically, Mexico has "vast untapped deposits of gas in domestic shale rock formations." However, some claim that because of lack of infrastructure and limited capacity, "it will take years for the country to unlock those reserves while facing a severe natural gas shortage in the meantime. Consequently, at least for the medium term new pipeline capacity will be needed" (Kilisek 2014, para. 6).

Emilio Lozoya, former CEO of PEMEX, was a major advocate of expanded pipeline capacity. According to Lozoya, "The Mexican economy needs more natural gas." While heading PEMEX, he recognized that Mexico has the natural gas but does not have the necessary pipelines. Therefore, in his view, there was a need to build "thousands of kilometers of natural gas pipelines" with the help of partners to finance them. Lozoya argued that in the next few years "the number of kilometers of natural gas pipelines [would] increase by 75% in the country." He saw "these as the arteries of the economy to bring natural gas to some parts of Mexico that today are very energy inefficient" (Sheehan 2015, para. 7). In this context, a number of U.S. pipeline projects to support additional natural gas exports to Mexico were recently constructed and are supposed "to double existing capacity" (U.S. Energy Information Administration 2013, para. 5; Correa-Cabrera 2019).

Recent proposed projects connect South Texas, a key center of production of natural gas, with key energy hubs in Mexico. One of these projects is the Nueces County to Brownsville pipeline, located in the United States, which moves natural gas from the Eagle Ford Shale to the border (Chapa 2015, para. 5). Another important project of this type is the South Texas–Tuxpan pipeline, worth an estimated US$3.1 billion and considered to be the biggest proposed natural gas pipeline project in South Texas. It seeks to move natural gas from the border to Tuxpan, Veracruz, via an underwater pipeline in the Gulf of Mexico interconnected with the Nueces-Brownsville and the Tuxpan-Tula pipelines (Black 2015; Chapa 2015).

Proposed by U.S. "energy companies to export gas from shale fields, which is extracted by the method of hydraulic fracturing, to buyers in Mexico and other countries," these projects are among many others for consideration. (Paterson 2014 para. 5). The U.S. Federal Energy Regulatory Commission (FERC) recently approved a permit for the construction of an additional cross-border natural gas pipeline projected for the export of shale gas from Hidalgo County, Texas, to Reynosa, Tamaulipas (Paterson 2014, paras. 1–2).

The Los Ramones natural gas pipeline is another key project designed to improve gas supply in central Mexico. It is considered the backbone of the country's natural gas system (Dorantes 2014; Paterson 2014). Los Ramones links "the prolific Eagle Ford shale formation . . . in south Texas to central Mexico's industrial heartland" (Kilisek 2014, para. 6). The construction of this massive project required an investment of more than US$2.5 billion, and it was built with the intent of supplying Mexico's manufacturing industry and increasing natural gas transportation capacity by nearly 40 percent. Los Ramones was initially expected to meet 20 percent of Mexico's natural gas demand (Rodríguez 2014). This extended natural gas pipeline network is complemented by the construction of the industrial interoceanic corridor in the Tehuantepec Isthmus. This project connects the Gulf of Mexico with the Pacific Ocean through a 300-kilometer facility, for the first time bringing natural gas through pipelines to Mexico's southern region (PEMEX 2015, para. 1).

U.S.-Canada Energy Cooperation

The close and durable energy ties between the United States and Canada have resulted in a unique relationship between the two countries that includes the way energy relations are managed. Governmental interactions between the United States and Canada typically occur through specialized and functional channels such as bilateral processes and agreements, operating "under the radar" and out of public view (Heyen and Higginbotham 2004, 22). Bilateral processes can be formal, such as summits between the president and prime minister. However, the majority are informal processes that are issue specific, ad hoc meetings with information sharing. Actors involved in bilateral processes in energy are located in the executive branches of both governments and include regulators, public servants, and semiautonomous public entities. Gattinger (2012) notes that these actors form a dense network responsible for managing everyday relations in the countries' energy sectors, connecting energy specialists so they can share information, collaborate on joint projects, and coordinate energy trade standards.

Another characteristic that the U.S. and Canada energy sectors share is the substantial regional and local roles individual states in the United States and Canada's provinces play in energy decisions. Provincial governments in Canada have authority over their energy resources through the constitution, while state governments in the United States have significant control over energy production, transmission, and sales within their respective state lines. Power sharing was clearly on display during the contentious Keystone XL negotiations in the United States—for example, in January 2016 the state of South Dakota approved sections of the pipeline planned on its state land even after the Obama administration had rejected the pipeline.

In addition, to day-to-day cooperation in their energy sectors, Canada and the United States have committed to a number of high-profile bilateral agreements in recent years. Important examples include the 2009 U.S.-Canada Clean Energy Dialogue, which encouraged the development of clean energy to reduce greenhouse gas emissions, and a 2014 memorandum of understanding between the U.S. Department of Energy and Natural Resources Canada to enhance binational energy collaboration. The two countries have also sought to improve cooperation with Mexico to enhance energy development and pursue the goal of energy independence across North America. In 2014, the energy ministers of the three countries met and agreed to strengthen government-to-government and business-to-business relations in the energy sector, outlining three areas for future cooperation: development of North American energy public data and continental mapping of commodities and infrastructure, adoption of sustainable best practices for the development of unconventional oil and natural gas resources, and the creation of a modern and resilient North American energy infrastructure.

Despite this long-standing history of binational cooperation, questions loom concerning future U.S.-Canadian cooperation in clean energy and reductions in carbon emissions. Donald Trump campaigned on the pledge to renew America's coal industry and additionally questioned the role of human activity in climate change. Furthermore, the Trump administration withdrew the United States from the Paris Climate Accord and has reversed a number of the

Obama administration's climate-change policies, including eliminating plans to cut carbon emissions from coal power plants and reversing the Obama-era moratorium prohibiting coal mining leases on federal lands. While cooperation on climate change between Canada and the Trump administration may be temporarily stalled, the Trudeau administration has continued to pursue collaboration in the reduction of carbon emissions by reaching out to the governor of Washington, who, along with California and New York, has been planning to honor carbon emission reductions outlined in the Paris Accord despite the Trump administration's decision to pull out of the agreement (Mindock 2017). In 2018, California, Quebec, and Ontario formally acted on this pledge and furthered state and province collaboration on climate change by holding their first cross-border auction of greenhouse gas emission credits (Malo 2018).

U.S.-Mexico Energy Cooperation

Following changes to the Mexican Constitution, key alliances have materialized that aim to further energy development and strengthen commercial and energy relations between Mexico and the United States. For example, in March 2014, the all-American city of Pharr, Texas, and the Port of Corpus Christi Authority signed a memorandum of understanding (MOU) to form a cooperative alliance for "generating new business by promoting the efficient logistical land and seaport route between the Bridge and the Port." This alliance is supposed to be "a mutually beneficial synergy due to the result of providing progressive, professional, and expedient logistical options ensuring the smooth flow of commerce." It would also further "economic growth by increasing the logistical attractiveness of the Port as well as the Bridge, thereby increasing job opportunities and revenues at both the Port and the Bridge" (Morales 2014, para. 2).

It is worth noting that Pharr is considered to be "the hub of South Texas' international commercial crossing," and many see the Pharr International Bridge as "the heart of the Rio Grande Valley's international economy" (Morales 2014, para. 1). The recent alliance between Pharr and the Port is very relevant in this new context for two reasons. The first is the partnership's strategic geographical location: Pharr's proximity to key energy hubs in Corpus Christi, Texas, Monterrey, Nuevo Léon, and the Mazatlán-Matamoros superhighway in Mexico will further energy development and trade on both sides of the border.[11] The agreement will "open the industrial and seaport areas of Western Mexico, specifically from the Mazatlán region, to the Pharr region, thereby saving hours and costs in logistical transportation" (Morales 2014, para. 3). The second is that the agreement benefits the region because of the fact that "Pharr is the only international commercial bridge that is ideally situated in an area that will be able to service roughly 80% of northern Mexico's fracking opportunities, which signifies that the future of oil and gas logistics will take place through the Pharr International Bridge" (Morales 2014, para. 4).

Another key and prescient trade arrangement between the two countries is the Transboundary Hydrocarbons Agreement. Mere days after the passage of Mexico's energy reform, the U.S. Congress approved a binational treaty that established a framework for U.S. offshore oil and gas companies and PEMEX to develop joint transboundary oil and natural gas reservoirs along the United States' and Mexico's maritime boundary in the Gulf of Mexico (Seelke et al. 2014). The agreement provides access to nearly 1.5 million acres of the U.S. outer continental shelf and paves the way for the development of common safety and environmental standards.[12]

Strategic bilateral agreements such as these, particularly the new energy infrastructure that has been recently built or projected for the coming years, have been strengthening business-led cross-border governance (Correa-Cabrera 2019). The partnerships seem to be part of a new trend toward a new development model centered on the energy sector, involving key players in two neighboring nations, and appearing to greatly benefit the transnational business community. This new trade and development reality between Mexico and the United States has also been shaped by the passage of further legislation and design proposals to protect economic interests and investment.

In the post-2016 U.S. presidential election context, Donald Trump called for a renegotiation of NAFTA. This process effectively took place and shaped the new USMCA. However, Trump never mentioned the energy sector as part of his plans to modify commercial relations with Mexico. Hence, U.S.-Mexico energy relations appeared to be moving forward as planned before the arrival of the new U.S. administration. The election of Andrés Manuel López Obrador, however, could potentially dampen the transnational business relations that have developed between Mexico and the United States as the new Mexican president has been opposed to foreign investment in the energy sector in the past and has spoken of revitalizing PEMEX. However, López Obrador and his top economic aides have noted that his administration would honor all current signed contracts (Mufson 2018).

Future Challenges for U.S.-Canada Energy Relations

The United States and Canada governments have heralded their energy relations as an exemplary model of binational interaction, producing a collaborative relationship with both nations working together to address energy issues and challenges. Conflicts between the two countries over energy have been rare, typically involving long-standing disagreements over the development of the Arctic National Wildlife Refuge or technical disagreements on the definition of renewable energy (Gattinger 2012). While energy relations between the two countries have generally been financially lucrative and politically harmonious, a number of issues could adversely affect their future cooperation, including the development of nonconventional energy resources, environmental concerns, and increased public opposition to energy projects.

Nonconventional energy sources that include oil sands, offshore oil and gas, heavy oil, tight gas, as well as shale oil and gas make up an increasingly large portion of U.S. and Canada energy resources, resulting in both countries having become net exporters of petroleum, a feat the United States accomplished in 2011 for the first time in sixty-two years (Pleven and Gold 2011). While the development of nonconventional energy resources is perceived as a positive innovation that could lead to North American energy independence in the coming years, the issue has created a number of problems between the two countries, such as the reduced U.S. reliance on Canadian energy imports and record-high U.S. natural gas exports to Canada, prompting tension between U.S. and Canada energy producers (Gattinger 2012). Development of nonconventional energy resources has also resulted in public opposition because of damaging environmental impacts related to their removal, such as shale oil and gas fracking, strip mining from oil-sands extraction, and safety concerns about offshore oil rigs.

Environmental concerns also pose a threat to binational energy relations. Addressing climate change will require governmental action to foster a wide variety of policies, including the promotion of renewable energy, carbon capture and storage, and fuel switching. Both Canada and the United States will have to develop policies that efficiently reduce carbon emissions in ways that minimize economic effects. Canada and the United States have sought to increase cooperation on climate-change issues, including the U.S.-Canada Clean Energy Dialogue. However, Gattinger (2012) notes that the agreement lacks an attempt to tackle the issue with a shared approach. Also, given the Trump administration's reluctance to acknowledge or address climate change, it is unclear whether there will be future bilateral dialogue on the issue during the Trump presidency. In addition to climate change, policy makers will also need to address other environmental concerns the two countries share, including safety concerns regarding energy exploration and development, clean-air initiatives, land use, habitat protection, water use, and water quality.

The final issue that could negatively affect U.S. energy relations in the future involves increased public opposition to energy projects, including those considered clean, that utilize renewable resources, such as hydroelectric and wind, as well as those that contribute to climate change and environmental degradation, such as the extraction of shale oil and gas and oil sands. Gattinger (2012) notes that public opposition has evolved from individual-based resistance related to the potential effect of energy projects on communities to principles-based resistance with people opposed to any and all energy projects. This shift has been defined as a move from away from NIMBYism toward the more extreme and defiant BANANA (build absolutely nothing anywhere near anything) syndrome. Gattinger (2012) argues that neither government has taken formal steps to address this problem: in order to effectively do so, both governments must involve civil society in energy policy decision making and make the process more open and transparent.

Mexico: The Biggest Challenge to North American Energy Integration

Possible complications may arise in future U.S. and Canada energy integration projects. However, the two countries have a long history of strong binational collaboration between their governments and private sectors that accompanies shared vested interests in continued cooperation, all of which mitigates against any serious future obstacles. In contrast, the main challenge in North America's energy integration is Mexico's successful inclusion into an emergent regional framework. At present, organized crime and security are the two main issues Mexico faces in its efforts to effectively implement desired energy reforms to fully bring about North America's energy independence. Possible social conflicts connected to land and water distribution are additional key issues that may hinder Mexico's full inclusion into the trilateral energy project. The challenges are all subject to Mexico's capacity to cope with its preeminent challenge—that is, its need to fight corruption by strengthening its rule of law.

Mexico's legislative changes, actual and proposed investments, commercial alliances, and further policies to promote energy development constitute what appears to be an excellent combination to further North American integration. However, Mexico's success in achieving this goal remains subject to a number of serious challenges and limitations that include organized crime and violence, corruption, environmental concerns, water availability constraints, fiscal constraints, potential land-related conflicts, and other forms of social unrest (Correa-Cabrera 2019).[13]

According to the National Infrastructure Program 2014–2018, Mexico's past administration was planning to build in collaboration with the private sector more than 740 major investment projects throughout the country. The plans involved the construction of major infrastructure projects, including roads, pipelines, hydroelectric dams, wind farms, and other ventures linked to the energy sector. The main aim of these projects was to develop or "transform Mexico." However, according to a number of human rights advocates, environmental groups, and other activists, these investments would incentivize the displacement of vulnerable communities, increase inequalities, damage the environment, provoke water shortages, and bring about significant losses for small and medium farmers and cattle ranchers (Ramírez 2013; Camarena 2014; Hernández Navarro 2014; Mayorga 2014; Correa-Cabrera 2019).

An additional challenge for Mexico's energy sector is persistent insecurity and extremely high levels of crime and violence. According to McCumber Hearst (2015), "While the large companies have experience dealing with potentially insecure environments, and in some cases have their own security, smaller players want assurances that gang activity in development areas will be controlled" (para. 12). In the past few years, some hydrocarbon-rich areas have registered a strong presence of armed groups. In fact, some energy companies situated in these zones, such as the Burgos Basin, Mexico's far northeast territory that forms a border with Texas as well as the Gulf of Mexico, have been making payments to groups such as the Zetas or the Jalisco New Generation Cartel (Cartel Jalisco Nueva Generación, CJNG) simply to operate (Corchado and Osborne 2014).

Although some progress has been made against some regional criminal organizations such as the Zetas, the Gulf Cartel, and the Knights Templar, many criminal groups and their members who operate in these strategic zones "still threaten, steal, extort, kidnap for ransom, and even terrorize the industry's personnel." PEMEX (the national oil company) itself has often been the target of extortion or theft by organized crime. The government of Mexico has not yet established "complete control of regions rich in hydrocarbons in the country." Its "failure to recover vast swaths of territory lost to [transnational criminal groups] and bring it into full government control under the rule of law" puts the reform initiative's promises and the stability of the new system at risk (Payan and Correa-Cabrera 2014a, 4).

A further key challenge to the project designed by Enrique Peña Nieto's (2014) administration regarding energy development in the framework of energy reform has to do with water availability constraints. Shale oil and gas development was a central part of the previous Mexican administration's strategy to develop its energy sector with the final aim of creating jobs and furthering economic growth. Shale energy development depends on ample water supply. Limited availability of fresh water is a debilitating hindrance for developing shale resources through fracking (Reig, Luo, and Proctor 2014). According to a 2014 World Resources Institute (WRI) Report titled *Global Shale Gas Development: Water Availability and Business Risks*, Mexico has abundant reservoirs of shale gas but limited supplies of fresh water.[14]

Finally, issues connected to land ownership and use in Mexico can also put at risk North America energy integration. The new legislation on land ownership and use under Mexico's energy reform stands to create an environment ripe for social conflicts. In fact, the development of Mexico's hydrocarbon resources may face "challenges ranging from peaceful local protests to potentially violent social unrest associated with the displacement of farmers, ranchers, and other land users, including indigenous peoples." It is plausible that "resistance movements, protests, social unrest, and even individual and communal standoffs against energy projects . . . arise in the near future" (Payan and Correa-Cabrera 2014b, 4).

Conclusion

Mexico is a less developed and less wealthy country, by any array of economic data points, so it is in the interest of all in the region—incumbent on them—to collaborate to solve the transnational problems discussed heretofore. Any solution requires a trilateral commitment by Canada, the United States, and Mexico. This chapter discusses the disappearance of borders in the North American energy sector; it is therefore desirable to comprehensively integrate the region. In time, one will see the gains made in energy markets if cooperation among the three countries continues. The election of Andrés Manuel López Obrador raises questions about future integration and cooperation. The current Mexican administration is expected to uphold energy reforms and honor all existing energy contracts; however, U.S. energy companies are concerned about future access, and environmentalists are fearful that López Obrador's campaign promise to address climate change will be undermined by his plans to rejuvenate PEMEX (Hares 2018). Additional uncertainty looms in the future policy initiatives of the Trump administration given recent stridency in renegotiating NAFTA and aversion to addressing climate change.

One potential hindrance to future cooperation may prove to be the high numbers of vacancies at FERC, which oversees interstate pipelines, natural gas exports, and wholesale electricity markets. It is estimated that US$13 billion worth of energy projects, such as natural gas pipelines and gas export terminals, are delayed because of vacancies that the administration has yet to fill at FERC. Wolff and Dixon (2017) note that this reflects a broader issue beyond the Trump administration's sluggishness in filling vacancies; it involves the increased politicization of energy projects within the agency and in the country as a whole.

The election of Donald Trump as president has raised hopes and concerns for the future of North American energy integration. While the Trump administration has demonstrated support for energy cooperation, as the approval of the Keystone XL pipeline shows, his past comments about renegotiating the terms of NAFTA raise concerns about the prospect for future cooperation to unite the countries into one single energy market. The concerns have been alleviated by the new trilateral agreement, dubbed the United States–Mexico–Canada Agreement, or USMCA, which is awaiting legislative approval in all three states. The oil and gas industries have been deemed big winners of the new deal because a number of favored NAFTA provisions that have supported an integrated market were left in the new agreement, including protections for energy investments abroad, eligibility for investor-state dispute settlement in which multinational energy companies can sue state governments if new regulations are passed, and the continuation of tax-free transport of raw and refined materials across borders (Grandoni 2018). Thus, as North America continues in the uncharted territory of the Trump administration, the continued elimination of North American energy borders appears to remain a singular and enduring certainty.

NOTES

1. Reform to Articles 25, 27, 28 and transitory articles of the constitution.

2. The reform will allegedly open up approximately 85 percent of shale gas and oil fields in Mexico to private investment. "Foreign energy companies also will be able to gain access to vast untapped oil reserves, including fields in the deep waters of the Gulf of Mexico (the majority of which lie off the coast of Tamaulipas and Veracruz)" (Haahr 2015, 6).

3. SHCP will establish the fiscal terms applicable to each contract type as well as royalty rates and taxes and will design the parameters of a new oil sovereign wealth fund, the Mexican Petroleum Fund for Stabilization and Development (FoMePe). This fund will be overseen by the Central Bank (O'Neil and Taylor 2014).

4. CENAGAS will own and operate the national pipeline systems, and CENACE will do the same with the electricity grid.

5. Additionally, Mexico's new energy regime includes three new types of contracts under which foreign companies can now book oil and gas reserves for financial reporting purposes (Cama 2014; Estévez 2014). This "is a particularly attractive incentive for investment in Mexico's energy sector" (Estévez 2014, para. 6). And again, the main potential investors will be U.S. energy firms.

6. Information in this section was also mentioned in Correa-Cabrera 2017, and Payan and Correa-Cabrera 2016.

7. There are many refineries located along the U.S. part of the Gulf, from south of the city of Houston to the port of New Orleans. There is also a large concentration of refineries in the area of Corpus Christi, Texas.

8. There are plans to construct an additional road that would connect the strategic region of the Rio Grande Valley (RGV) in the United States with other areas of energy development, both north and south of the border. This is State Highway 68 (SH 68), which is a proposed twenty-two-mile new road that will connect I-2/U.S. 83 to I-69C/ U.S. 281, thus providing an additional north-south route for the RGV region.

9. In 2015, plans were made to generate an additional 1,442 megawatts of power and lay down approximately 1,500 miles of natural gas pipeline as well as around 2,000 miles of power lines. This would represent more than US$9.8 billion in infrastructure investments (Chapa 2015, para. 3).

10. Natural gas demand from Mexico's electric power sector is expected to grow significantly in the coming years. There are plans in this country "to add about 28 gigawatts of new electric generating capacity between 2012 and 2027, mostly in northern Mexico." According to CFE estimates, this could considerably "raise natural gas needs for power generation" (U.S. Energy Information Administration 2013, para. 6).

11. The states connected through this highway represent more than nineteen million habitants and close to 23 percent of the Mexican GDP. This new highway has a total length of approximately 1,120 kilometers and is among the most modern in Latin America. Its construction has promoted national and international trade by connecting the markets of the Pacific with the northern, northeastern, and southeastern parts of the Mexican Republic. Through this highway, the port of Mazatlán, Sinaloa, becomes the

point of departure for northeastern Mexican products destined to the Pacific Ocean and the markets and production centers of Asia.

12. According to estimates of the Department of the Interior's Bureau of Ocean Energy Management (BOEM), this area contains approximately "172 million barrels of oil and 304 billion cubic feet of natural gas" (Department of the Interior 2014, para. 2).

13. This section is part of the conclusion in Correa-Cabrera (2019).

14. This report draws on WRI's Aqueduct Water Risk and is a global and country-specific resource to help stakeholders evaluate the availability of fresh water across shale plays worldwide. It has a special focus on eleven countries, including Mexico.

REFERENCES

Austen, Ian. 2015. "Keystone XL Decision by Obama Takes Weight Off Trudeau." *New York Times*, November 6. http://www.nytimes.com/2015/11/07/world/americas /obamas-call-on-keystone-xl-pipeline-takes-pressure-off-trudeau.html?ref=topics &_r=0.

Black, Bob. 2015. "U.S. Natural Gas Exports to Mexico Taking Off." *Financial Times*, August 3. http://www.forbes.com/sites/drillinginfo/2015/08/03/u-s-natural-gas -exports-to-mexico-taking-off/.

Cama, Timothy. 2014. "EIA Predicts 75 Percent Increase in Mexico's Oil Output." *The Hill*, August 24. http://thehill.com/policy/energy-environment/215923-eia-predicts -75-increase-in-mexicos-oil-output#.VB1awcUf2ts.facebook.

Camarena, Salvador. 2014. "Listos Para la Fiebre Petrolera?" *SinEmbargo*, February 4. Accessed December 27, 2014 (no longer posted). http://www.sinembargo.mx/opinion /04-02-2014/21345.

Chapa, Sergio. 2015. "A Look at 24 New Energy Projects up for Bid in Mexico." *San Antonio Business Journal*, June 23. http://www.bizjournals.com/sanantonio/blog/eagle -ford-shale-insight/2015/06/a-look-at-24-new-energy-projects-up-for-bid-in.html ?ana=e_hstn_nrg&u=mfJGhtX5JSlT/ATWytrhmg0779b38c&t=1435633918.

Clark, Steve. 2018. "LNG Terminal Construction Would Begin in 2020." *Brownsville Herald*, September 4. https://www.brownsvilleherald.com/news/local/lng-terminal -construction-would-begin-in/article_4e98f1b6-1470-5666-8825-040b83297b19.html.

Corchado, Alfredo, and James Osborne. 2014. "The New Border: Eyes Are on Mexi-co's Untapped Potential." *Dallas Morning News*, July 13. http://res.dallasnews.com/ interactives/border_energy/.

Correa-Cabrera, Guadalupe. 2019. "Transforming Mexico's Energy Field: The Intended Consequences of a Drug War." *Small Wars and Insurgencies* 30 (2): 489–517.

Dorantes, David. 2014. "Oil Sir, Welcome to Tamaulipas." *El Financiero*, April 8. http:// www.elfinanciero.com.mx/monterrey/oil-sir-welcome-to-tamaulipas.html.

Dukert, Joseph M. 2005. "North American Energy Cooperation: How Far Has it Come? How Far Can It Go?" Paper presented at American University's North American Program, Washington, D.C., July 12.

Embassy of the United States in Mexico. 2014. "Ambassador Applauds New Rail Bridge Across US-Mexican Border." Press release, September 12. Accessed November 4, 2014 (no longer posted). http://mexico.usembassy.gov/press-releases/ambassador -applauds-new-rail-bridge-across-US-mexican-border.html.

Estévez, Dolia. 2014. "Booking Oil Reserves Is an 'Attractive Incentive' for Foreign Companies in Mexico, Says US." *Forbes*, September 4. Accessed September 11, 2014 (no longer posted). http://www.forbes.com/sites/doliaestevez/2014/09/04/booking-oil -reserves-is-an-sattractive-incentive-for-foreign-companies-in-mexico-says-u-s/.

Flannery, Nathaniel P. 2018. "Will Mexico's New President Catalyze Economic Growth." *Forbes*, July 26. https://www.forbes.com/sites/nathanielparishflannery/2018/07/26 /will-mexicos-new-president-catalyze-economic-growth/#2ca3a40f56d2.

Gattinger, Monica. 2012. "Canada-United States Energy Relations: Making a MESS of Energy Policy." *American Review of Canadian Studies* 42:460–73.

Government of Mexico. 1958/2008. "Ley reglamentaria del artículo 27 constitucional en el ramo del petróleo." Law published November 29, 1958; last reform published on November 28, 2008; law abrogated on August 11, 2014. Mexico City: Official Gazette of the Federation.

Government of Mexico. 2014a. "Decreto por el que se expide la ley de hidrocarburos y se reforman diversas disposiciones de la ley de inversión extranjera; Ley minera, y ley de asociaciones público privadas." August 11. Mexico City: Official Gazette of the Federation.

Government of Mexico. 2014b. "Decreto por el que se expiden la ley de petróleos mexicanos y la ley de la comisión federal de electricidad, y se reforman y derogan diversas disposiciones de la ley federal de las entidades paraestatales; la ley de adquisiciones, arrendamientos y servicios del sector público y la ley de obras públicas y servicios relacionados con las mismas." August 11. Mexico City: Official Gazette of the Federation.

Grandoni, Dino. 2018. "The Energy 202: Big Oil and Gas Companies Are Winners in Trump's New Trade Deal." *Washington Post*, October 3. https://www.washingtonpost .com/news/powerpost/paloma/the-energy-202/2018/10/03/the-energy-202-big-oil -and-gas-companies-are-winners-in-trump-s-new-trade-deal/5bb39b531b326b7c 8a8d17cc/?utm_term=.fac0348c66ab.

Haahr, Kathryn. 2015. "Addressing the Concerns of the Oil Industry: Security Challenges in Northeastern Mexico and Government Responses." *Mexico Institute*, Working Paper, January. Washington, DC: Wilson Center.

Hares, Sophie. 2018. "Pressure to Secure Mexico Energy Supply Endangers Green Dream." *Reuters*, August 2. https://www.reuters.com/article/us-mexico-environment -politics-analysis/pressure-to-secure-mexico-energy-supply-endangers-green-dream -idUSKBN1KN1HA.

Hernández Navarro, Luis. 2014. "La reforma al campo, cuentos chinos." *La Jornada*, April 8. url.

Heyen, Jeff, and John Higginbotham. 2004. "Advancing Canadian Interests in the United States: A Practical Guide for Canadian Public Officials." Canada School of

Public Service Action Research Roundtable on Managing US Canada Relations, Canada School of Public Service, Gatineau, Quebec.

Hussain, Yadullah. 2015. "New Marcellus Pipelines from Northeastern U.S. Squeezing Out Canadian Natural Gas." *Financial Post*, September 10. http://business.financial post.com/news/energy/new-marcellus-pipelines-from-northeastern-u-s-squeezing -out-canadian-natural-gas?__lsa=4abe-6eac.

Kilisek, Roman. 2014. "Mexico's Energy Reforms: Can Mexico Emerge as a Prime Global Oil and Gas Industry Expansion Prospect?" *Breaking Energy*, January 8. http://breakingenergy.com/2014/01/08/mexicos-energy-reforms-can-mexico-emerge -as-a-prime-global-oil-gas-industry-expansion-prospect/.

Malo, Sebastien. 2018. "U.S., Canadian Provinces Launch First Cap-and-Trade Auction to Battle Climate Change." *Reuters*, February 21. https://www.reuters.com/article/us -canada-climatechange-carbonmarket/u-s-canadian-provinces-launch-first-cap-and -trade-auction-to-battle-climate-change-idUSKCN1G52T7.

Mayorga, Patricia. 2014. "La fracturación hidráulica es nociva para la salud: 'Chihuahua vs fracking.'" *Proceso*, September 4. http://www.proceso.com.mx/?p=381343.

McCumber Hearst, David. 2015. "Another Eagle Ford South of the Border?" *Laredo Morning Times*, January 31. http://lmtonline.com/business/article_9c9a3a5c-a9a2 -11e4-aace-076fd54814a3.html?mode=jqm.

Mindock, Clark. 2017. "Justin Trudeau Contacting US Politicians About Tackling Climate Change." *Independent*, June 2. http://www.independent.co.uk/news/world /americas/us-politics/justin-trudeau-trump-paris-agreement-climate-change-us -governors-talks-canada-a7769796.html.

Morales, Isidro. 2011. "The Energy Factor in Mexico-U.S. Relations." Prepared for the Study: *The Future of Oil in Mexico*, April 29. Houston, Tex.: James Baker Institute, Rice University. http://bakerinstitute.org/files/515/.

Morales, Pamela. 2014. "MOU Ceremony at Pharr City Hall." Press release, Pharr International Bridge, March 7. Accessed October 25, 2014 (no longer posted). http://pharr -tx.gov/2014/03/03/mou-ceremony-at-pharr-city-hall/.

Mufson, Steven. 2018. "The Energy 202: AMLO Seeks to Rejuvenate Mexico's Pemex." *Washington Post*, August 1. https://www.washingtonpost.com/news/powerpost/paloma /the-energy-202/2018/08/01/the-energy-202-amlo-seeks-to-rejuvenate-mexico-s -pemex/5b605ad41b326b0207955e6b/?utm_term=.f684e75e2920.

Natural Resources Canada. 2015. "FAQs Concerning Federally-Regulated Petroleum Pipelines in Canada." http://www.nrcan.gc.ca/energy/infrastructure/5893#h-1-4.

O'Neil, Shannon K., and James S. Taylor. 2014. "A Primer: Mexico Energy Reforms." *Vianovo*, March 16. http://vianovo.com/news/a-primer-mexico-energy-reforms.

Paley, Dawn Marie. 2014. *Drug War Capitalism*. Oakland, Calif.: AK Press.

Parfomak, Paul W., and Michael Ratner. 2011. The U.S.-Canada Energy Relationship: Joined at the Well. CRS Report no. R41875. Washington, D.C.: Congressional Research Service, 2011. https://www.fas.org/sgp/crs/row/R41875.pdf.

Paterson, Kent. 2014. "A New Gas Pipeline for Texas-Tamaulipas." *Frontera NorteSur News*, March 25. http://fnsnews.nmsu.edu/a-new-gas-pipeline-for-texas-tamaulipas/.

Payan, Tony, and Guadalupe Correa-Cabrera. 2014a. "Energy Reform and Security in Northeastern Mexico." Mexico Center, Issue Brief, May 6. Houston, Tex.: James Baker Institute, Rice University.

Payan, Tony, and Guadalupe Correa-Cabrera. 2014b. "Land Ownership and Use Under Mexico's Energy Reform." Mexico Center, Issue Brief, October 29. Houston, Tex.: James Baker Institute, Rice University.

Payan, Tony, and Guadalupe Correa-Cabrera. 2016. "Seguridad, estado de derecho y reforma energética en México." In *El Estado de derecho y la reforma energética*, edited by Tony Payan, Stephen Zamora, and José Ramón Cossío, 403–43. Mexico City: Tirant Lo Blanch.

PEMEX. 2015. "Con inversión de 200 millones de dólares inicia operaciones nuevo gasoducto del corredor interoceánico." Press release, January 5. Accessed January 5, 2015 (no longer posted). http://www.pemex.com/prensa/boletines_nacionales/Paginas/2015-001-nacional.aspx#.VKsgPNLF-Im.

Peña Nieto, Enrique. 2014. "Modernización y equipamiento del Puerto de Lázaro Cárdenas." *Mexico's Presidency* (blog), September 10. Accessed September 10, 2014 (no longer posted). http://www.presidencia.gob.mx/modernizacion-y-equipamiento-del-puerto-de-lazaro-cardenas/.

Pleven, Liam, and Russell Gold. 2011. "U.S. Nears Milestone: Net Fuel Exporter." *Wall Street Journal*, November 30. http://www.wsj.com/articles/SB10001424052970203441704577068670488306242.

Ramírez, Erika. 2014. "Programa nacional de infraestructura, despojos por venir." *Contralínea*, September 23. Accessed September 23, 2014 (no longer posted). http://contralinea.info/archivo-revista/index.php/2014/09/23/programa-nacional-de-infraestructura-despojos-por-venir/.

Ramírez, Jesús. 2013. "Los políticos mexicanos que son socios de petroleras extranjeras." *Vanguardia*, December 10. http://www.vanguardia.com.mx/lospoliticosmexicanosquesonsociosdepetrolerasextranjeras-1900041.html.

Reig, Paul, Tianyi Luo, and Jonathan N. Proctor. 2014. *Global Shale Gas Development: Water Availability and Business Risks*. Washington, D.C.: World Resources Institute.

Rodríguez, Israel. 2014. "Anuncia Pemex inicio de obras del gasoducto Los Ramones." *La Jornada*, March 27. Accessed December 13, 2014 (no longer posted). http://www.jornada.unam.mx/ultimas/2014/03/27/anuncia-pemex-inicio-de-proyecto-de-gas-natural-los-ramones-correra-de-tamaulipas-al-centro-del-pais-2760.html.

Rosner, David, and Scott Mckee. 2014. "U.S. Imports of Canadian Oil Sands Have Doubled Since 2005." Bipartisan Policy Center, March 28. http://bipartisanpolicy.org/blog/us-imports-canadian-oil-sands-have-doubled-2005/.

Seelke, Clare Ribando, Phillip Brown, Michael Ratner, and M. Angeles Villarreal. 2014. *Mexico's Oil and Gas Sector: Background, Reform Efforts, and Implications for the United States*. Washington, D.C.: Congressional Research Service.

Sheehan, John. 2015. "Mexico E&P Spend Could Double." *Hart Energy*, February 2. http://www.epmag.com/mexico-ep-spend-could-double-781356#p=full.

U.S. Department of the Interior. 2014. "Secretary Jewell Announces Award of First Oil and Gas Leases in Gulf of Mexico Subject to U.S.-Mexico Transboundary Hydrocarbons Agreement." U.S. Department of the Interior, May 30. https://www.doi.gov/news/pressreleases/secretary-jewell-announces-award-of-first-oil-and-gas-leases-in-gulf-of-mexico-subject-to-us-mexico-transboundary-hydrocarbons-agreement.

U.S. Energy Information Administration. 2013. "U.S. Natural Gas Exports to Mexico Reach Record High in 2012." *EIA*, March 13. http://www.eia.gov/todayinenergy/detail.cfm?id=10351#.

Wolff, Eric, and Darius Dixon. 2017. "Why Are These Billions in Pipeline Projects Stalled?" *Politico*, August 5. http://www.politico.com/story/2017/08/05/trump-energy-commission-pipeline-projects-delayed-241347.

CHAPTER 11

Maturing Cross-Border Cooperation for Economic Development

CHRISTOPHER WILSON

The idea that the coming together of diverse communities from across the U.S.-Mexico border could be used as a strategic driver of economic development goes back at least as far as the Border Industrialization Program, or maquiladora program, of the 1960s. At that time, a bet was made that special taxation and customs rules would attract "twin plant" manufacturing investments to the region with more complicated and capital-intensive parts of the operations on the U.S. side of the border and more labor-intensive production taking place in Mexico. In many ways, the project was a success; Mexico's northern border region is highly industrialized, and its factories have become a source of employment strong enough to attract workers from across the country. Unfortunately, neither the maquiladora program nor NAFTA, which expanded tariff benefits for cross-border manufacturers, ended up attracting many factories to the U.S. side of the border. In the end, the high-quality transportation infrastructure in the United States made the benefits of relocating factories to the U.S. side of the border insufficient to overcome the costs, and the twin plant vision was never realized.

There is no doubt that free trade within North America has been a huge boon for border communities. Indeed, as the home to major transportation and logistics industries, in addition to the Mexican manufacturing clusters, border-region economies tend to depend heavily on cross-border trade. But for many, especially on the U.S. side, they have become what locals term "pass-through economies." That is, by specializing in moving widgets into and out of their communities as fast as possible, there is very little local value added in the more than half-trillion dollars of commerce that crosses the U.S.-Mexico border each year. Despite the presence of maquiladoras, Mexican border communities face a similar challenge. They want to add more value to the products they are assembling in local plants and in particular seek to make higher skill and therefore higher value contributions to the products they are building.

The basic lesson of the past half century of economic development in the U.S.-Mexico border region is that while free trade has become a necessary component of economic development that derives from the strategic location of border communities, it is nonetheless insufficient as a driver of the type of development that residents of both U.S. and Mexican border communities aspire to deliver to their populations. In addition to a favorable regional trade framework, active local- and state-level collaboration is needed to bridge the gaps and barriers created by the many jurisdictional lines cutting through border communities and to take full advantage of the unique opportunities for development available to cross-border communities, which bring together divergent cost structures, regulatory systems, and talent pools in a compact geographic area.

Local and state-level cross-border collaboration for economic development is not a new phenomenon. The limitations of economic development driven by a free-trade framework and private-sector decisions to take advantage of that framework, however, have become more and more clear. As border communities aspire to create high-quality jobs, the need for more robust strategies for binational development has become increasingly apparent. Other works have documented both the existence of cross-border cooperation for economic development and opportunities for greater cooperation.[1] This chapter complements, with an emphasis on the recent past, earlier research by documenting the qualitative experience of various actors who have been on the forefront of the process over the past few decades. This study is based almost entirely on a series of interviews with current and retired community leaders with significant experience doing economic development work in the border region—whether based in economic-development organizations, the private sector, academia, or government—and is designed to capture the state of binational cooperation for economic development across the various subregions of the U.S.-Mexico border. The twelve interviews were conducted during the summer and fall of 2018.

The interviews confirm that there is, at least across much of the border region, a growing level of binational cooperation for economic development.

Nonetheless, clear differences in the depth and intensity of cooperation are found in the various pairs of cities and states on either side of the border. Though this analysis is too cursory to offer definitive explanations for these various levels of cooperation, the capacity of local institutions, especially government and civil society, appear to play an important role. At times, the institutional capacity of a community on one side of the border can be used to supplement lesser capacity on the other side, but the deepest and most effective collaboration comes when capable actors from both sides are able to develop initiatives that provide tangible benefits for communities on both sides of the border and transcend the life spans of the local and state governments that help support them.

Interviews with Border-Region Economic-Development Experts and Practitioners

Gerry Schwebel, Executive Vice President, IBC Bank

For several decades, Gerry Schwebel has worked in his native Laredo, Texas, and surrounding communities as a member of IBC Bank, a regional commercial bank oriented to meeting the banking needs of small businesses operating in Texas and across the border in Mexico.[2] The bank started in Texas and quickly came to hold the personal bank accounts of many Mexican clients. Even before NAFTA spurred a boom in manufacturing investment on the Mexican side of the border, IBC Bank began serving industrial plants operating on the Mexican side of the border, including the large manufacturing hub that was growing in Monterrey and Saltillo, Mexico.

With the experience of developing relationships with correspondent banks and industry on both sides of the border, Schwebel was an active participant in early discussions with other Texas-Mexico border business leaders to create a strategic plan to attract more jobs to the region. In the second half of the 1980s, a summit of business leaders was held (as the U.S.-Canada FTA went into force and talk of a potential North American free-trade agreement was on the rise), and they saw a need for greater binational cooperation to spur economic development in the region. This meeting led to the formation of the Border Trade Alliance (BTA), of which IBC Bank, represented by Gerry Schwebel, was a founding member. The BTA website describes the organization in the following manner:

Founded in 1986, the Border Trade Alliance (BTA) is a grassroots, non-profit organization that serves as a forum for participants to address key issues affecting trade, travel and security in North America. Working with entities in Canada, Mexico and the United States, the BTA advocates on behalf of policies and initiatives designed to improve border affairs and trade relations among the three nations. The BTA's mission is to initiate, monitor and influence public policy and private sector initiatives for the facilitation of international trade and commerce through advocacy, education, issue development, research and analysis, and strategic planning.

An early (and continuing) focus of the BTA was on attracting infrastructure development to the region, especially to the U.S. side of the border. Gerry notes that this was taking place at a time before the United States had a border czar, a binational executive committee for border planning, or many of the other policy-coordination mechanisms that have been developed in recent years. As such, the BTA, and local stakeholders more generally, played a vital role in connecting with Mexican mayors, governors, and federal officials to understand their infrastructure development plans and ensure that U.S. and Mexican projects would effectively connect the region.

In 1992, Schwebel became the president of BTA, and he led the organization as cross-border cooperation and advocacy in support of NAFTA was at its peak. The agreement was passed by the U.S. Congress in 1993. As an organization made up of small- and medium-size businesses from the border region, the BTA has never had the heft of larger business organizations such as the U.S. Chamber of Commerce and Business Round Table. However, BTA came to play an important role in advocating for NAFTA by partnering with those larger organizations and bringing small- and medium-size business leaders to meet with members of Congress to explain how trade growth would lead to greater economic opportunity both at the border and in other communities across the United States.

Schwebel laments that after the passage of NAFTA much of the coalition that had come together to lobby on behalf of U.S.-Mexico trade and represent the interests of border communities simply went back to their businesses to take advantage of the new opportunities created. In doing so, he saw an insufficient effort, especially from the private sector, to tell the success stories of border communities in the wake of NAFTA and thereby maintain political support for the agreement. He, along with many other border business leaders, got involved in advocating for NAFTA once again during the recent renegotiation process, reactivating many of the relationships that to a certain extent had gone dormant for a time.

Schwebel's experience exemplifies the major wave of binational cooperation and advocacy that developed around the negotiations and congressional debate on NAFTA in the first half of the 1990s. It also shows the overwhelming focus of private-sector participants (and indeed a large segment of all of those doing economic-development work in the border region) on issues of trade facilitation. The success of manufacturing companies and the businesses that support them depend heavily on the ability to efficiently move goods back and forth across the border. To do so, they need an open trading framework, adequate transportation infrastructure, and efficient port of entry management. Naturally, they have found ways to advocate for those goals.

Flavio Olivieri, Executive Director of Cali-Baja Binational Mega-Region Association

Flavio Olivieri has worked for thirty years in Tijuana and San Diego, including positions in the maquiladora industry, and with economic development and investment attraction organizations on both sides of the border. He is currently executive director of the Cali Baja Bi-National Mega-Region, Inc., which began in 2008 and functions as a consortium of economic-development organizations working to coordinate "the organization of a long-term economic-development strategy partnering San Diego County, Imperial County, and Baja California in Mexico for global competition."[3]

Flavio has observed a shift underway that involves a move away from the traditional model of industrialization in the border region that was built almost entirely around the combination of low labor costs and close geographic proximity to the U.S. market. He points to the increased human capital needs of newer industries, including medical tourism and software development. It is not that these industries do not rely on the wage gap across the border but that they find their niche in a higher skill and wage level than traditional assembly plants. To take advantage of and encourage this trend, Flavio sees the need for major human capital development efforts both to improve educational and training programs and to facilitate the immigration of highly skilled workers from across North America and the world to the Cali Baja region.

Flavio pointed to his work with the aerospace and medical device clusters in Baja California as examples of successful efforts to strengthen human capital. He stressed that cluster development is fundamentally about finding and implementing collective actions to strengthen the competitiveness of the firms that make up a particular cluster. Olivieri mentioned the importance of building relationships with universities and individual professors in order to create connections between industry and academia to develop successful internship programs and to codesign curricula that prepare students for jobs in growing local industries. These two cluster-development efforts were also involved in promoting STEM (Science, Technology, Engineering, and Math) at local schools. Flavio sees some of the region's biggest successes in creative efforts to bring together the assets of the two labor markets (San Diego and Tijuana). He points to the case of Thermo-Fischer Scientific, which was contemplating a move from San Diego to India in order to meet its labor needs. San Diego and the broader Cali Baja community came together to convince them instead to add operations in Tijuana while retaining their workforce in San Diego. The company is still looking for additional talent, but it is working with academic institutions to develop it locally.

The Cali Baja Bi-National Mega-Region Initiative began in 2008 when the Imperial Valley Economic Development Corporation got a grant from the U.S. Department of Commerce's Economic Development Administration to work with Mexicali and other regional partners in an effort to create jobs. Imperial Valley had a massive problem of unemployment during the Great Recession. Tim Kelley and others from Imperial Valley saw that their best opportunity for economic development involved leveraging the assets and cooperation of their neighboring jurisdictions, both in Mexico and San Diego (see section on Tim Kelley, below, for more information). Early conversations involving stakeholders from across the region identified aerospace, auto parts, medical devices, and agriculture as industries with important potential for advance through regional collaboration. Flavio sees the branding of the region as a single entity that goes beyond traditional boundaries and borders as perhaps the group's biggest success—he notes that Cali Baja has even become a clothing brand. Other efforts have included a mapping tool of regional assets, collaboration with other regional entities to analyze cross-border clusters, and the hosting of the 2016 World Forum for Foreign Direct Investment (FDI).

The California–Baja California region demonstrates some of the most advanced binational economic-development projects found in the U.S.-Mexico border region. At the level of San Diego and Tijuana, sophisticated efforts have taken root to not only do basic investment attraction work but also to improve

the competitiveness of existing firms and industries through cluster development and human capital creation and attraction. Nonetheless, even in this area
of both extensive cooperation and sophisticated economic-development work,
binational efforts that go beyond the fundamentals of investment attraction
and cross-border transportation facilitation are only nascent. Binational clusters
have been studied and initial attempts to promote their development have been
taken, but much work remains to fully implement more comprehensive, cross-
border, competitiveness-enhancing, economic-development strategies.

Jon Barela, CEO, The Borderplex Alliance

Jon Barela grew up in Las Cruces, New Mexico, and like many residents of the
border region, he recalls fondly an era of easier movement back and forth across
the border and the deep bonds that connected the communities on each side.
He worked in the private sector for many years before more recently holding
two positions responsible for economic-development work in the border region.
Jon was previously the economic-development cabinet secretary for the state
of New Mexico and is currently CEO of the Borderplex Alliance, a nonprofit
organization working to advance economic development and policy advocacy
in the El Paso, Texas; Las Cruces, New Mexico; and Ciudad Juárez, Chihuahua
region.[4]

While working under New Mexico governor Susana Martínez, Barela helped
develop and implement a series of measures designed to expand the state's trade
with Mexico and stimulate job growth in the area of southern New Mexico
along the border. Steps taken by the government included a locomotive fuel
tax deduction that helped attract Union Pacific to build an intermodal terminal near the Santa Teresa port of entry, a half-billion dollar investment. New
Mexico also created a zone along the border that allowed the operation of over-
weight trucks (Mexican regulations allow for heavier trucks), which decreased
the need for loading and unloading goods, thereby facilitating trade. The state
helped develop transportation and water infrastructure for the growth of industrial parks along the border and partnered with the state of Chihuahua to create
a master plan for a binational community in the Santa Teresa–San Jeronimo
area. To design these measures, Jon Barela and other state officials asked New
Mexico border business leaders and land owners what they could do to stimulate
trade and investment and then implemented as much of what was requested as
possible. These measures stimulated the filling of at least a million square feet

of previously vacant office space in the area and thirty-eight announcements of job-creating investments from the private sector.

Barela describes the creation of the Borderplex Alliance as the result of local businesspeople understanding that El Paso, Las Cruces, and Ciudad Juárez are a single community and could be more effective in their efforts to attract investment and develop the local economy by working in a coordinated, collaborative fashion than by simply pursuing the more disjointed efforts on which each of the jurisdictions had previously relied. The original mission of the organization focused exclusively on job creation, but more recently, the Borderplex Alliance has added policy advocacy at the local, state, and federal level as an explicit goal as well. The organization has advocated on issues of NAFTA, trade facilitation, and immigration policy.

Despite the recognition of the value of coordinated, cross-border cooperation across the border region, it is often difficult to turn these ideas into practice when elected officials and other community leaders are focused narrowly on attracting investment and creating jobs in their local community. In a practical sense, the Borderplex Alliance manages this by referring all business development leads to all three states/jurisdictions in which it operates. This location-agnostic approach to regional economic development works because stakeholders in all three communities understand that there are significant positive spillovers of business growth in the surrounding areas. As an example, Barela pointed out that when southern New Mexico lands a major investment, many of the workers hired by the company will live in El Paso, Texas. In a similar sense, studies have shown that the growth of manufacturing employment along the Mexican side of the border has positive employment spillovers for U.S. border communities—Barela notes that some 20–30 percent of El Paso retail business is supported by Mexican nationals.[5]

Barela believes that "the unity in this region, in the business community, in government leadership, educational institutions, and other nongovernmental institutions, has never been stronger." He credits the way that people in the region instinctively understand their interconnectedness across borders as well as the efforts of many community leaders and the work of the Borderplex Alliance itself. Barela notes a binational and bipartisan feeling that the border region has been under assault from Washington and a desire among the population to stand together and deliver a response from the border.

In terms of specific projects and accomplishments, Barela points to the eleven thousand jobs that they have helped bring to the region, including some recent investments for back-office support operations on the U.S. side of the border that depend on the bilingual and bicultural workforce found in the border region as well as the El Paso–Ciudad Juárez cooperation to develop a pedestrian corridor linking the two downtown areas called Avenida de las Luces.

Margie Emmermann, Former Executive Director of the Arizona-Mexico Commission

Margie Emmermann worked for the state of Arizona in efforts to strengthen relations with the state of Sonora and Mexico more generally over a career that spanned several decades. She served as Mexico policy advisor for Governors Symington and Hull, was director of the Arizona Office of Tourism under Governor Napolitano, and was executive director of the Arizona-Mexico Commission under Governor Brewer, among other government and private-sector posts.[6]

From these vantage points, she has observed the development of Arizona-Mexico relations, and she notes a strong period of binational development beginning during the administrations of Governors Symington and Beltrones of Arizona and Sonora. Binational work during the early 1990s was funded by a direct appropriation from the Arizona state legislature along with significant support from local universities from both sides of the border. During that period, Emmermann saw state-level government taking the lead, but she has noted a much expanded base of stakeholders including mayors, business leaders, nonprofit organizations, and others now supporting the binational relationship. She saw an initial reluctance to let so many different actors all do their own thing without the supervision or guidance of the state governments, but in the end she believes it has proven to be a very positive development, providing the cross-border relationship with a depth and stability that would have otherwise been impossible to achieve.

Providing the states with a more institutionalized forum for cooperation than most other border state pairs, the Arizona-Mexico Commission has existed for more than five decades. The Arizona-Mexico Commission has always had a focus on economic development and transportation infrastructure. Other topics rise and fall in importance, such as agriculture, education, environment, water, banking, real estate, tourism, and arts and culture. Emmermann notes that during periods of coinciding binational vision from the governors of each state, the commission has provided a vehicle to implement binational projects, while during difficult periods in top level Arizona-Sonora relations, the commission has served as a node for many other cross-border relationships, "ensuring that Arizona has a good relationship with Mexico regardless" of the personalities in leadership.

Mark Kroll, Former Dean and Full Professor, College of Business and Entrepreneurship, the University of Texas Rio Grande Valley (UTRGV)

Mark Kroll is a native of Harlingen, Texas, and for nine years served as the dean of the UTRGV College of Business and Entrepreneurship.[7] From his post at the university, Kroll has been deeply involved in several regional economic-development initiatives, including the ongoing BiNED (Binational Economic Development) project.

Kroll sees recent growth in binational cooperation for economic development, but he also notes serious challenges that need to be overcome to realize fully the potential of cross-border efforts in the region. Federal government initiatives, including the maquiladora program and NAFTA, spurred earlier waves of binational cooperation, which were driven especially by the private sector working to take advantage of the new opportunities created by these programs. However, in recent years, even in the absence of such federal initiatives (and in the face of a serious challenge to NAFTA), Kroll has noticed an increase in cross-border cooperation, primarily in the form of growing sophistication and participation from private-sector actors on the Mexican side of the border, including representatives of business coalitions such as CANCINTRA and Index Matamoros (Asociación de Maquiladoras de Matamoros). This stands in contrast to a continued lack of local and state-level government capacity in Tamaulipas, which has faced a long series of organized crime and public security challenges. While holding onto hope that new government officials in Tamaulipas will make progress, Kroll notes that these challenges are the principal obstacle to both stronger binational cooperation and stronger economic development for the region.

In the face of the limitations on extensive binational efforts, the BiNED project has found important success in transcending other very real borders in the Lower Rio Grande Valley, bringing together actors from Brownsville, Harlingen, McAllen, Weslaco, Mission, and other jurisdictions within the region to overcome tendencies toward competition and join together to define and develop themselves as a single economic region. Kroll points to the region's workforce as both an opportunity—a young population of willing workers during a time of an aging population at the national level—and a challenge—education levels are lower than they need to be. He also sees assets on the Mexican side of the border, such as the highly developed but labor-tight manufacturing hub of Monterrey/Saltillo, which creates opportunities for manufacturing growth in the binational Lower Rio Grande Valley region as a base for an expanded supplier network. The growth of Cardone Industries and the recent plans for a Black & Decker plant in the region exemplify the opportunities that exist to leverage regional manufacturing clusters on both sides of the border for local investment and job creation.

Paola Ávila, Vice President of International Business Affairs, San Diego Regional Chamber of Commerce, and Chair of the Board of Directors, Border Trade Alliance

Paola Ávila worked in city- and state-level government in California focusing on issues of economic development and binational affairs before joining the San Diego Regional Chamber of Commerce to lead its work in the same areas.[8] She currently also serves as chair of the Border Trade Alliance (BTA).[9]

    Ávila believes the recent growth in binational cooperation in the San Diego–Tijuana area is in large part the result of the vision and strong relationships developed between the mayors of the two cities in the mid-2000s. Over the past decade, she saw this binational city-to-city relationship strengthened and institutionalized, which has reduced the need for personal chemistry among the mayors and increased the stability of the relationship. Ávila notes that San Diego–area chambers of commerce and other community organizations followed the lead of the city governments, adding permanent places on their boards for representatives from Tijuana and otherwise cementing the binational nature of their work. These other organizations now help ensure that the vision for binational cooperation transcends the life span of elected officials.

    Ávila describes the main focus of the San Diego Regional Chamber's binational economic-development work taking place in the form of advocacy. The chamber works to ensure that state and federal governments on both sides of the border adopt public policies that are conducive to economic development in the region, focusing specifically on issues of border infrastructure, trade, and immigration. Ávila sees significant gaps in public policy and spending in each of these areas as major inhibitors of the binational economy. She points out that companies like Qualcomm, the telecommunications company based in San Diego, cannot hire enough engineers locally, but they could if immigration policy was changed to allow them to tap into the broader regional talent pool by sponsoring Tijuana natives for visas more easily. Similarly, long wait times to get across the border for both individuals and commercial traffic create divisions within the regional economy that lead to inefficiencies and missed opportunities for growth. Nonetheless, Ávila also sees important advances in developing the binational economy, noting the creation of multiple new software developers headquartered in San Diego but with offices in Tijuana and the expansion of academic partnerships designed to offer students on both sides of the border training that will be recognized and valued wherever they work.

Ávila describes the role of BTA as especially important in terms of its advocacy for border transportation infrastructure and the efficient management of border ports of entry. She also notes the role the organization has played in the 2017–2018 renegotiation of NAFTA. In recent years, BTA has hired a lobbyist in Washington, D.C., to work continuously as an advocate for better trade policy and trade facilitation. Both this permanent presence in Washington and the participation of BTA members in offering guidance to the U.S. and Mexican governments formally and informally has given the organization and the border region an important voice during the renegotiation of NAFTA.

Gustavo A. de la Fuente, Executive Director, Smart Border Coalition

Gustavo A. de la Fuente has been the executive director of the Smart Border Coalition since the beginning of 2017.[10] The coalition itself was formed in 2011 when James Clark, Malin Burnham, José Galicot, and others came together and decided that they needed to act to create a better, more efficient, and innovative border for the San Diego–Tijuana region. De La Fuente sees the SBC in some ways as an outgrowth of the innovative San Diego Dialogue, which was led by Charles Nathanson and Mary Walshok and brought together leaders not only from across San Diego but also Tijuana to talk about the challenges and opportunities facing the region. De La Fuente notes that important border facilitation and security advances, including the SENTRI trusted-traveler program (precursor of the Global Entry Program, providing expedited border crossings for individuals who have been prevetted by the U.S. government), were conceptualized and pushed forward by the San Diego Dialogue.

The founders of the Smart Border Coalition found that there was nonetheless a lack of cross-border dialogue on the "nuts and bolts" of managing the border. By creating a forum for citizens and business leaders to connect and dialogue with the officials from both the U.S. and Mexican federal government running regional border crossings, the Smart Border Coalition has been able to make simple but important improvements to the operation of the border. An SBC effort, including both advocacy and financial support, has improved signage ahead of the border crossing in Tijuana so that travelers returning to San Diego from Tijuana or Ensenada get into the correct lanes as they arrive at the border. The coalition has also been an important contributor to and advocate for bigger cross-border infrastructure projects, such as the major modernization of the San Ysidro port of entry that is currently underway. The SBC is now working on a concept for an improved preclearance program, better border wait-time measurement processes, and other plans to smooth the border-crossing experience in the region.

De La Fuente notes that it is not easy to move three levels of government on each side of the border to come together, identify problems, and prioritize solutions to border management issues. It is precisely because of the large number of actors that need to be on the same page that De La Fuente believes organizations like SBC are needed to help with the process of convening and then advocacy. He also believes the San Diego–Tijuana region could be even more effective in building an improved border if all of the many stakeholders who care about cross-border issues could be more unified in their approach, especially to advocacy.

Wolfram Federico Schaffler, Director, Texas Center for Border Economic and Enterprise Development, Texas A&M International University

Federico Schaffler directs the Texas Center for Border Economic and Enterprise Development at TAMIU in Laredo, Texas, where he studies issues of trade and economic development.[11] He has worked as a city official in Nuevo Laredo, Tamaulipas, in three different governments, and he also has served in the state government. Finally, Schaffler led the Instituto Interamericano de Fronteras y Aduanas, the professional training institute of the Mexican National Federation of Customs Brokers (Confederación de Asociaciones de Agentes Aduanales de la República Mexicana [CAAAREM]) after working for several years in the logistics industry in Nuevo Laredo.

The Laredo–Nuevo Laredo region is the largest commercial crossing along the U.S.-Mexico border, serving as the main gateway for products moving from central and northeastern Mexico to the eastern seaboard and industrial heartland of the United States. As such, it has become the largest hub of logistics and trade facilitation businesses along the border. Schaffler notes that those in the logistics industry have always had good working relationships across the border since they need one another to move products between the two countries (and actually needed each other even more so before NAFTA when the Mexican economy was less open, Schaffler notes).

Despite its advantageous position at the center of binational trade, Schaffler believes that the Laredo–Nuevo Laredo region has missed out on the opportunity to grow into a manufacturing hub and even to strengthen the logistics industry. He points to the long-term vision developed in McAllen, Texas, and Reynosa, Tamaulipas, in the 1980s to attract maquiladoras to the area as an example of more active and successful government and nongovernment cooperation to develop the regional economy (see the section on Keith Patridge, below, for more details). In the early 2000s, the City of Nuevo Laredo created an economic-development office for the first time and has subsequently been a more active promoter of regional development and investment rather than simply relying on the private sector to play this role.

Still, Schaffler credits moments of real vision, leadership, and cross-border cooperation in making Laredo–Nuevo Laredo the main gateway of binational trade. He notes that the City of Nuevo Laredo and private-sector entities took on significant debt to help fund the construction of the World Trade Bridge, which is the single largest commercial crossing along the U.S.-Mexico border. Schaffler laments the fact that the Mexican tolls from the bridge are all collected by the Mexican federal government and therefore do not support the repayment of construction loans. He nonetheless thinks this was a moment of long-term strategic vision that has cemented the region's status as the largest commercial crossing point and served as the principal driver of economic development for the region.

For Schaffler, the key to successful binational economic development is the creation and implementation of a long-term strategy that transcends the life span of any single local government. TAMIU has recently facilitated an update of the Nuevo Laredo economic-development plan, and the City of Laredo has a comprehensive development plan, but Schaffler sees a need for the two plans to be integrated into a truly binational vision of development for the region.

Tim Kelley, President and CEO, Imperial Valley Economic Development Corporation

As head of the Imperial Valley Economic Development Corporation, Tim Kelley sees the border and the counterpart community of Mexicali, Baja California, as key assets that he can leverage for the development of communities in Imperial County, California.[12] He notes the advantages in terms of supply-chain management that the close proximity to the large U.S. market brings to investors in the region. The additional and larger workforce of Mexicali can also serve to supplement the local labor pool when jobs are created in Imperial Valley, California. The Imperial Valley–Mexicali region has achieved important binational accomplishments that strengthen the entire region in terms of cross-border electrical connections and water storage agreements that allow for and regulate the utilization of infrastructure across the border in the case of emergencies and to fill in infrastructure gaps.

Kelley has been involved in the creation of two major binational coalitions of actors working for the development of the region. Along with colleagues in San Diego, Tijuana, and Mexicali, he helped create the Cali Baja Bi-National Mega-Region, Inc., in 2008 (see section on Flavio Olivieri, above). The Imperial Valley Economic Development Corporation (IVEDC) won a grant from the U.S. Department of Commerce that allowed for the creation of the initiative, and Kelley leveraged the grant to bring together actors from San Diego and Baja California under a vision of interconnectedness in which each realized they needed the others to promote economic development. He sees it as essentially a privately led effort from the U.S. side and a publicly led effort on the Mexican side of the border. Despite the important achievements of the mega-region group, Kelley admits that the uneven nature of the various IVEDCs that make up the association has presented challenges.

More recently, in 2013, Kelley was one of the key forces behind the creation of the Imperial-Mexicali Binational Alliance, which works on binational approaches in the areas of economic development, environment, infrastructure, and education. With representatives from various associations and groups from each side of the border attending, the alliance holds meetings every two months to discuss regional needs in each of the above areas. Kelley notes the special importance of dialogue in the development of cross-border transportation infrastructure given that the U.S. and Mexican systems must be working together in order to facilitate efficient connectivity. Transportation improvements in turn have a positive effect on the environment by reducing the time spent by vehicles idling.

Keith Patridge, President and CEO, McAllen Economic Development Corporation

For approximately thirty years, Keith Patridge has worked to attract businesses to the McAllen-Reynosa region, assisting over six hundred companies and helping create over 150,000 jobs.[13] Patridge got involved in economic development in McAllen in the mid-1980s after the region was hit by a series of economic shocks: back-to-back severe freezes that debilitated agricultural producers, the 1982 oil price collapse and ensuing Mexican debt crisis, and a decline in tourism to the region (partly a result of the death of many tropical plants during the freezes). The shocks resulted in skyrocketing unemployment and a clear realization by regional leaders that there was a need to diversify the economy. In 1998, this led to the creation of the McAllen EDC, and Patridge joined the first president, Mike Allen, as executive vice president because of his background in manufacturing.

Allen, Patridge, and others asked themselves why a company would choose to invest in McAllen. In a transcendent moment of transborder vision, the McAllen EDC decided the greatest opportunity for economic development in McAllen was actually the attraction of manufacturing operations in neighboring Reynosa, Tamaulipas. With the local community reeling from the crisis, local leaders were open to trying something new and different. The devaluation of the peso added to the already significant cost savings associated with low labor costs in Mexico, making Mexico a very attractive alternative to outsourcing to Asia. Investment in Reynosa would in turn stimulate retail business (see section on Jon Barela, above) and attract plant managers and service providers to live and work in McAllen. The McAllen EDC presented this concept to the mayor of Reynosa, who naturally supported it and essentially designated the McAllen EDC as the EDC for Reynosa as well, although the McAllen EDC intentionally has never received direct funding from the City of Reynosa, preferring to request specific investments by the City of Reynosa to help attract companies to the region.

Over time, and especially throughout the 1990s, the strategy yielded results for both Reynosa and McAllen, which was consistently ranked among the fastest-growing metro areas in the United States during this period. By presenting the communities as a united, single, larger economic entity with greater resources and coordinated leadership, the McAllen EDC was able to attract significant investments to the region, which cemented support for this approach to economic development. This model also allowed the stability of the McAllen EDC to smooth out the traditional challenge of implementing long-term economic-development strategies across municipal administrations in Mexico. One key success was the case of Alpine Electronics, an auto parts supplier to the big three U.S. auto makers (Ford, GM, Chrysler), which started operations in the region with just seventeen employees in the Reynosa area and none in McAllen, Texas, only to grow to some six thousand employees in the region, including three to four hundred employees and many corporate management functions being located in McAllen, Texas.

Patridge and the McAllen EDC are in the process of updating their basic model as the needs and priorities of companies change. He notes that cheap labor has fallen lower on the scale of priorities than it used to be as automation changes the cost structure of manufacturing and artificial intelligence does the same for other operations. The value proposition of investment in the McAllen-Reynosa area is now based largely on the flexibility that having access to talent pools, regulatory jurisdictions, and even macroeconomic conditions on the two sides of the border can offer businesses that choose to locate in the area. The McAllen EDC is now advocating for changes to visa policy (particularly U.S. L visas for intracompany transfers) to allow companies to have employees who are authorized to work on either side of the border depending on changing conditions and the needs of the purchaser of the product they are building.

Martha Rascon, Executive Director, Safe Border Trucking Association

Martha Rascon has served as the executive director of the Nogales-area Safe Border Trucking Association since its founding in 2014. Before that, Rascon worked at the U.S. consulate in Nogales, the Fresh Produce Association, and was a founding member of the Greater Nogales Santa Cruz County Port Authority.

The Safe Border Trucking Association was formed by forty-five trucking companies from both sides of the border because they found that trucks entering the United States through Nogales were facing a much higher level of inspection from the U.S. Department of Transportation (DOT) Federal Motor Carrier Safety Administration (FMCSA) than those entering at other ports of entry. A study found that trucks entering through Nogales faced rates of inspections (and fines) that were ten times that faced by trucks crossing into Texas. After presenting U.S., Mexican, and state officials with this data, the association found that local and federal entities concerned with promoting cross-border trade became their allies in addressing this issue. They also found that the U.S. DOT was willing to engage them in dialogue in a way that was not possible before the phenomenon was well documented and before the carriers were organized in a way that allowed them to engage in constructive dialogue. Importantly, this occurred at a time in which Arizona's government and private sector were very focused on increasing trade with Mexico. The association worked to educate member truckers regarding the ways in which they could document their compliance with U.S. regulations, worked with the FMCSA to apply its rules in a more consistent manner, and are now working with the Mexican Secretariat of Communications and Transportation (SCT) to see whether the Mexican government might be able to certify compliance in a way that is recognized by U.S. officials. The end result has been a concrete reduction in transaction costs for cross-border traders and an improvement in relations between Mexican truckers and U.S. officials.

Rick Van Schoik, Portfolio Director, North American Research Partnership

Rick Van Schoik has been the portfolio director for the North American Research Partnership since the organization was founded in 2013.[14] Before that, he was the director of the North American Center for Transborder Studies at Arizona State University and director of the Southwest Consortium for Environmental Research and Policy, as well as serving as a U.S. Navy SEAL. Throughout his career in working on binational issues along the U.S.-Mexico border, Van Schoik has witnessed a steady and gradual increase in cooperation at both the local and federal levels, though he worries that the current environment at the federal to federal level may be putting some of that progress at risk.

Van Schoik noted a wave of support for binational projects, including U.S. congressional support for the work on transborder environmental issues done by SCERP, that came after the implementation of NAFTA in 1994. Like others, he saw that wave of binationalism challenged by the increase in inspection and congestion at border crossings that followed the terrorist attacks of 2001, but Van Schoik sees resilience. In the wake of 9/11 and now in response to challenges to NAFTA, immigration, and broader border policy posed by the Trump administration, people in border communities are organizing to protect their interests and binational way of life. Van Schoik points to efforts by the Smart Border Coalition, the San Diego Regional Association of Governments, and the State of California as potential examples of local-level binationalism in the face of nationalism coming from Washington.

At the same time, Van Schoik recalls that progress on issues of binational cooperation has rarely been linear, and several important border-region institutions have come on hard times. The Border Governors Conference has failed to meet for several years, and the Border Legislative Conference, while continuing to meet, faces budgetary challenges. These organizations and others are being forced to redefine and reconfigure themselves in order to survive the cycles of rising and falling federal interest and support for local-level cross-border cooperation.

Conclusions

Cross-border cooperation for economic development is on the rise. In cities all along the U.S.-Mexico border, local officials, business owners, nonprofit organizations, and members of academia are promoting closer binational ties as a tool for economic development.

Throughout recent history, there have been several waves and drivers of efforts that could be considered binational economic development, some in the form of opportunities to be realized and others in the form of challenges for border communities to overcome. The maquiladora program was an early driver of industrialization, but aside from the Arizona-Mexico Commission, few local or state-level mechanisms for binational economic development from this era have survived. The roots of several modern initiatives can be found in the 1980s, such as the creation of the Border Trade Alliance, the San Diego Dialogue, and the creation of the McAllen EDC with its vision of promoting economic development through a series of positive cross-border spillovers. Some of these occurred as discussion of a potential North American free-trade agreement was underway, but others had independent drivers specific to the local context. The effort to complete and pass NAFTA in the early nineties as well as the implementation of the agreement itself greatly increased national-level support for binational cooperation in the border region in both Mexico and the United States, and a wave of local initiatives followed. These were not limited to economic development but included cooperative approaches to issues including public health, environmental protection, resource management, and more. Even as trade volumes grew under the framework of NAFTA, the terrorist attacks of 2001 pushed the U.S. government to tighten border controls and increase the inspection levels faced by border crossers. This resulted in time-consuming, expensive, and ultimately community-dividing levels of congestion at the border, but it also led to a new wave of advocacy and cooperation on the part of border communities to find creative ways to increase border efficiency while maintaining or even strengthening border security. The Great Recession in the United States and the resulting recession in Mexico again pushed border communities to seek new opportunities for economic development, and most recently several border communities have come together to defend NAFTA and more welcoming immigration policies at a time when they are at risk in Washington.

The drivers of cooperation, whether the macrodrivers listed above or the more local and specific agents of binational efforts that are unique to each cross-border community, appear to result in sustained cooperative efforts only when they engage a group of actors with the capacity to develop and maintain them. Several of the interviewees pointed to local and state government officials as the most important actors in driving binational cooperation. Beyond the direct government-to-government cooperation, officials were seen as setting a tone of cooperation that was often echoed and sustained by civil society. Nonetheless, most interviewees agreed that cooperation was the most robust and lasting when businesses, universities, and nonprofit organizations were all engaged in binational efforts for economic development. Interestingly, San Diego, which is probably the community that traditionally saw itself as (and perhaps was) least connected to the Mexican economy, has been a leader in developing innovative and advanced forms of binational cooperation for economic development. As a center of innovation and intellectual capital, the leadership of San Diego underscores the importance of capacity as a driver of transborder cooperation (certainly having the large and industrialized city of Tijuana across the border was an important factor as well).

In many places along the border, the spirit of binationalism is understood to be innate, but it is nonetheless challenging to overcome parochial mind-sets and incentive structures (the incentive issue is especially relevant for elected officials) in order to implement binational projects and activate transborder communities.

The creation of mechanisms to distribute the benefits of collaboration in what are perceived as just ways have been important for many border communities. In this vein, the jurisdiction-agnostic approach to investment attraction developed by The Borderplex Alliance has facilitated the successful development of an organization with a mission to serve three states, two nations, and one transborder community. In other regions, such as McAllen-Reynosa, the mechanism for distributing benefits is different, with a greater emphasis placed on attracting manufacturing businesses to the Mexican side of the border, but the implicit agreement has nonetheless worked well for the community for several decades. Many communities along the border continue to struggle to overcome such challenges, and the dividing lines just as often run north to south and east to west.

The main focus of binational economic-development efforts to date has been on issues of trade policy and connectivity, efforts to make the border less thick and more permeable. The border in this sense has been understood as a barrier to economic development that must be overcome, and indeed studies on the negative effect of border congestion and the positive effect of growing trade confirm that in many ways this is the case.[15] Whether in the form of BTA advocacy for NAFTA, the Smart Border Coalition's advocacy for port of entry modernization, or the Safe Border Trucking Association's work to minimize trucker fines and increase compliance, the most widespread and basic model for strengthening economic opportunity in the border region remains rooted in the notion of breaking down barriers that inhibit the full realization of the benefits of trade and travel across the region. These efforts have been present in the border region for decades, but this series of interviews suggests that the number of initiatives has expanded and the base of stakeholders supporting these initiatives has become broader over the past two decades.

At other times, and perhaps increasingly, the border and the diversity it sustains have been seen as a source—rather than inhibitor—of economic opportunity. The binational nature of businesses such as Alpine Electronics in Reynosa and McAllen or Thermo-Fischer in San Diego and Tijuana, which rely on the availability of differing cost structures and talent pools in the close proximity that border communities offer, are testaments to the unique value that doing business in the border region can provide. Economic-development organizations across the border region are shifting their investment attraction strategies away from a focus on only the low cost of labor in Mexico and toward the other unique assets available in the region: flexible manufacturing structures, a bilingual and bicultural workforce, close and quick access to major markets, and the ability to divide operations across the border in order to tap into the comparative advantages offered by each side.

Across the border—and indeed across North America and the world—the importance of talent has eclipsed the importance of low labor costs. This is driving economic-development professionals across the region to partner with universities and other educational institutions to a greater extent, and it is part of a broader shift toward understanding economic development not just as investment attraction but also as the facilitation of collective actions to strengthen the competitiveness of a cluster, industry, or region. It is in this shift that the greatest opportunities for binational economic development exist. Communities from Brownsville and Matamoros to San Diego and Tijuana are beginning to explore and experiment with efforts to create transborder public goods, whether a binational talent pool or a binational airport designed to serve the needs of residents on both sides of the border. The border region may in some ways be on the periphery of the United States and Mexico, but regional actors are reconceptualizing it as the heart of a binational region that leverages the competitive advantages of both countries.

NOTES

I would like to thank Miguel Garza for his excellent research assistance in the preparation of this essay.

1. Christopher Wilson, Erik Lee, and Alma Bezares, *Competitive Border Communities: Mapping and Developing US-Mexico Transborder Industries* (Washington, D.C.: Wilson Center, 2008); Christopher Wilson and Erik Lee, *The US-Mexico Border Economy in Transition* (Washington, D.C.: Wilson Center, 2015); Alejandro Brugues et al., *Jobs Without Borders: Employment, Industry Concentrations, and Comparative Advantage in the CaliBaja Region* (La Jolla and Tijuana: CaliBaja Mega Region Initiative; Center for U.S.-Mexican Studies, University of California, San Diego; Colegio de la Frontera Norte, 2014); Miguel Gonzalez et al., *Backward Integration of Manufacturing Supply Chains in the Brownsville-Matamoros Region: An Approach for Creating a Competitive Binational Advanced Manufacturing Cluster* (Brownsville, Tex.: Ambiotec Group, UTRGV, Wilson Center, 2017).

2. International Bank of Commerce, http://IBC.com.

3. The Cali Baja Bi-National Mega-Region, http://Calibaja.net.

4. The Borderplex Alliance, https://BorderplexAlliance.org/about-us/the-borderplex -alliance.

5. Jesus Cañas, Roberto Coronado, and Robert Gilberto, *Texas Border: Employment and Maquiladora Growth* (Dallas, Tex.: Federal Reserve Bank of Dallas, 2005).

6. The Arizona-Mexico Commission, http://azmc.org.

7. The University of Texas Rio Grande Valley, "Robert C. Vackar College of Business and Entrepreneurship," http://utrgv.edu/cobe.

8. San Diego Regional Chamber of Commerce, http://sdchamber.org.

9. The Border Trade Alliance, http://thebta.org.

10. Smart Border Coalition, http://smartbordercoalition.com.

11. Texas A&M International University, Texas Center for Border Economic and Enterprise Development, http://texascenter.tamiu.edu.

12. Imperial Valley Economic Development Cooperation online.

13. The McAllen Economic Development Corporation online, "Keith A. Patridge."

14. North American Research Partnership online.

15. For information on various studies documenting the costs of border congestion, see *Improving Security and Facilitating Commerce with Mexico at America's Southern Border: Hearing on H.R. Rep. Before the Subcommittee on the Western Hemisphere, Committee on Foreign Affairs*, Cong. 113 (2014) (statement of Christopher Wilson, Associate, Mexico Institute, Wilson Center). For an analysis of the effect of US-Mexico trade, see Christopher Wilson, *Growing Together: Economic Ties Between the United States and Mexico* (Washington, DC: Wilson Center, 2017).

CHAPTER 12

Comparative Examination of Binational Watershed Research in North America

From Case Studies to a Continental Gestalt

CHRISTOPHER BROWN

Abstract

Transboundary water resources and watersheds are, by their nature, very challenging to manage and offer a wide range of management issues that are frequently not resolved through unilateral means. The North American continent possesses two different yet related spatial contexts in which transboundary water resource-management issues can be examined: the arid region of the southwestern U.S.-Mexico borderlands and the humid region of the Canada-U.S. borderlands. Although these regions possess different physical and political geographies, comparative analyses of water resource-management issues in these border regions can be highly instructive to policy makers in each region who are responsible for international water resource management.

This chapter revisits a comparative examination of watershed management efforts that I have done for select watersheds on the U.S.-Canada border (Brown 2014). In this previous research, I interviewed key policy and decision makers who were actively engaged in efforts to advance effective transboundary water resource policy in these select watersheds. I also explored extensive archival sources that detailed a range of water resource-management efforts with a particular interest in the role of scale in the dynamics being examined. With this foundational review in place, I expand on my earlier research by examining the Tijuana River Watershed, an important binational watershed on the U.S.-Mexico Border. Through this comparative analysis of select U.S.-Canada and U.S.-Mexico binational watersheds, I ask and answer the following questions:

- What are the main governmental and nongovernmental institutions and schemata that have developed in these border contexts, how did they develop, and what has been the general experience of these institutions?
- To what degree are we seeing the focus of and major activity related to binational watershed management in these regions devolve from the federal to the state/provincial to the nonstate/provincial levels, and why is this happening?
- To what degree and how can the experiences from one of the border regions being examined inform water resource-management policy in other border regions?
- To what degree do these experiences support the idea of a "North American gestalt" of watershed management that is consistent with Robert Pastor's North American Idea (Pastor 2012)?[1]

Introduction

Transboundary water resources and watersheds demonstrate a range of management issues that by their binational nature can be very challenging to address. On both sides of the U.S.-Canada and U.S.-Mexico borders, we can see evidence of, and action by, numerous governmental units and mature management institutions. Despite their mature nature, the reach of these efforts is largely limited by provincial/state or international boundaries; watersheds and surface and subsurface hydrologic processes are not. Previous research has examined transboundary water resource-management issues in two very different spatial regions: the arid southwestern U.S.-Mexico border region and the humid U.S.-Canada border region. Specific issues that have been explored in the U.S.-Mexico border region include the manner in which a range of institutional arrangements have existed and performed; these institutional arrangements include both existing and new institutions and how these various entities have performed across spatial scale, from local to reginal to national to international (Brown 2010a; Brown and Mumme 2000; Fischhendler, Feitelson, and Eaton 2004; and Frisvold and Caswell 2000). Turning our attention to the northern border of the United States with Canada, we see similar questions being asked of how best to manage transboundary and binational water resources. In the last fifteen years, we see an increasing level of interest and effort in U.S.-Canadian watersheds to explore the degree to which regional and subnational efforts have gained prominence and how successful efforts have tended to be regionally grounded (Lovecraft 2007; Norman and Bakker 2009; Norman, Bakker, and Cook 2012; VanNijnatten 2003, 2006). This dynamic of how institutional efforts have emerged and to what degree they have been successful across scale warrants a comparative examination of U.S.-Canada and U.S.-Mexico watersheds within a North American context similar to Pastor's *The North American Idea* (Pastor 2012).

In this chapter, I advance a comparative examination of subregions of the Cascadia Corridor region, within which the Salish Sea and smaller nested watersheds lie, and the binational Tijuana River Watershed, within which portions of San Diego and Tijuana lie. Based on extensive fieldwork I completed as part of my dissertation research (conducted with a Canadian Studies Research Program grant; Brown 2010b) and related archival research, I examine how transboundary water resource management in these regions either does or does not support the following arguments that are of relevance to scholars and policy makers:

1. As noted above, previous researchers (Lovecraft 2007; Norman and Bakker 2009; Norman, Bakker, and Cook 2012; and VanNijnatten 2003 and 2006) have examined how national governmental agencies have in effect ceded their primary role of regional water resource management to subnationals actors in the U.S.-Canada borderlands and context. These authors argue that this has occurred as governmental agencies have become less engaged in regional environmental issues and nongovernmental actors with major stakes in these issues have organized, secured resources, and sought out successful partnerships. The result of these related processes is that the interest and ability to craft and implement successful water resource-management policy moves from national/international to provincial/state scales and from governmental to nongovernmental, local/regional actors. A specific question I ask and answer is, to what degree will the experiences examined in the regions of interest support this argument?

2. As a comparative regional geographer who has looked at binational watersheds in detail, I have found that geography and the manner in which local stakeholders are connected to water resources in the regions being examined matter.

As noted in the introduction of this chapter, management of both surface water and groundwater resources is in play. These dynamics offer opportunities to examine the specifics of cross-border cooperation on transboundary water resource management and to answer the question, how and to what degree does "geography matter" as regards binational water resource management?

3. Geographic or spatial scale is a foundational concept within regional geographic research. In this chapter, I examine the degree to which "scale matters," both spatial and hierarchical scale (Coe, Kelly, and Yeung 2017; McKinnon and Cumbers 2011). The concept of hierarchical scale is related to the argument noted above concerning how policy formation and implementation are devolving from national/governmental levels to local levels. Spatial scale deals with how extensive the water resources being examined are. Are we examining very large watersheds with thousands or tens of thousands of square kilometers and many stakeholders and agencies, or are we exploring less extensive resources that cover less territory with fewer stakeholders and policy-making players?

In this chapter I introduce the overall areas of investigation, the Salish Sea region on the U.S.-Canada border, and the Tijuana River Watershed on the U.S.-Mexico border. I also provide an overview of the various subregions that I have investigated. At various spatial scales, I examine the arguments posed above and extract from each regional experience an understanding of what efforts were effective (or not) and why. I also speak to the three arguments posed above. I close the article with some reflections on the concept that I introduce in the title of the chapter: namely, "Do the results obtained from examining these binational watersheds support the idea of a 'continental gestalt' as regards binational watershed management that is consistent with Robert Pastor's idea of *The North American Idea?*" (Pastor 2012)

Introduction to the Areas of Interest

The Salish Sea Region of the Cascade Corridor

The Cascade Corridor is the functional, binational region on the U.S.-Canada border within which Vancouver, British Colombia; Seattle and Bellingham, Washington; and other regional population centers lie. Within this region are several regional water resources of major importance, including Puget Sound (a very large marine region), the Boundary Bay region, the Abbotsford-Sumas Transboundary Aquifer, and several smaller watersheds of regional interest. During my fieldwork, I met several regional scholars who referred to this region as the Salish Sea. The name reflects a rich cultural heritage of Native American and First Nations peoples in the region and the recognition that the Salish Sea is a dynamic and important ecosystem defined by marine, inland water, and land resources that exist here (Groc 2011).[2] Map 12.1 depicts the Salish Sea, within which the following subregions lie and are the focus of this chapter.

- **The Bertrand and Fishtrap Watersheds**—These transboundary watersheds that lie approximately 15–20 kilometers inland from the Boundary Bay region have the smallest areal extent of any of the regions examined. Within these watersheds, watershed improvement districts (WIDs) have been developed by regional stakeholders with considerable utility to examine regional water resource issues.
- **The Boundary Bay region**—This embayment lies within the Strait of Georgia, south of the urban area of Vancouver, in which several municipalities share water quality and supply concerns.
- **The Abbotsford-Sumas region**—Twenty-five kilometers east of the Boundary Bay lies the transboundary urban area known as the Abbotsford Sumas region, within which a transboundary aquifer of major regional importance lies.
- **The Puget Sound region**—At the opposite end of the spatial scale of the regions examined above is Puget Sound, a very large marine area that lies within the Salish Sea. Within the sound, a long-term transboundary effort at examining quality of surface waters known as the Puget Sound Partnership (PSP) has emerged in the last few decades.

The Tijuana River Watershed (TRW)

While doing my dissertation research, I was very fortunate to "be in the right place at the right time, for a good long time." My advisors and mentors Richard Wright and Paul Ganster were very successful in securing multiyear funding to support an exhaustive examination of the TRW, and I was one of a fortunate group of students that were actively engaged in fieldwork and related GIS analysis in the region. The results of this were a large number of articles, book chapters, theses, and dissertations that tell the story of the basin as well as the

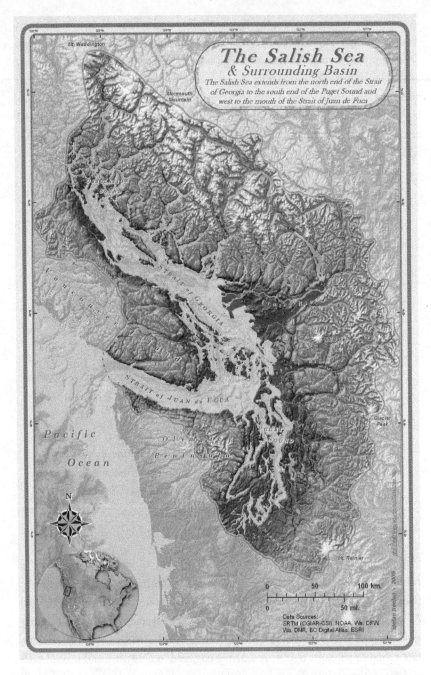

The Salish Sea
& Surrounding Basin
The Salish Sea extends from the north end of the Strait
of Georgia to the south end of the Puget Sound and
west to the mouth of the Strait of Juan de Fuca

Mt. Waddington

Monmouth
Mountain

STRAIT of GEORGIA

Fraser R.

Mt. Baker

STRAIT of JUAN de FUCA

Glacier
Peak

Pacific
Ocean

Olympic
Peninsula

PUGET
SOUND

N

Mt. Rainier

0   50   100 km.

0   50 ml.

Data Sources:
SRTM (CGIAR-CSI), NOAA, Wa. DFW,
Wa. DNR, BC Digital Atlas, ESRI

MAP 12.1 Salish Sea and surrounding basin (Area defined by Bert Webber, retired marine biologist, Western Washington University. Map compiled by Stefan Freelan 2009. Used by permission.)

creation of the Tijuana River Watershed Atlas (Institute for Regional Studies of the Californias and San Diego State University Department of Geography 2005a, 2005b).

The TRW is a binational watershed in the westernmost portion of the arid U.S.-Mexico border region within which San Diego, California, and Tijuana, Baja California Norte, lie. Map 12.2 provides a useful regional overview of the watershed and its location in the border region. As of 2007, the combined population of these twin cities was estimated to be just under five million people (World Gazetter 2007), and a majority of them live in the watershed. The basin covers approximately 1,735 square miles, with 70 percent in Mexico and 30 percent in the United States (Brown 1998). The headwaters of the watershed are in two regions, the Rio de las Palmas subbasin in Mexico, and the Cottonwood Creek subbasin in the United States. The topography of the basin is highly variable, with elevations ranging from sea level in the coastal region to over five thousand feet above sea level in the upper reaches (see map 12.3). This topography is such that surface water runoff from urban areas discharges into the Pacific Ocean where the Tijuana River Estuary meets the beach. Large volumes of untreated and marginally treated wastewater have generated serious surface water quality issues since the 1950s, when the region began to see rapid urbanization (Brown 1998). For decades, water quality issues within the basin have been both a source of regional conflict and a point of regional cooperation, both of which are examined in this chapter.

Regional Water Resource Issues and Emerging Policy Tools in the Salish Sea Region

In this section, I revisit work done previously (Brown 2014) in the Salish Sea Region in which I examined the four subregions identified above and discussed the most pressing binational water resource-management issues. As noted in the introduction to this chapter, the issue of scale is both documented in previous work and is of special interest to me as a regional geographer with a special interest in the political ecology of transboundary water resource management. Accordingly, I start this discussion at the local scale by looking at regions with water resources of regional importance that have the smallest area extent and then "move upscale" to the more spatially expansive regions of interest. I close each subsection with a review of efforts that have been advanced in

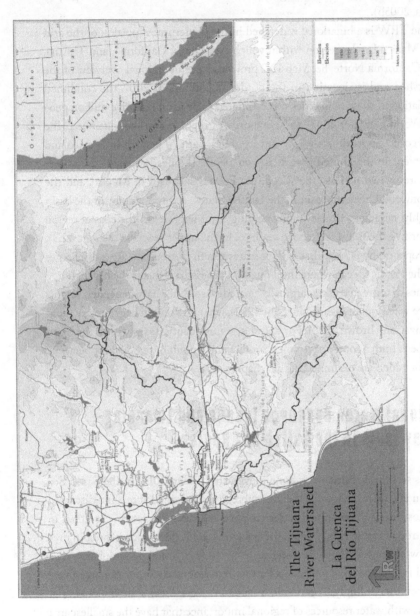

MAP 12.2 Overview of the Tijuana River Watershed (Source: Institute for Regional Studies of the Californias and San Diego State University Department of Geography 2005a. Used by permission.)

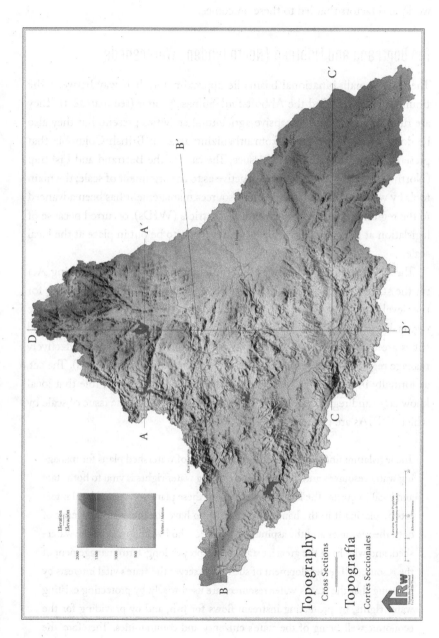

MAP 12.3 Topographic map of the Tijuana River Watershed showing relief that drives surface water flows (Source: Institute for Regional Studies of the Californias and San Diego State University Department of Geography 2005a. Used by permission.)

each subregion, drawing some conclusions concerning what worked (or did not work) and factors that led to these outcomes.

The Bertrand and Fishtrap (North Lynden) Watersheds

These two small, binational basins lie approximately half way between the Boundary Bay area and the Abbottsford-Sumas Aquifer (see map 12.4). They are rural in nature, with extensive agricultural activities present, but they also lie downstream/down basin from urbanizing areas in British Columbia that present a range of water quality issues. The case of the Bertrand and Fishtrap (North Lynden) Watersheds is instructive as to the argument of scale; the main tools by which transboundary water resources management has been advanced in the region, Watershed Improvement Districts (WIDs), occurred because of legislation at the state level allowing innovations to be put in place at the local scale.

The 1998 State of Washington Comprehensive Watershed Planning Act set the stage for innovative water resource-management efforts by calling for the development of Water Resource Inventory Areas (WRIAs). WRIAs are regionally grounded efforts by which local residents, governmental agencies, and tribes are able to work together to create watershed plans to more effectively manage regional water resources (Washington State Legislature 1998). The act, as formally introduced below, clearly establishes the important role that local knowledge and regional geography play and also speaks to the issue of scale by which WRIAs are created:

> The legislature finds that the local development of watershed plans for manag-
> ing water resources and for protecting existing water rights is vital to both state
> and local interests. The local development of these plans serves vital local inter-
> ests by placing it in the hands of people: Who have the greatest knowledge of
> both the resources and the aspirations of those who live and work in the water-
> shed; and who have the greatest stake in the proper, long-term management of
> the resources. The development of such plans serves the state's vital interests by
> ensuring that the state's water resources are used wisely, by protecting existing
> water rights, by protecting instream flows for fish, and by providing for the
> economic well-being of the state's citizenry and communities. Therefore, the
> legislature believes it necessary for units of local government throughout the
> state to engage in the orderly development of these watershed plans.[3]

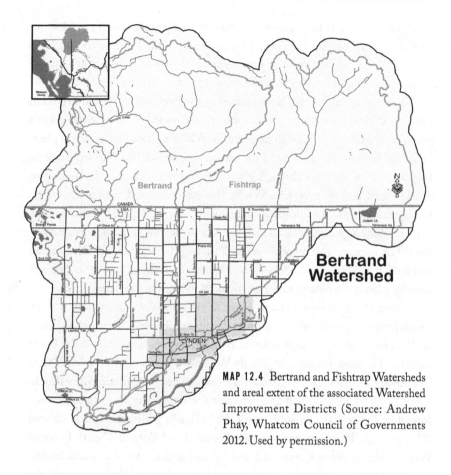

MAP 12.4 Bertrand and Fishtrap Watersheds and areal extent of the associated Watershed Improvement Districts (Source: Andrew Phay, Whatcom Council of Governments 2012. Used by permission.)

Consistent with this legislation, stakeholders in the Bertrand and Fishtrap (North Lynden) Watersheds established two WIDs, and these WIDs are state-sanctioned mechanisms by which local stakeholders can use local knowledge to advance regional watershed management efforts. Both the Bertrand and Fishtrap (North Lynden) WIDs were established via local elections, with approximately 70 percent of voters supporting the creation of the Bertrand WID and 90 percent of voters supporting the creation of the Fishtrap (North Lynden) WID (Bierlink 2010).[4]

Examining specific issues within each WID is instructive in exploring similarities and trends in these management efforts. Specific issues examined within the Bertrand WID include in-stream flows, water storage projects, deep aquifer research, a regional water transfer study, market approaches to resource management, efforts to improve fish passage facilities and habitat, and water quality monitoring. Research topics explored within the Fishtrap (North Lynden) WID include stormwater management, in-stream flows, water quality monitoring, irrigation efficiency, and condition of aquatic habitat.[5]

What lessons can we take from examining the Bertrand and Fishtrap (North Lynden) WIDs? First, the legal framework that allowed WIDs to be created was put in place by State of Washington statute. With this state framework in place, local stakeholders then mobilized and secured funds from the Washington State Department of Ecology through grants dedicated to watershed planning to develop, staff, and support these WIDs. This experience indicates policy efforts moving across scale; the initial legal framework was put in place by actions of the State of Washington, then local stakeholders deploying local knowledge made the WIDs happen. This is consistent with findings by Norman (2009), Norman and Bakker (2009), and VanNijnatten (2003) that document activity and energy devolving from the federal to state/provincial to local and regional scales.

Second, efforts to create and mobilize the WIDs were actively supported by researchers at regional universities, namely, the Border Policy Research Institute at Western Washington University in Bellingham, Washington, and the Environmental Studies Program at Trinity Western University in Langley, British Columbia.[6] Last, local efforts based on local knowledge have been successful in building trust and good will among regional stakeholders, and this is demonstrated by the very strong support for the WIDs in the elections that allowed them to form. This examination of the Bertrand and Fishtrap (North Lynden) WIDs clearly answers questions 1 and 2 posed at the start of this article concerning the arc of water resource-management efforts in the region and the degree to which this region is seeing the devolution of these efforts from federal to state/provincial and to the nonstate/provincial levels.

I close this section with a somewhat surprising finding concerning these WIDs. Although the watersheds are binational in nature and the region sees considerable transboundary interactions, the WIDs have largely remained rooted and active in the United States. Interactions with Canadian municipalities and other stakeholders are limited to informal relationships. This is due to the root of these organizations coming from State of Washington laws and funds; limited, if any, means exist to formally extend the reach of the WIDs into Canada. Ideas being examined in the region to make WIDs more transboundary in nature include having Canadian stakeholders join the WIDs as ex officio members, working with Canadian nongovernmental organizations, or working with other informal mechanisms such as the Shared Waters Roundtable that came out of participation by researchers at Western Washington University.[7]

The Boundary Bay Area

In this coastal region that lies south of the urban area of Vancouver, the major water resource concerns that face the region are poor surface water quality driven by discharges of stormwater and wastewater (see map 12.5). In 1976, the negative effects that these discharges had on environmental quality and human health led to Environment Canada formally closing the bay to the harvesting and consumption of shellfish, an important economic and cultural resource to the region's First Nations residents (Boundary Bay Assessment and Monitoring Partnership 2010). In the late 1990s and early 2000s, two institutions/groups formed and took action to improve regional water quality in the Bay:

- **The Shared Waters Alliance** was a binational group that worked to monitor the region's surface water quality, examine the results of this monitoring, and identify the sources of water quality problems in the Bay.
- **The Boundary Bay Assessment and Monitoring Partnership (BBAMP)** introduced above is a collection of governmental agencies and First Nations' peoples that built on this early work and established an extensive water quality monitoring network that continues its work to the present. As such, this can be seen as a regional and collaborative effort focused on a shared binational water resource, the Boundary Bay, that has been effective at long-term monitoring and the analysis and sharing of relevant data (Boundary Bay Assessment and Monitoring Partnership 2010; Riddell and Peterson 2009). As such, this is a well-recognized and successful effort to understand and positively affect binational water quality issues along the U.S.-Canada border.

Two aspects of this work are noteworthy in terms of the questions posed in this chapter. The first of these is that both of these efforts focused on a shared water resource that was important to a wide range of people and groups. An example of this connection is a periodic canoe expedition led by the local First Nations peoples in which numerous stakeholders explore the bay by canoe to learn about relevant issues (Boundary Bay Assessment and Monitoring Partnership 2010). The second aspect worth noting is that these efforts were locally driven by community leaders and leadership of regional agencies, not state/

MAP 12.5 Boundary Bay region of the Straight of Georgia (Source: Google Earth. Used under Fair Use Doctrine as outlined in U.S. copyright law consistent with Google Earth terms and conditions.)

provincial or federal agencies. Of special note is the fact that these local efforts see no influence from the International Joint Commission (IJC), the binational federal agency established by the 1909 Boundary Waters Treaty between the United States and Canada. Given previous research into the IJC and its International Watersheds Initiative (IWI), I found this surprising and noteworthy. This lack of a connection to the IJC is consistent with previous research by Norman (2009), Norman and Bakker (2009) and VanNijnatten (2003) that documented how local/regional interest and activities were having a greater influence on solving transboundary environmental issues than national-level actors. In fact, VanNijnatten specifically states that "these actors have become a key, perhaps the key component, of the Canada-US environmental relationship" (VanNijnatten 2003, 1). As is the case with the Bertrand and Fishtrap (North Lynden) WIDs, the Boundary Bay case study clearly answers questions 1 and 2 posed at the start of this article—what is the arc of water resource-management efforts in the region, and to what degree are we seeing the devolution of these efforts from federal to state/provincial and to the nonstate/provincial levels?

The Abbotsford-Sumas Region

As introduced above, this transboundary urban area contains an aquifer that is an important source of water supply for the region (see map 12.6). Approximately 140,000 people live in this binational region, and resulting pressures on the aquifer generate negative effects on water quality (Andzans 2010). Primary among these are increasing nitrate concentrations in groundwater that have been linked to inputs and outputs of agricultural activities, specifically manure from dairy and poultry operations and fertilizer applied to large-scale raspberry operations (U.S. Geological Survey, U.S. Department of the Interior 1999; Wassenar 1995; and Zebarth et al. 1998). Two regional organizations emerged from a shared concern for water quality in the aquifer: the Abbotsford–Sumas Aquifer International Task Force (Task Force) and the Abbotsford–Sumas Aquifer Stakeholders Group (Stakeholders Group; Andzans 2010). Attention to water quality concerns was facilitated by the signing of the Environmental Cooperation Agreement by the Premier of British Columbia and the governor of Washington. This agreement in turn led to the creation of the BC-WA Environmental Cooperation Council (Alper 1996), which had similar goals to the two organizations detailed below.

- **The Abbotsford-Sumas Aquifer International Task Force** is a binational group of officials and researchers from state/provincial agencies, regional universities, and local governmental units that brought a shared concern and high level of technical expertise to issues at hand (Andzans 2010). The five topical priority areas where the task force devoted energy and resources are
  - Establishing and mapping the spatial extent of the aquifer
  - Determining regional land uses of concern and examining how legislation can help protect groundwater quality
  - Exploring public health issues effected by groundwater quality[8]
  - Exploring both technical data needed to better understand issues being examined and the gaps that existed in the available data
  - Developing ideas to help close the data gaps identified and exploring how best to share the results of research being conducted through educational and outreach activities.[9]

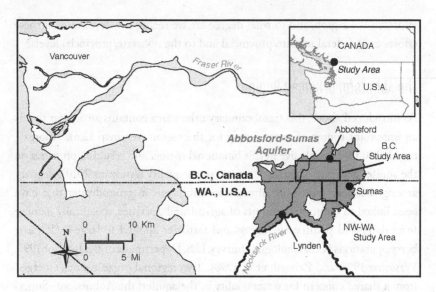

MAP 12.6 Abbotsford-Sumas region (Source: Mitchell et al. 2005. Used by permission.)

- **The Abbotsford-Sumas Aquifer Stakeholders Group**—In contrast to the task force, the stakeholders group was mostly a Canadian-led effort driven by local stakeholders looking for practical solutions to regional groundwater issues. Specific parties involved were those that relied on regional groundwater resources to support local industry and business as well as community people concerned with general environmental issues.

What insights can we gain from looking at the experiences of the task force and stakeholders group? Both efforts were voluntary in nature and driven by stakeholders, officials, and researchers with an interest in the issues at hand. Neither group has any regulatory power to control the use of land and water resources. Both groups benefitted indirectly from the Environmental Cooperation Agreement and the BC–WA Environmental Cooperation Council. These efforts facilitated leadership on regional environmental issues, and regional stakeholders have argued these mechanisms created a public policy environment that was conducive to regional cooperation among stakeholders, officials, and researchers (Andzans 2010). The successes of the task force and stakeholders group were due to efforts and resources at various levels of government, including seed funding provided by the British Columbia Ministry of the Environment and local efforts to codify productive environmental policies.

As was the case with the Boundary Bay experiences, two variables were in play in the Abbotsford-Sumas region—a strong and shared local connection to a transboundary water resource of value and concern to regional people at all scales, and the role of local/regional leadership in municipal agencies, business/industry players, and local and regional groups. Of special note in the Abbotsford-Sumas case is the "cascade dynamic" whereby events and actions at the state/provincial level coupled with federal resources in Canada and local energy and leadership to support these two successful transboundary water resource-management efforts. Again, this finding is consistent with the concept of activity and energy devolving from the federal to state/provincial to local and regional scales documented by Norman (2009), Norman and Bakker (2009), and VanNijnatten (2003).

The Puget Sound Region and Partnership

The last of the subregions of the Salish Sea being examined is that of Puget Sound, within which the Puget Sound Partnership (PSP) has evolved to address regional water resource issues (see map 12.7). The PSP functions over a much larger areal extent than any of the other subregions previously examined and offers an enhanced opportunity to examine the role of scale. The initial seed for this regional partnership was the Puget Sound Water Quality Authority (PSWQA), this in turn being an outcome of the U.S. Clean Water Act (Section 20) and the designation of the Puget Sound as an area of concern with national effects. The PSP evolved from the PSWQA because of an agreement signed by the governor of Washington and the premier of British Columbia, this in turn being the outcome of the Joint Statement of Cooperation on the Georgia Basin and Puget Sound Ecosystem, an agreement between the Canadian minister of environment and the administrator of the U.S. Environmental Protection Agency that was signed on January 19, 2000.[10] This evolution of the PSP is another case of the "cascade dynamic" noted above whereby action at the federal/binational level leads to state/provincial action that is grounded to a regional water resource.

In a manner not dissimilar to how the State of Washington established the framework for the WIDs examined above, the idea of an integrated, regional approach to water resource-management issues in the sound was codified in the text of Engrossed Substitute Senate Bill 5372 (State of Washington, 60th Legislature 2007):

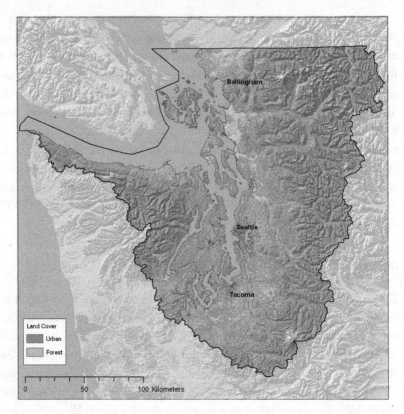

MAP 12.7 Puget Sound subregion of the Salish Sea ecosystem (Source: United States Geological Survey [USGS], 2016, https://archive.usgs.gov/archive/sites/geography.wr .usgs.gov/pugetSound/ps.html. Used under Fair Use Doctrine as outlined in US copyright law.)

The legislature intends for the Puget Sound Partnership to define a strategic, basin-wide plan that prioritizes necessary actions, and create an approach that addresses all of the complex connections among the land, water, web of species, and human needs. The legislature finds that immediate and concerted action is needed to save the national treasure that is Puget Sound, and that we must fundamentally change our approach toward restoring the health of Puget Sound. To this end, the Puget Sound partnership is tasked with using, supporting, building upon, and unifying the existing efforts from organizations and from all levels of government.[11]

Two specific actions were advanced in the early work of the PSP: the establishment of the Georgia Basin/Puget Sound Research Conference and the development of *Environmental Indicators for the Puget Sound Partnership: A Regional Effort to Select Provisional Indicators* (O'Neill, Bravo, and Collier 2008). The conference is an annual binational meeting that is considered the best effort by researchers in the region to share relevant research findings, and it has evolved into the Salish Sea Ecosystem Conference.[12] The *Environmental Indicators* document sought to develop a series of technically based, comprehensive indicators of regional water quality, human health, habitats, and mechanisms by which these habitats support a regional species and food web (O'Neill, Bravo, and Collier 2008). In 2012 the Washington State Academy of Sciences (WSAS 2012) conducted an evaluation of these indicators that sought to answer the question, how well do the indicators perform at measuring the ability of the sound to support a healthy ecosystem and the human health and well-being of the people living there? The results of this analysis noted that problems existed with the development of dashboard metrics and how well synchronized the metrics were with efforts to improve water quality. Human health and well-being indicators also lagged behind ecosystem indicators. Despite these shortcomings, the WSAS study noted that given the complexity of the task at hand, this work on environmental indicators provided a useful foundation on which future research and policy making can be advanced (Washington State Academy of Sciences 2012).

I close this section of this review of water resource issues and efforts to address them in the Puget Sound region by asking the question posed in the previous three regional studies: how can the Puget Sound Partnership experience inform our discussion of the three arguments posed at the start of the chapter? As was the case with regions examined previously, a cascade dynamic was found whereby federal and binational efforts to set the stage for regional work did just this. Legislation passed by the State of Washington and binational agreements between the United States and Canada provided mechanisms by which regionally grounded work could be conducted, and regional researchers, stakeholders, and government officials engaged in a wide range of activities. The grounding of this work with the sound and the people living there connected local knowledge and stakeholders in a manner that tells us that yes, geography in the sound matters. These connections are reflected in the renaming of the Georgia Bay/Puget Sound Research Conference to the Salish Sea Ecosystem

Conference in 2009, which parallels the broader acknowledgment of the Salish Sea region documented earlier (Groc 2011).

What of the issue of scale? The PSP experience unfolded over a much larger areal extent than the other cases, and it involved many more players across spatial scale in the region of the sound. This broader scale offers more stakeholders, agencies, and perspectives a seat at the table, but this also adds considerable institutional complexity to the work of the PSP. Despite this complexity, the PSP has been effective at working at the regional and local scale. Collaborative work with the BBAMP in developing sampling and monitoring protocols discussed above is evidence of this ability to effectively work across scale.

As we look at the sum of the regional explorations in the Salish Sea region that are discussed above, I offer table 12.1 as a comparison of how these experiences inform questions posed earlier in the chapter—what is the role of devolution of policy initiatives, regional grounding of policy options explored, and the role of scale? All regions examined see variations of how these variables interact to generate the policy landscape that exists in these regions. I will revisit this concurrence of trends later in the chapter. Discussion now turns to exploring the Tijuana River Watershed.

Regional Water Resource Issues and Emerging Policy Tools in the Tijuana River Watershed (TRW)

As noted in the introduction to this chapter, the TRW is a binational basin within which much of the urbanized portions of the *municipio* of Tijuana, Baja California Norte, and the city and county of San Diego, California, lie. As such, the watershed can be seen as an excellent laboratory within which transboundary water resource-management issues can be explored. Of special note, Tijuana, as an urban area in the developing world, lies immediately adjacent to the developed region of the city and county of San Diego. As noted in the introduction to the chapter, the topography of the region results in the urbanized areas of Tijuana, where a majority of the sources of water quality issues lie, being at a higher elevation. Therefore, these areas lie upstream of San Diego, the Tijuana River Estuary, and the marine waters of the Pacific Ocean, where all surface runoff in the basin discharges. Accordingly, water quality issues of surface waters that originate in the Mexican portion of the basin cause major downstream effects north of the border.

TABLE 12.1 Matrix of how research arguments examined in the Salish Sea connect to regional experiences

Region/effort being examined	Devolution/subnational actors	Regional grounding	Role of spatial scale
Boundary Bay	Partnership driven by local partners' leadership and resources; limited federal interaction	Focus is Boundary Bay, a well-recognized region with strong cultural connection	Small-scale effort focused solely on bay with limited linkages to larger scale
Abbotsford–Sumas	Active local groups driven by shared resource; foundation provided by state/provincial agreement	Focus is on shared aquifer and attendant risks facing region	Focus is solely on regional resource, yet state/provincial actors are also active
Bertrand/Fishtrap watersheds	Local watershed improvement districts (WIDs) driven by focus on local water rights, flows, and quality; state legislation was key to formation	Small transboundary basins are focus; regional cooperation is key to actions of WIDs	Focus is solely on small basins; local leadership is key, as are linkages to regional universities
Shared waters information roundtable	Effort came from regional acknowledgment that small basins not likely to see state, provincial, or federal action	No specific regional focus; effort was a convening tool for small basins	Small spatial scale of basins involved drove entire discussion
Puget Sound Partnership (PSP)	Considerable federal, state and provincial participation is evident; initial step toward formation is result of U.S. Clean Water Act	Regional connection to the sound is evident in entire history, with wide scale recognition of sound's importance	PSP is largest scale case of all examined, posing considerable management and operational challenges

Source: Brown 2014.

Previous research has documented these issues, including Dedina's (1991) work on the political ecology of wastewater issues in the basin, Kelly's (1994) work on "sewage diplomacy," and Brown (1998). Review of this literature finds that, as is the case of any rapidly urbanizing region in development, the TRW has longed faced considerable challenges in the areas of water supply, flood control, water quality, and wastewater management. In this section, I focus my attention on challenges of effective wastewater management and explore how a regional watershed approach to relevant issues may be advanced.

Following the end of World War II, the entire border region saw large-scale increases in industrialization and urbanization due to large federal investments in the region by both the Mexican and U.S. governments. These investments coupled with major changes in the labor force in the region due to the development and termination of the bracero, or guest worker, program. The bracero program was established in 1942 to provide a source of much-needed Mexican labor to fill the void resulting from large-scale military deployments in the United States. Large numbers of Mexicans relocated to the United States, and with the termination of the program and repatriation of Mexican nationals to Mexico in the 1960s, Mexican border cites saw huge increases in population. (Herzog 1990; Hoffman 1983; Huntley et al. 1993).

Further changes in labor flows and border industrialization occurred in the early to mid-1960s that had marked impacts on economic development and population growth in border twin cities. In 1961, the federal government in Mexico established La Programa Nacional Fronterizo (PRONAF), with the intent to improve border infrastructure and enhance commercial opportunities in Mexican border cites. Commercial areas were built in Mexican portions of twin cities to draw more commerce to these regions; the Rio Grande Mall in Ciudad Juárez was an example (Ganster and Lorey 2016). In 1965, the federal government in Mexico developed a second program, the Border Industrialization Program (BIP), which called for the development of the maquiladora program whereby firms outside of Mexico could build industrial capacity in Mexican border cities and employ large numbers of Mexican workers at wages much lower than in the firms' countries (Dillman 1970a, 1970b, 1976; Hoffman 1983). The result of the BIP was a very large increase in the number of jobs in Mexican border cities and an attendant increase in population. NAFTA exacerbated both the industrialization and population growth in Mexican cities with a special focus on border cities. Tijuana was no exception; population increased from 65,000 in 1950 to 991,000 in 1995 and to a current population of 1.7 million people in 2019 (Brown 1998).[13]

The management, treatment, and disposal of wastewater in the TRW are especially vexing problems. The urbanization, industrialization, and population growth detailed above results in large quantities of wastewater being generated in Tijuana, much of which is marginally treated at best or disposed of as untreated effluent at worse. Untreated or marginally treated effluent and renegade sewage flows cross the U.S.-Mexico border into the Tijuana River Estuary and eventually into the immediate offshore environment of the Pacific Ocean. Effects on human health and quality of life are highly negative and well documented (Herzog 1990; Meyer 1983).[14] Personal experience with these flows in the marine environment by Serge Dedina led to his 1991 thesis in which he researched the political ecology of wastewater flows in the TRW (Dedina 1991). Of special note, Dedina was elected to be the mayor of Imperial Beach, California, in 2014, and he pursues an active agenda to improve the quality of life and the environment in the region.

During the period from the 1970s to the early 1990s when the population in Tijuana greatly increased, various defensive measures to prevent the release and discharge of marginally or untreated effluent were put in place by the Comisión Estatal de Servicios Publicos de Tijuana (CESPT), the state of Baja California's agency charged with public works provision for the Tijuana region.[15] These measures were only marginally successful, and the challenges with managing wastewater originating in Tijuana remained largely unmet. In 1983, a blue-ribbon panel of local municipalities in the United States developed the blueprint for a comprehensive solution to the transboundary wastewater flows (Lowry and Associates 1993). On July 2, 1990, officials with the International Boundary and Water Commission (IBWC)/Comisión Internacional de Límites y Aguas (CILA) signed Minute 283, "Conceptual Plan for the International Solution to the Border Sanitation Problem in San Diego/Tijuana" in El Paso, Texas (International Boundary and Water Commission 1990).[16] The comprehensive plan that the blue-ribbon committee had developed was agreed on by the United States and Mexico; the specifics of a solution were at long last in place.

Construction of the South Bay International Wastewater Treatment Plant (SBIWTP) began in 1992, and the project consisted of the following elements.

- A secondary wastewater treatment plant at a site on Dairymart Road, approximately two miles east of the Pacific Ocean

- Collection infrastructure to capture renegade flows in several canyons in the lowest part of the watershed
- A land outfall facility to convey treated effluent from the treatment plant to the Pacific Ocean
- An ocean outfall to convey treated wastewater from the termination of the land outfall to a series of diverters and risers that discharge treated effluent into the Pacific Ocean approximately 18,700 feet offshore.[17]

The SBIWTP was completed in 1996, and the plant is operated by the IBWC under a series of National Pollutant Discharge Elimination System (NPDES) permits that the State of California Region 19 Water Quality Control Board administers. As the above process unfolded and resulted in the completion and operation of SBIWTP, CESPT undertook a series of planning and construction efforts that increased the coverage of areas in the Municipio de Tijuana for collection and treatment of wastewater. Despite these improvements, persistent problems still exist with marginally treated wastewater being discharged into the ocean environment, leading to beach closures in Imperial Beach and Coronado, California. In the last three to five years, large amounts of solid waste and sediment originating in Tijuana have become another challenge of the region; these solid waste and flows result in massive piles of trash and sediment that generate quality of life issues in the U.S. portion of the basin and also pose problems with the operation of various wastewater treatment and collection works (Horn 2018).

Related University Research Efforts
Work by Teams at San Diego State University and Their Partners

As steps toward putting in place a solution to the TRW wastewater problems proceeded, research was being undertaken at San Diego State University (SDSU) and its regional partners that would significantly inform the discussion of watershed and wastewater management in TRW. In the early 1990s, Paul Ganster, director of SDSU Institute for the Regional Studies of the Californias (IRSC), and Richard Wright, director of the SDSU Center for Earth Systems Analysis Research (CESAR) Laboratory, began collaborating on a series of externally funded projects focusing on the TRW. Sources of funds included the National Oceanic and Atmosphere Administration, the California Coastal

Conservancy, and the U.S. Environmental Protection Agency. These funds
supported a series of related projects that comprehensively mapped and documented water resources and resource-management issues in the TRW.

Notable outcomes of these projects included the following:

- **The "poster worth a 1000 words."** A large format poster of the watershed,
  including a five-meter SPOT satellite image on which key elements were
  mapped, and a series of maps depicting land use, vegetation, hydrology,
  and climate.[18] The poster, published in 1997 by a consortium of government
  agencies and university partners, is completely bilingual, and all maps seamlessly cover the watershed. As such, this was the first effort at mapping the
  watershed with binationally coordinated data for all variables mapped. The
  "poster worth a 1000 words" was extremely well received and widely distributed, and a large number of regional-planning and resource-management
  agencies in both San Diego and Tijuana displayed the poster prominently.
- **The Tijuana River Watershed Atlas.** A publication that followed the poster
  and greatly expanded the range of resources being mapped (Institute for
  Regional Studies of the Californias and San Diego State University Department of Geography 2005a). Again, this was a partnership of a large number
  of academic researchers and funding agencies, and the end result was an
  extensive, seamless, and binational mapping inventory of the watershed
  that included all relevant social and physical geographic variables. The atlas
  contains thirty color plates of all relevant resources and remains the most
  comprehensive mapping project of the TRW to date.
- **TRW Binational Vision Project.** Another collaborative effort among
  university researchers in the area that included SDSU, El Colegio de la
  Frontera Norte, and La Universidad Autonoma de Baja California. The
  research team from these institutions convened the Binational Watershed
  Advisory Council (BWAC). Members of the team included a wide range of
  stakeholders in the TRW who met and worked together to develop a very
  extensive vision document that outlined the "state of the watershed" that
  stakeholders wanted and a series of strategies and actions that would bring
  this vision to reality (Institute for Regional Studies of the Californias and
  San Diego State University Department of Geography 2005b).
- **Numerous MS theses and related research articles.** These include
  - A large number of theses and one dissertation that documented a range
    of research projects that were either directly or indirectly involved with

the projects (water quality, soils mapping, binational watershed policy, and environmental education, to name but a few)

- A PC-based tool allowing interactive research into the databases and maps described above (this was literally a "watershed app" before smart phones and apps existed)
- A series of very well-integrated research partnerships among university researchers, members of the community, and agency officials that had a long-term influence on the science and public policy of the TRW[19]

The SDSU experience documented above helps answer questions 1 and 2 posed at the start of this article concerning players involved in regional water resource-management efforts and the devolution process discussed earlier in the section of the chapter on the Salish Sea. International and state-level efforts and funding drove a wide range of regional research efforts among citizen stakeholders and regional U.S. and Mexican universities, which, as I will discuss later in the chapter, in turn linked back to efforts of the IBWC to advance a watershed-based framework to address regional water quality concerns.

Companion Work with Colleagues at the Utton Center, Colorado State University (CSU), and the Colegio de la Frontera Norte (COLEF)

Owing to the success of the TRW Binational Vision Project that Paul Ganster and colleagues at SDSU and other regional partners advanced, discussions emerged with researchers at CSU and the Utton Transboundary Resources Center at the University of New Mexico Law School concerning how the ideas for watershed research and planning could be leveraged into action by the IBWC/CILA. Out of these discussions, we developed a document, *US-Mexico Border Basin Advisory Boards*, that shared ideas in the outcomes of the visioning process.[20] These ideas concerned specific actions that IBWC/CILA could take to advance comprehensive, watershed-based research and planning efforts. In discussions with IBWC commissioner Carlos Marín in the summer of 2008, our research team shared this draft document with the commissioner and discussed the ideas it contained. Commissioner Marín was very interested in these ideas and was in the process of discussing these ideas with his Mexican counterpart, Arturo Herrera, when a horrible tragedy struck the borderlands. On

September 17, 2008, a light aircraft carrying Commissioners Marín and Herrera and Jake Brisbin, county judge of Presidio, Texas, crashed in the Lower Rio Grande Valley while surveying flood damage. All aboard perished. With this tragedy, the borderlands lost three highly committed officials who had worked together for decades and the 100-plus years of experience that they brought to their jobs. Carlos Rincon, U.S. EPA staff person directing the El Paso, Texas, EPA office described the tragedy most aptly: "Today, we have a thorn in our heart as we mourn the loss of these fine people."

Despite the tragic loss of these policy makers, discussions continued between academics with interest in the TRW, members of nongovernmental organizations, and public officials that led to productive discussions. From May 14 to 16, 2013, the Southwest Consortium for Environmental Research and Policy (SCERP), San Diego State University, and the El Colegio de la Frontera Norte (El COLEF) convened Managing the Binational Tijuana River Watershed: A Workshop (Brown and Mumme 2013; Dibble 2013).[21] This three-day, binational workshop had open public sessions in both San Diego and Tijuana, and many potentially fruitful ideas came out of this workshop that warranted further exploration, including

- Reconstitute and reactivate the Binational Watershed Advisory Council that was active in the TRW Binational Vision Project
- Establish public meeting space at the SBIWTP that would allow binational meeting participation without having to clear the San Diego/Tijuana Port of Entry, a major barrier to true binational discussions
- Explore expanding the spatial reach of the IBWC Citizens Forums (currently U.S. domestic efforts) to include Mexican members and make these forums binational in nature
- Develop an IBWC/CILA minute on controlling trash and sediment that are currently posing major problems in the lowest reaches of the watershed by looking upstream for options for better source control of trash and sediment
- Call for offices of the State of California to be more active in discussions to advance watershed management in the TRW
- Explore how the role of U.S. and Mexican consul general offices in San Diego and Tijuana could take advantage of the Border Liaison Mechanism[22] to advance binational cooperation on issues of interest in the watershed
- Explore some form of Joint Powers Agreement (JPA) among U.S. and Mexican agencies to advance watershed management[23]

- Enlist regional-planning agencies in the U.S. (San Diego Association of Government—SANDAG) and in Mexico (Instituto Metropolitano de Planeación de Tijuana) to engage on watershed management.[24]

Out of these discussions at the 2013 workshop, I worked with Steve Mumme (CSU), Carlos de la Parra (COLEF), and Paul Ganster to refine the ideas explored at the San Diego/Tijuana workshop. Based on our work together, we developed two papers that continued to explore binational watershed management in the TRW: "Proposed Action Plan for Advancing Binational Cooperation in Managing the Tijuana River Watershed (TRW)" (Brown and Mumme 2013) and "Proposed Conference for Advancing Binational Cooperation in Managing the Tijuana River Watershed" (Brown et al. 2014).

Although neither of these papers was published and we were not able to secure funding for the conference, several specific ideas came from these discussions that inform the questions posed in this chapter. Admittedly, the issues facing the basin are complex and by their very nature transboundary, yet specific policy instruments do exist that either allow or call for binational action:

- The historic 1944 U.S.-Mexican Water Treaty incorporates the Tijuana River with the Colorado and the Rio Grande in its treaty regime for international rivers. Article 16 actually requires the IBWC to engage in specific actions in the TRW—"In order to improve existing uses and to assure any feasible further development, the Commission shall study and investigate, and shall submit to the two Governments for their approval recommendations for the equitable distribution between the two countries of the waters of the Tijuana River system and plans for storage and flood control to promote and develop domestic, irrigation and other feasible uses of the waters of this system" (United States of America and Mexico 1944, art. 16).

- The IBWC/CILA minutes mentioned previously can be implemented on specific technical issues such as binational watershed management in the TRW. In fact, Brown and Mumme (2013) specifically called for the IBWC/CILA to develop a treaty minute on trash and sediment in the lowest reaches of the river based on previous technical research conducted by IBWC/CILA. We also asked the IBWC/CILA to explore a second minute that would establish an integrated, binational management framework, be it a binational watershed council (*consejo de cuenca*), an enhanced IBWC binational citizens' forum (USIBWC framework), or a locally driven, integrated

TRW commission that is larger than the urban areas of the watershed. Such a commission was proposed at the May 2013 workshop that Paul Ganster organized by Walter Raul Zúñiga Castillo, a highly knowledgeable expert on the basin from the Universidad Autónoma de Baja California.

- We reiterated a concept that came out of the 2013 workshop, that the Border Liaison Mechanism be deployed to draw TRW stakeholders together to incubate binational dialogue and build consensus on a desirable mix of policy initiatives for addressing sustainable management of the river's resources.

Regional Connections of Note

The TRW Binational Vision Project, the conferences detailed above, and related documents and discussions clearly reflect a very strong connection between stakeholders in the watershed and the land and water resources that define the watershed. Implicit in this connection is very extensive local knowledge and a shared commitment to work collaboratively on the major issues facing the watershed.

IBWC Efforts to Develop an IBWC/CILA Minute for the Tijuana River Watershed

In discussions that select academic researchers had with key IBWC staff from 2014 to 2017, we proposed exploring the very successful model of binational cooperation on a shared binational watershed that was advanced in the Rio Colorado Delta under IBWC/CILA Minute 317, Minute 319, and Minute 323 (International Boundary and Water Commission 2010, 2012, 2017). As these discussions were occurring, IBWC and CILA held a binational public meeting in Tijuana on April 24, 2014, at which the main elements of a binational TRW management mechanism were discussed.[25] Out of these discussions, IBWC/CILA Minute 320, "General Framework for Binational Cooperation on Transboundary Issues in the Tijuana River Basin," was developed and then signed on October 15, 2015. After almost two decades of research and discussion by U.S. and Mexican researchers and agency officials, a comprehensive framework for binational watershed management in the TRW was a reality. Specific tools that are part of this successful effort include (IBWC 2015)

- Topic-specific working groups (water quality, sediment, and solid waste)[26]
- A high-level binational consultative council (Binational Core Group [BCG]) composed of IBWC/CILA staff and representatives of state and federal governmental agencies in the United States and Mexico
- Active participation by nongovernmental organizations in the United States and Mexico

Specific actions to be advanced by the working groups and BCG are noted below, these being taken from the text of the minute (International Boundary and Water Commission 2015).

- Determine issues of mutual interest and importance
- Identify institutions that should be at the table
- Outline and carry out studies, inventories, and other research efforts to fully inform members of the working groups and BCG of issues in play
- Define short- and long-term issues and actions in areas of mutual interest
- Develop actionable ideas and strategies to advance sustainable outcomes
- Create mechanisms by which the project can be implemented
- Develop cost estimates of work to be done and seek funding to support the work
- Develop and implement a public outreach and education plan to inform the communities involved of progress on the above actions and ideas
- Develop a monitoring plan to provide data needed to prioritize issues to examine

What has been the experience of the comprehensive approach to watershed management in the TRW that IBWC/CILA Minute 320 seeks to advance? One of the specific actions called for in the minute is to define and implement an outreach and education plan to inform the communities where the work is taking place. To meet this objective, IBWC has developed two means of informing the public, an exhaustive list of reports that includes progress on Minute 320,[27] and a monthly newsletter, *Transboundary Issues in the Tijuana River Basin Newsletter.*[28] As detailed in these web portals, the following major efforts have been undertaken. ·

- Development of an outreach tool that reviews the framework of the project and the issues it will examine

- Specific research and mitigation efforts in process related to surface water spills, monitoring work, identification of key source areas for sediment flows, solid waste removal efforts, and infrastructure assessment
- Development of specifications for specific projects, including costs and technical issues involved; note should be made that many of these projects involve binational cooperation among members of the working groups and BCG
- A comprehensive effort at examining issues of concern within a binational watershed framework that is consistent with previous research into watershed councils/*consejos de cuencas*, similar work being done on the U.S.-Canada border, and the manner in which engaged entities work across scale from the federal/binational to the local and regional levels. (As someone that has studied binational watershed management in the U.S.-Mexico border region for over twenty years, I was very heartened to see that this type of approach—well grounded to the watershed and local communities—is at long last a reality in the Tijuana River Watershed.)

"What worked" in the TRW that advanced the idea of an integrated watershed approach to issues of concern? Several ingredients were in play in the watershed, stakeholder groups, and agencies that moved this approach forward. First, very strong local interest, leadership, and motivation existed to address the solid waste and sediment flows that were having such highly visible and negative effects on the lowest reaches of the watershed. The Tijuana River Recovery Team, a group of thirty U.S. and Mexican agencies and regional stakeholders, worked since their formation in 2008 to develop ideas to reduce the trash and sediment flows that are negatively affecting the lowest reaches of the basin.[29] Second, the importance of strong and committed local leadership cannot be overstated. In my most recent research for this chapter, I was "reintroduced" to a large number of leaders in academia, agencies, and the communities involved who have worked for decades to advance this effort. Third, the U.S. and Mexican sections of the IBWC/CILA worked very hard as well. In this work, agency staff needed to determine whether a comprehensive framework offered the highest likelihood of success or a case by case effort would have been more effective. The comprehensive approach was the result of these discussions, and both sections have worked diligently to make this work. Finally, the model of regional binational cooperation that the IBWC/CILA, other federal agencies, and nongovernmental organizations advanced in the Colorado River Delta under IBWC/CILA Minutes 317 and 323 offered valuable lessons. Borrowing lessons concerning the manner in which the management framework, nongovernmental groups, and collaborative stakeholder participation were advanced in the Colorado River Delta region was key to the success of the effort in the TRW.

To what degree does the TRW experience answer questions posed earlier in this chapter about agencies, nongovernmental organizations (NGOs), and citizens involved in regional water resource-management efforts and the devolution process discussed earlier? The experience detailed above directly speaks to the manner in which governmental efforts at the national and state level drove, funded, and guided local and regional efforts. Place-based knowledge and experience were brought to resulting discussions by engaged citizens and NGOs, and the result was a series of highly informed discussions that helped advance solutions to regional water resources management issues. Of special note in the TRW experience is the manner in which these locally and regional driven discussions coalesced with efforts by the IBWC/CILA to produce IBWC/CILA Minute 320, *General Framework for Binational Cooperation on Transboundary Issues in the Tijuana River Basin*. The discussion has come full circle from a national/international treaty to locally and regionally driven efforts involving regional university researchers and finally to a new IBWC/CILA minute with much promise to resolve regional water resources management issues.

Closing the Loop on the "Question of the North American Watershed Gestalt"

In this chapter, several watersheds of interest on the U.S.-Canada and U.S.-Mexico borders were examined. This limited sampling of basins is by no means comprehensive, but several shared elements help inform the questions raised in the chapter. First, local participation and leadership are key to successful efforts at transboundary watershed management; both local advocates and informed stakeholders are highly evident in the successful cases. Second, all cases visited demonstrated the manner in which activity, energy, and success are devolving from federal/binational to state/provincial to regional/local scales, consistent with previous research (Lovecraft 2007; Norman and Bakker 2009; Norman, Bakker, and Cook 2012; VanNijnatten 2003, 2006). Yes, "scale does matter in all cases examined; also, geography matters" a good deal. All cases examined saw a very strong connection to important water resources from agency staff, policy makers, and citizen stakeholders.

Back to the "question about the North American watershed gestalt." Do the experiences and regions explored support the idea of a unified approach to watershed management that is consistent with Robert Pastor's North American Idea? (Pastor 2012). To a degree, yes, and to a degree, no. Yes, I believe that these experiences demonstrated the value of a comparative approach to different basins on the U.S.-Canada and U.S.-Mexico borders. Experience and insight from basins in one border region *do* inform the manner in which similar efforts to resolve transboundary water resource challenges are advanced in other basins. Given this insight, do these results support the notion of a "North American watershed gestalt?" The answer to this really lies with the reader. How universal and portable are the lessons and experiences explored? I close this chapter with the idea that the North American watershed gestalt is illusive at best, but certainly worthy of future research.

NOTES

1. Pastor's North America Idea is an argument that states that the United States, Canada, and Mexico are best served (both individually and collectively) in resolving the many challenges they face by taking a distinctively North American continental perspective (Pastor 2012). Pastor doesn't argue that a "North American Union" similar to the European Union be advanced; rather, he advocates for a regional geographic approach to the challenges that Canada, Mexico, and the United States face that draws on the range of connections and interactions that currently exist and could be enhanced in the future.

2. Interview with Don Alper, director of the Border Policy Research Institute at Western Washington University, Bellingham, July 2, 2010.

3. Comprehensive Watershed Planning Act of 1998, chap. 90.82.010.

4. Interview with Henry Bierlink, founding director of the Bertrand and Fishtrap (North Lynden) Watershed Improvement Districts, North Lynden, Washington, June 30, 2010.

5. https://www.bertrandwid.com; http://www.northlyndenwid.com; Bierlink interview; Brown 2014; Steensma et al. 2006.

6. Bierlink interview; Brown 2014.

7. Bierlink interview.

8. A particular issue of concern was how to better understand the relationship between regional health concerns and levels of nitrates in regional groundwater.

9. http://www.env.gov.bc.ca/wsd/plan_protect_sustain/groundwater/aquifers/absu mas.html; Brown 2014; Davidson 2010.

10. Interview with Judith Leckrone Lee, USEPA Region 10 staff person, on detail to Puget Sound Partnership, June 30, 2010.

11. Engrossed Substitute Senate Bill 5372, Section 101, points 4 and 5.

12. http://www.salishseaconference.org/index.php.

13. http://worldpopulationreview.com/world-cities/tijuana-population/.

14. Joint IBWC/Imperial Beach City Council meeting to address the proposed action for additional interim works to capture and return Mexican sewage to Mexico, October 6, 1993, Imperial Beach, CA.

15. See https://www.cespt.gob.mx for details of CESPT's operations.

16. The International Boundary and Water Commission/Comisión Internacional de Límites y Aguas (IBWC/CILA) is a binational agency housed within the U.S. Department of State and the Secretaría de Relaciones Exteriores, the Department of State's counterpart in Mexico. IBWC and CILA have parallel staffs and leadership teams that work on specific boundary and water issues, and these discussions lead to IBWC/CILA minutes that commit staff to work together to plan, design, fund, and build infrastructure. IBWC/CILA also deals with other boundary and water issues (Brown and Mumme 2000).

17. https://www.waterboards.ca.gov/sandiego/water_issues/programs/iwtp/. International Boundary and Water Commission 1990.

18. http://trw.sdsu.edu/English/index.html.

19. As late as 2014, SDSU researchers and alumni shared policy research with the International Boundary and Water Commission (IBWC) that spoke to issues at the heart of *IBWC/CILA Minute 320, General Framework for Binational Cooperation on Transboundary Issues in the Tijuana River Basin*, to be discussed in detail in the latter part of this chapter (IBWC 2015).

20. Unpublished document outlining ideas on binational U.S.-Mexico border basin advisory board as a toll for binational watershed management.

21. http://trw.sdsu.edu/English/index.html.

22. As noted in a study done at Texas A&M International University, "The Border Liaison Mechanism (BLM) is a local binational meeting that US and Mexican consuls convene to address cross-border issues. . . . The BLMs came into existence in 1993 as the result of a bilateral agreement between the United States and Mexico" (http://www.tamiu.edu/binationalcenter/BLM.shtml).

23. Early management of the Tijuana River National Estuarine Research Reserve was handled by such a JPA.

24. SANDAG's Commission on Binational Regional Opportunities, a U.S.-based research arm of SANDAG, offers considerable promise to advance these discussions. See https://www.sandag.org/index.asp?committeeid=34&fuseaction=committees.detail for specific details on COBRO.

25. Binational meeting on draft minute points for an IBWC/CILA minute on a watershed-wide approach to water resource-management challenges, Tijuana, Baja California, April 24, 2014.

26. Solid waste and sediment have become highly problematics of late, as they are carried by stormwater across the border where they dissipate and pose major threats to human health and quality of life.

27. https://www.ibwc.gov/EMD/reports_studies.html#Minute320—documents on Minute 320 are at page bottom.

28. https://www.ibwc.gov/Files/Tijuana_Transboundary_Issues_092917.pdf.

29. See the Alter Terra website (http://alterterra.org/?p=59).

REFERENCES

Alper, D. 1996. "The Idea of Cascadia: Emergent Transborder Regionalisms in Pacific Northwest-Western Canada." *Journal of Borderlands Studies* 11 (2): 1–22.

Andzans, P. 2010. Interview with Peter Andzans, City of Abbotsford Manager of Community Sustainability. Abbotsford, British Columbia, Canada. June 29, 2010.

Boundary Bay Assessment and Monitoring Partnership. 2010. Interview of BBAMP participants conducted by the author in a briefing session. White Rock, British Columbia, Canada. June 29, 2010.

Brown, C. 1998. "A Watershed and Ecosystem Approach to Transboundary Wastewater Management in the Tijuana River Watershed." PhD diss., San Diego State University and University of California, Santa Barbara.

Brown, C. 2010a. "Comparative Approaches to Governance and Management of Water Resources. in North America." *VertigO: La revue électronique en sciences de l'environnement*, 7. http://vertigo.revues.org/9721.

Brown, C. 2010b. *Research into Transboundary Water Resource Management in North America: A Comparative Perspective*. Proposal submitted to the Canadian Studies Research Program, Canadian Embassy, Washington, D.C.

Brown, C. 2014. "Scale and Subnational Resource Management: Transnational Initiatives in the Salish Sea Region." *Review of Policy Research* 32 (1): 60–78.

Brown, C., C. de la Parra, P. Ganster, and S. Mumme. 2014. "Proposed Conference for Advancing Binational Cooperation in Managing the Tijuana River Watershed." Unpublished concept paper outlining ideas for binational conference to explore binational watershed management.

Brown, C. and S. Mumme. 2000. "Applied and Theoretical Aspects of Binational Watershed Councils (*Consejos de Cuencas*) in the US-Mexico Borderlands." *Natural Resources Journal* 40 (4): 895–929.

Brown, C and S. Mumme. 2013. "Proposed Action Plan for Advancing Binational Cooperation in Managing the Tijuana River Watershed (TRW)." Unpublished concept paper outlining ideas for binational watershed management.

Coe, N., P. Kelly, and H. Yeung. 2017. *Economic Geography: A Contemporary Introduction*. New York: John Wiley.

Davidson, D. 2010. Interview with David Davidson, Assistant Director of the Border Policy Research Institute at Western Washington University, Bellingham, WA. June 3, 2010.

Dedina, S. 1991. "The Political Ecology of Transboundary Development: Land Use, Flood Control, and Politics in the Tijuana River Valley." Master's thesis, University of Wisconsin–Madison.

Dibble, S. 2013. "Tijuana River Watershed Topic of Binational Conference." *San Diego Union-Tribune*, May 14. http://www.sandiegouniontribune.com/news/border-baja-california/sdut-tijuana-river-watershed-topic-of-bi-national-confe-2013may14-story.html.

Dillman, C. 1970a. "Recent Developments in Mexico's Northern Border Program." *Professional Geographer* 22 (5): 243–47.

Dillman, C. 1970b. "Urban Growth Along Mexico's Northern Border and the Mexican National Border Program." *Journal of Developing Areas* 4 (4): 487–508.

Dillman, C. 1976. "Maquiladoras in Mexico's Northern Border Communities and the Border Industrialization Program." *Tijdschrift voor Economische en Sociale Geografie* 67 (3): 138–50.

Fischhendler, I., E. Feitelson, and D. Eaton, 2004. "The Short-Term and Long-Term Ramifications of Linkages Involving Natural Resources: The US–Mexico Transboundary Water Case." *Environment and Planning C* 22 (5): 633–50.

Fishtrap (North Lynden) Watershed Improvement District (WID). N.d. Management plan for drainage, flooding, irrigation and fish issues. https://www.northlyndenwid.com/.

Freelan, Stefan. 2009. *Map of the Salish Sea and Surrounding Basin.* http://maps.stefanfreelan.com/salishsea/.

Frisvold, G., and F. Casswell. 2000. "Transboundary Water Management Game-Theoretic Lessons for Projects on the US–Mexico Border." *Agricultural Economics* 24 (1): 101–11.

Ganster, P., and D. Lorey. 2016. *The US-Mexico Border Today: Conflict and Cooperation in Historical Perspective.* Lanham, Md.: Rowman and Littlefield.

Groc, I. 2011. "Salish Sea Change: A New Name Brings Together the Strait of Georgia, the Juan de Fuca Strait, and Puget Sound." *Canadian Geographic*, June. http://www.canadiangeographic.ca/article/salish-sea-change.

Herzog, L. 1990. *Where North Meets South: Cities, Space, and Politics on the US-Mexico Border.* Austin: Center for Mexican American Studies, University of Texas, Austin.

Hoffman, P. 1983. "The Internal Structure of Mexican Border Cities." PhD diss., University of California, Los Angeles.

Horn, J. 2018. "Tijuana Steps Up Efforts to Keep Sewage out of US." *10 News*, June 22. https://www.10news.com/news/tijuana-steps-up-efforts-to-keep-sewage-out-of-us.

Huntley, N., J. Bortz, D. Lorey, and A. Pahissa. 1993. *Transformation and Integration: The Borderlands, 1940–1990.* Unpublished manuscript.

Institute for Regional Studies of the Californias and San Diego State University Department of Geography. 2005a. *Tijuana River Watershed Atlas.* San Diego, Calif.: San Diego State University Press. https://irsc.sdsu.edu/docs/pubs/TRWAtlas.pdf.

Institute for Regional Studies of the Californias and San Diego State University Department of Geography. 2005b. *A Binational Vision for the Tijuana River Watershed.* San Diego, Calif.: SDSU, IRSC, and SDSU Department of Geography. http://trw.sdsu.edu/English/Vision/Documents/Docs/Final_Binational_Vision_Document_9-16-05.pdf.

International Boundary and Water Commission. 1990. *IBWC/CILA Minute 283, "Conceptual Plan for the International Solution to the Border Sanitation Problem in San Diego/ Tijuana."* El Paso, Tex.: IBWC. https://www.ibwc.gov/Files/Minutes/Minute283.pdf.

International Boundary and Water Commission. 2010. *IBWC/CILA Minute 317, Conceptual Framework for US Mexico Discussions on Colorado River Cooperative Actions.* El Paso, Tex.: IBWC https://www.ibwc.gov/Files/Minutes/Minute_317.pdf.

International Boundary and Water Commission. 2012. *IBWC/CILA Minute 319, Interim International Cooperative Measures in the Colorado River Basin Through 2017 and Extension of Minute 318 Cooperative Measures to Address the Continued Effects of the April 2010 Earthquake in the Mexicali Valley, Baja California.* El Paso, Tex.: IBWC https://www.ibwc.gov/Files/Minutes/Minute_319.pdf.

International Boundary and Water Commission. 2015. *IBWC/CILA Minute 320, General Framework for Binational Cooperation on Transboundary Issues in the Tijuana River Basin.* Tijuana, Baja California: IBWC/CILA. https://www.ibwc.gov/Files/Minutes /Minute_320.pdf.

International Boundary and Water Commission. 2017. *IBWC/CILA Minute 323, Extension of Cooperative Measures and Adoption of a Binational Water Scarcity Contingency Plan in the Colorado River Basin.* El Paso, Tex.: IBWC. https://www.ibwc.gov/Files /Minutes/Min323.pdf.

Kelly, T. 1994. "Sewage Diplomacy: The Political Geography of Cross-Broder Swage Flows at San Diego-Tijuana." PhD diss., Tufts University.

Lovecraft, A. L. 2007. "Transnational Environmental Management: US-Canadian Institutions at the Interlocal Scale." *American Review of Canadian Studies* 37 (2): 218–45.

Lowry and Associates. 1993. *Proposed Joint International Wastewater Treatment Plant.* San Diego, Calif.: Lowry and Associates.

McKinnon, D., and A. Cumbers. 2011. *Introduction to Economic Geography: Globalization, Uneven Development, and Place.* 2nd ed. London: Routledge.

Meyer, E. 1983. *Staff Report: History of Sewerage Facilities Serving the City of Tijuana, Baja California, Mexico.* San Diego, Calif.: California Regional Water Quality Control Board, Region 9.

Mitchell, R., S. Babcock, H. Hirsch, L. McKee, R. Matthews, and J. Vandersypen. 2005. *Water Quality: Abbotsford-Sumas Final Report.* Bellingham: Western Washington University. http://kula.geol.wwu.edu/rjmitch/Report_2005.pdf.

Norman, E. S. 2009. "Navigating Bordered Geographies: Water Governance Along the Canada–United States Border." PhD diss., University of British Columbia.

Norman, E. S., and K. Bakker. 2009. "Transgressing Scales: Water Governance Across the Canada–US Border." *Annals of the Association of American Geographers* 99 (1): 99–117.

Norman, E. S., K. Bakker, and C. Cook. 2012. "Introduction to the Themed Section: Water Governance and the Politics of Scale." *Water Alternatives* 5 (1): 52–61.

O'Neill, S., C. Bravo, and T. Collier. 2008. *Environmental Indicators for the Puget Sound Partnership: A Regional Effort to Select Provisional Indicators.* Technical document submitted to the Science Panel of the Puget Sound Partnership. Seattle, WA: NOAA Fisheries, Northwest Fisheries Science Center. http://psp.wa.gov/downloads/SP2009/IndicatorSummaryReport(Final)120108.doc.

Pastor, R. 2012. *The North American Idea: A Vision of a Continental Future*. Oxford: Oxford University Press.

Phay, Andrew. 2012. *Map of the Beltran and Fishtrap Watersheds and Areal Extent of the Associated Watershed Improvement Districts*. Lynden, Wash.: Whatcom Conservation District.

Riddell, E., and L. Peterson. 2009. "Boundary Bay Assessment and Monitoring Partnership." Presentation made to the Environmental Monitoring Committee, Metro Vancouver, British Columbia, September. http://trw.sdsu.edu/English/index.html.

Steensma, K. M. M., B. Chisholm, S. Tang, S. Stoner, A. Phay, and S. Koole. 2006. *Bertrand Creek State of the Watershed Report*. Lynden, Wash.: Bertrand Creek Watershed Improvement District, Nooksack Recovery Team, and Whatcom County.

U.S. Geological Survey, U.S. Department of the Interior. 1999. *Hydrogeology, Ground-Water Quality, and Sources of Nitrate in Lowland Glacial aquifers of Whatcom County, Washington and British Columbia, Canada*. Water Resources Investigations Report no. 98–4195. Tacoma, Wash.: USGS.

United States of America and Mexico. 1944. *Water Treaty for the "Utilization of Waters of the Colorado and Tijuana Rivers and of the Rio Grande."* Binational treaty signed by the United States and Mexico, February 3, 1944. https://www.ibwc.gov/Files/1944Treaty.pdf.

VanNijnatten, D. L. 2003. "Analyzing the Canada-US Environmental Relationship: A Multi-Faceted Approach." *American Review of Canadian Studies* 33 (1): 93–120.

VanNijnatten, D. L. 2006. "Towards Cross-Border Environmental Policy Spaces in North America: Province-State Linkages on the Canada-U.S. Border." *AmeriQuests* 3 (1). http://ejournals.library.vanderbilt.edu/index.php/ameriquests/article/view/54.

Washington State Academy of Sciences. 2012. *Sound Indicators: A Review for the Puget Sound Partnership*. Olympia, Wash.: WSAS. http://www.washacad.org/wp-content/uploads/2016/12/WSAS_Sound_Indicators_wv1.pdf.

Washington State Legislature. 1998. *Enabling Legislation for State-Wide Watershed Planning Efforts in the State of Washington*. http://app.leg.wa.gov/RCW/default.aspx?cite=90.82.010.

Wassenar, L. 1995. "Evaluation of the Origin and Fate of Nitrate in the Abbotsford Aquifer Using the Isotopes of 15N and 18O in NO3-." *Applied Geochemistry* 10:391–405.

Zebarth, B. J., B. Hii, H. Leibscher, K. Chipperfield, J. Paul, G. Grove, and S. Szeto. 1998. "Agricultural Land Use Practices and Nitrate Contamination in the Abbotsford Aquifer, British Columbia, Canada." *Agriculture, Ecosystems and Environment* 69:99–112.

CHAPTER 13

A Model for Trilateral Collaboration

The Commission for Environmental Cooperation:
Whither the CEC?

IRASEMA CORONADO

Introduction

Evaluating the effectiveness of environmental institutions and international environmental regimes is a challenge for academics and policy makers. Scholars are asking, "Is the quality of the environment or resource better because of the institution?" (Haas, Keohane, and Levy 1993, 7). Does the creation of environmental protection institutions by nations, states, provinces, or local governments or the signing of the Geneva Convention on Long-Range Transboundary Air Pollution (CLRTAP) in 1979 or the 1985 Vienna Convention for the Protection of the Ozone Layer and the 1987 Montreal Protocol on Substances that Deplete the Ozone Layer, to list a few examples, make a difference in improving the environment writ large? Have institutions such as the United States Environmental Protection Agency (EPA) or the Texas Commission on Environmental Quality (TCEQ) addressed the issues of transboundary air pollution or reduced ozone depleting substances? Academics have tried to demonstrate the existence and strength of causal links between the creation of institutions and environmental regimes and changes in the problem. They have devised indexes that can be used to measure empirically the performance of individual regimes. However, both of these approaches provide analytical and methodological challenges (Young 2010). Public policy scholars have focused on project evaluation as a key component of the standard public policy cycle examining the effectiveness of educational institutions, health care programs, and pilot projects addressing recidivism, for example. These evaluations tend to measure the performance of an institution or project using measurable outcomes: how many children were immunized in a certain time period, how many probationers committed a crime, and so forth. In the environmental arena, this type of programmatic evaluation proves to be more difficult because of the complexity of environmental problems and the inordinate number of intervening variables that one must analyze when trying to determine whether air and water quality, habitats, ecosystems, and human health have improved over time. Adding another variable to the equation of successful environmental protection is working across boundaries with other sovereign nations and determining the effectiveness of environmental institutions or policies; this adds another layer of complexity because of the transboundary effects of environmental pollution.

The purpose of this chapter is to analyze the effectiveness and performance of the Commission for Environmental Cooperation (CEC) and to shed light on the conditions and variables that allow this trinational institution to carry out its intended mission. The CEC was created in 1993 by Canada, Mexico, and the United States to implement the North American Agreement on Environmental Cooperation (NAAEC), the environmental side accord of the North American Free Trade Agreement (NAFTA). I contend that the CEC contributes to the formulation of environmental policy and adoption of trinational standards and practices, showcases emerging science, and produces tangible outcomes. Recognizing that environmental problems loom large throughout North America, I will focus on the incremental steps and the contributions that the CEC has made in this area. This chapter will unfold in three parts: (1) a history and structure of the CEC, (2) highlighting the successful environmental outcomes and institutional adaptation of the CEC based on personal observations as executive director of the institution, and (3) a discussion of the future of the CEC in light of the renegotiation of NAFTA evolving into the United States–Mexico–Canada Agreement (USMCA). This new agreement could conceivably challenge the very existence of the CEC, though it has survived and thrived in spite of the fact that many heads of states with different agendas have come to power in Canada, Mexico, and the United States. How all of these aforementioned issues can potentially affect the cooperative environmental work of the CEC will be discussed.

History of the CEC

The North American Free Trade Agreement (NAFTA) between Canada, Mexico, and the United States took effect on January 1, 1994, creating one of the world's largest free-trade blocks. The aim of the pact was to promote closer economic and trade ties among the three countries, but there was concern that an increase in cross-border commercial activity could harm the shared North American environment if proper environmental safeguards were not put in place. Trade liberalization was expected to lead to an expansion of the flow of goods, people, and commerce in North America but perhaps also place a higher demand on the vast region's natural resources, including fresh water. It could also exacerbate issues such as the treatment and disposal of waste stemming from an increased use of chemicals harmful to the environment or human health.

Additionally, the broader, higher levels of trade across an expanded marketplace would require the development of infrastructure for road, rail, air, and maritime transport, raising the prospect of a range of effects on everything from air and water quality to the retention of natural habitat. Environmental and labor activists in the three countries warned of dire consequences, arguing that business and industry would flock to Mexico to take advantage of lower labor costs and weaker environmental protection standards. Environmental organizations speculated that increased trade would lead to a "race to the bottom" and that pollution havens would emerge in areas where environmental regulations were not enforced. Scholars contributed to this debate (Hufbauer and Yee 2003; Vaughan 2004; Wisner and Epstein 2005; Sheldon 2006).

In order to assuage these concerns, the governments of Canada, Mexico, and the United States negotiated the adoption of a companion environmental pact to NAFTA known as the North American Agreement on Environmental Cooperation (NAAEC). Through NAAEC, the three countries (referred to as the Parties in NAFTA and NAAEC) created the Commission for Environmental Cooperation (CEC) of North America and designated Montreal, Quebec, as the host city for its secretariat. NAFTA was the first international agreement to link environmental cooperation with trade relations, reinforcing the obligation of each country to protect its domestic environment and meet its international commitments. (Hufbauer et al. 2000). During the signing ceremony for the two NAFTA side agreements, the NAAEC and the North American Agreement on Labor Cooperation; President Clinton stated that it would make it difficult for businesses to relocate because of low wages or lax environmental rules and highlighted that trade sanctions would be applied if a country failed to enforce its own environmental laws (Clinton 1993). William Reilly, EPA administrator during the George H. W. Bush administration, stated that NAFTA is the most environmentally sensitive, the greenest free-trade agreement ever negotiated anywhere. NAFTA was being presented as possibly the "greenest trade agreement" ever signed, though not everyone agreed with that assessment (Vaughan 2004).

It is important to note that during the NAFTA negotiations and the elaboration of the NAAEC, the North American public participated in a series of hearings held throughout border cities, especially on the U.S-Mexico border. Nongovernmental organizations (NGOs) located in Canada, Mexico, and the United States working arduously on environmental and labor arenas provided input and made public comments throughout the NAFTA negotiations. At these public hearings, the public noted that access to water was a major problem throughout the border region, especially in colonias located throughout Texas and in large cities in Mexico's northern border. Air quality problems exacerbated by the large number of trucks idling waiting to cross the border into the United States were noted as well as concerns with the transportation and disposal of hazardous chemicals used by the maquiladora industry in Mexico. The NGO community was actively engaged in the development of the environmental side agreement (Staudt and Coronado 2002).

The three governments created the North American Development Bank (NADBANK), the Border Environment Cooperation Commission (BECC), and the Commission for Environmental Cooperation (CEC). These organizations were originally located in San Antonio, Texas; Ciudad Juárez, Chihuahua; and Montreal, Quebec, respectively; hence, each country would host one of these newly formed institutions. In 2017, the BECC and NADBANK merged to create a single binational institution.

Structure of the CEC

NAAEC set forth a set of principles and objectives to conserve and protect the environment in the three countries and to further promote cooperation on these matters. The CEC's tripartite structure included a council composed of the cabinet-level environmental representatives of the parties. The minister of what was then Environment Canada (now Environment and Climate

Change Canada), the *secretario* of the Secretaría de Medio Ambiente y Recursos Naturales (SEMARNAT), and the U.S. EPA administrator headed a fifteen-member (five from each country) joint public advisory committee (JPAC) of volunteers from civil society and a permanent secretariat. Most importantly, the CEC's mandate supported efforts to foster public input and engagement on environmental issues and on the effective enforcement of environmental laws through the Citizen Submission Process.[1]

The CEC council is a high-level nexus of cooperation between the three countries on environmental matters that fall within the scope of NAAEC. It oversees the implementation of the agreement and meets in person in regular session once a year with the meeting venues rotated through the three countries. The council's annual regular session is open to the public and includes a town hall type question and answer session with the three environment ministers. These council meetings have taken place in various locations, including Yellowknife, Northwest Territories; Morelia, Michoacán; and Denver, Colorado, to name a few. It is important to note that during the council session in 2017, hosted by the Canadian government on Prince Edward Island, Scott Pruitt did not attend. Canada turned over the chair of the council to the United States. The U.S. representatives attending the council session accepted and stated that the next council meeting in 2018 would take place in Oklahoma City, Oklahoma, Scott Pruitt's hometown. However, by the time that the council meeting took place, Scott Pruitt did not attend and a few days later he resigned as EPA administrator.

The council sessions are geared toward advancing the commission's cooperative environmental agenda. The July 2015 session of the council in Boston, Massachusetts, for example, focused on the theme of climate-change adaptation and resilience. At that meeting, the council appointed a fifteen-person advisory roster of experts in traditional ecological knowledge to incorporate the valuable input that local and Indigenous communities can bring to environmental management activities.[2] The council also approved funding the grants under the North American Partnership for Environmental Community Action (NAPECA), supporting community environmental projects that are as grassroots as possible.[3]

Joint Public Advisory Committee

NAAEC provides for active citizen participation in the work of the CEC, and much of this happens through the work of JPAC, a nongovernmental group of volunteer professionals who provide advice to the parties on the work of the CEC and environmental protection issues. Each country names five individuals to serve as volunteers on JPAC. In Mexico and Canada, the environment ministers appoint their JPAC members, while in the United States, the president has that purview. Canada names its JPAC members for a three-year term, while Mexico and the United States do not have fixed terms.[4] Some JPAC members from Mexico have served for several years, even rotating off and on the committee.

On average, JPAC members meet in person three times a year to discuss issues related to the full scope of CEC cooperative work, including its North American Partnership for Community Environmental Action (NAPECA) grant program as well as the Submissions on Enforcement Matters (SEM) process. The committee's fifteen members are drawn from a variety of stakeholder groups—academia, NGOs, business, industry, and wider civil society—and all have experience in environmental issues. The North American public is invited to participate at JPAC's open forums in person or via webcast, social media, and videoconference hubs. Interpretation services are offered in English, French, and Spanish for these meetings, and agendas and other materials are available in the three languages. Through JPAC, the public can also provide feedback on both the Strategic Plan (SP) and Operational Plan (OP) of the CEC.

JPAC's commitment to public participation and transparency in its advisory role is evident in the publication of its advice and letters to council on key matters as well as meeting agendas, presentations, background papers, and speaker biographies. The agendas for JPAC's public forums are generally aligned with the priorities laid out in the SP and OP, but discussions can address any issue that is pertinent to the shared North American environment. JPAC's public session held in conjunction with the twenty-second regular session of council in mid-July 2015, for example, focused on how green infrastructure and land-use planning can help communities manage the effects of changing stormwater patterns. This input is expected to inform public policy makers in the three countries.

JPAC members have access to their environmental ministers in a formal and semiformal manner. A Mexican environmental minister met regularly with JPAC members for lunch meetings and for discussions. Several Canadian JPAC members had direct access to the environmental minister and kept them apprised of the work of the CEC. The U.S. EPA scheduled regular phone calls with JPAC members to discuss issues related to the CEC. Therefore, JPAC members play a key role in keeping environmental ministers apprised of the

CEC's work; though not all JPAC members have that access, those who do certainly play a key role in keeping the CEC on the agenda of their respective minister.

CEC Secretariat

Canada, Mexico, and the United States contribute equally to the CEC budget. The three countries provide equal contributions, US$3 million dollars per year. This includes funding for the secretariat, which along with council and JPAC is one of the commission's constituent bodies. The secretariat provides technical, administrative, and operational support to the council, including management of its cooperative work projects. Another important feature of the CEC is that there is rotating leadership at the executive director level. The countries take turns appointing the executive director for a three-year term. The equal financial contributions and the rotating leadership counters the notion of power asymmetry that border scholars often refer to when describing relationships between two countries (Bustamante 1997; Krasner 1989).

The secretariat also has the mandate to prepare independent reports on environmental matters and the state of the North American environment. These reports have helped broaden knowledge on key issues such as opportunities to make freight transportation more sustainable, to limit the long-range migration through the air of persistent pollutants, and to reform the trade in spent lead-acid batteries. However, it is important to note that these independent reports fall short of documenting the state of the North American environment, a data gathering project that would provide detailed and quantifiable measures and indicators that would enable further analysis.

Through the Submissions on Enforcement Matters (SEM) process, one of the CEC's unique responsibilities is to consider submissions from any North American NGO or resident asserting that a party is failing to enforce effectively its environmental law. The secretariat's SEM unit reviews the submissions and determines whether they meet eligibility criteria for further consideration and, based on the response from the party, whether to recommend to the council that a "factual record" be prepared regarding the facts associated with the enforcement issue in question. Ultimately, council decides whether the secretariat should produce and release a factual record. As of March of 2019, this vital work has resulted in ninety-five public submissions and twenty-four factual records helping to "bring the facts to light" on the related environmental enforcement issues, such as the operation of a limestone quarry in a national park in Mexico or air pollution issues from automobiles in the province of Quebec. The work of the SEM unit has a new online tracking tool that provides updates on the process and has led to more transparency and efficiency.[5]

Role of Government Experts

The CEC has strengthened the three countries' capacities to inform public policy and better manage their domestic and shared environmental challenges and opportunities. High-level government officials at the EPA, Environment and Climate Change Canada (EC) and Mexico's Secretaría de Medio Ambiente y Recursos Naturales (SEMARNAT) appoint experts—a working group or steering committee—from their organizations to work together on the implementation of the SP and OP. With professional support from the secretariat, these experts devise the cooperative work program projects that gather and share scientifically rigorous information.

High-level government officials help craft the projects in their respective areas of expertise and develop the expected outcomes. Although an expert from one government may take the lead in the development of a particular project, this is done in close consultation with the experts from the other two countries. The projects are approved for funding only after the parties' vetting of budgets, timelines and proposed tangible outcomes. Most importantly, the public can provide input on the chosen projects through the CEC's fifteen-member Joint Public Advisory Committee (JPAC). The public can submit comments on the proposed projects online and during the public comment session held during JPAC meetings. Public participation in North American environmental issues has waned in part because of the demise in the number of environmental NGOS due to a lack of funding (Coronado 2014).

Strategic Priorities and Cooperative Work

The CEC's strategic priorities and cooperative work have engaged issues that are relevant to diverse stakeholders across the three countries and have had measurable influence on managing environmental issues affecting local regions and people. Research indicates that the CEC's strategic priorities and cooperative work program has evolved over time and has yielded some positive and tangible outcomes, such as the Sound Management of Chemicals Initiative and the North American Action Plans (NARAP) for the management and control of persistent and toxic substances (Block 2003, 30–31). The Pollutant Release and Transfer Registry (PRTR) has evolved over time into a comprehensive data base where over thirty-five thousand facilities in North America report their pollutant releases and transfers.[6] Another hallmark project of the CEC is the North American Bird Conservation Initiative (NABCI), which promoted biologically driven and land-oriented private and public partnerships to identify critical migratory pathways at the local level (Block 2003, 34).

Over the years, CEC projects have ranged from cooperative conservation work on blue carbon, the carbon that is captured by the oceans and coastal habitats, grasslands, and transboundary ecosystems, to shared approaches on managing green building, monitoring black carbon emissions, and recycling spent lead-acid batteries. New projects and emerging fields of interest—such as food waste, organic waste, and ISO 50001 energy standards—have emerged as part of the CEC cooperative work program.

The CEC has developed tools and initiatives to contribute to the body of knowledge on the North American environment. These include an online virtual library that has more than four hundred CEC publications and reports on over 630 projects and grants in the three official languages, and all can be downloaded free. The CEC's North American Environmental Atlas provides updated geospatial data that helps experts map changes in environmental conditions. The CEC's North American Portal on Climate Pollutants supports the comparability of data that makes it easier to cooperate on regional climate-change adaptation and mitigation strategies.[7] One added benefit of data gathering at the CEC, so that it is comparable across countries, addresses the methodological nationalism concerns that have plagued nation-states and scholars when collecting data (Anderson and Gerber 2008).

Unique Approach to Environmental Cooperation

The CEC has had an important role in helping the three parties meet their domestic and international objectives in conserving, protecting, and enhancing the environment. Based on the principle that cooperation on the environment is the best way forward, the CEC has served as a catalyst to promote an environmentally sustainable integration and development of trade in North America.

Each of the three countries has its individual environmental institutions and priorities. But in complementing the initiatives taken by each national government domestically and internationally, the CEC has proven to be a model of trilateral environmental cooperation focused on sharing knowledge. More than twenty-five years later, academics and experts are still debating whether the implementation of NAFTA has had a positive, a negative, or simply a varied effect in the three countries. Intraregional trade flows have quadrupled, and cross-border investment and travel have grown significantly since NAFTA's inception (McBride and Sergie 2017, 1). Wisner and Epstein (2005) contend that NAFTA and NAAEC pushed the Mexican government to create new oversight agencies, pass new environmental laws, and strengthen enforcement actions; coupled with consumer demands from Canada and the United States, Mexican industries responded favorably and in turn positively affected environmental performance.

However, it is also important to note that while the CEC is not a perfect institution, the parties and the CEC secretariat have taken into account the observations and comments that academics and the public of North America have made. Changes have been proposed, such as modernization of the submissions on enforcement process, focusing on fewer, more specific cooperative program projects and reinstituting the grant program for communities. To its credit, the institution has responded to these concerns.

Though the CEC regime, while innovative, is neither well institutionalized nor well grounded in the political support, it may need to move aggressively in implementing its mandate (Mumme and Duncan 1997). It is clear that the three governments will have to play a key role in strengthening and supporting the institution in the near future.

National Government Transitions

Over time, the CEC has dealt with changes in the executive fifteen times: five U.S. presidents, six Mexican presidents, and four Canadian prime ministers. Based on conversations with longtime staff members at the CEC, Environment and Climate Change Canada (EC), the EPA, and the Secretaría de Medio Ambiente y Recursos Naturales (SEMARNAT), these transitions do have an effect on the work of the CEC. Although the work of the CEC continues once

TABLE 13.1 The three nations' leaders during CEC's existence

	Years in office
Canada Prime Minister	
Jean Chretien	1993–2003
Paul Martin	2003–2006
Stephen Harper	2006–2015
Justin Trudeau	2015–present
Mexico President	
Carlos Salinas de Gortari	1988–1994
Ernesto Zedillo Ponce de León	1994–2000
Vicente Fox	2000–2006
Felipe de Jesús Calderón Hinojosa	2006–2012
Enrique Peña Nieto	2012–2018
Andrés Manuel López Obrador	2018–present
United States President	
Bill Clinton	1993–2001
George W. Bush	2001–2009
Barack Obama	2009–2017
Donald J. Trump	2017–present

a new executive is sworn into office and starts making decisions and political appointments, it might slow down the work of the CEC. Staffers noted that when there are upcoming elections in any of the three countries, the assigned federal government staff members take a wait and see attitude until the elections take place and political appointments are made. There are staff members at Environment and Climate Change Canada, the U.S. EPA, and SEMARNAT that have been working on this file for several years and are equipped to immediately brief new personnel and to navigate through changes in administrations.

In 2006, during the George W. Bush administration, government scientists and contractors reported that they were being "chastised" by administration officials for speaking to the media regarding policy questions. Scientists reported that administration officials had removed references to global warming from their reports, news releases, and conference websites (Eilperin 2006; Donaghy et al. 2007). This policy also affected the CEC. CEC staffers (current and former) reported that they were discouraged from using the words *climate change* and *global warming* in their discussions and documents as well. CEC staff indicated that obtaining clearance for publication of a project was impeded by Bush administration officials. Since the three countries needed to approve the final publication of all CEC reports and documents, to their credit, CEC staff worked diligently to facilitate and achieve compromise on the language used so as to please the three governments and publish the outcomes of the projects.

In 2008, the Canadian government implemented a policy that directed federal scientists to convey all media inquiries regarding their research to national headquarters and not talk to reporters about their work. During the Harper administration, climate change was downplayed, much like the Bush administration's practices in the United States. In 2012 the Canadian Parliament passed a bill that cut funding at research institutes and stripped away environmental protections. Government scientists lost their jobs, and monitoring stations shut down; the effects of these actions on scientists and scientific research were captured in a documentary titled *Silence of the Labs* that was presented on Canadian Television in 2014 (CBC, 2013–2014). CEC staff reported that the Harper administration's policies affected their work, but again, because the work of the CEC requires trilateral approval, one country can try to change the course of the CEC, but it must be aligned and timed with development of the Strategic Plan and the Operational Plan, and everyone must be in agreement with the new theme, focus, or direction.

Enter Trump

Presidential candidate Trump's anti-environment, anti-Mexico, and anti-NAFTA comments sent distress signals to the CEC and to other institutions such as the Border Environment Cooperation Commission and the North American Development Bank. Trump's statements that the EPA was responsible for the loss of jobs and that enforcement of regulations affected businesses adversely concerned environmental activists and staff at EPA. Trump stated that if elected, he would dismantle the EPA. The appointment of Scott Pruitt, an anti-environmentalist, as head of the EPA upset several members of Congress and environmental activists. As attorney general for the state of Oklahoma, Pruitt had sued the EPA twenty-eight times, accusing it of overreaching its mandate. Trump and Pruitt proposed cutting the staff and budget, including all international programs and activities, the section responsible for the CEC portfolio. Trump and Pruitt intended to overturn key decisions that had been made by the Obama administration, specifically coal production and withdrawing from the Paris Climate Change Agreement.

Mustafa Ali and Elizabeth Southerland, two long-term staff members at the EPA, resigned (Geiling 2017). Ali was the chief environmental justice official at EPA.[8] Southerland had worked at the EPA for thirty years, most recently, as director of the Office and Technology in the Water Office. These two high-profile departures were in clear opposition to the policy changes of the new administration. The administration was sending an anti-environmental message that alarmed people at the local and international level.

Anti-Mexico

Trump's anti-environment rhetoric, coupled with the anti-Mexico and Mexican comments, were magnified on January 25, 2017, when he issued Executive Order 13767, titled Border Security and Immigration Improvements. The order directs a wall to be built along the U.S.-Mexico Border. This wall would completely ignore the potential negative environmental effects. Additionally, Trump demanded that Mexico pay for it, upsetting people on both sides of the border. How can one promote environmental cooperation on the one hand and on the other insult your neighbor and trade partner and build a wall? Never mind that pieces of border wall have been erected since 1990 in various locations along the U.S.-Mexico border. In July 2017, the *Texas Observer* reported that Santa Ana Wildlife Refuge in South Texas, located on the U.S.-Mexico border, ten miles southeast of McAllen, Texas, was the site selected by the Trump administration to build part of the wall. The Santa Ana Wildlife Refuge was established in 1943 and is one of the top birding destinations in North America, home to at least 400 bird species and 450 species of plans. Two federal officials who were working on the plans at that site anonymously shared with the *Texas Observer* that the construction of a concrete levee topped with steel bollards would take place. The Santa Ana Wildlife Refuge was selected because it is federally owned land. Customs and Border Protection spokesperson Carlos Díaz reported that the Department of Homeland Security might transfer money from within the agency to build the segment of the wall if Congress did not approve the budget. However, he also stated that "everything is unpredictable with this presidency" (del Bosque 2017). Since 2007, the United States Fish and Wildlife Service opposed the wall and reiterated their concerns that erecting the wall would have serious wildlife consequences and habitat loss and damage.[9] In the summer of

2017, the National Butterfly Center (NBC) in Mission, Texas, reported that Customs and Border Protection (CBP), without notice, hearing permission, or condemnation judgment entered NBC's private property and cleared vegetation, supposedly to prepare the terrain for the building of the border wall (Mumme and Duncan 1997).

As candidate Trump alienated certain sectors of Mexican society and border residents, and investors expressed concern when he said that he would renegotiate NAFTA, numerous chambers of commerce on the U.S.-Mexico border went on a public relations campaigns highlighting the economic importance of NAFTA and lauding the extensive supply chains that had been established throughout North America, especially in the automotive industry. They also cited the number of exports and imports between the three countries. Jon Barela, chief executive officer of the Borderplex Alliance, a binational economic-development organization located in El Paso, Texas, and Ciudad Juarez, Chihuahua, lamented that "the uncertainty of future trade policies is having a chilling effect on investments in our region. Dozens of projects I am aware of have been put on hold" (Kolenc 2017). EPA and CEC staff members were nervous about losing their jobs and, most importantly, seeing their work being dismantled and setting the clock back on environmental protections and successes that had been achieved.

Donald Trump sent a tweet on August 17, 2017, stating, "We are in the NAFTA (worst trade deal ever made) renegotiation process with Mexico and Canada"; he continued, "Both are being very difficult, may have to terminate?" As NAFTA renegotiations were taking place and the new United States–Mexico–Canada Agreement (USMCA) was being hammered out, President Trump was hinting that the United States might withdraw from the trade agreement, thereby creating more uncertainty among CEC staff as to what the future might bring. Would withdrawing from NAFTA render the NAAEC and the CEC null and void? Trump's political style coupled with his anti-NAFTA, anti-environment, and anti-Mexico declarations certainly adversely affected the morale at the CEC. How could the institution promote environmental cooperation amid such antagonistic declarations? On the one hand, the CEC is tasked with promoting environmental cooperation between the three countries, and on the other hand, how can you reach out to a government when the president of the United States is spewing insults to the country that you are trying to work with to uphold and advance the mandate of the CEC?

United States-Mexico-Canada Agreement (USMCA)

In November 2018, negotiators and representatives from the three NAFTA countries signed the USMCA. The negotiations were described by some as testy, trying, and tough, especially when President Trump would threaten to walk away from the talks and in the process criticize the Canadian negotiators. To students, supporters, and observers of the CEC, of utmost importance turned out to be the environmental chapter. The CEC survived! Chapter 24 reiterates that the USMCA parties cooperate to protect and conserve the environment and take into account the rights of Indigenous peoples and consult with them on environmental protection efforts. The CEC has made progress on those two fronts.

Additionally, chapter 24 includes the continuation of the Submissions on Enforcement Matters (SEM), a unique feature of the CEC, that has helped to bring facts to light on environmental problems in Lake Chapala, enforcement of the Migratory Bird Act in the United States, and the impact of logging in Ontario.[10] However, Chapter 24 states that all three parties must agree to the development of a factual record, and presently, only two countries need to agree; this new requirement could negatively affect this process. Why would a country agree to the development of a factual record if they are not enforcing their environmental laws?

The USMCA's Chapter 24 is yet to be ratified, there are many unanswered questions regarding the exact role that the CEC will have in the future. Nevertheless, there are many opportunities for the CEC to continue promoting trilateral environmental cooperation and to capitalize on its successes.

Conclusion

The CEC is a strong, resilient and relevant organization and has developed into an institution that can adapt to changes in national governments because of (1) long-standing staff members assigned to work this file in the respective environmental agencies; (2) the creation of five-year strategic plans and two-year operational plans where the deliverables are agreed on and contracts are issued to accomplish the goals of the work plan coupled with the necessary, albeit limited budgets; (3) the role of the Joint Public Advisory Committee's direct contact with decision makers in the respective environmental agencies and the importance of the roster of traditional ecological knowledge experts who can provide expert advice on environmental protection; and (4) the yearly council sessions that include a meeting with the environmental ministers and administrator. This yearly council allows for the three governments to set priorities and highlight successes vis-à-vis environmental and natural resource protection. It would behoove the three countries to maintain the CEC as an institution. The foundation is set, and with increased financial and political support, the CEC can capitalize on its past successes and expand its mandate to work on more pressing environmental issues. Finally, the parties to the USMCA could and should consult with CEC staff as well as their respective government officials assigned to work on this file in order to better implement Chapter 24. There are many lessons learned and best practices that have emanated from the CEC's twenty-four-year trajectory in protecting and conserving the environment in North America.

NOTES

1. http://www.cec.org/, https://www.epa.gov/international-cooperation/epas-role-north-american-commission-environmental-cooperation-cec.

2. http://www.cec.org/about-us/jpac/tek-members.

3. http://www.cec.org/our-work/napeca.

4. http://www.cec.org/about-us/jpac/joint-public-advisory-committee-jpac.

5. http://www.cec.org/sem-submissions/sem.

6. http://www.cec.org/resources/tracking-pollutant-releases-and-transfers-north-america.

7. http://www.cec.org/home/index.cfm.

8. https://insideclimatenews.org/news/09032017/epa-environmental-justice-mustafa-ali-flint-water-crisis-dakota-access-pipeline-trump-scott-pruitt.

9. http://investigations.blog.statesman.com/2017/09/29/emails-u-s-fish-and-wildlife-officials-still-have-concerns-about-border-wall-at-santa-ana-refuge/.

10. http://www.cec.org/sem-submissions/factual-records.

REFERENCES

Anderson, Joan B., and James Gerber. 2008. *Fifty Years of Change on the US-Mexico Border: Growth, Development, and Quality of Life.* Austin: University of Texas Press.

Block, Greg. 2003. "The CEC Cooperative Work of Program: A North American Agenda for Action." In *Greening NAFTA the North American Commission for Environmental Cooperation,* edited by David Markell and John H. Knox, 2–37. Stanford, Calif: Stanford University Press.

Bustamante, Jorge A. 1997. "Mexico-United States Labor Migration Flows." *International Migration Review* 31 (4): 1112.

CBC. 2013–2014. "Silence of the Labs." *The Fifth Estate*. Season 39. http://www.cbc.ca /fifth/episodes/2013-2014/the-silence-of-the-labs.

Clinton, William J. 1993. "Remarks at the Signing Ceremony for the Supplemental Agreements to the North American Free Trade Agreement." In *The American Presidency Project*, edited by Gerhard Peters and John T. Woolley, September 14. https://www .presidency.ucsb.edu/documents/remarks-the-signing-ceremony-for-the-supplemental -agreements-the-north-american-free-trade.

Coronado, Irasema. 2014. "Whither the Environmental Nongovernmental Organizations on Multiple Regions of the US-Mexico Border?" *Journal of Borderlands Studies* 29 (4): 449–64.

del Bosque, Melissa. 2017. "Trump Administration Preparing Texas Wildlife Refuge for First Border Wall Segment." *Texas Observer*, July 14. https://www.texasobserver.org /trump-border-wall-texas-wildlife-refuge-breaking/.

Donaghy, Timothy, Jennifer Freeman, Francesca Grifo, Karly Kaufman, Tarek Maassarani, and Lexi Shultz. 2007. *Atmosphere of Pressure: Political Interference in Federal Climate Science*. JSTOR Research Report. https://www.jstor.org/stable/resrep00051.

Eilperin, Juliet. 2006. "Climate Researchers Feeling Heat from White House." *Washington Post*, April 6. http://www.washingtonpost.com/wp-dyn/content/article/2006 /04/05/AR2006040502150_pf.html.

Geiling, Natasha. 2017. "Senior EPA Official Resigns with Scathing Message for Trump and Pruitt." *Think Progress*, August 1. https://thinkprogress.org/epa-southerland -resignation-letter-ca62895b0c47/.

Haas, Peter M., Robert O. Keohane, and Marc A. Levy. 1993. *Institutions for the Earth: Sources of Effective International Environmental Protection*. Cambridge, Mass.: MIT Press.

Hufbauer, Gary Clyde, et. al. 2000. *NAFTA and the Environment: Seven Years Later*. Washington, D.C.: Institute for International Economics.

Hufbauer, Gary C., and Wong Yee. 2003. "Security and the Economy in the North American Context: The Road Ahead for NAFTA." *Canada-United States Law Journal* 29:53–69.

Kolenc, Vic. 2017. "Trump Barrage Hurts Border Business, Leaders Say." *USA Today*. January 26. https://www.usatoday.com/story/news/2017/01/26/el-paso-mexico -border-trump-economy/97099428/.

Krasner, Stephen D. 1989. *Power Asymmetries and Relations Between Mexico and the United States*. Stanford, Calif.: Americas Program, Stanford University.

McBride, James, and Mohammed Aly Sergie. 2017. "NAFTA's Economic Impact." Council on Foreign Relations. https://www.cfr.org/backgrounder/naftas-economic -impact.

Mumme, Stephen P., and Pamela Duncan. 1997. "The Commission for Environmental Cooperation and Environmental Management in the Americas." *Journal of Interamerican Studies and World Affairs* 39 (4): 41–62.

Sheldon, Ian. 2006. "Trade and Environmental Policy: A Race to the Bottom?" *Journal of Agricultural Economics* 57 (3): 365–92.

Staudt, Kathleen A., and Irasema Coronado. 2002. *Fronteras no más: Toward Social Justice at the US-Mexico Border*. New York: Palgrave Macmillan.

Vaughan, Scott. 2004. "How Green is NAFTA?" *Environment* 46 (2): 26–42.

Wisner, Priscilla S., and Marc J. Epstein. 2005. "'Push' and 'Pull' Impacts of NAFTA on Environmental Responsiveness and Performance in Mexican Industry." *MIR: Management International Review* 45 (3): 327–47.

Young, Oran R. 2010. *Institutional Dynamics: Emergent Patterns in International Environmental Governance*. Cambridge, Mass.: MIT Press.

Toward North American Integration?

VICTOR KONRAD AND GUADALUPE CORREA-CABRERA

T hroughout this book, contributing authors have critically examined the U.S.-Mexico border, the Canada-U.S. border, or both. Our objectives have been at once to decenter the assumed hegemonic role of the United States in border affairs in North America so that we can view the borderlands more clearly and to acknowledge that, yes, the United States is at the geographical and policy center of borders and bordering in North America. The United States of America maintains a centrality in defining current border processes in North America as it has done for centuries, and yet Canada and Mexico, both global as well as continental forces, play a major role in shaping borders and borderlands. The asymmetries of border engagement—between Canada and the United States and between Mexico and the United States— remain in the twenty-first century and are sustained by an immense U.S. market economy and a robust U.S. military stance at the boundaries and within the borderlands.

Clearly, there are differences in how the United States faces Mexico and how it faces Canada, and border management practices reflect these differences. In the post–9/11 George W. Bush administration, initial U.S. Homeland Security approaches defined one consistent perimeter around the country but soon eased into separate practices at the Mexico and Canada borders. Initially, the Obama administration also announced one border policy but soon differentiated U.S.-Mexico and U.S.-Canada border practice. Now, in the Trump administration, although differences in practice remain, the two international borders are increasingly subjected to the same narratives of edge space and place, a cross-border zone of concern and scrutiny, a space where walls belong. This situation alone seeks a comparative analysis of the borders of the United States.

A comparative analysis is also required to answer the question of what happened to North American integration. What role did borders and borderlands play in the late twentieth-century thrust toward integration? How has this role changed in the early twenty-first century? A comparative analysis of North America's borders enables a better understanding of the borders and borderlands, and the comparative analysis also allows a more incisive assessment of the current state and future of North America. The North American continent is both constructed and contradicted by its borders. Borders define a multiscalar complex of jurisdictional boundaries throughout the continent—international, state/provincial, regional, municipal, ward, and neighborhood. This is the North American border construct that intuitively cascades through distinctive multiscalar boundary complexes within each nation-state container. Yet borders also cut across these lines at all scales to define political, cultural, economic, and social boundaries between people according to their beliefs, values, wealth, race, and other aspects of identity.

With the advent of accelerated globalization built on advances in technology, communication, and mobility, the constantly changing and shifting borders between people have emerged to challenge and even to contradict national border complexes as people align together with or against each other along boundaries of ethnicity, gender, religion, net monetary worth, and other distinctions. Illicit flows also play an important role in the new border complexes. People all across North America create different spaces of affiliation within these borders. Some of these spaces emerge as distinctive borderlands and "third" spaces of transition and hybridization (U.S.-Mexico borderlands), but many are zones or areas of like-mindedness that range from relatively stable and long term (Bible Belts) to sudden and ephemeral (crowdfunding spaces). Consequently, whereas North American borders, and particularly national boundaries, may appear to be so simply configured and delineated, they are in fact disguising an intricate, variable, multiscalar, and dynamic border complex.

This border complex may appear to be everywhere because it is socially constructed by a growing number of interest groups (border communities, the business sector, border politicians, labor unions, and the border-security complex) both within and across national boundaries in North America. Yet the borders are also somewhere. That is, the borders are defined spatially, and they may be recorded and situated through technologies such as the global positioning system (GPS). Furthermore, the North American border complex may be situated in time as well as space to help us comprehend the processes of bordering in addition to the documentation of borderlines. Ultimately, the contribution of border studies, then, is to help us understand the process of becoming North America and North Americans and the meaning of North America—not only as a region but also as a concept.

Unfortunately, for many people in North America, borders are viewed primarily as limits. Moving across borders is considered transgression by those comfortable within these limits. Transgression is codified and enforced as trespassing by a growing and increasingly powerful "border security/military industrial complex" (Miller 2014; Correa-Cabrera 2017) ostensibly invigorated to deter and prevent illegal flows. Yet the securitization of borders has led to an elevated level of control of all flows. Only the elites are allowed and enabled to transcend the entire border complex within the nation-state and beyond its borders. Only the "compliant" are permitted to cross selected boundaries within the nation-state, and only the documented citizenry are permitted to venture across international borders. Also, inequalities have grown between the northern and southern borders. Our comparative analysis allows us to see more clearly these inequalities and the contradictions associated with them.

In an increasingly bordered North America, the sheer weight and volume of border constructions and their accumulated contradictions cloud any possible visions of a North American entity. North America in 2019 may be one of the most highly connected spaces in the world, yet this connectivity has not yielded extensive integration but rather discernable division. This division is remarkable in its intensive polarization resulting in manifestations such as neonationalism buoyed by populism. Concurrently, globalization, once considered a force for equalization, has, in fact, led to greater inequalities in North America. It appears that in a North America made up of Canada, the United States, and Mexico, the differences between Americans, Mexicans, and Canadians have grown even as distances have diminished. Our comparative analysis offers a prism through which to view and evaluate the inequalities and contradictions driven by globalization, securitization, and the new political contexts of the three countries.

As recently as 2011, Robert Pastor, in his book *The North American Idea*, espoused a vision for the future of North America. He begins cautiously with the question, "Should we fear North America?" In his introduction, he details hopes and fears of NAFTA and the dread of sovereignty at risk, not only in Canada and Mexico but also in the United States. Consequently, the forces driving the emergence of North America are countered constantly by forces aligned against a North American entity even remotely akin to the European Union. The promise of the North American idea, once fed by the successes of NAFTA as well as accords in environmental protection cooperation and defense partnerships, has become elusive. Now North American trade is defined in an acronym that clearly places "America First" over Mexico and Canada—the so-called new United States–Mexico–Canada Agreement (USMCA), and makes no mention of North America. Even though millions of Mexicans work and reside in the United States and some in Canada, and even though millions of Canadians reside at least seasonally in the United States and in Mexico, the continent remains three distinct nation-states where visitors and residents from the other countries remain identifiable, and often at risk. The North American idea remains far from realization.

In our book, we have tried to look not only at the idea of North America but also to discern what parts or expressions of this idea work and what is clearly beyond realization. We have done this through a perspective on borders rather than from the more traditional approach of comparing nation-states. However, this is also a comparative analysis of borders overall. "Seeing like a border" (Rumford 2011) allows us to view the North American relationship from the edges rather than from the centers of component states. Also, this perspective allows us to examine important questions of how and where North America works. To be explicit, does enhanced connectivity and integration lead to greater cooperation and exchange? Or, as is evident in North America today, does interconnection and interdependence actually contribute to inequalities, polarization, and extremism?

The view from the edges is clear. There is a North American "advantage," and it does work in the borderlands of Mexico and the United States where millions of people depend on interaction and exchange. Similarly, the Canada-U.S. borderlands, which arguably contain most of the populated parts of Canada, show some of the most extensive and sophisticated exchange networks on the planet. Despite recent difficulties between Canada and the United States in renegotiating NAFTA, the cross-border regions remain viable and effective conduits of the world's foremost trading relationship. Yet the edges of North America remain very unequal, and as stated previously, it is through comparison that these significant inequalities may become more evident.

The edges are also the primary spaces of contestation between the United States and its neighbors. Here, "holding the line" (Nicol and Townsend-Gault 2005) remains an imperative. In 2019, Trump's "wall" remains a very real possibility. In March 2019, the president of the United States vetoed a congressional effort to deny proclamation of a national emergency at the U.S.-Mexico border in another effort to assure construction of "his wall." Although the rhetoric of the barrier comes and goes and has subsided somewhat as other issues take precedence in the United States, the expanded "wall" is taking shape. Nevertheless, the paradox, that the edges in North America are also the foremost spaces of integration, remains as viable as it ever was since the boundaries were drawn (Widdis 2015).

Although the paradox of North American borders remains—and it is important to acknowledge and understand that borders sort flows rather than just allow or disallow passage—it is most important to understand just how this new era of sorting has come about and how it works in both distinctive border contexts. This is the focus of most of the chapters in this book. The aim has been to show how North Americans transcend borders in the twenty-first century as opposed to how they crossed borders in previous eras. As Pastor (2011) explains, the borders are still there, but there are "new faces" at the borders to manage them and make them work more effectively. In some sectors (energy, for example), transcending borders has worked exceptionally well, and the North American energy grid is an effective system.

Unfortunately, illicit markets in firearms and prohibited drugs have also been adept in transcending the border. Overall, the flows allowed and facilitated are selective, chosen and regulated by elites who use increasingly discerning technologies to enforce flow management. Advances in forwarding a virtual border have, in part, addressed both the need for enhancing sanctioned flows and interdicting noncompliant flows. Indeed, there has been a growing realization in all three countries that flows across both territorial and aterritorial borders are components of emerging global networks that transcend national and continental borders.

Borders are in motion; they "are born in motion, conduct motion and create motion" (Konrad 2015, 1). This is evident throughout North America where borders juggle, increasingly, purpose, efficacy, passage, and effect in globalization. Also, increasingly, motion becomes the constant—rather than static boundaries—as borders become mobile and aterritorial in their nature. In an effort to harness and control mobility, North Americans are building and enhancing north-south corridors the length of the continent. Yet as Pastor (2011) argues, even though we envision and create North American "superhighways" to cross borders, inevitable and irreversible "speed-bumps," "potholes," "roadblocks," "walls," and "hidden tolls" remain or are constructed to slow down the even more inevitable forces of connectivity and transformation.

Another paradox emerges. The very initiatives undertaken by all three countries, but primarily by the United States, to stem inflows of terrorists, illegal migrants, and prohibited substances have in fact become transnational projects. In North America, national and public security is inherently transnational as well, and this characteristic has grown with the "war on terror" and the "war on drugs." Similarly, efforts by the Trump administration to adjust the economic playing field of NAFTA in favor of the United States have led to the facilitation of more effective exchange platforms in all three countries. Whereas the trade agreement now called USMCA remains a blueprint at this point, there are signs that nonconformities, such as the dairy supply management system in Canada, are being addressed to create a more effective North American trade and distribution system in all economic sectors. The overall effect of these transnational transformations may yet be to forward the North American advantage, albeit quietly and cautiously, at the same time that national agendas have been touted and extolled. But at this time, it is difficult to see beyond the emphasis on "America First" and the fact that the centrality of the idea of North America, at least implicit in NAFTA and the side agreements, has been lost.

This discussion brings us back to the subject of this book, North American borders in comparative perspective. On the one hand, we have North American borders that are distinctively North American, yet on the other hand, these borders—south and north—are distinctive in their own right. This inequality, two borders with different dynamics, allows us to compare these borders and draw out the inequalities. As discussed previously in this book, this inequality is one reason that the Mexico-U.S. border and the Canada-U.S. border are only occasionally considered together and rarely compared. Now, as North America as a transnational construct is very much in question, it is imperative that we do compare the borders in order to comprehend how they work both separately and in concert and how these borders operate to hinge as well as divide contemporary North America.

The chapters in this book have accomplished this. In part 1, we explore the twenty-first-century replacement of borders between Mexico, the United States, and Canada. The boundary lines themselves remain in place but the border constructs are placed both at and beyond the border. All of the chapters in this section underline the interconnectedness and multilayered space that emerges in evolving North American borders. Collectively, the papers establish that North American borders are increasingly aterritorial, constructed in imagined spaces, fuzzy, flexible, and multifaceted in contradiction to the fixed and stable entities that they portray. Clearly, national claims of intransigent and sacred borders, primarily by the U.S. authority, are blurred in the wake of contemporary bordering, debordering, and rebordering processes. A major border disconnect is the result as the borders that North Americans imagine and construct fail to coincide or engage with the borders enforced by the nation-states.

A significant contribution to the complexity and confusion at the border-line is the large number of actors and interests that reside, engage, collide, and ultimately try to control border space. In the first chapter, Tony Payan assesses border issues facing policymakers and residents at the U.S.-Mexico borderlands. He observes that there is a contemporary, paradoxical opening of the border with exchange and a closing of the border with security that has reconfigured the governance system and that prevails. The U.S.-Mexico border is governed by a multiplicity of border actors in a "Strategic Action Field." The actors all seek control of this complex, multilayered space through a combination of forceful actions and negotiations. Because of the fluid nature of this interaction, institutions are lacking. Instead, "governance in the region is more of an amalgam of actors constantly jockeying in a highly competitive space with low levels of cooperation to achieve true democratic governance."

In the second chapter, Victor Konrad examines the imaginaries of the border between Canada and the United States. It is enticing, he states, to reimagine the U.S.-Canada border as a line diminished in geopolitical significance where aligned security, transparent biopolitical screening, coordinated and scaled management, and rationalized flows mesh at a multicultural, balanced and efficient border. But instead we see security primacy, centralized and flailing border policy and management, and images of a predominant American culture. The border is imagined quite differently in Canada and in the United States, and this difference appears to be increasing rather than decreasing in globalization. Whether, the great misalignment of the United States and Canada at the border is both an indication of a short-term difficulty and a long-term benefit remains to be seen. Yet the growing discontinuity at the border is also a sign of upheaval and change in North America and a call for an overdue redefinition of North America.

In the third chapter, Rick Van Schoik concludes that while North American borders, compared with borders around the globe, appear more fixed and definitive, they are actually considerably more complex because they are, concurrently, fuzzy, flexible, fluid, and to a degree, free. Borders are more fixed for security, but sovereignty is more shared, particularly by subnational governments. Our state-challenged and border-challenged world, according to Van Schoik, is a world "complex" with "ambiguous outcomes," "volatile costs," and "error-prone systems." In North America, borders are increasingly affected by stateless actors; threats are generally not targeted; risks occur across domains of defense; and hazards multiply. This is a challenge to complacency and a call for action. Van Schoik's chapter keys the volume with a decidedly incised practitioners' viewpoint.

Overall, the chapters in part 1 confirm that North American borders must be viewed concurrently as both distinctive and parts of a set. These borders are also part of a world system, and they must be viewed in this light as well. Moreover, North American borders are in transition, and as such, it may be difficult to define how, why, and where they work. What we do know is that regardless of neonationalistic pronouncements, primarily in the United States, the borders with Mexico and Canada are continental and global linkage points as well as conduits of flows and motion that resonate more with the global than with the national pitch. The continental scale, however, continues to elude recognition and acknowledgment as forces in the United States proclaim "America First" in the face of mounting evidence that something bigger is going on and that this something is articulated at local, global, and continental scales.

Part 2, "Spaces, Divisions, and Connectivity in North American Borderlands," again features three chapters. Here, the focus is on borderlands space and place, transborder community, robust cross-border regional entities, and the creativity of coexistence in the reality of North American exchange. Coexistence in North American borderlands, as in many other borderlands around the world, has actually opened up closed off or bounded space to enable and even promote creativity in the use of this bounded space. Moreover, coexistence has formed cross-border community and extended *communitas* to regional and supranational scales. The multiscalar affiliations of borderlands space and borderlands places are demonstratively transnational, exhibiting at once local transborder, regional borderlands, binational, and global connections. In this regard, North American borderlands, like North American "world cities," engage the world not only across prescribed national boundaries but also at multiple levels all at once.

In chapter 4, Francisco Lara-Valencia offers a comparative analysis of trans-border spaces and regional identity in North America through an examination of the different ways borders are perceived and related to. Similar elements of regional identity define contours of contrasting ideas of what the border means and what it contributes to border communities. The study evaluates the asymmetries in border narratives to illustrate different intensities and modalities of cross-border regionalism, particularly with regard to border-city pairs that may develop strong narratives of cross-border regionalism or rivalries. He defines three significant aspects to conclude that there is a historically contingent nature of all identity formation and cross-border regional processes, nationalistic views of war and conflict continue to play a role in identity formation, and discourses of identity shift and adapt to opportunities and challenges perceived by public and private actors.

In chapter 5, Don Alper addresses the shifting meanings of borders in the North American borderlands and concludes that there are two simultaneous tendencies in contradiction: the "closing-off effect" and the "opening-up effect." The first is illustrated by enhanced security and militarization of the border. The second is the combination of economic, environmental, and cultural exchanges and flows. Together these forces shift the meanings of borders by affecting sovereignty and operating at several spatial scales. The interspatial interaction is focused on the borderlands of intertwined and intense spaces. So, suggests Alper, we need to focus our studies on this coexistence and develop policies to nurture cross-border regional processes that enliven the mix and develop creative institutions that operate across traditional jurisdictional boundaries. These robust regional institutions, PNWER (Pacific Northwest Economic Region) for example, provide mechanisms for actors at various scales to shape collective action across border domains. In the process of doing this, these institutions project outward to North Americans the vital workings and functions of the borderlands.

Finally, in chapter 6, Alan Bersin provides a practitioner's viewpoint on the reconfiguration of lines and flows. The author, a former senior official in the U.S. Department of Homeland Security, provides an inside look at the massive paradigm shift that has moved our perception of borders from lines to movements and how a border viewed as flows obliges security agencies to work beyond homeland and national security to a network-based focus on transnational security. Border management depends now more on big data, compliance checks, and risk assessment. To identify threats, rather than trying to find a needle in a haystack, the haystack needs to be made smaller. Consequently, an emphasis has been placed on segmentation of traffic flows and the development of various trusted-traveler and carrier programs to enable this approach. The Department of Homeland Security has evolved, but course corrections are being called for. The "intermestic" (international/domestic) reality of North American exchange and relations is challenged now by the populist agendas and neonationalism in the United States.

Border Governance in North America is the focus of part 3. Yet border governance in twenty-first-century North America needs to acknowledge the shifting, unstable, mobile, and multiscalar nature of borders in globalization. All the authors contributing to this section agree that border governance needs to capture this essence of mobile rights and goods that are negotiated across as opposed to within territorial boundaries. Yet border governance remains caught in between a global nexus of policy making and the container of territorial governance. This leads to forms of both territorial and aterritorial border governance evident in border regions with the result that the border continues to promote inequalities. Concurrently, some border regions develop gateways and corridors to empower borderlands and produce models for binational governance articulated at subnational levels.

In chapter 7, Emmanuel Brunet-Jailly analyzes twenty-first-century globalization and border governance and questions whether borderland governance can be both or either territorial or aterritorial. He argues that the geopolitical governance of borders is shifting and in transition from territorial bordering to regional and plausibly global bordering through connectivity. Brunet-Jailly reflects on China's current belt and road initiative to illustrate his central argument that in the twenty-first century, borders are either territorial or they are functional. He concludes that borders of globalization are much less stable than territorially grounded borderscapes because their essence is to serve the functions of multiple forms of flows and mobility: trade flows, human movements, and their infrastructure of connectivity. Thus, they demarcate mobile goods, ascertaining their rights to movement. Brunet-Jailly also argues there are no spatial or territorial attachments to mobile rights because they are negotiated across multiple territories and with policy makers, states, and private and nonprofit policy actors of the global nexus; they are aterritorial because they are dependent on global nexus policy makers.

In chapter 8, Kathleen Staudt explores the range of short-term and long-term preparation for democratic cross-border governance in the central part of the U.S.-Mexico borderlands. She analyzes the changing narratives over the last decade in border trade and security rhetoric. Her analysis reveals the "shallow commitment to long-term prosperity in the central borderlands of El Paso and Ciudad Juárez, particularly the low minimum wages in the latter." Staudt criticizes "the neoliberal discourse of global competitiveness and the way it leads to the perpetuation of low-cost labor in the border region." Hence, according to Staudt, border public institutions should consider it a major priority to reduce inequalities at the border and should focus on elevating net wages. She finally advocates for "fairer wage policies, inequality reduction, and proactive programs at multiple levels of government." She concludes by saying that the United States and Mexico "should move to embrace these policies so that some semblance of democracy can survive."

In this section the practitioner's viewpoint is offered in chapter 9 by Bruce Agnew, who shows how the gateways and corridors of Cascadia and the Pacific Northwest empower borderlands. He sees the Pacific Northwest Economic Region (PNWER) as the model for binational governance, and he highlights its success as an environmental movement in the Cascadia region. In his analysis Agnew highlights the critical blending of commerce and conservation initiatives, the commitment of multilevels of government to data-driven decision making, and the fresh energy of private-sector technology companies to push the binational region to greater integration. According to Agnew, this experience could serve as inspiration to other borderlands to further empowerment of regional stakeholders in the face of globalization and political nationalization of security. He concludes that advocates for cross-border economic and environmental cooperation in North America should work cooperatively and through legislative initiatives to empower cross-border governance structures. According to him, the best approach is "a multigovernmental decision-making structure providing flexibility to local inspection agencies and a healthy dose of private-sector interest, equity capital, and industry leadership."

Part 4 evaluates border-policy directions in North America and how these are advancing integration or sustaining bilateral constructs. Sectoral policy—whether in energy, water resource management, economic development, conservation, or any one of a vast number of policy fields—often extends beyond Canadian, American, and Mexican policy-making bodies to encompass international regions and even the continent of North America. Some of these sectors have experienced legislated trilateral cooperation, as in the case of the Commission for Environmental Cooperation (CEC) developed out of a side agreement of NAFTA, with a mandate, funding from all three countries, and a secretariat in Montreal. Other sectors—watershed and water resource management, for example—linked to geographical contexts and well-established rules and traditions, retain bilateral models, although advances in policy making are shared across the continent. Energy policy, often led by regional interests, remains largely in the domain of national policy, although in some aspects, hydroelectric grids and pipelines for example, there is extensive bilateral and multilateral cooperation and integration. Overall, a range of sectoral policy frameworks are evident, and each of these is dynamic, affected by forces originating in government, industry lobbies, nongovernmental agencies, public representation, and from agencies external to North America.

The initial chapter in this set approaches North American energy integration along two "unequal" borders. The authors of chapter 10, Guadalupe Correa-Cabrera and Michelle Keck, describe the most recent advances toward energy integration in both border regions, highlighting the differences and limitations of these processes. According to their research, the primary areas of concern are potential environmental issues that affect the entire North American energy region and security and corruption problems that jeopardize the future inclusion of Mexico into a successfully integrated North American energy region. New economic agendas of the U.S. government and a new Mexican administration might add to these concerns and might limit further energy integration.

Christopher Wilson of the Wilson Center rounds out the discussion in chapter 11 with a qualitative analysis of cross-border cooperation for economic development on the U.S.-Mexico border. The interviews he conducted for this study confirm that there is, "at least across much of the border region, a growing level of binational cooperation for economic development. Nonetheless, clear differences in the depth and intensity of cooperation are found in the various pairs of cities and states on either side of the border." Wilson's research demonstrates to some extent that the capacity of local institutions, especially government and civil society, plays an important role. He concludes by saying that "at times the institutional capacity of a community on one side of the border can be used to supplement lesser capacity on the other side, but the deepest and most effective collaboration comes when capable actors from both sides are able to develop initiatives that provide tangible benefits for communities on both sides of the border and transcend the life spans of the local and state governments that help support them."

In chapter 12, Christopher Brown offers a comparative examination of watershed research on the two borders. More specifically, he examines transboundary water resource management issues both in the arid region of the southwestern U.S.-Mexico borderlands and the humid region of the Canada-U.S. borderlands. By making this comparison, Brown concludes that local participation and leadership are key in successful efforts at transboundary watershed management. In his view, scale and geography matter. At the same time, he sees "a very strong connection to important water resources from agency staff, policy makers, and citizen stakeholders." He is ambivalent about the idea of a unified approach to watershed management or a "North American watershed gestalt" but recognizes the value of a comparative approach to different basins on the U.S.-Mexico and U.S.-Canada borders.

In chapter 13, Irasema Coronado, a former director of the North American Commission for Environmental Cooperation (CEC), discusses the commission as a model for trilateral cooperation. She analyzes the effectiveness and performance of the CEC and highlights the conditions and variables that have allowed this trinational institution to carry out its intended mission. Coronado also mentions the challenges that are being experienced today in this area—particularly since the beginning of the Trump era. For Coronado, the CEC represents a unique approach to environmental cooperation. In her view, the commission has helped the three North American countries to "meet their domestic and international objectives in conserving, protecting, and enhancing the environment" and has served as "a catalyst to promote an environmentally sustainable integration and development of trade" in the region.

Any effort to draw summary conclusions needs to be tempered by the acknowledgment that these conclusions are possibly illusory and certainly premature because North American borders are very much in process and caught up in motions both connected to globalization and pitted against it. What we do know is that North American borders have seen a paradigm shift. As former U.S. Homeland Security deputy director Alan Bersin confirms and all the chapters in this book have elucidated, North American borders have been reimagined, reconfigured, and undeniably altered since the events of 9/11. The demarcation lines remain the same, but the borders are simultaneously opening and closing according to new imperatives, regulations, and forces originated both in North America and around the globe. The two different borders—U.S.-Mexico and U.S.-Canada—remain distinctive, and they are emerging as more unequal despite the leveling forces of globalization, securitization, and cooperation.

Multiscalar expressions of bordering both at, near, and removed from the boundaries, complicate and cloud the view. The essence of understanding North American borders lies in understanding the flows that are also multiscalar. These flows are facilitated, filtered, expedited, rerouted, amalgamated, diminished, and arrested at "border points" in an increasingly complex set of networks. Consequently, border management has been obliged to reorient its approach, and this remains a work in progress. Similarly, border governance remains caught between a slowly emerging consensus that borders have moved from being territorial to more aterritorial in nature and a reluctant admission that border governance needs to be practiced at scales from community to national levels to be effective. All of these shifts in the meanings, configurations, workings, effects, and governance of North American borders call for policy adjustments and new directions. Many of the advances in cooperation across the borders, particularly in energy flow management and environmental protection, are currently undermined by challenges from a vocal, extremist administration in the United States. The efficacy of North American borders and the sustainability of the idea of North America are both in jeopardy.

What are the implications of knowing more about North American borders? Will it help us to understand North America better? Will it help us to understand borders better? Clearly, the answer to both questions is yes. As this book has emphasized, there is an intersection of North American borders and the idea of North America. We cannot understand North America without a comprehension of its borders at all scales. And we cannot understand how these borders work without an overview of what is being bordered, where these borders prevail, and why bordering has come to dominate in the continent and particularly in the American psyche. Although North America is a paragon of integration, North America's borders prevail over integration. There is currently no indication that this condition will change. Nevertheless, the buoyancy of the North American idea prevails as well to emerge regularly as a leitmotif and a potential framework for cooperation, greater democracy, civil society, and progress. The idea of North America is inextricable from the ideals that constitute civil and just society in Mexico, the United States, and Canada, yet notions of borders, barriers, fences, and walls are also constructed and enshrined in the social fabric of all three countries. Our goal, then, must be to understand the ideas and processes that lead to both North American integration and North

American polarization and how they intersect. Knowledge and understanding of this intersection is fundamental to shaping a future for North America.

In this book we have introduced concepts and tools to enable this understanding from the perspective of border studies. Among these concepts are foundational ideas in the study of borders, such as border regions, borderlands, edge spaces, bordering, and more. Also, there are concepts recently developed to assist in our understanding of borders in globalization such as aterritorial borders, borderities, seeing like a border, borderscapes, and borders in motion. The study of North American borders, and ultimately an understanding of North America in the context of its borders, depends on our continued exploration and debate of all of these concepts and their assessment in the context of both North America and more widely in the global arena. Currently, there is no inclusive paradigm that enables understanding borders, and as we have learned in this book, there is no conceptual framework for understanding and relating North American borders. Yet this book has enabled a more thorough understanding of how borders in North America work and do not work. In pursuit of this understanding, we have encountered a better sense of how connectivity, networks, integration, and cooperation operate within North America and across its increasingly complex borders. We have examined these processes in the context of globalization. Also, we have focused on the inequalities produced by borders and inherent in the process of bordering. In North America, once viewed as a bastion of progressive ideals, equalization, democracy, and opportunity, increasing division and polarization now predominate in multiply bordered spaces at all scales. To address and hopefully to ameliorate this condition, it is necessary to learn the language of borders that now constrains North America.

As we completed the draft of these conclusions, a migrant group (the caravan) of thousands of refugees from Central America was traveling through Mexico in the direction of the U.S. border. Although Mexican authorities watched the movement, they did not halt it. Of course the media was watching closely as well and anticipating the collision of this force with the barriers at the United States border. The movement came as the United States prepared for midterm elections in early November. Although this migration apparently lost its momentum, U.S. border authorities now have cautioned that a new wave of migrant families is coming and that no wall will deter them because they will aim to seek asylum at official border crossings.

Meanwhile, along the Canada-U.S. border, it appears to be business as usual. Asylum seekers continue to cross the border from the United States to Canada.

Canada, in an effort to stem the flow, has determined that the United States is safe for the return of these migrants. A looming border issue is occasioned by the legalization of cannabis in Canada and an insistence by U.S. authorities that cannabis users will be inadmissible in the United States. Although central authorities in the United States are adamant about this "anti-pot" stance, an increasing number of states have legalized cannabis use. The paradoxes of North American borders continue to unfurl.

These illustrations underline that although the U.S. borders with Mexico and Canada are very different, both borders are affected by currents that sweep across the continent and beyond. Migrations originating in Central America are peopled by asylum seekers who aim for the United States but find themselves opting for Canada as they are deflected from the United States. The borders may be different, but the trajectories across them are similar and extend throughout the continent. At a point, major flows develop the momentum to cross both borders. It remains to be seen how the legalization of cannabis will extend into and across the United States, and how this flow will play at the U.S.-Mexico border.

Current events, our evolving theories about borders, and the research on borders in North America all confirm that flows of increasing magnitude and effect are both challenging and creating borders beyond the territorial boundaries that were once established to delineate the continental space. This book has provided insights from scholars and practitioners about how borders in the twenty-first century are not only dividing North America but also how the complex of borders, bordering, and borderlands is an integral component of what North America has become. For better or worse, borders are here to stay. It is incumbent on all North Americans to comprehend borders and try to understand how they help to shape the living spaces, communities, regions, and countries where we work, play, and visit. As North Americans continue to extend activities and imaginations across more and more space, they confront and construct an expanding array of borders. Only through recognition and comprehension of borders may we reconcile our experience of the twenty-first-century bordered world.

REFERENCES

Correa-Cabrera, Guadalupe. 2017. *Los Zetas. Inc.: Criminal Corporations, Energy, and Civil War in Mexico*. Austin: University of Texas Press.

Konrad, Victor. 2015. "Toward a Theory of Borders in Motion." *Journal of Borderlands Studies* 30 (1): 1–17.

Miller, Todd. 2014. *Border Patrol Nation: Dispatches from the Front Lines of Homeland Security.* San Francisco: City Lights.

Nicol, Heather N., and Ian Townsend-Gault. 2005. *Holding the Line: Borders in a Global World.* Vancouver, BC: UBC Press.

Pastor, Robert A. 2011. *The North American Idea: A Vision of a Continental Future.* New York: Oxford University Press.

Rumford, Chris. 2011. "Seeing Like a Border." *Political Geography* 30:67–68.

Widdis, Randy W. 2015. "Looking Through the Mirror: A Historical Geographical View of the Canadian-American Borderlands." *Journal of Borderlands Studies* 30 (2): 175–88.

Contributors

Bruce Agnew has directed the Cascadia Center at Discovery Institute in Seattle since 1995, leading the Northwest Cascadia initiative. He is the co-chair of the Transportation Work Group of the Pacific Northwest Economic Region and charter member of the Can Am Border Trade Alliance based in New York.

Donald K. Alper is professor emeritus of political science and a research fellow at the Border Policy Research Institute, Western Washington University. He is the former director of the Center for Canadian-American Studies (1993–2014) and founder and director of the Border Policy Research Institute (2005–2014).

Alan F. J. Artibise was appointed as provost emeritus at the University of Texas Rio Grande Valley in fall 2015. He was formerly vice president for academic affairs and provost at the University of Texas at Brownsville and Texas Southmost College (a legacy UTRGV institution). He also served as executive dean, dean of social sciences, and executive director of the Institute for Social Science Research in the College of Liberal Arts and Sciences at Arizona State University. In previous positions, he has been a professor and administrator at several other North American universities, including the University of New Orleans, the University of Missouri–St. Louis, and the Universities of British Columbia, Winnipeg, Victoria, and Manitoba.

Alan D. Bersin served as commissioner of U.S. Customs and Border Protection (2010–2011) and as assistant secretary of policy and international affairs and chief diplomatic officer at the Department of Homeland Security (2012–2017). He served previously as United States attorney in the Southern District of California and the attorney general's Southwest border representative ("Border Czar") during the Clinton administration. He serves currently as an inaugural senior fellow in the Homeland Security Project at the Belfer Center of the Harvard Kennedy School of Government; as a Global Fellow at the Woodrow Wilson Center for International Scholars in Washington, D.C.; and as inaugural North American fellow at the Canada Institute and the Mexico Institute (Wilson Center).

Christopher Brown is associate professor in the department of geography at New Mexico State University. He is also director of NMSU's Spatial Applications Research Center and chair of the faculty senate. He is past president of the Western Social Science Association.

Emmanuel Brunet-Jailly is professor at the University of Victoria, British Columbia, Canada. He is Jean Monnet Chair in European Urban and Border Region Policy and president of the Association for Borderlands Studies. He is the director and principal investigator of the Borders in Globalization project. He is also editor of the *Canadian American Public Policy* journal and *Borders in Globalization Review*.

Irasema Coronado is professor in the department of political science, a contributing faculty member of the environmental science and engineering doctoral program, and former associate provost at the University of Texas at El Paso. She is also the former executive director of the North American Commission for Environmental Cooperation.

Guadalupe Correa-Cabrera is associate professor at the Schar School of Policy and Government, George Mason University. Her areas of expertise are Mexico-U.S. relations, organized crime, immigration, border security, and human trafficking. Her newest book is titled *Los Zetas Inc.: Criminal Corporations, Energy, and Civil War in Mexico* (University of Texas Press, 2017; Spanish version, Planeta, 2018). She was recently the principal investigator of a research grant supported by the department of state's Office to Monitor and Combat Trafficking in Persons to study organized crime and trafficking in persons in Central America and along Mexico's eastern migration routes. She is past president of the Association for Borderlands Studies and a global fellow at the Woodrow Wilson International Center for Scholars as well as a non-resident scholar at the Baker Institute's Mexico Center (Rice University). She is also coeditor of the *International Studies Perspectives* journal. She is now working on a new book project that analyzes the main political, cultural, and ideological aspects of Mexican irregular immigration in the United States and U.S. immigration policy titled *"Illegal Aliens": The Human Problem of Mexican Undocumented Migration*. She is also finalizing a book titled *An Improvised War: Personal Stories and Political Perspectives of Mexico's Security* (co-authored with Tony Payan).

Michelle Keck is associate professor and associate chair in the department of political science at the University of Texas Rio Grande Valley.

Victor Konrad teaches geography at Carleton University in Ottawa, Canada. Recently he was visiting professor at Yunnan Normal University, China; Radboud University, Nijmegen, Netherlands; and the Karelian Institute of the University of Eastern Finland. In 2009, he was visiting fellow at the Border Policy Research Institute, Western Washington University. From 1990 to 2001, he established the Canada-U.S. Fulbright program and the Foundation for Educational Exchange between Canada and the United States. During the 1970s and 1980s, he was a professor of geography and anthropology at the University of Maine and director of the Canadian-American Center. He was president of the Association of Canadian Studies in the United States and recipient of the Donner Medal. Recently, he was president of the Association for Borderlands Studies. His current research is on various aspects of borders but primarily on border culture. He is the author of more than one hundred publications including *Beyond Walls: Re-Inventing the Canada-United States Borderlands*. Currently he is codirector of the Borders in Globalization Project and serves on the editorial board of the *Journal of Borderlands Studies*.

Francisco Lara-Valencia is associate professor in the School of Transborder Studies and Southwest Borderland Scholar at Arizona State University. He is also director of the Program for Transborder Communities and senior sustainability scientist of the Global Institute of Sustainability at ASU. He is currently president and executive secretary and treasurer of the Association for Border-lands Studies.

Tony Payan is the Françoise and Edward Djerejian Fellow for Mexico Stud-ies and director of the Mexico Center at the Baker Institute. He is also an adjunct associate professor at Rice University and a professor at the Universidad Autónoma de Ciudad Juárez. Between 2001 and 2015, Payan was a professor of political science at University of Texas at El Paso.

Kathleen Staudt is professor emerita of political science at the University of Texas at El Paso. She was professor of political science (1977–2017) and endowed professor of Western Hemispheric Trade Policy Studies at UTEP. From 1998 to 2008, she founded and led UTEP's Center for Civic Engagement.

Rick Van Schoik serves as portfolio director of the North American Research Partnership. He was previously the director of the North American Center for Transborder Studies at Arizona State University and of the Southwest Con-sortium for Environmental Research and Policy.

Christopher Wilson is Deputy Director of the Mexico Institute at the Wood-row Wilson International Center for Scholars, where he leads the institute's research and programming on regional economic integration and U.S.-Mexico border affairs. He previously worked as a contractor doing Mexico analysis for the U.S. military and as a researcher at American University's Center for North American Studies.

Index